The dBASE III Programming Handbook

Cary N. Prague and
James E. Hammitt

Notices
dBASE, dBASE II, dBASE III, Framework, Friday!, and RUNTIME are all registered trademarks of Ashton-Tate, Inc. This document was produced using Framework.
Turbo Pascal and Sidekick are registered trademarks of Borland, International.
IBM PC, PC-XT and PC-AT, Professional Editor, and Personal Editor are all trademarks of IBM. PC-DOS is a trademark of IBM, and was written by Microsoft Corporation.
Compaq and Compaq Plus are trademarks of Compaq.
The Norton Utilities are copyright 1982, 1983, and 1984 by Peter Norton.
KEDIT is a trademark of the Mansfield Software Group of Storrs, Connecticut.
MS-DOS is a trademark of Microsoft Corporation.
WordStar and MailMerge are trademarks of Micro Pro.
Brief is a trademark of Solution Systems.
FirsTime and FirsTime for dBASE III are trademarks of Spruce Technology Corporation.
SPF/PC is a trademark of Command Technology Corporation.

FIRST EDITION
THIRD PRINTING

Copyright © 1986 by TAB BOOKS Inc.
Printed in the United States of America

Reproduction or publication of the content in any manner, without express permission of the publisher, is prohibited. No liability is assumed with respect to the use of the information herein.

Library of Congress Cataloging in Publication Data

Prague, Cary N.
The dBASE III programming handbook.

Includes index.
1. dBASE III (Computer program) 2. Microcomputers—Programming. I. Hammitt, James E. II. Title.
QA76.9.D3P726 1986   005.75'65   85-27711
ISBN 0-8306-0676-9
ISBN 0-8306-2676-X (pbk.)

Contents

Acknowledgments v

Introduction vii

SECTION I: Data and Databases

1 Designing Data 1
2 An Overview of dBASE III Components 10
3 Dates, Times, and Conversions 19
4 Memo Fields and Files 25
5 Fred's Gourmet Seafood 30

SECTION II: Techniques for Programming

6 Programming for Efficiency 39
7 Memory Variables 48
8 Creating and Using Procedures 53
9 Full Screen Operations 59
10 Reporting Techniques 72
11 Programming Techniques 81

| 12 | Fred Discovers SOUNDEX | 90 |

SECTION III: Technical Considerations

13	Beyond dBASE III	97
14	Technical Techniques	107
15	dBASE III Hardware and System Considerations	113
16	dBASE III File Structures	120
17	Fred, Inc.	125

SECTION IV: Peripheral Packages

18	Report Writers	131
19	Screen and Program Generators	146
20	Debugging Tools	170
21	dBASE Compilers	179
22	Other Software Programs	181
23	dBASE Publications	190
24	dBASE User Groups	193

Appendix A	Common dBASE III Error Messages	195
Appendix B	A Sample Data Dictionary System	197
Appendix C	Some Development Tools	201
Appendix D	SOUNDEX Routines	213
Appendix E	A List of Peripheral Packages and Publications	221

| Glossary | 223 |
| Index | 226 |

Acknowledgments

We would like to especially thank the following people and companies for their help in producing this book:

Susan Cohen of Fox and Geller for their entire dBASE III series.

Alun Wyn-Jones at WallSoft Systems for dFlow—a true gem.

The Software Bottling Company of New York, makers of FlashCode and Screen Sculptor, for their truly remarkable packages.

Nantucket Software, whose public relations agency sent a cheese-and-crackers gift pack along with their Clipper compiler, with orders to lock ourselves in a room and learn it.

Special thanks to Nico Mak, wizard-without-portfolio.

To my wife Karen, for taking care of things while I write.
    —CNP

To my parents, and my wife, and to all the others that made this possible.
    —JEH

Introduction

Fully explaining a software package as extensive as dBASE III in a single book is very difficult. Although dBASE III is advertised as a user-friendly database management system, only experienced computer users seem to use the system to its fullest. Experience in the actual use of the software brings to light many idiosyncrasies and features of the package not immediately understood or recognized. Many of the features of dBASE III work in conjunction with other features to produce a whole far greater than the sum of its parts.

The dBASE III Programming Handbook is a sequel to our *Programming with dBASE III* (TAB book No. 1976) and takes the ideas expressed in that book farther. For the user who is already experienced, this book offers help in using the dBASE III functions not fully explained elsewhere and provides examples of algorithms for business use.

Technical subjects are treated on a very basic level. The casual computer user has no real need to understand the intricate melding of programs within a system. *The dBASE III Programming Handbook* will introduce the hardware and software considerations of using this powerful DBMS.

The first section of the book shows the practical results of good, solid design work when building a dBASE system. The most important part of the system, the data itself, is overlooked or designed "on the fly," causing incompatibility and confusion. This book shows how to avoid this trap and how to build systems that are more efficient because of their data, not in spite of it.

Section II gives examples and descriptions of various programming techniques and how they can be applied to a dBASE III system. One of these algorithms, SOUNDEX, is used to give words that sound alike a similar key, so that phonetic searches are possible. This book also provides the Turbo Pascal source code for a program that can be used to implement SOUNDEX in dBASE III and a version of SOUNDEX written in dBASE III itself.

Section III discusses the technical detail of making dBASE III "talk" to the rest of the world, using other programs from within a dBASE ".PRG," and utilizing the actual contents of the various dBASE files. This section also discusses programs, such as Ashton-Tate's RUNTIME compiler, which can speed the execution of programs by creating machine-code routines that do not require processing by the interpreter. The disk caching programs, print spoolers, and other PC-DOS utilities that can speed up dBASE III operations are also investigated. Pascal source code is provided for two utilities, CRUSHER and PXREF, which can be used to aid in programming for dBASE III.

The last section in the book will review various packages available from third-party vendors for use with dBASE III, including compilers, report writers and applications generators. Buyers and prospective buyers will find Section IV an excellent guide to the capabilities and limitations of these packages.

The dBASE III Programming Handbook is for the experienced user looking for shortcuts and for novices looking for tips on building systems that work for their businesses.

Please note that all routines, processes, and programs used as examples in this book have been tested on a Compaq portable computer with two floppy-disk drives and 640K of memory. Memory size was varied (using a RAM-disk) to simulate smaller configurations. The packages in Section IV were tested on an IBM PC/XT with two floppy-disk drives, a 10M hard-disk, and 640K of memory.

Chapter 1
Designing Data

One of the major problems in contemporary computer application development is that while many person-hours are spent in the design and meticulous coding of a program, little thought is given to the design of the data. The most important company asset in the Information Age is its data—and the uses to which it can be put.

The design of a company's *database* (all the data available to the company) will affect the direction and capabilities of all future application development efforts. This fact points out the need for a company-wide computer plan to guide development of the database; new applications should fit into the plan easily. The plan itself should be flexible enough to take advantage of new technology and also to allow for company growth.

DATA ENTITIES

The most effective method of data design is called the *data entity* approach, which is also known as *structured data design*. Through a process called *normalization*, the relationships between pieces of information are discovered, allowing the entity to be developed with no repetition of data items.

There are four steps in the normalization process, called first-, second-, third-, and fourth-form normalization. Each form reduces the amount of data that must be stored to complete the entity, and each form increases the amount of time before errors begin to creep in.

A data entity is defined as something, real or abstract, that we want to store data about. Each item of data to be stored is referred to either as a *data item* or *field*. The first step in the normalization process is to identify all of the data items to be included in this entity. This identification is also the first step to building the system's *data dictionary*. These *fields* are then placed in a table so that their interrelationships can be examined. This table is called the *flat file* view of the entity, because this is how the data would look if stored in a single sequential, or flat, file.

The first form of data normalization involves examining this table of data items for groups of items that appear more than once for each occurrence, also called an *instance*, of an entity. In an entity called Employee, all of the data items for Smith represent one instance of the entity, while all those for Jones represent a second instance, and so forth. Figure 1-1 shows the first normal form.

The terms used to describe the relationships of repeating groups of data items are *one-to-one* and *one-to-many*. Each group split out in such a manner will have some sort of key field that will identify that particular group. When the repeating groups have been split out into separate physical files the database is said to be first-form normalized.

The change to second-form normalization requires the grouping of data items that depend on the entire key field for identification. A key field can be made up of several data items, creating a unique identification for the record. If a data item is dependent on one part of a key, but not the whole key, there is a new *functional dependency* that should be split out. When all of the functional dependencies have been removed, the database is in second normal form. Figure 1-2 shows the second normal form.

A transitive dependency can occur when a data item is sometimes dependent on another, non-key data item. If a data item is dependent on both the key and another data item, they can be split out to yield another file. When all of these *transitive dependencies* are split out, the database is in the third normal form. Figure 1-3 shows the third normal form.

The fourth normal form is extremely complicated and not used by most database managers. The dependencies it reduces are unlikely to occur in any but the most complex database relationships. Fourth-form normalization uses the process of *canonical synthesis* to split out *non-trivial multivalued dependencies* into other records, thus removing the last of the dependencies. If no such dependencies exist, the third normal form also constitutes the fourth normal form.

Each entity has a name, such as Employee, Inventory, and Customer, that reflects the type of data it contains. Within each entity can be *subentities*, which would be named with both the primary entity name and the subentity name; for example,

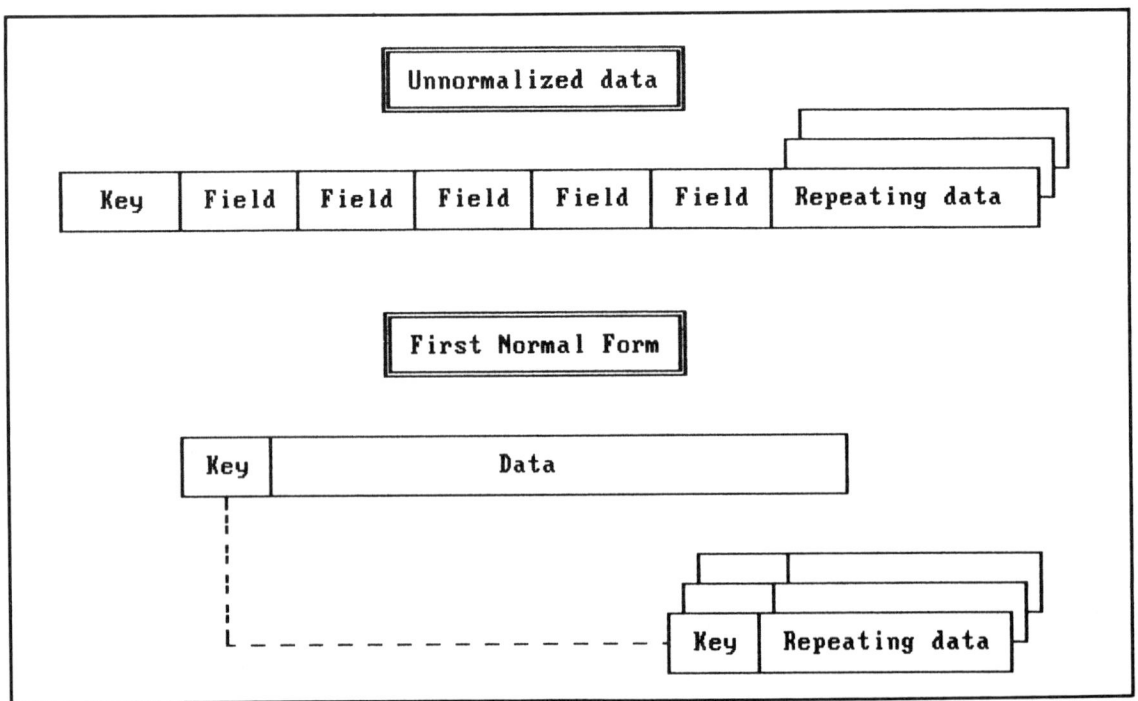

Fig. 1-1. The first normal form.

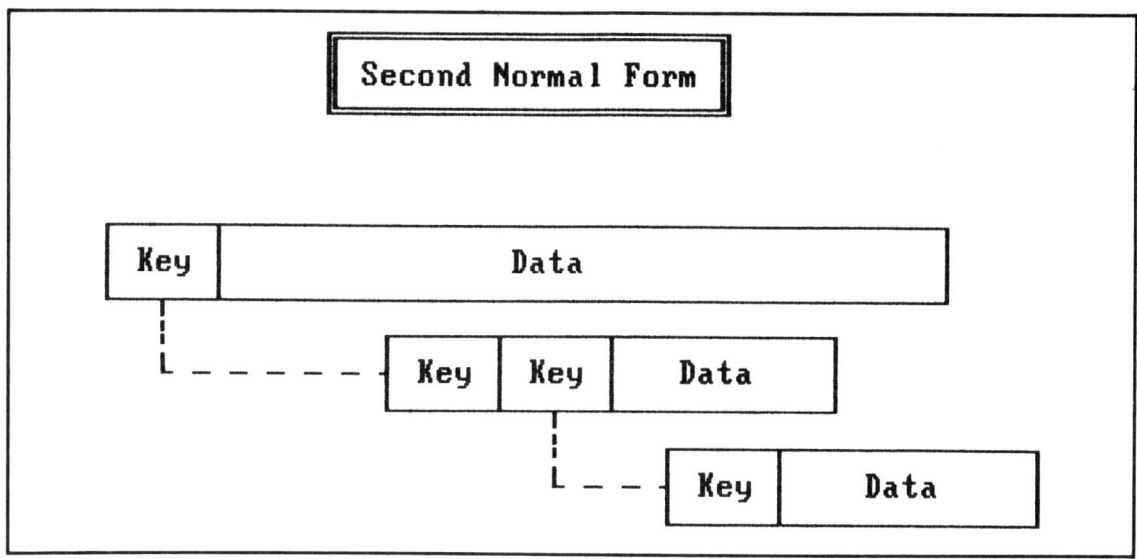

Fig. 1-2. The second normal form.

Employee Skill and Inventory Descriptions are names of subentities.

An entity can be contained in a single file, but most likely it is spread among several files, which are related by a key field. The physical arrangement of the data should not affect the functions of the system—that is the primary goal of data independence.

dBASE relational databases lend themselves well to the entity design of data, because dBASE allows you to add fields to an entity without changing existing programs. Since all field accessing is

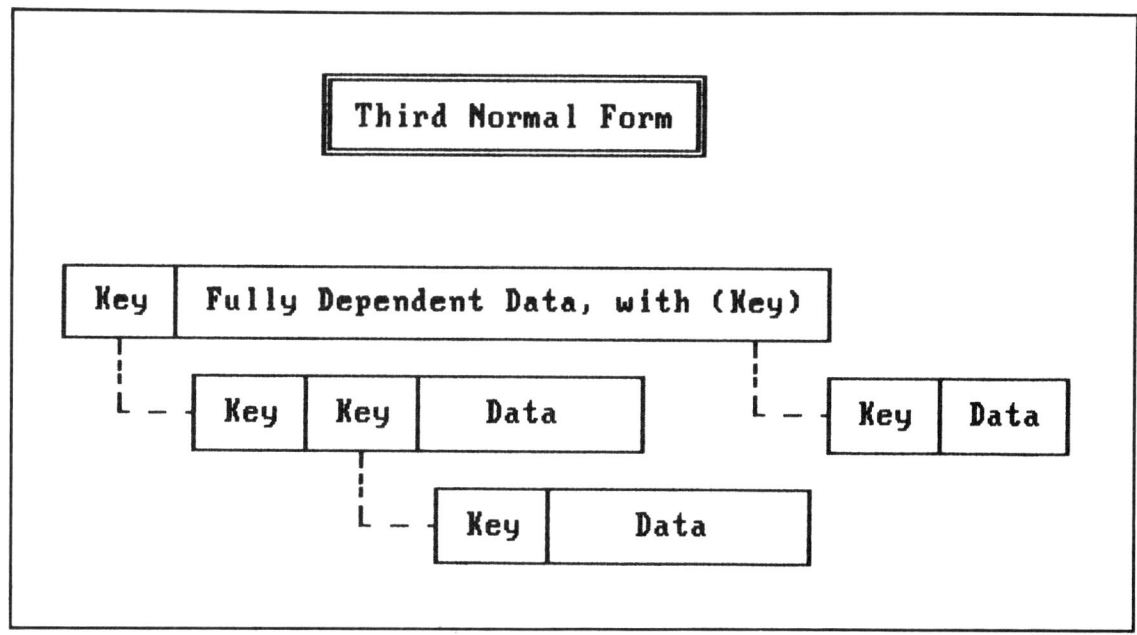

Fig. 1-3. The third normal form.

done by the field name given the field when you create a database, new fields can be added easily. This is called *format independence* because programs do not need to know the physical layout of the data.

THE DATA DICTIONARY

The foundation of a data design is the *data dictionary*. This document is a functional description of every item of data within the installation. This description includes the file in which it can be found, its format, length, and the entity to which it applies.

These descriptions are maintained in a file of some sort, possibly a database. The advantages of having such a dictionary are very important for a growing organization. The major impact of a data dictionary is that it provides a common definition of the data stored in the installation. It is surprising how little agreement there is on what a field like POLICYHOLDER'S NAME contains!

In an existing installation, the use of a data dictionary can weed out existing data redundancies. The cost of maintaining the same data in multiple files is a consideration, but more importantly, the data can become "out of synch," meaning that different files contain different data for the same person or other entity.

When a new application is being developed, the data dictionary becomes a valuable source for reference. It provides a trustworthy body of common descriptions that are agreed upon by everyone. It is also a guide for developing ad-hoc reports; the location and descriptions of each data item will lead the on-the-fly programmer through the relationships needed to produce any report. Figure 1-4 shows the information that belongs in a data dictionary.

The data dictionary should contain the following basic information about each data item:

Field name: the actual data name used for this field in a program.

Field data type: the type of field: character, numeric, logical, date, or memo.

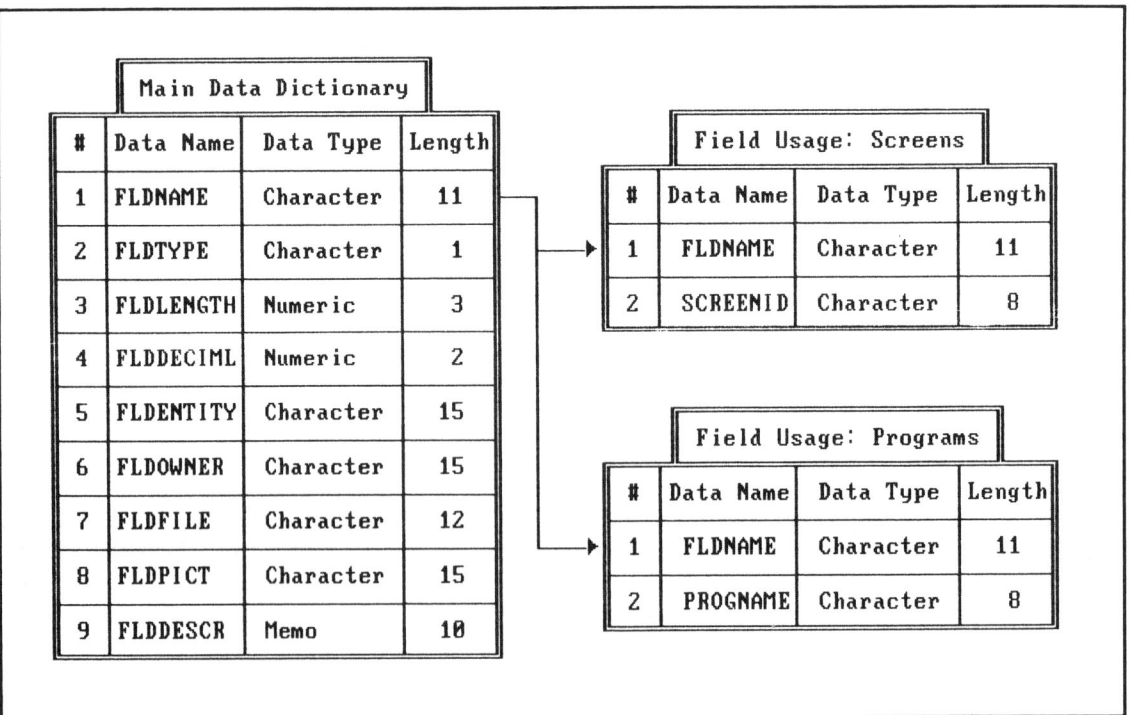

Fig. 1-4. Data dictionary data.

```
         --- Data Dictionary ---
         Fred's Friendly Fish Market

                                          Contained in
  utes   Entity          Owner            File

    0    EMPLOYEE        PERSONNEL        EMPLOYEE.DBF
    0    EMPLOYEE        PERSONNEL        EMPLOYEE.DBF
    0    EMPLOYEE        PERSONNEL        EMPLOYEE.DBF
```

report.

ength of the field.
he number assigned
icluded in the overall length.

Narrative description: a noncomputer description of the data contained in the field. A memo field might be used, if the description is very involved. Otherwise, 50 characters should be enough.

Entity: the entity which this field is a part of.

Project/owner: the area or person responsible for this data item. In smaller shops, this field might be eliminated.

Filename: the name of the database file where this data item is physically stored.

Optionally, the screens on which the data item is displayed can also be contained (in a separate file, since there could be multiple screens). The usual picture template can also be stored on the data dictionary. Figure 1-5 shows a sample data dictionary report.

There are two types of data dictionaries in use on mainframe computers: *passive* and *active*. Active data dictionaries are those that monitor programs for violations of standards or even write the data structure code necessary for the program. dBASE data structures, however, are set at the times of the CREATE for the database; a truly active dictionary has no real use in dBASE III.

The passive data dictionary is used for creating system documentation. The data is updated by the usual data entry methods, and a printed copy of the dictionary is produced. With a passive data dictionary, the maintenance of standards and conformity to the company's information design are the responsibility of the programmer.

An example of a passive data dictionary system is included in Appendix B.

COLLECTING DATA FROM SEVERAL SOURCES

Programs don't particularly care where the data comes from. In an effort to simplify the programming task, programs are made data independent, so that a database can change format without causing changes to all of the programs.

Mainframe database management systems use a type of *window* to change the database view for a particular program. This view is called the *database schema*, in technical terms. The actual physical format of the database is called the *sub-schema*.

The schema is used to gather all of the data items that make up the entity. This identifies to the end user the function of the data and its interdependencies.

The sub-schema is used by the programmer to develop the routines that will access the physical files and return only the data requested to the program. Making these routines separate from the program is a very important part of data independent design.

As shown in Fig. 1-6, the components of a data entity can be contained in several physical files or databases. It is the job of the interface program to provide the data to the application program for processing. The interface program also controls the modification of database records.

Most likely, if a data item is contained in a separate file from the main entity, it is because that particular data item can occur multiple times for a single entity. For example, one requirement of a personnel system might be the maintenance of a skills inventory for every employee. Each employee will most likely have more than one skill that is necessary for his job or promotion, so the skill information will be contained in a separate Employee/Skills database.

One technique in using dBASE (or any other DBMS) for data entities is to create an interface program that retrieves the necessary information for a particular entity and stores the information into memory variables. The memory variables can be used within the program, be modified, and passed back to the interface program for storing out to the database.

DATABASE ALIASES

When several databases are open at the same time, it may become difficult to remember which database is in which partition. To aid in avoiding this confusion, dBASE III allows the programmer to assign an alias to the various partitions, giving a meaningful name to use in pointing and selecting.

The SELECT statement is used to move from partition to partition. The partitions are numbered 1 through 10, and have built-in aliases A through J. These aliases can be used to identify database fields referenced when a different partition is SELECTed, by using the "pointing" operator (->). This method of identification becomes more readable when meaningful alias names are used—it is rather difficult to unravel the code surrounding something like A->NAME.

A meaningful alias can be assigned in the USE statement which is used to open the file. The code segment in Fig. 1-7 shows the alias EMP assigned to the A partition. Later references to fields contained in the database USEd in partition A may be made using EMP->. The A->NAME now becomes EMP->NAME, which makes more sense.

A default alias is also assigned to each database; the database name itself becomes the alias if no other alias is specified.

RELATING DATABASES TO EACH OTHER

When processing sales slips in an accounts receivable system, it is usually necessary to access information that is on the customer file but does not exist on the sales slip file. The sales slip file, however, does contain the key of the customer's

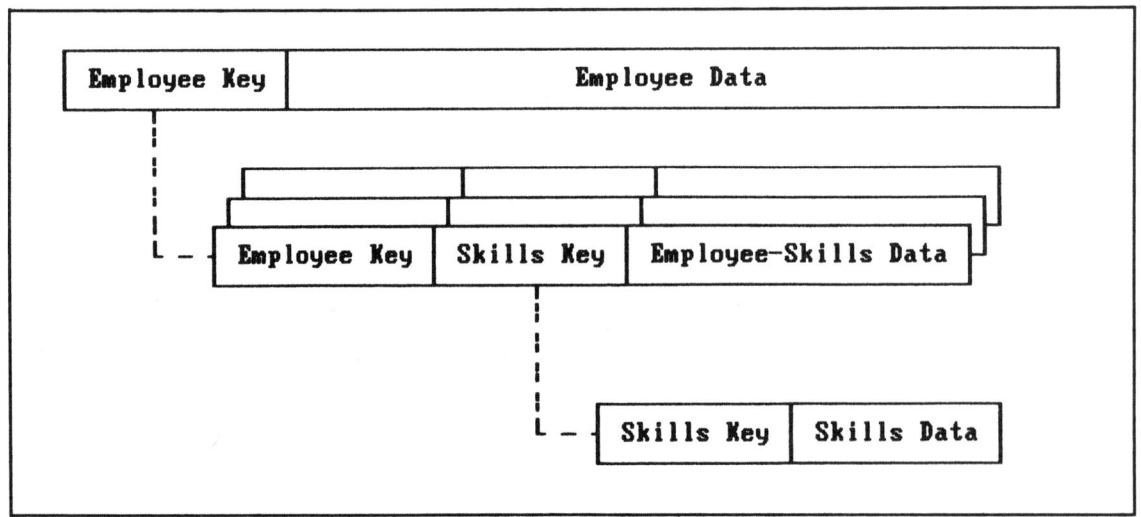

Fig. 1-6. Database connections.

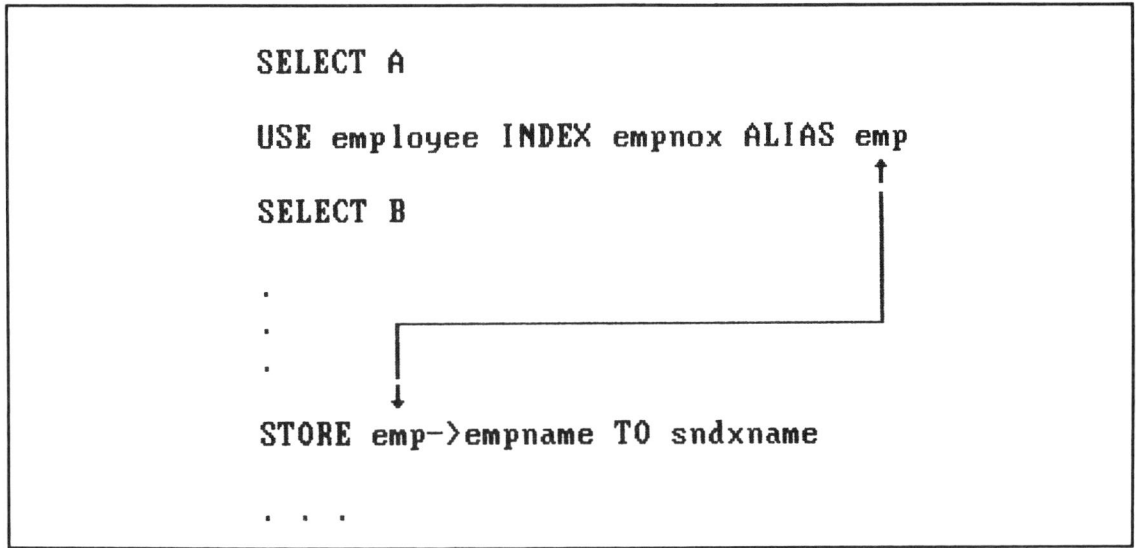

Fig. 1-7. The use of an alias.

record, and it is a relatively simple matter to open the customer database and LOCATE the record or use SEEK/FIND to locate it via the index. dBASE III also provides a method for performing this function automatically.

An indexed database may be related by its key field to other databases using the SET RELATION TO command. This command tells dBASE to reposition the related file each time the relation field, in this case Customer number, is changed. Thus, when your program is processing a sales slip, the customer information is instantly available by referencing the alias to qualify the "outside" information.

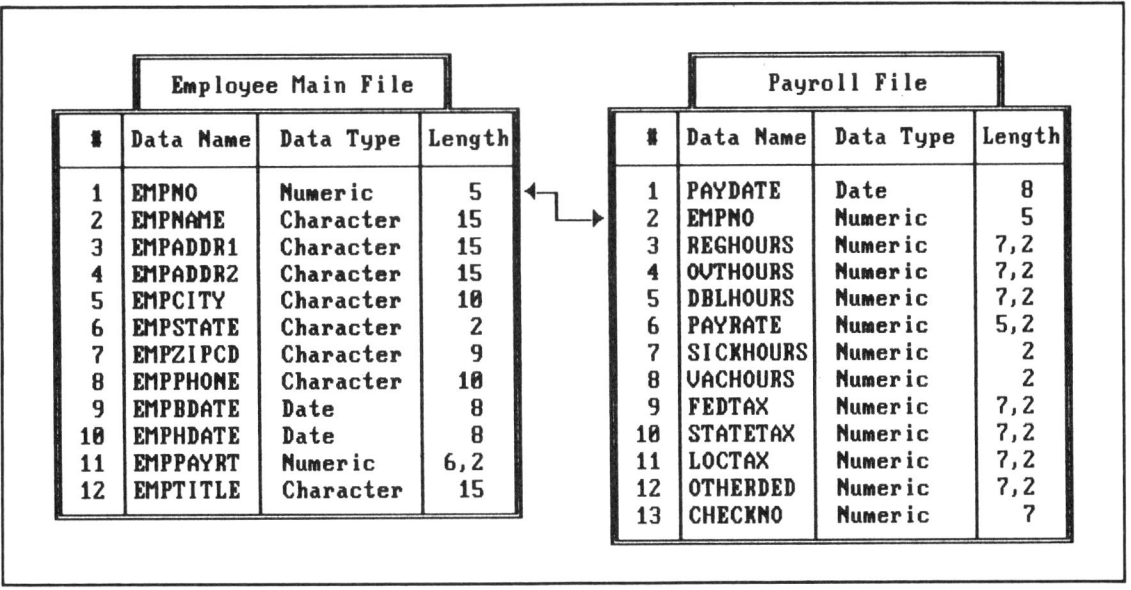

Fig. 1-8. Employee and Payroll databases.

7

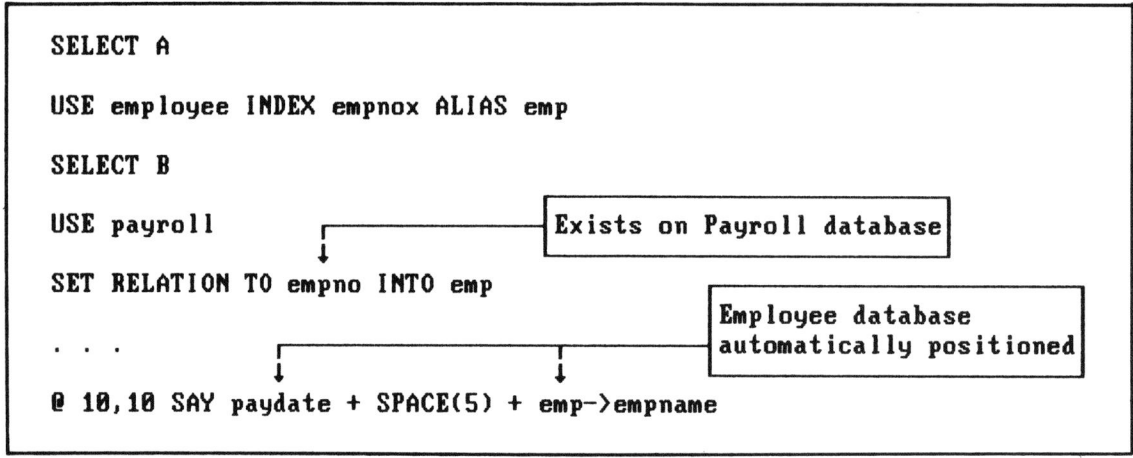

Fig. 1-9. Using the SET RELAtion command.

The format of the command is:

SET RELAtion TO <field name> INTO <alias>

The database identified by the alias must be indexed by the field referenced by <field name>. This must also be a field present on the database USEd in the current partition. Each time a new value is received into the current partition, the database <alias> is repositioned automatically.

This feature allows you to sequentially process one file and refer to related data in another without extra processing. For example, as shown in Fig. 1-8 the employee payroll file contains the employee number to identify the employee being paid. The pay rate is contained on the employee master file, along with all other nonrepeating information.

As shown in Fig. 1-9 by using SET RELAtion TO, the employee master file can automatically be positioned to the correct employee each time a new

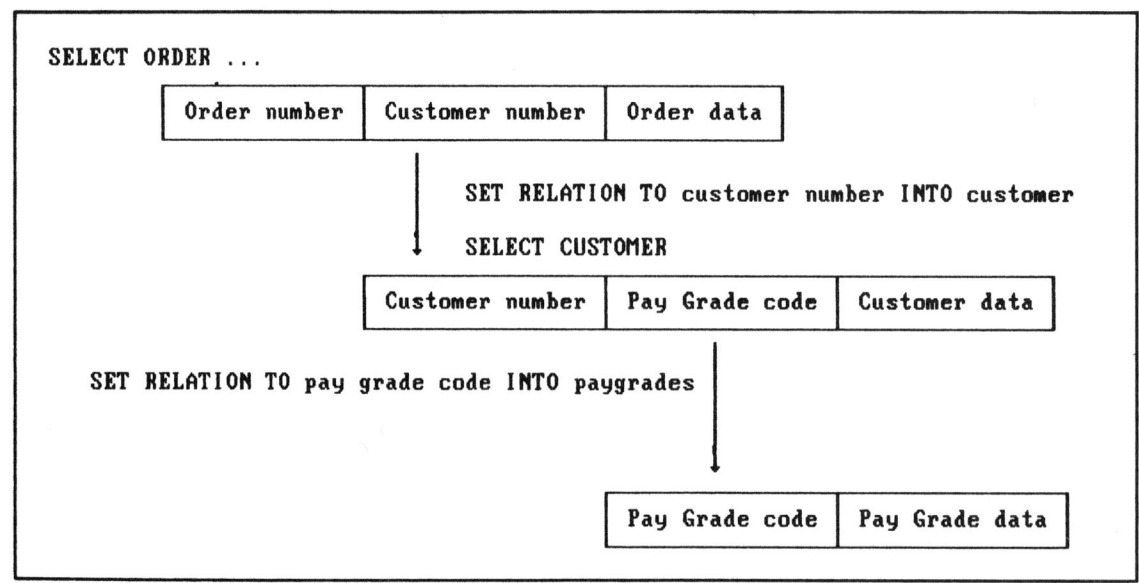

Fig. 1-10. Chaining relations.

payroll file record is read. Related files may be used to produce a report format that includes fields from multiple databases.

Only one SET RELAtion is allowed for each partition, which can be a drawback in some cases. However, multiple files can be accessed via relations by setting relations from one file to another, and then from that file to still another, and so forth. In a payroll system, the Payroll records may be related to the main Employee field by Employee number, while the Employee file is related to a Pay Grade description file by Pay Grade code. This technique is called *chaining*.

In processing a file like the Employee/Skills file, the SET RELAtion can be used to automatically access either the Skills Description file by the Skill code, or the Employee file by Employee number, but not by both at the same time. The database to SET RELAtion into should be the potentially largest file; in this case, the main Employee file. The Skills Description file, being smaller than the main Employee file, can quickly be accessed using SEEK or FIND. Figure 1-10 shows a sample of chaining relations.

Sometimes, although it is not a frequent occurrence, dBASE III seems to lose its place during an operation on related databases. This usually occurs when the related database is repositioned independently of the active database. dBASE will automatically reposition the related database, but it will do so only if the record in the active database is reaccessed. This can be done simply by GOing to the current record, with the statement "GO RECNO( )" while the active database is SELEcted.

Chapter 2
An Overview of dBASE III Components

The dBASE III software is designed to work with databases generated in a specific way. dBASE is relatively inflexible in its capabilities of data and file manipulation. Learning to operate within these constraints is possibly the most difficult part of producing a dBASE system.

Because these limitations do exist, it is necessary to "slant" the design slightly. The usual design methodology states that a system design should be independent of computer hardware and software. This can still be done with a proposed dBASE system at the earliest stage of system design, the problem definition. Slanting occurs when some system attributes affect the course of the design.

The programmer must be aware of the fundamental field and file capabilities of dBASE when designing the overall database. This chapter, and the two that follow, examine the uses of dBASE data types and files. This will help form the foundation of dBASE data design techniques.

COMMON FIELD TYPES AND THEIR USAGE

dBASE III allows for five types of fields that can contain factual data. The three most frequently used of these types of fields are character, numeric, and logical fields. There are also date and memo fields, whose purposes are self evident and whose functions will be discussed in later chapters. There is also an unseen field that is used in dealing with deleted records.

Character Fields

Character fields are used to store names, addresses, and other small amounts of textual data. A character field, defined on screen without a picture, will accept any character.

When combined with the PICTURE clause, character fields can contain any type of data in any format. This can be useful in temporary storage of dates in formats other than the common dBASE date formats. Figure 2-1 shows the character field specifications.

```
┌─────────────────────┐
│ Character Fields:   │
└─────────────────────┘
     ┌─────────────────────────────────────────────────────┐
     │ Data type:         C                                │
     ├─────────────────────────────────────────────────────┤
     │ Maximum Length:    254 characters                   │
     ├─────────────────────────────────────────────────────┤
     │ Minimum Length:    1 character                      │
     ├─────────────────────────────────────────────────────┤
     │ Allowable Values:  All codes* from X'00' to X'FF'   │
     │                    Usually alphanumeric             │
     └─────────────────────────────────────────────────────┘

     *Exception: Ctrl-Z (X'1A') which marks end of file.
```

Fig. 2-1. Character field specifications.

Character fields can also be used to approximate the table or array concept, using specialized functions like AT( ) and SUBSTR( ). One character string is used to contain the positioning data and another of the same length contains the data to be found. The data is placed so that when the AT( ) function is used to find the position of the positioning data in its character string, a SUBSTR( ) can be used to pull the result from the other character string.

Character fields are stored as a string and padded with blanks. The LEN( ) function will return a numeric value that is the length of the character string. This only applies to memory variables that are assigned strings of varying lengths. Character fields residing on a database always will show a length that is the same as the field length, unless the TRIM( ) function is used as well.

Numeric Fields

Numeric fields can be used for any type of arithmetic data. Any purely mathematical function or operation must have numeric variables as its component operands.

Numeric fields are stored as character strings in a dBASE database, right justified and blank filled. dBASE translates these numbers into binary/hexadecimal values for calculations.

The length of a database numeric field is specified on the Create screen, including the sign and decimal point. A field of length 7 with 2 decimal places can contain values in the range 9999.99 to −999.99. Figure 2-2 shows the numeric field specifications.

In dBASE, almost any place a numeric value may be used, a numeric result of a calculation or function may be substituted. The calculation or function is done first, and the resulting value is then used in the statement.

Logical Fields

The dBASE Logical data type is for fields that contain simple yes or no values. Logical fields are also known as binary (or bit) switches, because they have only two possible values.

Logical fields provide a way to readably test control information in a program. The logical field name can be created in such a way as to make decision statements understandable at a glance.

For example, the Employee database has a field that indicates whether or not a person is a veteran of one of the armed forces. Rather than using the following statement to interrogate the value:

IF EMPLOYEE – >VETIND = 'Y' . . .

this much more readable statement can be used:

IF EMPLOYEE – >VETERAN . . .

Figure 2-3 shows the logical field specifications.

Logical fields are stored in a database record as single characters (length 1) with values of T, t, Y, and y interpreted as true; the characters F, f, N, and n are considered false.

The @ . . . SAY . . . GET command displays the actual value of the field, so that Y or N answers are allowed for a logical field. When tested in an IF statement, the logical field will test as .T. or .F.. This is also the format that will be shown if the ?, DISP, or LIST commands are used to display the logical field.

The Unseen Field

Each database record includes a one-character field as its first field. This is used to mark a record for deletion. This is the extra character noted on the DISPLAY STRUCTURE report, where the field lengths do not seem to total correctly. Figure 2-4 shows the structure of the unseen field.

When the DELETE command is issued for a record on a database, dBASE places an asterisk (*) in the first character of the record. This will indicate to commands like PACK which records are not to be copied.

The function DELETED( ) can access this unseen field, providing a true/false indicator. DELETED( ) always works with the current database record.

The SET DELEted TO command can set the dBASE environment to accept or reject deleted records. If SET DELEted is ON, most dBASE commands will ignore deleted records; with SET DELEted turned OFF, the deleted records are treated as any other record. The DELETED( ) function can then be used for processing dependent on this fact.

Database records can be "undeleted" simply by moving a space into this unseen field in the rec-

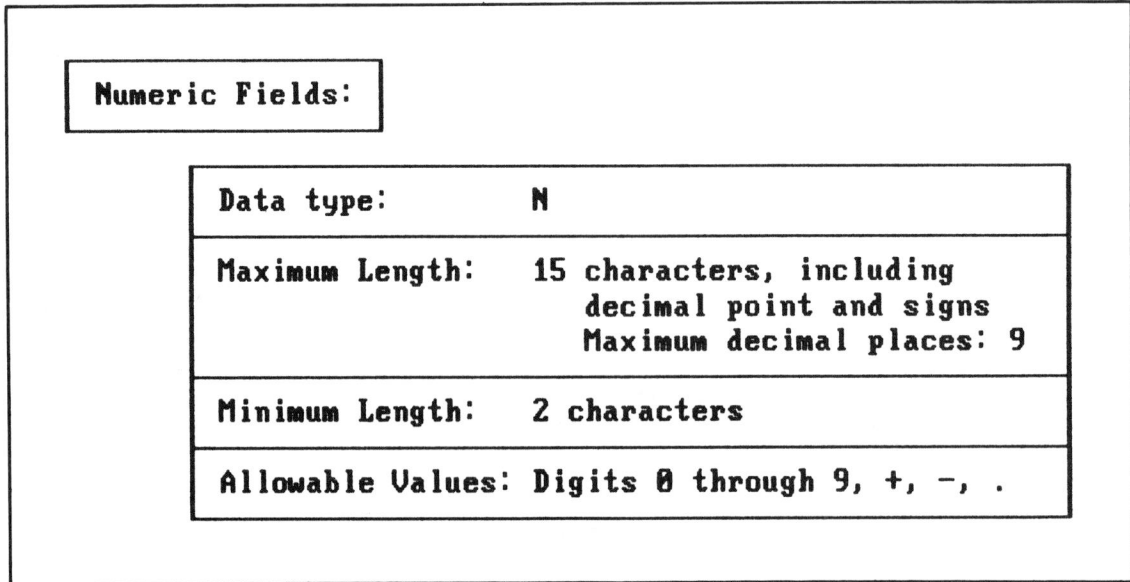

Fig. 2-2. Numeric field specifications.

```
┌─────────────────────────────────────────────────────────┐
│  ┌──────────────────┐                                   │
│  │ Logical Fields:  │                                   │
│  └──────────────────┘                                   │
│       ┌─────────────────────────────────────────────┐   │
│       │ Data type:         L                        │   │
│       ├─────────────────────────────────────────────┤   │
│       │ Maximum Length:    1 character              │   │
│       ├─────────────────────────────────────────────┤   │
│       │ Minimum Length:    1 character              │   │
│       ├─────────────────────────────────────────────┤   │
│       │ Allowable Values:  T, t, F, f, Y, y, N, n   │   │
│       └─────────────────────────────────────────────┘   │
└─────────────────────────────────────────────────────────┘
```

Fig. 2-3. Logical field specifications.

ord. The programmer, however, cannot directly access this field. The dBASE command RECALL will recall deleted records in this manner. Note that a RECALL ALL will not work with SET DELETED ON.

Deleted records are always indexed, and direct-access commands like DISPLAY RECORD 7 or GO 7 will display/access the record even when it is deleted and SET DELETED is ON.

FILE TYPES AND THEIR USAGE

As shown in Fig. 2-5, dBASE III uses nine different kinds of files, each of which serves a different purpose. The seven most important types are described on the following pages.

Database Files

Database files, the files that actually contain the

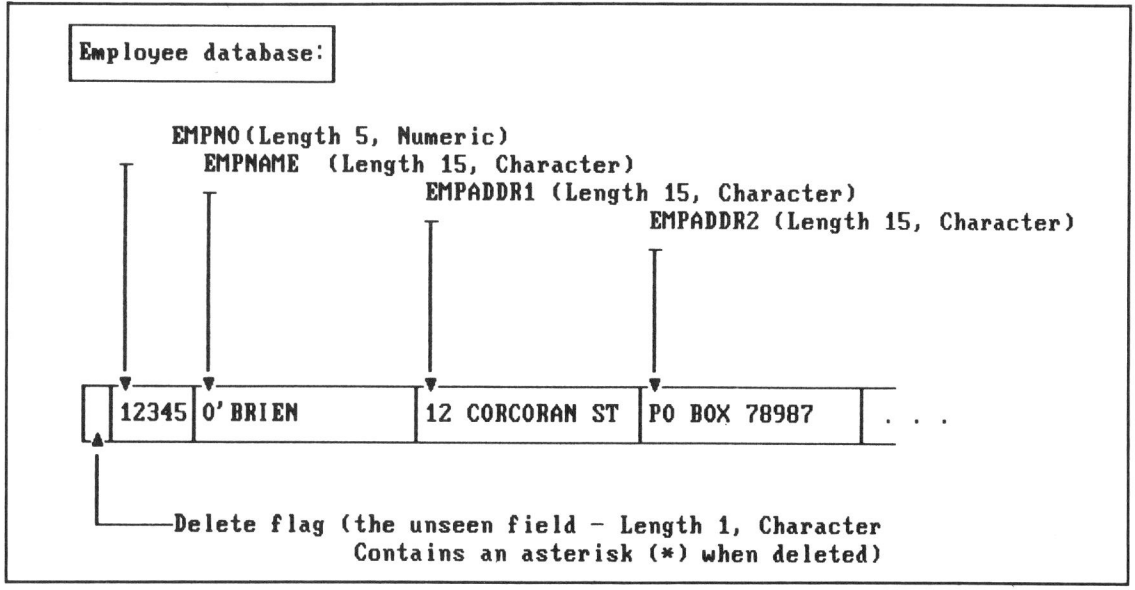

Fig. 2-4. The Unseen field.

Type of File	dBASE default extension
Database	.DBF
Memo field file	.DBT
Index	.NDX
Saved memory variable file	.MEM
Program/procedure file	.PRG
Screen format file	.FMT
Report format file	.FRM
Text output files	.TXT
Label format file	.LBL

Fig. 2-5. The dBASE file types.

data, are the main feature of dBASE III. The data area of the file contains all of the information entered or updated in the file. The data are all stored in "plain text" ASCII format, or, in other terms, character strings. dBASE retrieves the data from the file and converts it for use by the computer.

The database file contains an area of information about the database, called a database header. The database header information contains the date of the last update of the database and the number of records currently contained, including deleted records.

The database file also contains information about the fields in the database records, including the field name, length, number of decimals, and the data type (character, numeric, date, logical, or memo) of the field. This information is used by dBASE in setting up the memory areas it uses to hold database file records.

It is necessary, before deciding on the use of a particular storage medium, to estimate the size of the database that will be created. The database file size computation is:

```
32 +
(<number of fields> * 32) +
3 +
<number of records> * (<sum of field lengths> + 1)
```

The first line is the length of the dBASE header area. The second line yields the overall length of the field description areas. The third line represents the three characters that separate the field descriptions from the data. Line four computes the length of the entire data area. The "+ 1" is the length of the unseen field—the deletion indicator. Figure 2-6 shows how the database size is calculated.

Database records are located by a record

number. The current record number is always available to a program through the use of the RECNO( ) function. RECNO( ) should never be used to form a key—it is a variable number. If records are deleted and the file PACKed, the record number will be changed.

Index Files

Index files contain information necessary to quickly locate a particular record in a database. The key field of the record, which in dBASE can be literally any field in the record, is stored in a tree-type chain; this means that the desired record number can be obtained with a minimal number of disk reads. The record is accessed directly, so that the search-and-wait time is very short.

An index is created by the INDEX ON command. The field specified after the ON becomes the key field for that particular index. The key and the record number of each record are stored in the index, and the tree structure is built. The name of the index is specified in the TO clause; this name is given a file extension .NDX and becomes the name of the physical file containing the index.

A dBASE index is a structure known as a B+tree. Originally named *binary trees*, further refinement of the structure lead to *B–trees*, and finally the *B+tree*. The B+tree checks the key (requested via SEEK, FIND, or SET RELAtion) against node keys that it has made part of the tree structure. If the requested key is greater than the node key one branch is followed, and if less, another branch is followed. Several levels of nodes and branches are followed to retrieve the record number.

It takes much less time to index a database than it does to sort it. The index stores much less data than the database, so actual physical rearrangement is unnecessary. This reduces disk input/output (I/O) operations, which always speeds up a process.

One method of sorting a database without using the dBASE SORT command is to first INDEX the database into the order you wish to sort it and then use the COPY TO command to copy it to another file. This actually takes about 75 percent of the time that is necessary to do a sort, because the constant

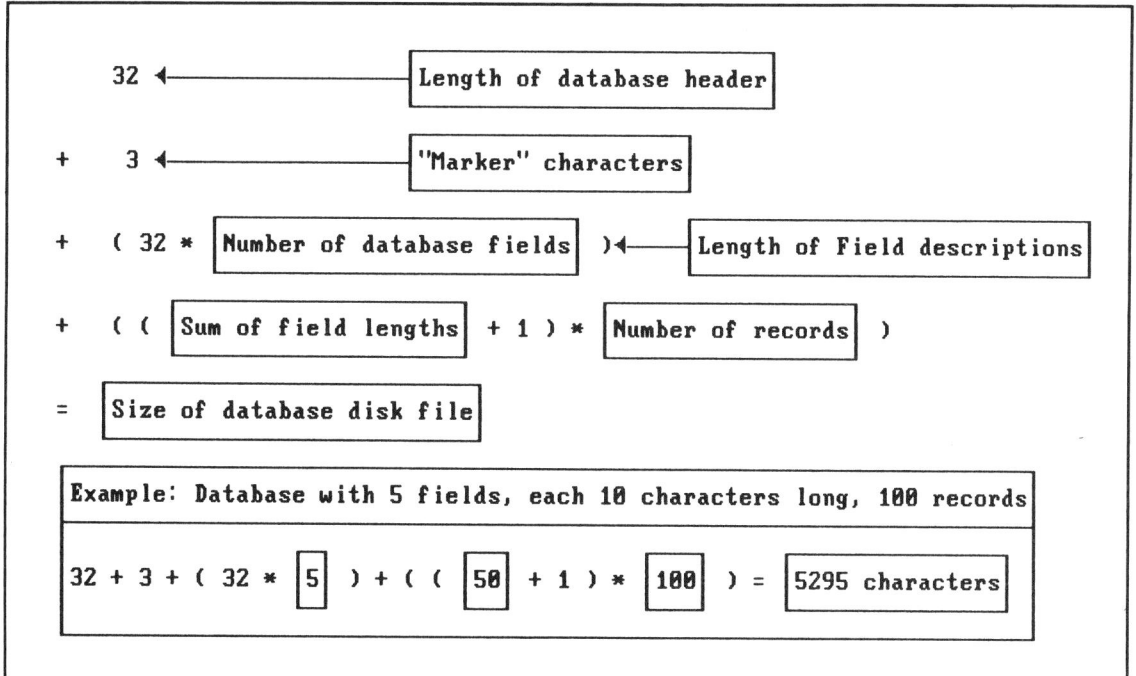

Fig. 2-6. Calculating the database size.

passing of records between memory and disk is avoided to a large degree.

Memory Variable Files

dBASE III sets a limit of 256 as the number of memory variables defined in one program. There is also a space limit, which can be managed by a parameter in the CONFIG.DB file discussed later in this chapter. Memory variables can also be "swapped out" to a file when they are not being used; this frees up storage and enlarges the number of memory variables that can be used in a system.

The SAVE command saves memory variables to a disk file, and the RESTORE command retrieves them and makes them available to the program again. The disk file has the extension .MEM, and the name is specified by a TO clause on the SAVE command.

Memory variables can be retrieved from the file using the command RESTore FROM <filename> [ADDItive]. The word ADDItive tells dBASE not to clear out the current memory variables, but to add the memory variables stored in the file to those already in memory. This allows the temporary transfer of memory variables to a file; these variables can be restored later and added to the already existing memory variables.

Memo Field Files

The text contained in a memo field is stored separately from the database record it appears to be on. This is because the database record contains a ten-character long pointer field that indicates the location of the text.

The text is actually stored in a file with the same name as the database file it is related to, but with the extension of .DBT. This file contains the text for all of the memo fields in the entire database.

Memo fields can only be accessed by pressing the Ctrl-PgDn key while in an interactive command, such as EDIT, APPEnd, INSErt, and CHANge. They are ignored during COPY operations.

Memo fields are discussed in more detail in Chapter 4.

Program/Procedure Files

Program and procedure files both have the file extension of .PRG. These files contain the dBASE commands that make up a program. Although procedure files have the .PRG extension, they are not directly executable.

A program file can be executed with the DO command. Parameters can be passed by using the WITH clause of the DO statement and including the PARAmeters statement as the first executable line of the subprogram.

A procedure file is used by a program file as storage for a group of subroutines. Access to those subroutines is gained through the SET PROCedure TO <filename> command. dBASE will load the procedure file into memory; there the subroutines contained in the file are available immediately. Without the wait for the program to load from disk, the program appears to work faster.

There is a limit of thirty-two (32) procedures that can be placed in a procedure file. Any procedures after the 32nd one in the procedure file are ignored. If a name referenced by a DO command is not found in the current procedure file, the disk is searched for a program file with that name.

Screen Format Files

Screen format files contain @ ... SAY ... GET commands to define a full-screen format for input or output. The file extension expected by dBASE for a screen format file is .FMT, but it can be any extension you want to use.

The advantage of placing the screens in a separate file is to remove what is really unnecessary code from the main program. The @ ... SAY ... GET commands position text on the screen and define areas for input. These functions can be removed from the main program code, which allows you to rearrange your screens without modifying the program file.

The screen format is accessed by the SET FORMat TO <filename> command. Once the format is SET, the GETS must be activated by the READ, CHANge, INSErt, EDIT, or APPEnd command.

Report Format Files

Report format files are identified by the file extension .FRM. (If you have difficulty remembering which type of file has the .FMT extension and which has the .FRM extension, just remember that report is the one that has the R in it.)

Report formats can only be created interactively with the dBASE CREATE REPOrt command. This process leads the user through some questions about the report, and generates the report based on the specifications entered. The data fields of the current database are displayed at the top of the screen for reference. Report formats can be changed with the MODIfy REPOrt command.

The reports are generated either interactively or from a program with the command REPOrt FORM <format name> [TO PRINT] [PLAIN]. The TO PRINT tells dBASE to send the generated report to the printer; the PLAIN option removes the automatic date and page number included in the heading.

USING CONFIG.DB

The CONFIG.DB file contains commands that can change dBASE to suit the user's needs. The entire dBASE environment can be tailored using this file; the file can even specify a program to run immediately upon entry into dBASE.

Values for all of the SET commands may be specified in CONFIG.DB, thus creating new default values for those switches. There are also several other options available. The dBASE III disks do not contain a sample of this file, so there is some confusion as to its use.

Besides the SET commands, the following parameters and switches may be set using CONFIG.DB:

PROMPT. This specifies the character or string of characters that dBASE will use to prompt for input from the keyboard. For example, the usual dBASE prompt is a single period. If this is all that appears on the screen, a novice user might have trouble determining what is going on. A more readily identifiable prompt would be dBASE>, which indicates the software package that is prompting for input. This can be implemented via a statement in the CONFIG.DB file: PROMPT = <char>, where <char> is the prompt of your choice. In this case, the command would be PROMPT = dBASE>.

F2 through F10. You can specify the commands associated with the PC's function keys using CONFIG.DB. Any function key (except F1, which is HELP) can be changed to alter its function; the character string following the = sign can be any string or command.

TEDIT and WP. These parameters allow you to use editors other than the built-in editors of dBASE. TEDIT specifies the full path and filename of the editor to be used when the command MODIfy COMMand is used. This editor is then accessed as if it too were built-in to dBASE; of course, some time is lost waiting for the editor to load from disk, since dBASE's editor is internal. WP indicates the editor to be used for memo field editing.

BUCKET and GETS. BUCKET specified the amount of memory to be reserved for PICTURE clauses and RANGE values from the @ ... GET commands. The default value is 2K but may be changed to any value between 1 and 31, representing the number of kilobytes to be reserved. GETS sets the total number of GETS that may be active at once. The default value is 128, but it can be changed from 35 to 1023.

MVARSIZ. This parameter affects the way memory is arranged in dBASE, just as the BUCKETS parameter does. MVARSIZ adjusts the amount of memory that is used to store memory variables. The default MVARSIZ is 6000 characters, and the size can be adjusted from 1 to 31, each number representing that number of kilobytes.

MAXMEM is the highest memory location that dBASE keeps exclusively for its own use. This is not to say that it will not use memory above this point; this is simply the point in memory above which external commands can be executed.

COMMAND. This parameter identifies the name of a program (.PRG) file that is to be executed

17

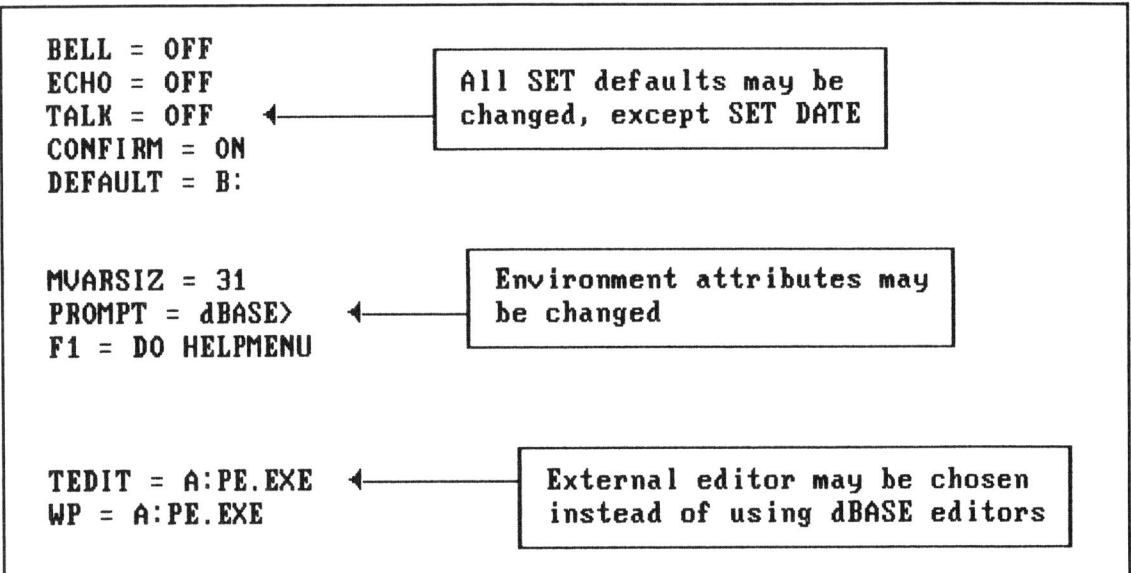

Fig. 2-7. An example of CONFIG.DB.

as the first command to dBASE. The program file is loaded off of disk and executed immediately after dBASE III's initialization is complete, just as if you had typed DO <program name> from the dBASE prompt. Figure 2-7 shows an example of a CONFIG.DB file. The CONFIG.DB file can save the tedious steps necessary to tailor the environment to the needs of the individual dBASE user, developer, and system.

Chapter 3
Dates, Times, and Conversions

dBASE III offers both time and date functions. Date fields are a new addition to dBASE III. The date fields provide flexibility when dealing with date-oriented comparisons and calculations. Date fields are also automatically edited for correctness, so a separate edit is not required.

Date fields are stored as character strings eight (8) characters long, in the format YYYYMMDD. This is the most utilitarian format of the Gregorian date in common use. The advantage of storing dates in this format is that numeric comparisons of greater or lesser values will work correctly, without the need for multiple comparisons and conversions.

DATE USAGE

Figure 3-1 shows the Date programming functions that dBASE III offers. dBASE III also allows a limited range of calculations to be performed on date fields. Days may be added to a date, yielding another date; dates may also be subtracted from one another, yielding the number of days between them.

Dates in dBASE can be stored with up to 5 digits of century, allowing a vast range of dates to be stored. This means that historical scholars could create a time-line using dBASE III, using memo fields to store a narrative text. The database could then be used to produce time-lines and other educational aids.

The century may not be entered when entering a date with @ . . . GET; the format is strictly MM/DD/YY. Using this format, the century number 19 is always assumed. Dates greater than 12/31/1999 and less than 01/01/1900 can be used in calculations but cannot be displayed in a date field.

The correct century can be stored and accessed by using the YEAR( ) function. By using PICTURE, the CTOD( ) function, and a memory variable, dates outside of the 20th century can be stored in dBASE date format.

dBASE III can be used to store other date formats as well, but they are not (yet) software supported—which means, of course, if you want to do it, you must program it yourself. This is only

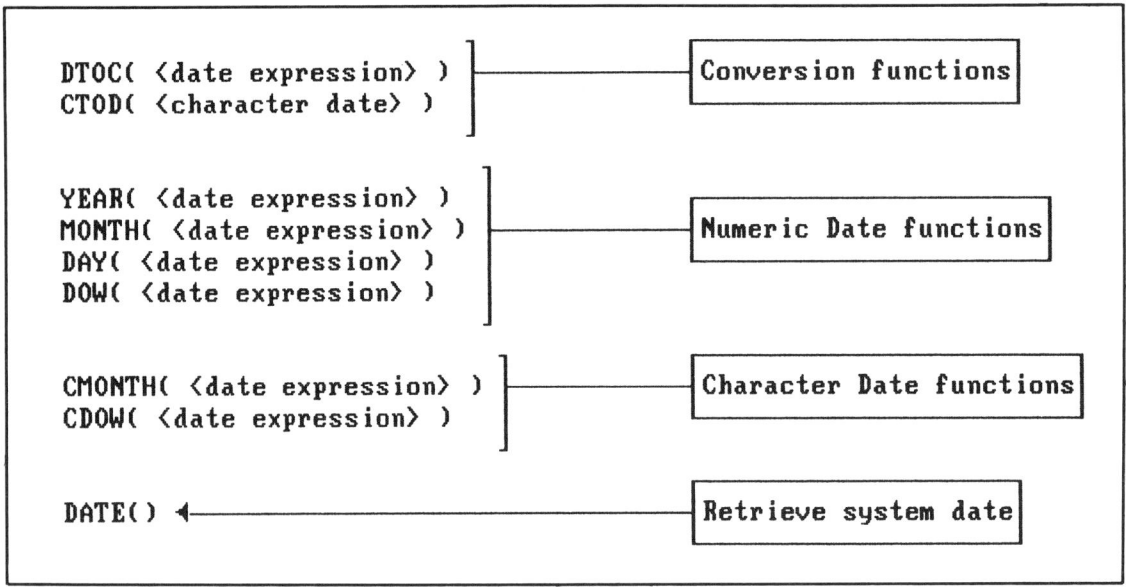

Fig. 3-1. Date programming functions.

possible in a language that has the functions necessary to complete the conversion; dBASE III has these functions, if you know where to look.

DIFFERENT TYPES OF DATES

dBASE III only accepts input into Date fields in the format MM/DD/YY. The year, even though only two digits long, will be stored as 19YY on the database. The 19 is assumed on every date entered.

This is useful for a current-time system, or any system that deals with dates in a fifteen-year range or smaller. For some systems, such as historical research data, genealogies, science-fiction character files, or municipal records, this limitation may be unacceptable . . . and the year 2000 is rapidly approaching. Most likely, the dBASE III language and access methods will be changed before then to accept a four-digit year.

To use dates in other than the dBASE III date format now, however, requires working around the limitations. If you could choose a standard date format with an entry in CONFIG.DB, that would probably be best, since you would want all date entry consistent.

dBASE III date fields are still usable as storage fields, because dates up to 12/31/9999 will work in calculations and comparisons.

The most useful form of date is the YYYYMMDD format of the standard Gregorian date that dBASE stores its dates in. This format allows dates to be compared, since the format is in ascending order of change. This means that the date 19860704 will test to be greater than 19851231. This would not be the case using any other arrangement.

dBASE III allows several formats of Gregorian date, notably the American, ANSI (American National Standards Institute), British, French, German, and Italian.

Another useful date form is the Julian, or relative-day date. The months and days of the Gregorian format are replaced with a single, three-digit number, denoting the day number relative to the year; January 1 is day 001, December 31 is day 365, or 366 during leap years. The most useful format of a Julian date is YYYYDDD.

Julian dates are useful because they can be added to and subtracted from easily. This format of date is rare in a dBASE III system, since dBASE

III can properly add and subtract days from a date. However, some people prefer the Julian format to the Gregorian.

Figure 3-2 shows the various date formats allowed by dBASE III. The differently-formatted dates may be used in a dBASE III system by programmatically arranging the date into an "MM/DD/YYYY" format and then using the CTOD( ) function to store the date in dBASE format. The CTOD( ) function will correctly store the four-digit year.

Getting the date into dBASE can also be done, by @ . . . GETting each portion of the date (month, day, year) as a different field, performing range and numeric checks, and then using STR( ) to concatenate all the parts, including the slashes, into one character string. CTOD( ) takes care of the rest. However, correct use of the PICTURE clause can save you the hassles of juggling multiple fields.

The PICTURE function "@R", when used with a template, tells dBASE that the literals in the template are not to be stored with the variable. This way you can store dates as character strings, and by using SUBSTR( ) you can manipulate the information into any desired format. Also, using template "99/99/9999" without the "@R" will save the "/" characters as a part of the field, making the conversion to a date variable even easier. You must still edit the date for correctness, since dBASE does not perform this function on any but Date-type fields.

DATE FUNCTIONS

The dBASE III functions that deal with date processing make it easy to use dates in an effective manner from within a program. The functions can also lend an air of superiority to your programs, by performing some very sophisticated tasks that would otherwise be impossible.

The functions can be divided into functions that work with the whole date, year functions, month functions, and day functions.

DATE( ). The DATE( ) function returns the

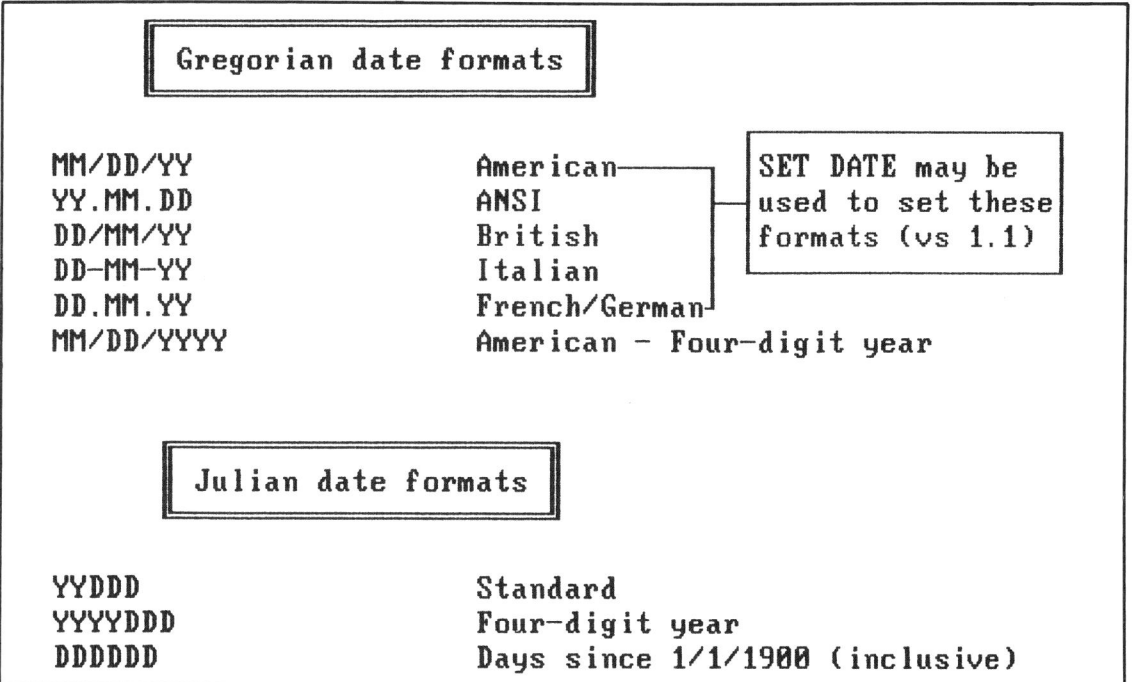

Fig. 3-2. Other date formats.

value of the current system date. This is set by a clock-calendar built into the PC, which can be set with the DATE and TIME PC-DOS commands. The value returned is of the Date data type. If you wish to use the current date in a character string, you must convert it to character. No expression goes in the parentheses.

CTOD(<character expression>) and DTOC(<date expression>). These are the two date conversion functions. CTOD( ) converts a character string into the Date data type. The character string must be in the format "MM/DD/YYYY" for dates outside of the 20th century, and "MM/DD/YY" for 20th century dates. The CTOD( ) function will accept dates in the range 1/1/100 to "12/31/32767". The DTOC( ) function reverses the process, changing a Date variable into a character string of the format "MM/DD/YY".

YEAR(<date expression>). The YEAR( ) function returns a numeric value that is the full year of the date expression. The correct century is returned, and the value may be used in any expression where a numeric variable can be used.

MONTH(<date expression>). MONTH( ) returns the numeric value of the month of the date expression. Date expressions can be any date field or variable, or a calculation that returns a date value.

CMONTH(<date expression>). The CMONTH( ) is one of the dBASE III built-in functions that does not exist in most programming languages. This function returns a character string that is the month name of the date expression enclosed in the parentheses. This is extremely useful in producing very sophisticated output reports and even form letters. For example, if you want to set an appointment for 90 days hence, you might include these character expressions:

". . . so our appointment is set for " + DTOC (DATE( ) + 90) + "."
"See you in " + CMONTH(DATE( ) + 90) + "!"

These strings would be translated (for a system date of 08/03/1985) into the following text:

". . . so our appointment is set for 11/01/1985."
"See you in November!"

CDOW( ), DOW( ), and DAY( ). These functions work with the day portion of a date expression. The DAY( ) function returns a numeric value that is the day: 31 for 12/31/85, for example. The DOW( ) function returns a numeric value for the day of the week: Sunday is 1, Monday is 2, and so on. Finally, the CDOW( ) function returns a character string that is the name of the day of the week.

The date functions can be used as expressions to other date functions. By mixing the date functions (always taking care to end up with a character string), you can create sophisticated formats to enhance your output. The example in Fig. 3-3 shows how the current date can be formatted for output in the classic format.

THE TIME FUNCTION

The time can also be included in output, whether screen or print, where it is needed. No calculations can be performed with the time, however, and no functions exist (yet) for time processing.

The TIME( ) function returns a character string that is the current time in the format "HH:MM:SS". The TIME( ) function, like the DATE( ) function, returns a system value, so there is no value placed in the parentheses.

One way to effectively use the TIME( ) function is to display a time on the screen for operator reference. By continuously writing the time to the same position on the screen, the impression of a running clock can be given.

Another use for the TIME( ) function is for audit trail purposes. If a log of changes is being kept, the log can be date and time stamped for more accurate reporting. The time can also be placed in a file or database to note updates, additions, or other actions.

USING DATES TO BUILD OTHER VARIABLES

The date functions allow more than just normal internal processing. They can be used to affect areas usually outside the normal programming sphere.

Since dates can be broken into their numeric components using the DAY( ), MONTH( ), and YEAR( ) functions, the various portions can be used to create unique names for output files. This is possible by mixing the date functions with macro substitution (&), to create unique character strings. This can be used to produce files for back-up. The files can also be archived by date using a routine similar to the one shown in Fig. 3-4.

The trick is in padding the numeric months and days with zeroes when the values are less than two digits long. By using the length parameter of STR( ), you can concatenate leading zeroes to the month and day. The example routine in Fig. 3-4 does NOT take the year into account, although the same method should work there, as well.

The syntax of the STR( ) function is:

STR(<numeric expression> , <length>)

where *numeric expression* is the number to be turned into a string, and *length* is the length of that string. So, to produce a two-digit month:

```
IF MONTH(DATE( )) < 10
    STORE '0' + STR(MONTH(DATE( )),1) TO MM
ELSE
    STORE STR(MONTH(DATE( )),2) TO MM
ENDIF
```

The IF statement determines whether or not padding is needed. If it is, the first STORE concatenates zero to the one-digit month. Otherwise, the two digit month is used (second STORE instruction). Days are handled in the same way:

```
IF DAY(DATE( )) < 10
    STORE '0' + STR(DAY(DATE( )),1) TO MM
ELSE
    STORE STR(DAY(DATE( )),2) TO MM
ENDIF
```

▶ Given: System date of 08/30/1985

▶ Formatted with the following functions:

```
STORE CDOW( DATE() )+', ';
    + CMONTH( DATE() )+' ';
    + STR( DAY( DATE() ),2)+', ';
    + STR( YEAR( DATE() ),4) TO bigdate
```

▶ Yields the date in full date format:

```
"Friday, August 30, 1985"
```

Fig. 3-3. Using the date functions.

```
PROCEDURE ARCHIVE
SELECT A                [database to be archived]
USE ...
STORE SPACE(2) TO YR    [setup the memory variables]
STORE SPACE(2) TO MM
STORE SPACE(2) TO DD
STORE SUBSTR(STR(YEAR(DATE()),4),3) TO YR
IF MONTH(DATE()) < 10   [find out if padding is needed]
    STORE '0'+STR(MONTH(DATE()),1) TO MM
ELSE
    STORE STR(MONTH(DATE()),2) TO MM
ENDIF
IF DAY(DATE()) < 10
    STORE '0'+STR(DAY(DATE()),1) TO DD
ELSE
    STORE STR(DAY(DATE()),2) TO DD
ENDIF
STORE 'xx'+YR+MM+DD TO FN    [xx: identification]
COPY TO &FN        [copy to the filename we just made up]
ZAP                [optional: refresh database]
USE
RETURN
```

Fig. 3-4. The archival routine.

Once the year, month, and day are turned into two-character strings, the COPY TO statement can be used to copy the database to a filename made up of two other characters plus the date:

STORE 'xx' + YY + MM + DD TO FN
COPY TO &FN

The xx is a two-character identifier for the file, for example, RT for register tape or MR for monthly report. The &FN tells dBASE to replace the &FN with the value of FN in this statement. Optionally, a file extension can be added, and the data copied to a System Data Format (SDF) file (which is what dBASE calls a straight ASCII file). Finally, you can ZAP the database for reuse, because you have created a backup dynamically, directly from your program.

Chapter 4
Memo Fields and Files

Database systems do not often offer a way of storing large amounts of textual data. After all, that is not really a function of a database, because text, rather than being in a readily-identifiable format, is random. There is no easy way of breaking the text into discrete items of data, since most text is meaningful only in conjunction with the rest of the text in the document.

dBASE III, however, allows text lines (i.e., a document) to be stored separately from the "real" data, but related to it by means of a memo field.

The memo field on the database record is not a field that the dBASE user can access. It contains information that will help dBASE find the textual information, which is really stored in another file. Such referencing fields are called *pointers*. The memo field points to the stored text.

Memo fields can be used for several purposes, depending on the requirements of the dBASE user (you). One way of using a memo field is use it to hold a history of changes made to a particular database record, which is called a *change log*. When a record is changed, the operator can enter the memo text and add a line describing the change, the date, and so forth. This type of "honor-system" audit trail can save confusion later, especially when the order in which changes occurred is being disputed.

Another way that a memo field could be used is to store resumes in a personnel system, or a work history for an employee. They can be used to store descriptions of items, appointment reminders, and exceptional processing conditions for the record.

USING MEMO FIELDS

A memo field is created by entering M as the field type of a field on the Create menu. Each memo field takes up ten characters in the database record and contains a pointer to the text information. The text is stored in another file, which has an extension .DBT, meaning Database Text.

Once a memo field is defined, it can be displayed like any other field type. EDIT and the other interactive modes, like @ ... SAY ... GET, display a four character field that says "memo." This is to identify the memo field to the operator.

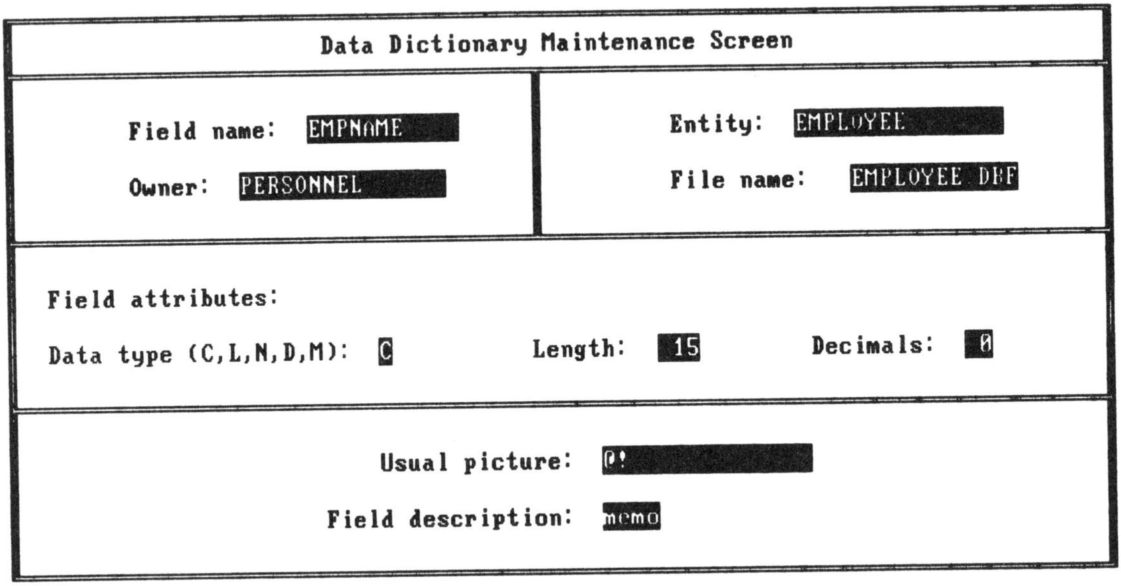

```
┌─────────────────────────────────────────────────────────────────┐
│              Data Dictionary Maintenance Screen                 │
├──────────────────────────────────┬──────────────────────────────┤
│  Field name:  EMPNAME            │  Entity:     EMPLOYEE        │
│  Owner:       PERSONNEL          │  File name:  EMPLOYEE.DBF    │
├──────────────────────────────────┴──────────────────────────────┤
│  Field attributes:                                              │
│  Data type (C,L,N,D,M):  C       Length:  15    Decimals:  0    │
├─────────────────────────────────────────────────────────────────┤
│                    Usual picture:  @!                           │
│                Field description:  memo                         │
└─────────────────────────────────────────────────────────────────┘
```

Fig. 4-1. The memo field displayed on screen.

Figure 4-1 shows how the memo field is displayed on the screen.

You cannot put data into the field in the usual manner. The screen display will just say "memo" until you press the Control-PgDn key. Doing this will open up the dBASE Word Processor editor, where you may add text lines to the memo.

Once the word processor is activated, dBASE retrieves the text from the memo-storage file. The contents of the memo field are then displayed over the current screen. The screen is not erased from memory—dBASE just overlays the screen with the full-screen text editor. This process is called *windowing*; pressing Ctrl-PgDn opens a window to the memo text.

The operator may make any additions or changes to the text using the commands for the dBASE word processor or the other editor that you specified in CONFIG.DB. The operator could also just look at the contents without changing them.

ACCESSING STORED MEMO FIELDS

As mentioned before, the text contained in a memo field is retrieved when the operator presses the Ctrl-PgDn key while the cursor is on the screen field, which reads simply "memo". The word processor is then executed, bringing the text to the screen. You can store several pages of text, which can then be examined or modified using the word processor commands.

Stored memo fields can only be accessed using the interactive commands EDIT, APPEND, INSERT, and CHANGE. Using READ to access a memo field in an @ . . . GET does not work. There is a work-around for interactive systems that are program-driven—use CHANGE in the program instead of READ.

Since CHANGE will automatically try to skip to the next record when you pass the last data field on the screen, a small repositioning is necessary, as shown in Fig. 4-2. By saving the record number of the record to be CHANGEd, the database can be repositioned at the correct record for editing. Using the RECORD scope for the CHANGE command, the operator will not be able to page forward and backward through the database, which is a usual feature of CHANGE.

If a memo field is entered as a display field in a report, the report will print each line of the memo field on a single line of the report. The other fields on the report line are not repeated.

Figures 4-3 through 4-5 show the use of memo

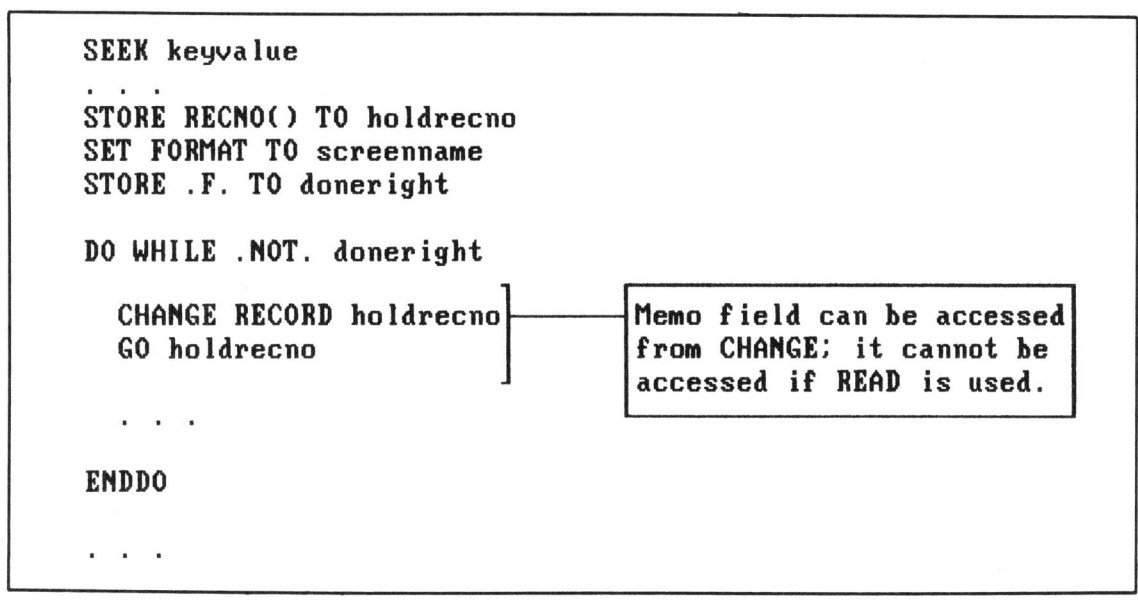

Fig. 4-2. Memo field access from a program.

fields as a resume in a personnel system. The Employee Resume database includes one record for each detail section of the resume. Information on the base employee record can be formatted for the top portion of the resume, with the more detailed sections following. Memo fields can only be displayed using REPORT, DISPLAY, LIST, or "?".

BRINGING OUTSIDE DATA INTO MEMO FIELDS

Data in a dBASE memo file can be copied from

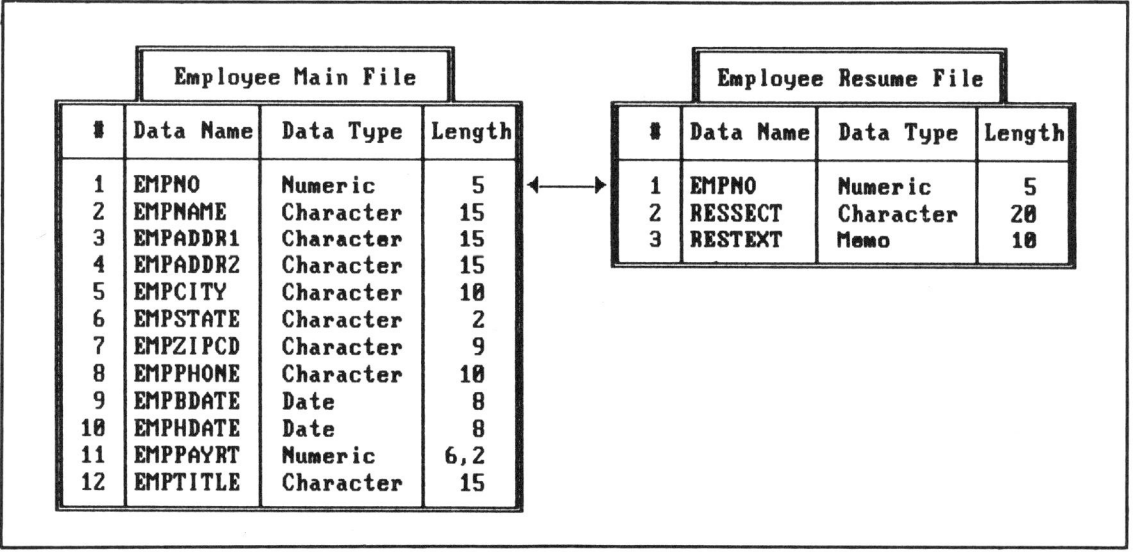

Fig. 4-3. The employee file and the employee resume file.

27

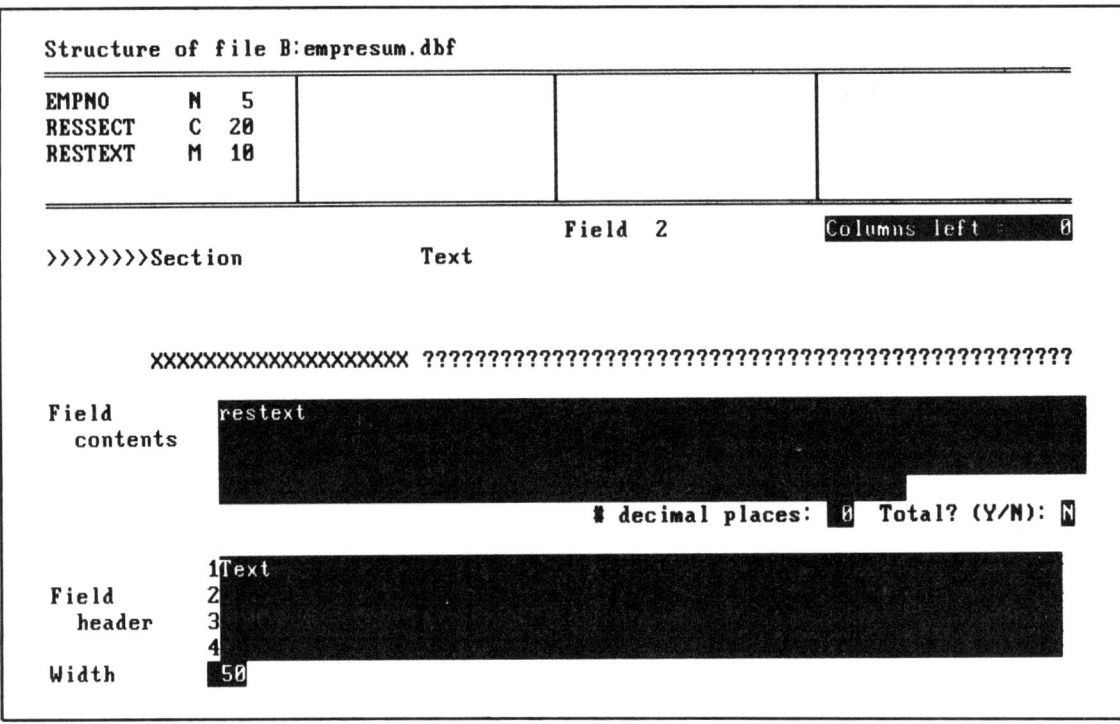

Fig. 4-4. The resume report format.

```
SELECT 1
USE EMPLOYEE INDEX empnox ALIAS emp
SELECT 2
USE EMPRESUM
SET RELATION TO empno INTO emp
SET DEVICE TO PRINT
GO TOP
DO WHILE .NOT. EOF()
   @ 1,1 SAY 'Employee overview: '+DTOC(DATE())
   @ 5,10 SAY emp->empname
   @ 5,50 SAY 'Birth date: '+DTOC(emp->empbdate)
   @ 6,10 SAY emp->empaddr1
   @ 6,50 SAY 'Hire date: '+DTOC(emp->emphdate)
   @ 7,10 SAY TRIM(emp->empcity)+', '+emp->empstate
   @ 7,50 SAY emp->empphone PICTURE '@R Phone number: (999)999-9999'
   @ 8,20 SAY emp->empzipcd PICTURE '@R 99999-9999'
   REPORT FORM hybrid TO PRINT PLAIN NOEJECT RECORD RECNO()
   @ ROW()+1,10 SAY emp->emptitle
   SKIP 1
ENDDO
CLOSE DATABASES
RETURN
```

Fig. 4-5. The resume report program.

an external text file by using the features of the editor you have chosen in CONFIG.DB. The editor's usual commands to bring in a file or a portion of a file can be used to augment the text. The size of a memo field is limited to 5000 characters, including carriage returns.

The built-in dBASE Word Processor allows the user to copy external text files. The command is a WordStar-like key sequence Ctrl-K-R, entered by holding the control (Ctrl) key down and then pressing k and r in succession. The WP will then prompt you for the name of the file to be copied, retrieves this file, and places it in the memo field at the cursor position.

Knowledge of this capability leads to the discovery of another—the ability to take a series of character fields and store them in a memo field.

A common practice before the advent of dBASE III and memo fields was to store textual information in a file as a group of character fields. These pseudo-text records would be stored on a separate database, related by the key field of the record they applied to. The only other field on the record would be a 50 character field, containing one line of text. This pseudo-text database could be manipulated, edited, and printed like any other. The widespread use of this type of text manipulation lead to the creation of the memo field.

People who use this technique now want to change their character-field text data into a memo field, thus reducing or eliminating the programming necessary for the use of the character databases. In small systems, this can be done very easily.

First, the character fields for each main record are copied to separate SDF (Standard Data Format) files, which become the external text files. Then the main database can be modified to include the new memo field. Finally, the database is edited, the memo fields accessed, and each external text file copied into the memo field with Ctrl-K-R. This technique is only useful when small amounts of data are involved.

Chapter 5

Fred's Gourmet Seafood

It's late on a Thursday evening; the baseball game has gone off the air, and we see a small businessman hunched over the console of his IBM PC/XT, sweating profusely and muttering under his breath. This person started using dBASE III about six months ago and is plodding through the creation of a payroll system.

This is Fred, owner, manager, and programmer for Fred's Friendly Fish Market. Fred learned to use dBASE III to develop a customer order and inventory system; now, he is trying to automate his personnel system, as well. Not only does he have the fish market employees, but he owns a warehouse and several trucks; the total is about 50 employees.

Developing a personnel system requires adding a new entity, employee, to the overall database. This entity will be comprised of all data fields that relate to a single employee. This includes personnel information such as name and address, payroll information such as pay rate and number of dependents, and performance information (employee reviews). Fred has decided that he wants as little trouble as possible with this database. He is being very methodical in his second development effort, because he has heard of the dreaded "Second-System Syndrome."

SSS happens to most programmers, usually when they begin to design their second system immediately after their first. The structured programming principles which are listed in Fig. 5-1, so laboriously followed in the first system fade away in a flurry of excuses; direction is lost as the details take on greater than their share of importance. Top-down coding becomes bottom-up or even middle-out. Another symptom of SSS is that the programmer attempts to add extra little features to the functions of the system, possibly losing sight of the original purpose. Such "bells-and-whistles" programming may give the user functions beyond those that can be used effectively, while making the program code ten times more complex than it needs to be.

SSS (also known as *Babbage's disease*) can be avoided by methodically proceeding in the development of the second system, being sure to touch all

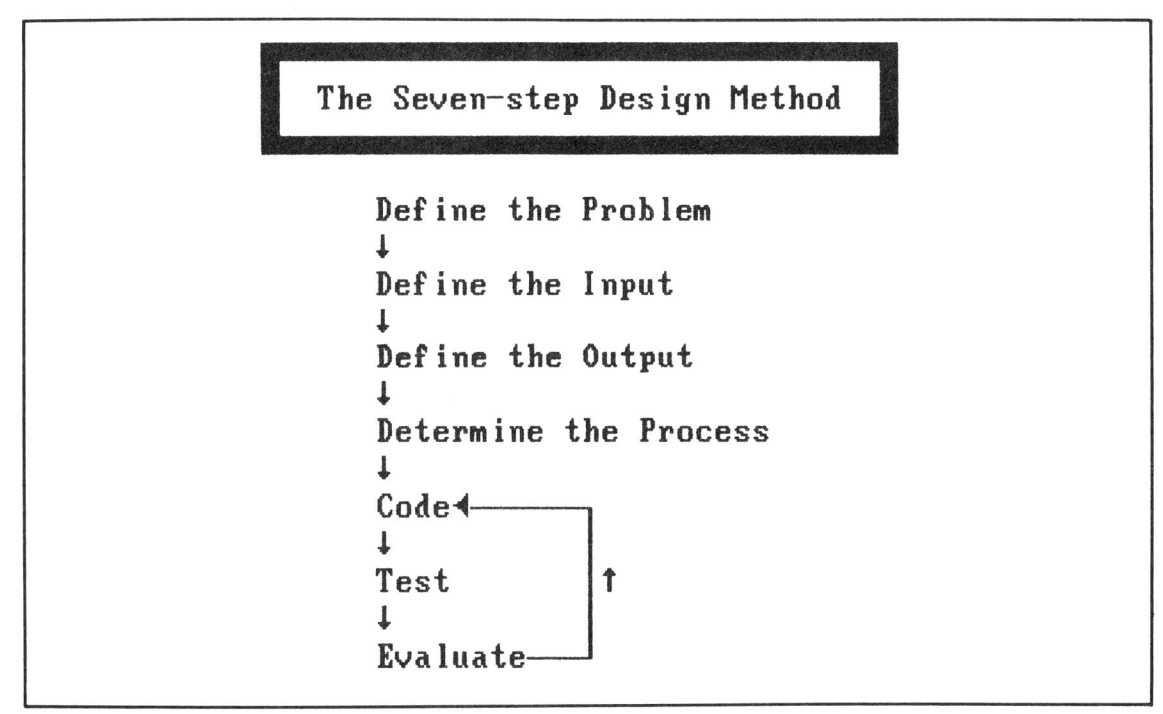

```
       The Seven-step Design Method

              Define the Problem
                    ↓
              Define the Input
                    ↓
              Define the Output
                    ↓
              Determine the Process
                    ↓
              Code ←─────────┐
                    ↓        │
              Test           ↑
                    ↓        │
              Evaluate ──────┘
```

Fig. 5-1. The seven-steps of system design.

of the bases. All written documents should be completed before starting to write program code.

DESIGNING A PAYROLL SYSTEM

Fred has already defined the data items he will need for output. He also has accumulated the input and calculated fields into a long list of data to be stored in database files.

So, to start the design of the employee databases, Fred writes down all of the data items that he wants to store for each employee (Fig. 5-2). This will be the start of his data dictionary; it is not necessary to use data names or program variable names—the title of each item is sufficient at this point.

His next step is to identify groups of data items that repeat; that is, those fields into which more than one piece of information will be entered for each employee. These repeating groups must be separated from the rest of the data items to form separate physical files. Once they have been split out, the database will be in first normal form.

The first repeating group is the skills information. Each employee can have many skills; thus the employee number must also become a part of the key for the Employee-Skills records. The next repeating group is the Payroll information, which will occur once for each pay period. Finally, the year-to-date and this-quarter accumulated information occurs once for each year that the employee has worked for Fred. The employee performance review information is also used on a yearly basis, which is why it is placed in the year-to-date repeating group as well. The "this-quarter" information is needed for tax purposes. Figure 5-3 shows the first normal form for the Employee database.

Fred now looks for dependencies in his data items. To evolve the second normal form of the database, Fred must split out data items that are not dependent on the entire key of the record. The key of a record is the concatenation of all data items required to uniquely identify the record.

In the case of the Employee-Skills record, the concatenated key of the record is "skill number" + "social security number". The skill descrip-

```
                Entity: employee
                Data items:

Social Security Number      skill description       YTD local tax
Name (last, first m)        years experience        YTD other deductions
address line 1                                      YTD sick hours
address line 2              regular hours           YTD vacation hours
city                        overtime hours          YTD regular hours
state                       sick hours              YTD overtime hours
zipcode                     vacation hours          YTD non-pay hours
home phone                  non-pay hours           QTD gross pay
emergency phone             gross pay               QTD federal tax
pay rate                    federal tax             QTD state tax
pay grade code              state tax               QTD local tax
pay grade title             local tax               QTD other deductions
hire date                   other deductions        QTD sick hours
birth date                                          QTD vacation hours
termination date            YTD gross pay           QTD regular hours
sex                         YTD federal tax         QTD overtime hours
number of dependents        YTD state tax           QTD non-pay hours

                                                    Performance review
```

Fig. 5-2. The unnormalized Employee entity.

```
                Entity: employee
                Data items:
One per employee:           Many per employee:

Social Security Number      skill description       YTD local tax
Name (last, first m)        years experience        YTD other deductions
address line 1                                      YTD sick hours
address line 2              regular hours           YTD vacation hours
city                        overtime hours          YTD regular hours
state                       sick hours              YTD overtime hours
zipcode                     vacation hours          YTD non-pay hours
home phone                  non-pay hours
emergency phone             gross pay               QTD gross pay
pay rate                    federal tax             QTD federal tax
pay grade code              state tax               QTD state tax
pay grade title             local tax               QTD local tax
hire date                   other deductions        QTD other deductions
birth date                                          QTD sick hours
termination date            YTD gross pay           QTD vacation hours
sex                         YTD federal tax         QTD regular hours
number of dependents        YTD state tax           QTD overtime hours
Performance review          (continued)             QTD non-pay hours
```

Fig. 5-3. The Employee first normal form.

tion is dependent on the skill number but not on the SSN, and therefore must be split out into a new file, the Skills database. The other databases have no such dependencies, because each data item on the records is uniquely identified only by the entire concatenated key. The key of the Payroll database is "social security number" + "pay date"; the complete key of the Payroll Summary (yearly) file is "social security number" + "year". Figure 5-4 shows the second normal form of the Employee database. The precise definition of the second normal form is a database that is in first normal form and has no data items in a record that are not dependent on the entire key of that record.

Fred then derives the third normal form of the database by removing data items from the record that are dependent on data items not in the key. This is to find fields that are fully dependent on the entire key, but also dependent on other fields.

There is an occurrence of this type of dependency, called a *transitive dependency*, in the Employee record. The pay grade description of an employee is dependent on the primary key of the Employee record, but it is also dependent on the pay grade code. Splitting this into another file, the Pay Grade Description database, the transitive dependency is removed, and the database is now in third normal form (Fig. 5-5).

Now, Fred examines the step necessary to convert the database to fourth normal form—and finds that he has already achieved it. The fourth normal form of a database is one on which multivalued dependencies (like Employee Skill in this database) do not coexist on records that also have single-valued dependencies (like Name or Address). Since the conversion to the first normal form tends to remove this type of dependency where it is most obvious, the third normal form almost always constitutes the fourth normal form as well.

The Employee entity is now completely normalized and ready for implementation as a dBASE III database. Each separate record split out of the Employee data items will become a separate dBASE database. The data records should be in-

```
Entity: Employee
                                    Split out items not fully dependent
                                                       on the entire key.

  ┌─────────────────────────────┐      ┌──────────────────────────────┐
  │ Social Security Number (key)│◄────►│ Social Security Number       │
  │ Name (last, first m)        │      │ Skill Code                   │
  │ address line 1              │      │ Years experience             │
  │ address line 2              │      └──────────────────────────────┘
  │ city                        │
  │ state                       │
  │ zipcode                     │
  │ home phone                  │      ┌──────────────────────────────┐
  │ emergency phone             │─────►│ Skill Code (key)             │
  │ pay rate                    │      │ Skill description            │
  │ pay grade code              │      └──────────────────────────────┘
  │ pay grade title             │
  │ hire date                   │
  │ birth date                  │
  │   . . .                     │
  └─────────────────────────────┘
```

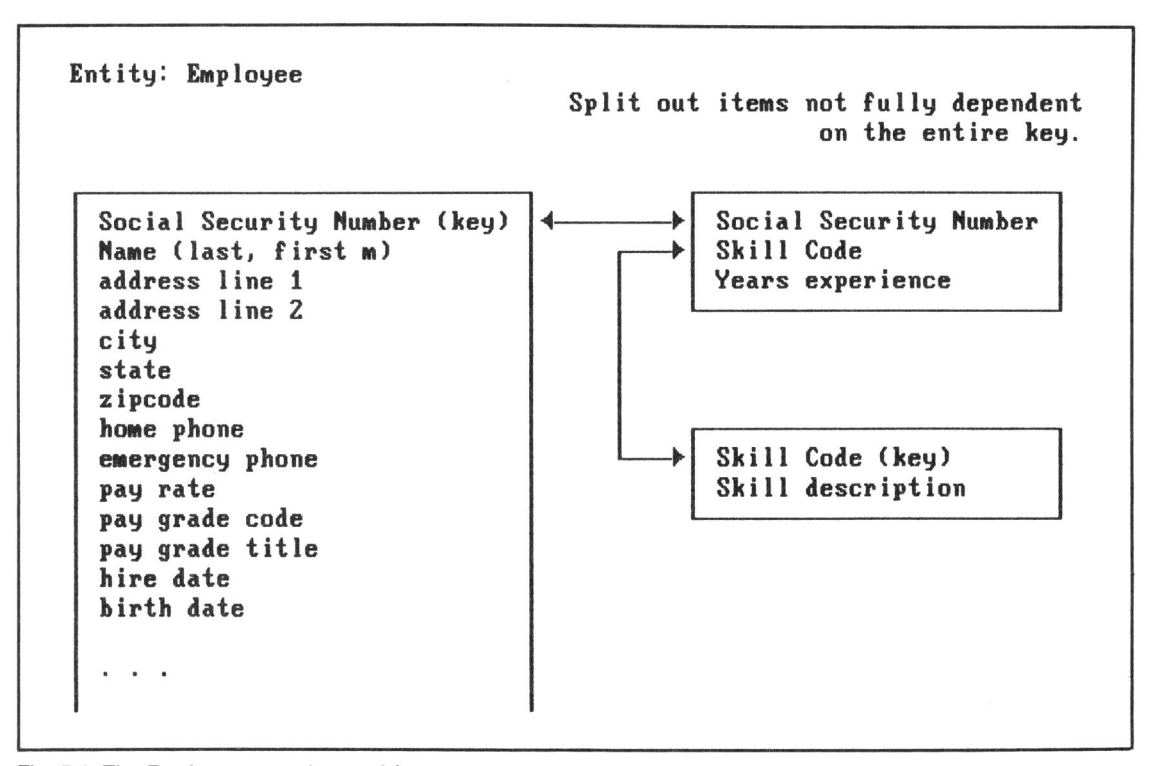

Fig. 5-4. The Employee second normal form.

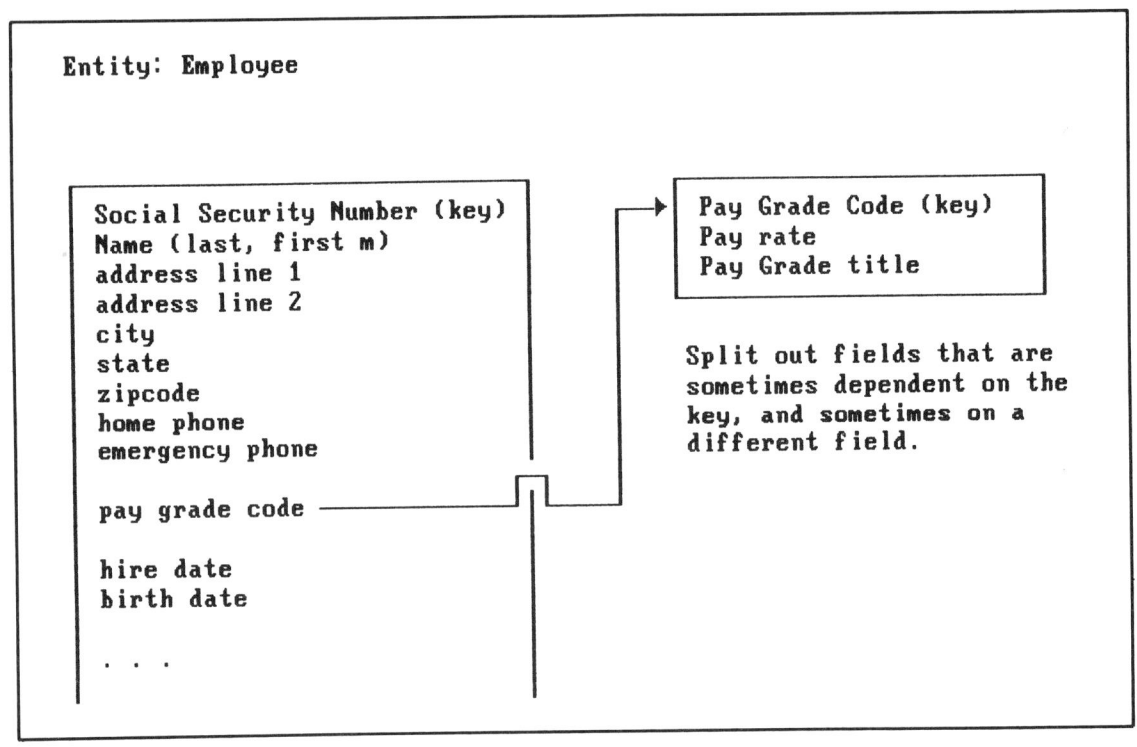

```
Entity: Employee


  ┌─────────────────────────────────┐      ┌──────────────────────────┐
  │ Social Security Number (key)    │   ┌─▶│ Pay Grade Code (key)     │
  │ Name (last, first m)            │   │  │ Pay rate                 │
  │ address line 1                  │   │  │ Pay Grade title          │
  │ address line 2                  │   │  └──────────────────────────┘
  │ city                            │   │
  │ state                           │   │   Split out fields that are
  │ zipcode                         │   │   sometimes dependent on the
  │ home phone                      │   │   key, and sometimes on a
  │ emergency phone                 │   │   different field.
  │                                 │   │
  │ pay grade code ─────────────────┼───┘
  │                                 │
  │ hire date                       │
  │ birth date                      │
  │                                 │
  │ . . .                           │
  │                                 │
  └─────────────────────────────────┘
```

Fig. 5-5. The Employee third normal form.

dexed by their entire keys. This means that the Employee-Skills file, the Employee Payroll file, and the Employee Payroll Summary files will be indexed by employee number first and their unique keys second. This will keep each employee's information "together" on the database, so that the multiple records for each employee are available together and therefore retrieved faster.

ARCHIVING OLD FILES

Now that Fred has defined the contents of his Employee databases, he reexamines the design for ways in which to make the physical arrangement of the databases improve the efficiency of the functions to be performed. Once he has produced the functional description of his system, Fred can look for places where experience has taught him to expect inefficiencies.

The major problem with functions that must do sequential access of a database is that they often bypass most of the records to process a few. Fred notices that if all of the Employee Payroll records are kept on the same file, the payroll file will grow each pay period by the number of employees receiving checks. That means that the payroll process will take longer and longer to complete each time it is run.

One method of overcoming this problem is to create an *archive* database to contain the Employee Payroll information for prior pay periods. The main Payroll database will contain records for only the current pay period.

The function that actually processes the payroll, when it is written, will now only have to go sequentially through one period's information, instead of through a steadily increasing number of records.

Fred has found that, when he is attempting a new process using dBASE III, it is a good idea to review the dBASE programming commands necessary to perform the process. He finds how to fit them together to accomplish the process, writes the idea down on a piece of paper, and then places it with his other notes, for use when writing the actual programs. It is common for insights to happen before they are needed, as with following the step-by-step route. Fred keeps good notes and uses them to his advantage during the coding phase.

In this case, the dBASE commands to archive the old payroll records can be performed at the end of the payroll process. Before the program finishes, Fred must:

```
USE <payroll archive>
APPEND FROM <current payroll>
USE
```

Fred also notices that, if the records are indexed primarily on Employee (SS) Number, all of the employee's records for skills and payroll (archived) will appear to be together on the database. This will also increase the system's efficiency; the process will be discussed in the next section. Figure 5-6 shows the archival process.

THE FARLEY FILE

Fred has noticed that he has grown out-of-touch with his employees lately. The problem is, of course, that now with almost fifty people working for him, Fred has too many names to remember. Heck, those new kids he can hardly tell apart, but he knows that the birthday cards and other little reminders are important to the employees and thereby to the company.

One day, while having lunch with his local congressional representative Ima Gogetter, he brought up this problem. Ima laughed and asked him to try to remember hundreds of people by name, nickname, activity, position, and political party!

Fred groaned.

Then Ima told him about the Farley file, and how it had helped her climb the party ladder.

The Farley file (derivation of the name is unknown) is an old politician's trick where information about a person is saved in a file of three-by-five cards for reference. The information is not sought out, just noted down for later transfer to the file. Names, nicknames, titles, and usually one activity that the person engages in or is associated with are noted.

This way, Ima explained, just before an interview with a person, she can pull the Farley card on that person and know whether or not to wish them a happy birthday or inquire about their golf game, bowling, aerobics class, or whatever. The personal touch this imparts to her meetings has charmed even the most hard-hearted of her constituency. She explained to Fred that there is nothing

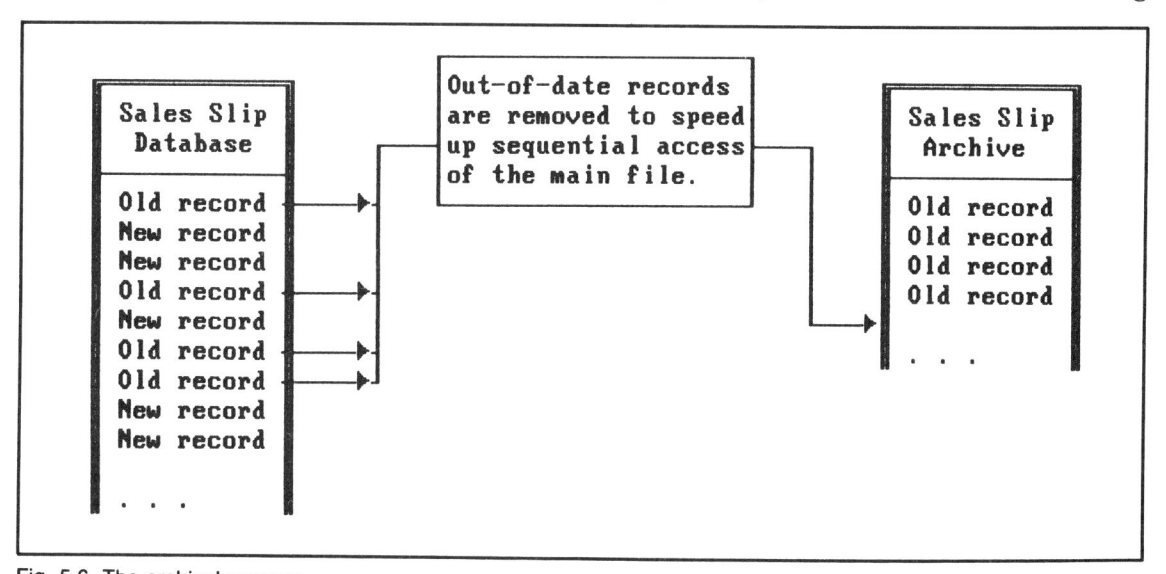

Fig. 5-6. The archival process.

```
Structure for database : B:FARLEY.DBF
Number of data records :      30
Date of last update    : 08/09/85
Field  Field name   Type          Width     Dec
    1  LASTNAME     Character        20
    2  FIRSTNAME    Character        20
    3  NICKNAME     Character        10
    4  BIRTHDATE    Date              8
    5  PERSONAL     Memo             10
** Total **                          69
```

Fig. 5-7. The Farley database.

cynical about this; it's just a practical method to keep from hurting anyone's feelings by not remembering.

Fred got more and more excited as he listened to Ima G. "That's the perfect solution to my problem!" he cried. Ima told him about a shop around the corner that sold three-by-five cards by the case, because he was going to need a lot of them.

Fred smiled. "Who uses cards anymore?" he asked slyly.

After Ima complained about having enough 3 × 5 cards to contain a local library's card catalog, Fred asked if she used a personal computer. One thing lead to another, and sure enough in a couple of weeks, Ima Gogetter got herself a copy of dBASE III, and Fred installed her Farley database

```
             Structure for database : B:employee.dbf
             Number of data records :       0
             Date of last update    : 08/05/85
             Field  Field name   Type          Width     Dec
                 1  EMPNO        Numeric          5
                 2  EMPNAME      Character       15
                 3  EMPADDR1     Character       15
                 4  EMPADDR2     Character       15
                 5  EMPCITY      Character       10
                 6  EMPSTATE     Character        2
                 7  EMPZIPCD     Character        9
                 8  EMPPHONE     Character       10
                 9  EMPBDATE     Date             8
                10  EMPHDATE     Date             8
                11  EMPPAYRT     Numeric          6         2
                12  EMPTITLE     Character       15
>>>>>>>>>>>>>>>>13  FARLEY       Memo            10
             ** Total **                        129
```

Fig. 5-8. The Farley field.

(Fig. 5-7). Her secretary Joe got to type in all the cards. Fred solved his own problem by adding a memo field, to the main Employee record, named (appropriately) Farley as shown in Fig. 5-8. Since the format of the database records do not affect dBASE programs, none of the so-far completed programs for the Employee system need be changed. In fact, Fred decides, the file will NOT be accessed by the program; only he will update it from interactive mode, so that no one will even know of the file's existence.

Now, since Fred has only about fifty employees, he can try his best to memorize the organized file for convenience; but before a face-to-face meeting with an employee, he can retrieve that employee's Farley to help his memory along.

Chapter 6
Programming for Efficiency

The programming language that is built-in to dBASE III almost requires that you properly structure your programs. There are no labels in the language, and therefore no unconditional branch-to-label statements. The logical structures formed in pseudocode are exactly mirrored in the syntax of the language. Figure 6-1 shows the logical constructs.

Structured coding means more than just eliminating GO TO statements from a language. It also means that each discrete group of code lines, or *module*, must be self-contained. Each procedure or program should have one and only one entry point and one and only one exit point.

dBASE will allow you to return control to a calling routine just by using the RETURN statement. In a structured environment, there should only be one of these in a routine.

As with most rules, the structured programming guidelines are made to be bent. In an interactive program, especially in systems with several levels of menus, the operator may require that there be a way to avoid the intervening menus when going back to the top. This means at least one extra RETURN statement, the RETURN TO MASTER, must be included in the lower-level menus. RETURN TO MASTER tells dBASE to return control to the first routine in the hierarchy, the top-most level.

This is an excellent example of coding trade-offs during application development. The coding necessary to reproduce the workings of the RETURN TO MASTER statement would take a prohibitive amount of time. The possible bending of structured programming guidelines can be weighed against the ease of coding and the understandability of the final code. The RETURN TO MASTER statement is obvious in its intent, and requires no further coding.

There are two other "unstructured" commands in dBASE III: the LOOP and EXIT statements. As shown in Fig. 6-2, these are used to bypass normal DO WHILE loop processing.

The EXIT statement causes control to pass from inside a DO WHILE loop to the first statement following the ENDDO; the condition is not

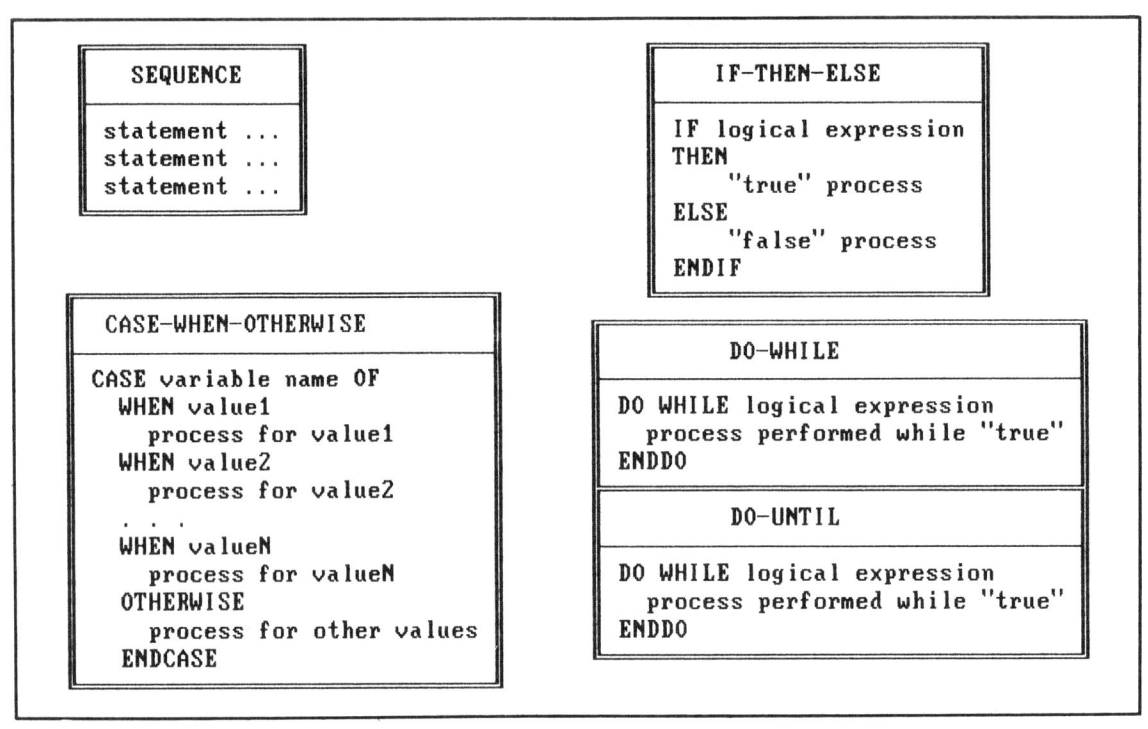

```
      SEQUENCE                                IF-THEN-ELSE

   statement ...                          IF logical expression
   statement ...                          THEN
   statement ...                              "true" process
                                           ELSE
                                               "false" process
                                           ENDIF


   CASE-WHEN-OTHERWISE                           DO-WHILE

   CASE variable name OF                   DO WHILE logical expression
     WHEN value1                               process performed while "true"
        process for value1                  ENDDO
     WHEN value2
        process for value2                          DO-UNTIL
     . . .
     WHEN valueN                           DO WHILE logical expression
        process for valueN                     process performed while "true"
     OTHERWISE                             ENDDO
        process for other values
   ENDCASE
```

Fig. 6-1. The logical constructs.

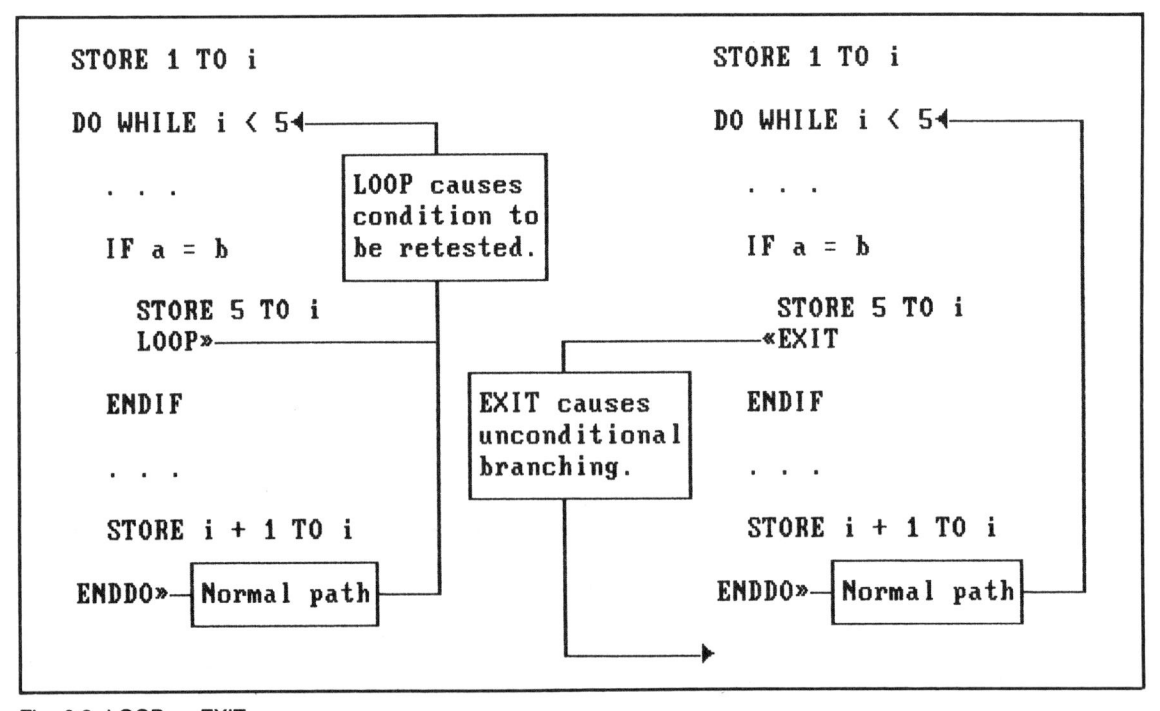

```
   STORE 1 TO i                            STORE 1 TO i

   DO WHILE i < 5◄────┐                    DO WHILE i < 5◄────┐
                      │                                       │
      . . .       ┌───────────┐               . . .           │
                  │LOOP causes│                               │
      IF a = b    │condition to│              IF a = b        │
                  │be retested.│                              │
         STORE 5 TO i│         │                 STORE 5 TO i │
         LOOP»──────┘                            «EXIT────────┼──┐
                                                              │  │
      ENDIF        ┌───────────┐               ENDIF          │  │
                   │EXIT causes│                              │  │
      . . .        │unconditional│             . . .          │  │
                   │branching. │                              │  │
      STORE i + 1 TO i                        STORE i + 1 TO i│  │
                                                              │  │
   ENDDO»──┤Normal path│                      ENDDO»──┤Normal path│
                                                              ▼
```

Fig. 6-2. LOOP vs EXIT.

tested again. The EXIT statement constitutes a second exit point from the loop, which can itself be considered a subroutine. Use of this statement, therefore, is a flagrant violation of structured principles, and should be avoided at all costs.

The LOOP statement, on the other hand, is a bender, not a breaker. LOOP tells dBASE to go immediately to the top of the DO WHILE loop, to once again test the condition. This can be necessary, since it bypasses unwanted processing without actually exiting the loop.

The efficiency of any program can be improved by skipping over statements that are truly unnecessary, based on certain conditions. The key here is the term *conditions*, because they are what slows down a program.

Any statement that requires a decision on the part of the interpreter takes longer than those that don't. This is another common-sense rule: the more a single statement has to do, the longer it will take. The statements that take the least amounts of time are STOREs (assignment statements). The value to store is in memory, and the area it is being stored in is in memory; the move is all but instantaneous.

DO WHILE loops, IF-THEN-ELSE conditions, and CASE structures take more time. In these cases, dBASE is retrieving two or more values from memory, comparing them character by character, and then storing a value (true or false) to yet another area of memory.

The statements that take the most time are input/output statements such as LOCATE and REPLACE. The interpreter must call the operating system to actually get the record and place it at a certain point in memory (called the buffer).

Keeping this in mind, you should begin to see little ways in which your programs can be made more efficient. Contrary to the beliefs of some programmers, when the code is complete and the program works, the project is NOT finished.

The source-code post mortem is another of the tools used by professional programmers to increase the efficiency of the systems that they write. This means going line-by-line through the final version and looking for places to tighten it up. This can be aided by having another programmer or other disinterested party sit down with you to walk through the code.

For example, a program might need to check for a certain character to be in a specific position in a character string. If the character is A, the remainder of the field contains one format, if it is B there is a slightly different format, and so forth. Rather than checking each possibility with SUBSTR( ), it is much better to use SUBSTR( ) once, at the beginning, move the value to a memory variable, and then test that variable instead of the substring. Figure 6-3 shows how this can be done.

Another "speed-eater" occurs when statements are performed within a loop. If the same value is being moved to the same variable each time through the loop, the statement can be moved outside the loop, probably to a position just before it. Even though a STORE statement does not take much time, when repeated over and over again in a loop, the time can add up.

SEQUENTIAL DATABASE PROCESSING

A major obstacle to quick database processing is the fact that some dBASE III commands force the data manager to do sequential database processing. Sequential processing means that each record is retrieved and checked; then the next record is retrieved, and so on, until the desired record is found.

A 3-by-5 card file without tabs becomes a sequential file. Each card must be examined to determine if that card is the one wanted. You cannot read card number 50 without first reading (and doing all the necessary I/O and buffer management for) the first 49.

A dBASE database is physically what programmers call an *ISAM* file. ISAM (Indexed Sequential Access Method, pronounced "EYE-sam") was originally designed by IBM to fill in the gap between sequential and random files. Some people will tell you that ISAM is a combination of sequential and random processing, incorporating all of the worst features of both. The idea is to have a sequential file of data that can be processed sequentially just like a card file; this file is coupled with an index

```
Poor code should be tightened ...

   IF (SUBSTR( TEST, 1, 1) = 'A') .OR. (SUBSTR( TEST, 1, 1) = 'B')

              ... so that unnecessary functions are eliminated.

      STORE SUBSTR( TEST, 1, 1) TO TEST2

      IF (TEST2 = 'A') .OR. (TEST2 = 'B')
```

Fig. 6-3. Tightening the code.

file that contains the key field values for each record in the data file and a pointer to the record's position in the file. When the programmer wishes to do random processing, the file is accessed via the index file.

An ISAM file is like a card file with tabs. The tab cards contain information that can position the reader to the proper card more quickly by giving a key or partial key to the card sought. Then only a small amount of sequential processing is necessary before the correct card is found.

dBASE takes the ISAM idea far beyond the original idea, because a database can be accessed randomly without an index by referencing the record number directly. This returns the requested record almost instantaneously, although it is not good to use the record number itself as a key, because the key will change with the first PACK command (if deleted records exist).

There are several dBASE commands that perform sequential database processing. If a condition is placed on them, such as with a WHILE or FOR clause, the database is processed sequentially until the condition is found, and then the rest of the database is processed sequentially until its end.

Needless to say, sequential access is performed much more slowly than direct accessing a record, but direct access is not always desirable or workable. For example, when processing unpaid sales slips in an accounts-receivable system, the slips need to be accessed sequentially, while the customer/client file is accessed as needed.

One way of speeding up sequential access is to read only those records that you need to read and then to exit when finished. This can be accomplished by indexing the database by the field that you would normally LOCATE . . . FOR. With this index in place, the unwanted records can be easily ignored, by using a FIND or SEEK to locate the first desired record. You can then process just those records by using a WHILE clause instead of FOR; another alternative is to use a DO WHILE loop for the processing.

Figure 6-4 shows how this process can be used in a payroll system for year-to-date type lookups. For example, our Employee database contains:

Employee number (key)
Name
Address
Pay rate
. . .

The file that needs to be processed sequentially is the Payroll database. Its format is:

Pay Date
Employee number
Pay rate
Regular hours worked
Overtime hours worked
Doubletime hours worked
. . .

First, the payroll database can be INDEXed by Employee number. Indexing takes approximately one quarter of the time that sorting does because no actual data is moved. An index file is built using the value of the key specified in the INDEX statement and the record number of that record.

Next, a FIND or SEEK command is used to retrieve the first record with the desired Employee number. This is called *positioning* the database, since now the record pointer is positioned to the first of the series.

The remainder of the series can be retrieved using a DO WHILE loop. The WHILE condition will terminate processing when a different Employee number is retrieved. This will mean that the desired series is complete. The remainder of the database contains no other records with that Employee number, since the INDEX "put them together." Other statements that use a WHILE clause, like REPOrt or TOTAl, can be used in place of a processing loop.

Of course, a better way to do this kind of processing is to have the database indexed that way in the first place. The drawback is that you will need to include the (in this case) Employee number index in the INDEXED BY clause in the USE statement wherever the database is updated. This means that there will be another file open, and this is a consideration in systems with large numbers of files.

RANDOM DATABASE PROCESSING

There are basically two types of random database processing. One situation occurs where the operator enters a key to retrieve, delete, or modify a particular record. dBASE will then use the index file to ascertain the correct record number and retrieve that record (when YOU tell it to, of course!).

The second situation in which random processing is used is in sequentially processing a different file. For example, you might be sequentially processing the payroll file, while accessing the employee database based on a key field contained in the payroll file.

Random database processing is usually performed via the use of an index. The FIND and SEEK commands are used to find a specific record on the database and are used mostly for the first type of processing mentioned above.

The SET RELATION feature of dBASE takes care of the second situation very nicely. The database mentioned in the INTO clause is automatically positioned each time the key field changes. Using the payroll example, each sequential access of the Payroll database will (possibly) change the key field, employee number, indicating the employee whose payroll record this is. The Employee record may then be used, as if a SEEK

```
SELECT A
USE PAYROLL INDEX PEMPNOX          [indexed by employee number]

. . .

FIND 12345

DO WHILE PAYROLL->EMPNO = 12345 .AND. .NOT. (EOF() .OR. BOF())

    . . .

    SKIP 1          [processes sequentially, as long as EMPNO = 12345]

ENDDO
```

Fig. 6-4. "Direct sequential" processing.

or FIND had already been done, to access the pay rate and other needed information.

The dBASE command GO and the function RECNO( ) allow the programmer to perform direct access into any database by record number. Since this is a number that can be changed by processes outside of a program, it is not a good key value. However, there is another use for random processing—to get around a dBASE III limitation.

The manual says that up to ten database files may be used at one time. This, however, is a dBASE specification. In the CONFIG.SYS file that the manual suggests, the parameter "FILES = 20" is telling PC-DOS that 20 files (of ANY type) may be open at once—and no more. This includes procedure files, format files, indexes, memo field files, and program files. dBASE sets an upper limit of 15 on the number of files that may be open at one time.

One way around this limitation, if you have reached it, is to temporarily save the current record number and release the database (via USE) to free the file. This is called *saving position* on the database. You can now open another file, process it, and release it; then you can reopen the first database and reposition by using the GO <record number> statement. Figure 6-5 illustrates this procedure.

dBASE III ERROR MESSAGES

When dBASE encounters an error while interpreting a statement, it displays an error message that indicates the nature of the problem and its position (if applicable) in the statement. Interpreting the messages is sometimes difficult; the manual does not include a section that explains the error messages.

Most of the error messages are helpful and quickly point out the root cause and probable solution. Some messages, however, are ambiguous and require arcane solutions.

The position of a syntax error is noted by a ? that appears on the line above the error, either directly over it or just after. If, for example, an attempt is made to query the contents of a memory variable that does not exist, the message "VARIABLE NOT FOUND" would appear, and a question mark would be placed above the variable name.

Other errors are not as easy to decipher. The most common of the arcane errors is "Out of Memory Error," which occurs when dBASE has exhausted the amount of RAM memory available on the computer. There are several causes for this particular error, not all of which point to ordering more memory. One case where this might happen is if the BUFFERS parameter in CONFIG.SYS (the PC-

```
SELECT A
USE PAYROLL

. . .

FIND 12345
STORE RECNO( ) TO SPAYREC
USE EMPLOYEE INDEX EMPNOX      [closes PAYROLL]

. . .

USE PAYROLL
GO SPAYREC                     [returned to the saved position]
```

Fig. 6-5. Saving position on the database.

DOS configuration file) is greater than twenty, and there is not more than 256K of available memory. This occurs because the buffers themselves take up memory, and dBASE must rearrange its own workspace. When a file is opened that causes the use of a buffer that cannot be allocated, the "Out of Memory error" is received. Figure 6-6 shows some of the common dBASE error messages.

TROUBLESHOOTING

Testing a dBASE program leads to the resolution of syntax errors, because they occur each time the interpreter encounters one and they usually end in the termination of the program. When all of the syntax is correct, however, is the time to discover the logic errors.

As sometimes occurs, programmers can find themselves staring at a program that seemed to work properly. When the database is listed, however, the data is found to be totally "fubar" (Fouled Up Beyond All Recognition). The programmer then sits back, scratches his or her head, and proceeds to track down the cause in a process known as debugging.

There are several peripheral packages that can aid the dBASE programmer in debugging program and procedure files; these packages will be discussed in detail in Section IV of this book. There are many debugging aids included in the dBASE software that can ease the debugging process.

SET ECHO ON. This is the command that makes dBASE "echo" each command to the screen as it is read. Using ECHO, the programmer can see the exact order in which statements are executed. This is also called tracing a program, and it is very effective in finding logic and looping errors.

SET TALK ON. This dBASE parameter causes the results of various operations to be displayed on the screen. This can be helpful in finding the exact values of comparisons and calculations. TALK can also be used in determining where bottlenecks or slow-ups occur.

?. Another debugging technique can be used to discover the exact values contained in a variable at a specific time. The variable is printed on the console via the question mark (?) command, sometimes with an identifying message. The programmer can then use this information to discover the problem. This technique is called exhibiting a variable. This technique is used only when the value of the variable is critical, because it requires changes to the source code.

DISPlay MEMOry, DISPlay STATus, DISPlay RECOrd RECNO( ). These commands can be used to monitor the status of the entire dBASE environment. DISPlay MEMOry provides the complete picture of the contents of all current memory variables. The name, value, and number and size of memory variable storage are displayed. DISPlay STATus displays the status of all open database files and indexes, including any set rela-

Message	Problem
Data type mismatch	Attempt to mix data types without conversion
File does not exist	File operation on file not on current directory
Too many files are open	More than the maximum number of files (13) open
Unrecognized command verb	Misspelled command
Variable not found	Attempt to use undeclared memory variable
Zero divide	Cannot divide by zero

Fig. 6-6. Common dBASE error messages.

```
dBASE>disp stat

Select area -  1, Database in use: B:employee.dbf    Alias - EMPLOYEE
     Index file: B:empnox.ndx   key - empno

Select area -  2, Database in use: B:payroll.dbf     Alias - PAYROLL
     Related to: EMPLOYEE

Currently selected database:
Select area -  3, Database in use: B:empresum.dbf    Alias - EMPRESUM

Press any key to continue...
```

Fig. 6-7. The DISPlay STATus output, page 1.

tions and the current index key. DISPlay RECOrd RECNO( ) displays the current database record. Figure 6-7 shows the first screen of the DISPlay STATus output, and Fig. 6-8 shows the second screen.

SET STEP ON. Stepping a program means stopping execution after each statement to examine the result before proceeding to the next instruction. This is a last-resort debugging tool, because it sometimes means hours of hitting the spacebar to see the result of a specific calculation. STEP can be set on during a program, however, and stepping performed for only a part of the process.

Any debugging method that requires additional program code should be saved, and methods that use small amounts of change should be tried before you change large amounts of code. Additional code requires debugging and syntax checking; if the time

```
File search path:
Default disk drive: B:
ALTERNATE   - OFF  DEBUG       - OFF  ESCAPE      - ON   MENU        - OFF
BELL        - OFF  DELETED     - OFF  EXACT       - OFF  PRINT       - OFF
CARRY       - OFF  DELIMITERS  - OFF  HEADING     - ON   SAFETY      - ON
CONFIRM     - ON   DEVICE      - SCRN HELP        - ON   STEP        - OFF
CONSOLE     - ON   ECHO        - OFF  INTENSITY   - ON   TALK        - OFF
UNIQUE      - OFF

Margin =     0

Function key  F1  - help;
Function key  F2  - assist;
Function key  F3  - list;
Function key  F4  - dir;
Function key  F5  - display structure;
Function key  F6  - display status;
Function key  F7  - display memory;
Function key  F8  - display;
Function key  F9  - append;
Function key  F10 - edit;
```

Fig. 6-8. The DISPlay STATus output, page 2.

```
. . .
SET ALTERNATE TO buglog.txt
. . .
USE employee INDEX empnox
. . .
FIND &enumb
IF .NOT. (EOF() .OR. BOF())
   SET ALTERNATE ON
   ? employee->empno+' has been retrieved.'
   SET ALTERNATE OFF
ENDIF


. . .

REPLACE empname WITH enamein, . . .

SET ALTERNATE ON
? employee->empno+' has been updated.'
SET ALTERNATE OFF

. . .
```

Fig. 6-9. Using an alternate output file.

required for the additions is not worth it, another debugging method should be tried.

If code is added to a program for debugging purposes, comment lines should be added also to identify the temporary statements. The debugging statements can also be deactivated by placing an asterisk (*) in the first column of each statement, making it a comment. The asterisks can be removed to activate the debugging statements.

Another dBASE feature that can be used to aid debugging is the SET ALTErnate statement. The results of screen printing operations, excluding the full screen operations like EDIT, APPEnd, and @ . . . SAY, can be sent to a text file rather than being displayed during full screen operations. The alternate output file is defined in the SET ALTErnate TO <filename> statement. Alternate output can be activated by SET ALTErnate ON and deactivated with SET ALTErnate OFF.

An alternate output file can be used to send the DISPlay and ? debugging output to a file, where it can be examined at a later time. It is important to identify the displays in the alternate file, so that the timing can readily be determined. Additional ? commands can be used for this purpose. Figure 6-9 shows the use of an alternate output file.

Chapter 7

Memory Variables

Memory variables are created by the dBASE assignment statement STORE (or =). These fields are not part of any database; they are stored in memory for use in calculations, screen displays, database updating, and passing data between subroutines.

The term for the area in memory which holds these variables is *working storage*. In an interactive program, this area is also known as a *scratchpad*. Each level of the system hierarchy can have its own memory variables, or they can be shared among all programs and procedures. Figure 7-1 shows the memory variable specifications.

The currently allocated memory variables can be displayed using the LIST MEMOry or DISPlay MEMOry commands. These commands report the status of the memory variables, their contents, data type, and other useful information. The commands can be used as excellent debugging tools; when a program stops because of an error, the current memory variable values can be obtained to help trace the problem.

Memory variables can be used to store intermediate results, constants, system variables, logical switches and other control data needed in the program but not necessarily on the database. Memory variables can also be used to temporarily store whole database records, if they are being retrieved by a separate program, as in entity programming.

The data type of a memory variable is determined by the data type of the data or expression STOREd in it. Character data will create a character memory variable; all data types (except Memo) can be stored in memory variables.

dBASE allows an area of 6000 characters, or about 6 kilobytes, for memory variable storage. This value is adjustable by using the MVARSIZ parameter in the CONFIG.DB file, provided you have more than the minimum 256K of memory on your PC. This area holds more than just the memory variable values, so the required size should be at least ten percent larger than absolutely required. The LIST or DISPlay MEMOry commands show the number of characters used and available. Figure 7-2 shows some sample DISPlay MEMOry output.

```
┌─────────────────────────────────────────────────────────────────┐
│  ┌─────────────────────────┐                                    │
│  │ Memory Variables:       │                                    │
│  └─────────────────────────┘                                    │
│    ┌───────────────────────────────────────────────────────┐    │
│    │  Allowable data types:   C, L, N, D                   │    │
│    ├───────────────────────────────────────────────────────┤    │
│    │  Maximum Length:    Standard for data type            │    │
│    ├───────────────────────────────────────────────────────┤    │
│    │  Minimum Length:    Standard for data type            │    │
│    ├───────────────────────────────────────────────────────┤    │
│    │  Total number allowed:  256 variables                 │    │
│    ├───────────────────────────────────────────────────────┤    │
│    │  Overall memory variable area:                        │    │
│    │    ┌─────────────────────────────┐                    │    │
│    │    │ Maximum length: 31K         │  (Changed via the  │    │
│    │    ├─────────────────────────────┤   MVARSIZ parameter│    │
│    │    │ Minimum length:  1K         │   set in CONFIG.DB)│    │
│    │    ├─────────────────────────────┤                    │    │
│    │    │ Default length:  6K         │                    │    │
│    │    └─────────────────────────────┘                    │    │
│    └───────────────────────────────────────────────────────┘    │
└─────────────────────────────────────────────────────────────────┘
```

Fig. 7-1. Memory variable specifications.

STORING MEMORY VARIABLES IN A FILE

dBASE III includes a feature for storing the values of memory variables and then retrieving them later. dBASE will also allow you to clear working storage to make room for more memory variables.

The commands SAVE, RESTore, RELEase, and CLEAr MEMOry, coupled with the MVARSIZ parameter of CONFIG.DB, give the dBASE programmer complete control over the allocation of memory variable space. All of these commands can be limited in scope; a single memory variable, a

```
dBASE>disp memo

ARCHDATE     pub   D  05/11/85
FUNDDATE     pub   (hidden)  D  08/09/85
MONTHLYIND   pub   L  .F.
ANSWER       priv  N           42 (         42.00000000)      B:mv1.prg
FUNDDATE     priv  D  08/04/85                                B:mv2.prg
TITLE        priv  C  "Fred's Friendly Fish Market"           B:mv2.prg
     6 variables defined,          67 bytes used
   250 variables available,      5933 bytes available
```

Fig. 7-2. DISPlay MEMOry output.

group of variables, or the entire area may be cleared, stored and/or retrieved.

The SAVE command takes the values of memory variables and stores them into a file with the extension .MEM. The values are not removed from memory by the SAVE command; they are just copied to the file. The CLEAr MEMOry statement or RELEase statement must be used to remove variables from memory.

There are several reasons for storing memory variables in a file. One example is to save all of the fields on a database record into memory variables; each of these special memory variables should start with the same characters, like EMP for employee. As shown in Fig. 7-3, the variables can then be saved to a file with the statement "SAVE ALL LIKE EMP*."

After the variables are saved to the .MEM file, the space used in memory for their storage can be made available to dBASE by using the RELEase statement. Then, when the record is subsequently updated, the memory variables can be recovered from the file with the RESTore statement, and compared against the new values. This way, you can create a detailed audit trail, including the fields that were changed and the values before and after the change.

Another reason for saving the memory variables to a file is to move them from memory when their number is getting close to the maximum limit of 256. Unneeded variables can be SAVEd to a file, RELEased, and the space used for more memory variables. This can be avoided by proper program design, but in large systems of programs, the limit might be approached.

CLEARING MEMORY VARIABLES

As mentioned previously, memory variables take up space in the (usually) 6000 character area reserved for them. It is possible to delete memory variables and give that space back to dBASE to be used for other memory variables. Programmers call this activity *freeing* the variables.

Memory variables are freed by the RELEase and CLEAr MEMOry commands. CLEAR MEMORY releases all currently allocated memory variables and leaves the area empty. The RELEASE statement may define what variables are to be freed with an ALL LIKE or EXCEPT clause

```
dBASE>disp memo

NUMB1         pub    N         123  (        123.00000000)
TITLE         pub    C    "Fred's Friendly Fish Market"
EMPSSN        pub    N     181727383  ( 181727383.00000000)
EMPLNAME      pub    C    "Burke"
EMPFNAME      pub    C    "Bruce"

    5 variables defined,       61 bytes used
  251 variables available,  31683 bytes available

dBASE>save all like emp* to empsave


dBASE>         ... data is saved.
```

Fig. 7-3. Saving a group of memory variables.

```
dBASE>release all like emp*

dBASE>disp memo

NUMB1         pub   N        123 (        123.00000000)
TITLE         pub   C   "Fred's Friendly Fish Market"

    2 variables defined,      38 bytes used
  254 variables available,   31706 bytes available

dBASE>
```

Fig. 7-4. Clearing a group of memory variables.

```
dBASE>disp memo

NUMB1         pub   N        123 (        123.00000000)
TITLE         pub   C   "Fred's Friendly Fish Market"

    2 variables defined,      38 bytes used
  254 variables available,   31706 bytes available

dBASE>restore from empsave additive

dBASE>disp memo

NUMB1         pub   N        123 (        123.00000000)
TITLE         pub   C   "Fred's Friendly Fish Market"
EMPSSN        pub   N    181727383 (  181727383.00000000)
EMPLNAME      pub   C   "Burke"
EMPFNAME      pub   C   "Bruce"

    5 variables defined,      61 bytes used
  251 variables available,   31683 bytes available

dBASE>
```

Fig. 7-5. Restoring memory variables.

specifying a name template (like EMP*, for example).

From this description, it would seem that RELEASE ALL and CLEAR MEMORY should perform the same functions, but this is only true when you are using dBASE in its interactive mode. In a program, RELEASE ALL merely releases those private memory variables declared in the module in which the statement is located. PUBLIC variables and those declared at higher levels are not released. The RELEASE ALL statement releases the same memory that would be released at the module's RETURN to the calling routine. Figure 7-4 shows the result of clearing a group of memory variables.

RESTORING MEMORY VARIABLES

The stored memory variables can be retrieved and replaced in memory with the RESTore command. This command generally clears all memory and replaces it with the memory variables from the file. Any currently allocated variables are released and their values lost.

There is, however, an alternative to this scenario: the ADDItive option. This option tells dBASE to add the memory variables in the file to the currently existing ones in memory. Any memory variables with the same name as a variable stored on the file will be wiped out by the restored variable.

Restored variables are also automatically declared PRIVATE to the routine containing the RESTore command, because this attribute is not saved as a part of the .MEM file. If, however, a memory variable is stored as PUBLIC with the same name as a variable in the file to be restored, the variable will be stored as PUBLIC. Figure 7-5 shows how memory variables can be restored.

The entire process of memory variable manipulation can be used to keep variable values from session to session or to share them between different functions. Key values, like Employee number or Skill code can be passed among different programs or be saved overnight and the function continued the next day, even after the computer has been rebooted.

A small amount of time is used to read a stored memory variable file and then to allocate the memory variables in working storage. If response time is a major bottle neck in the system, some other method of passing values should be used or the code rearranged to minimize the effect.

Chapter 8
Creating and Using Procedures

A program file is an ASCII text file containing dBASE III commands and instructions. The file is given an extension of .PRG to differentiate it from database and index files, although procedure files are also given the same extension. Programs are executed from within dBASE via the DO command or can be specified on the command line with the "dBASE" command.

CREATING A PROGRAM

Programs can be created using any text editor or word processor. dBASE has a built-in text editor for creating PRG files, but many people prefer an editor that they have used more often, or has more generic capabilities.

The need for an external editor is proportional to the amount of program development that there is to be done. If you do not have many programs to write or will write programs infrequently, the built-in dBASE text editor will probably fill your needs. A major development effort, however, needs some more powerful features.

There are several very fine editors on the market. These range from real professional development tools to the EDLIN editor included with PC-DOS. There are so many choices that anyone should be able to find an editor that fits their style and needs. Figure 8-1 shows some of the text editors that are available.

Another professional development tool is the source code control system. This can be either a series of programs or a feature of some of the more advanced editors. A source code control system records changes to the source code, saving both a base copy to record changes from and the latest changed copy.

The source code control system allows changes to be "backed out" of the source code when the need arises to do so. If a change causes worse problems that it fixes, the program can be recreated as it was before the change took place. This does not really fix any problems; it just wipes the slate clean so that the program can be run and/or the changes retried.

Editor package:	Supplier:
KEDIT	Mansfield Software
Professional Editor Personal Editor	IBM
Brief	Solution Systems
SPF/PC	Command Technology Corp.
FirsTime for dBASE III	Spruce Technology Corp.
Wordstar	Micro Pro

Fig. 8-1. Table of selected text editors.

You may specify the editor that dBASE is to use for the MODIfy COMMand process in the CONFIG.DB file. The parameters TEDIT (for "text editor") and WP (for "word processor") may be altered to utilize any editor you choose. The TEDIT editor is invoked for MODIfy COMMand, and the WP editor is invoked when you are accessing a memo field.

The editor specified in TEDIT must reside on the same disk as the dBASE.OVL file—that is, System Disk #2. This disk is not copy-protected, so that multiple versions of editors, CONFIG.DB, and so on may be created for different purposes. Perhaps, each person that uses your system will have their own System Disk #2, and the environment will be different for each person.

SUBPROCEDURES AND SUBPROGRAMS

dBASE III allows common procedures to be separated from programs in a procedure file. The file can contain up to 32 procedures; each procedure begins with a PROCEDURE <name> statement, and (at least in structured coding) it ends with a RETURN.

A subroutine should contain detailed coding pertaining to one basic system function. The level of the operation is decided by the programmer, but with only 32 procedures to work with (33 counting the main program), there must be practical decisions made about "how low to go."

The top-level menu program is usually a program file; in a multifunction system, with employee, customer, accounts receivable, and so forth, on the same menu, the second level may also be a program. This program would set up the procedure file for the rest of the functions. The procedure file contains all of the detailed coding for each overall function, such as Employee.

The advantage of the subroutine call is that control is returned to the calling program when the subroutine finishes. A main program, one in the upper levels of the hierarchy, may contain very few statements other than subroutine calls.

A subroutine can reside either as a program file or as one PROCEDURE in a procedure file. When a DO is issued for a subroutine, dBASE first checks the stored PROCEDUREs; if the requested procedure is not present, the system then tries to find a program file on the default disk drive. Therefore, generic modules used across many procedure files may be stored as small programs, to be called when necessary. Repeating the code in several procedure files may make the process a little faster, but it can be a nightmare when modifying and/or testing that particular routine.

A *generic* subroutine usually does not use database fields; in fact, it may only perform a minor process in the conversion, editing, or tabulating of database data. A generic function can be either one that is performed so often that it is inefficient to repeat the code or a function that, because of size or coding structure, would be impractical to include in the main program.

One example of a generic module would be the routine shown in Fig. 8-2, which converts a dBASE Date-format memory variable into a character string containing the Julian date. This subroutine could be called using the DO . . . WITH command, because the subroutine will use unique memory variable names; the subroutine may also use PUBLIC memory variables for its receiving and sending areas. Whenever the Date-to-Julian conversion is to occur, this subroutine is called to perform the task.

THE SCOPE OF VARIABLES

One of the most important concerns in systems that have multiple levels of procedures is the temporary data work area that is available to each procedure. In dBASE III, this temporary work area is the memory variables; the way dBASE handles those variables can shape the structure of dBASE systems.

The range of subroutines that a variable is available in is called the *scope* of the variable. The problems of scope must be addressed in every computer language that allows you to allocate areas in memory for variable storage in lower-level procedures. This includes dBASE, since the STORE statement creates the memory variable, instead of a formal declaration at the beginning of the topmost module.

The general rule of thumb in determining

```
STORE '  1  2  3  4  5  6  7  8  9 10 11 12 ' TO monsrch
STORE '000031059090120151181212243273304334 ' TO daysb4

STORE CTOD('10/15/1975') TO gdate

STORE VAL(SUBSTR(daysb4,AT(' '+STR(MONTH(gdate),2),monsrch),3)) TO jdays

STORE jdays + DAY(gdate) to jdays

IF MONTH(gdate) > 2
   IF INT(YEAR(gdate)/100) # (YEAR(gdate)/100)
      IF INT(YEAR(gdate)/4) = (YEAR(gdate)/4)
         STORE jdays + 1 TO jdays
      ENDIF
   ELSE
      IF INT(YEAR(gdate)/400) = (YEAR(gdate)/400)
         STORE jdays + 1 TO jdays
      ENDIF
   ENDIF
ENDIF

STORE INT(YEAR(gdate) * 1000) + jdays) TO jdate
```

Fig. 8-2. The Julian-Date conversion subroutine.

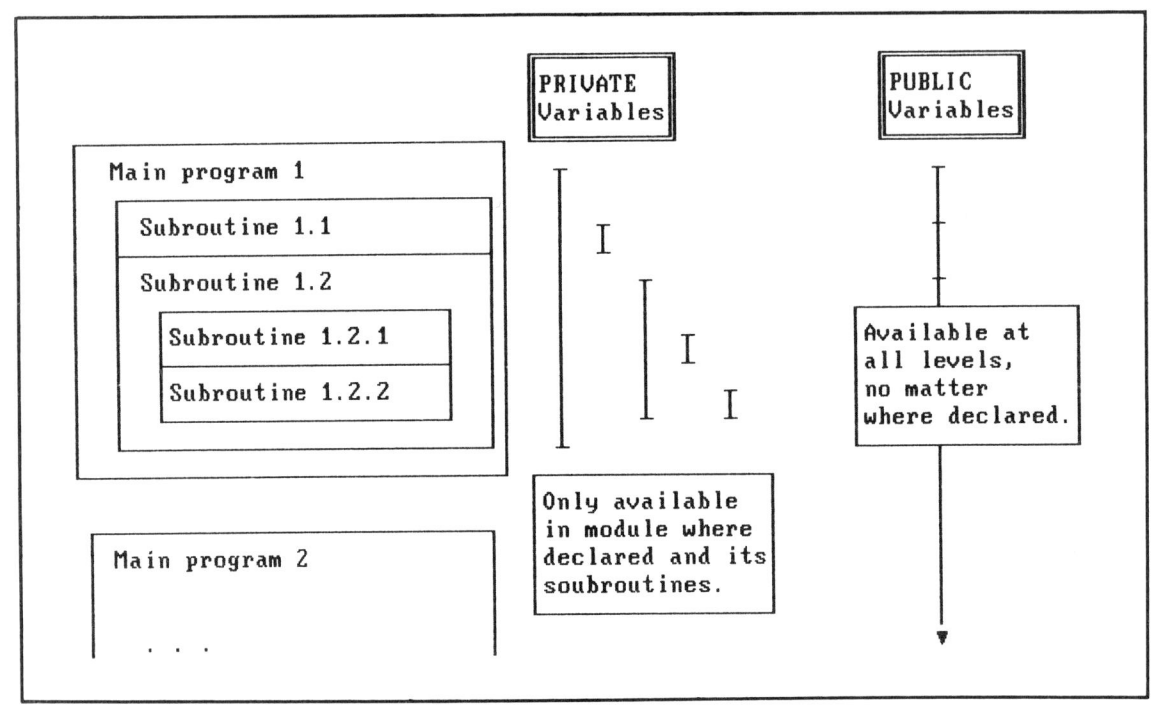

```
+-------------------------------------------------------------------------+
|                                    +----------+      +----------+       |
|                                    | PRIVATE  |      | PUBLIC   |       |
|                                    | Variables|      | Variables|       |
|                                    +----------+      +----------+       |
|  +-----------------------------+                                        |
|  | Main program 1              |                                        |
|  |  +------------------------+ |                                        |
|  |  | Subroutine 1.1         | |    I                                   |
|  |  +------------------------+ |                                        |
|  |  | Subroutine 1.2         | |    |                                   |
|  |  |  +-------------------+ | |    |           +-----------------+     |
|  |  |  | Subroutine 1.2.1  | | |    I           | Available at    |     |
|  |  |  +-------------------+ | |                | all levels,     |     |
|  |  |  | Subroutine 1.2.2  | | |                | no matter       |     |
|  |  |  +-------------------+ | |    I           | where declared. |     |
|  |  +------------------------+ |                +-----------------+     |
|  +-----------------------------+                                        |
|                                     +----------------+                  |
|                                     | Only available |                  |
|  +-----------------------------+    | in module where|                  |
|  | Main program 2              |    | declared and its|                 |
|  |                             |    | soubroutines.  |                  |
|  |  . . .                      |    +----------------+                  |
|  +-----------------------------+                                        |
|                                                                  ▼      |
+-------------------------------------------------------------------------+
```

Fig. 8-3. Variable scope.

variable scope is that a memory variable is known to the routine wherein it is declared and to all lower level submodules called, either directly or indirectly, from that routine. The *declaration*, in the case of dBASE, is the assignment statement. dBASE allocates a memory variable dependent on the type of data being STOREd into it. If the value is a character string, dBASE allocates a character variable; a numeric literal will be stored in a numeric variable, and so forth.

At the RETURN from a subroutine, dBASE releases all memory variables that were defined in that subroutine. Once the higher-level module regains control, the memory is gone, to be allocated to another variable at a later time. There are exceptions to this, since dBASE does allow you to perform some operations with scope, as shown in Fig. 8-3.

The statements PRIVATE and PUBLIC allow you to partially control the scope of memory variables in a dBASE III system. The default scope of a variable is PRIVATE, which means that the variable is available to the routine where it is declared and to all routines farther down the branches of the hierarchy that lead from that routine.

A memory variable declared PUBLIC is available at any level, no matter where it is declared PUBLIC. The effect is as if you had declared the variable at the highest level of the system, because PUBLIC variables are not released when the module containing them ends. The variable may be used and changed by any module in the system.

Note that a memory variable declared PRIVATE at the highest level of the hierarchy is really PUBLIC, but only up to a point. There is one hierarchical level above the top level in any system—the dBASE software itself. Memory variables declared PUBLIC are available after the program terminates and the dBASE prompt is once again displayed. This means that you could use the memory variables to store the execution status (that is, whether the program worked or not) in a PUBLIC variable and be able to LIST or DISPlay MEMOry to see the values.

When using DO . . . WITH, the only memory

variables not available to the submodule with their original names are those passed in the WITH and received by the PARAMETERS statement. Others are available, as usual. The WITH variables are effectively renamed for the duration of the submodule.

The scope of database fields is more simply explained than that of memory variables. Database fields are available any time that the database is open. However, if the particular partition is not currently SELECTed, an alias name can be used to qualify the name with the *pointer* (−>).

It is never a recommended practice to give memory variables and file variables the same names, nor is it good to give a PUBLIC memory variable and a PRIVATE memory variable the same name. Theoretically, dBASE should take the memory variable first, while requiring a pointer for the file variable; forcing dBASE into this position, however, is poor programming practice. Memory variables can be identified with an M−> pointer, if the problem arises.

If a PUBLIC memory variable and a PRIVATE memory variable are given the same names (that is, the PRIVATE command is used to specifically declare the name private), dBASE will hide the public value until the subroutine wherein it is declared PRIVATE is finished. The PUBLIC variable will still contain the value it contained prior to being hidden.

The LIST MEMOry or DISPlay MEMOry commands will display the currently allocated memory variables, their values, data types, and some overall information about the status of the area where they are stored. Both commands produce the same output. Any private memory variables are also identified by the name of the program they were declared PRIVATE in. Figure 8-4 demonstrates scope in the DISPlay MEMOry report.

PASSING DATA TO SUBROUTINES

As noted in the previous section, data may be shared among programs with the use of PUBLIC memory variables. Any subroutine may then use the variables, change them, or declare new ones for its own use. PRIVATE variables may also be passed to any subroutines lower in the hierarchy that branch from the subroutine where they are declared.

There are two ways of passing data to subroutines. In the first way, the data that is passed may be used, but not changed, by the routine. In the second way, changed data is available to the calling routine. dBASE employs the second of these methods by making the same storage areas available to all subroutines.

The DO . . . WITH command effectively changes the names of the passed memory variables for the called subroutine. All other PUBLIC and previously declared PRIVATE variables are available to the subroutine by their original names.

```
                                              Name of creating procedure
                                                    shown in this
                                                    column.
ARCHDATE      pub   D   05/11/85                       .
FUNDDATE      pub   (hidden)  D  08/09/85              .
MONTHLYIND    pub   L   .F.                            .
ANSWER        priv  N         42 (        42.00000000)  B:mv1.prg
FUNDDATE      priv  D   08/04/85                       B:mv2.prg
TITLE         priv  C   "Fred's Friendly Fish Market"  B:mv2.prg

      6 variables defined,        67 bytes used
    250 variables available,    5933 bytes available
```

Fig. 8-4. Scope in the DISPlay MEMOry report.

Only the variables listed in the WITH parameter are renamed to the corresponding name in the subroutine's PARAMETERS statement.

Renaming the variables accomplishes several goals. First, the subroutine may be called from widely separate areas of the system and still use the same names for the variables it uses. Second, the calling routine can receive a result or modified value in a passed variable and then use that variable without retrieving the values from an intermediate area. This is because the subroutine accesses the same area of memory that is used by the calling routine; the area is just renamed.

A general rule should be that generic functions, those that can be called from more than one program, are always called using DO . . . WITH. Modules in the direct line of the function that are only called from one place are usually called using a plain DO statement.

Chapter 9
Full Screen Operations

One of the obstacles facing the programmer who wants to write readable modules in dBASE III is programming the input, output, and text areas of the screen. The preponderance of commands necessary to draw a screen for a menu or full-screen input function can "clutter" a program.

Screen formats, once decided, change rarely over the life of the system. During development of the system, they may change more frequently, but not as much as the surrounding code.

THE SCREEN FORMAT FILE

There was nothing to do about the difficulties of designing a screen until the screen format file was added to dBASE, starting with dBASE II version 2.43. Screen format files allow the programmer to separate the screen formats from the program code, making both sets easier to understand and work with.

The screen format file contains the @ ... SAY ... GET commands necessary to build the screen and define the input fields. The file can be viewed as a type of .PRG file, since it contains executable statements.

Another advantage to using screen format files is that if the textual information is changed or new fields are added to the screen, the existing programs would not have to be changed. For example, the company name (usually) appears at the top of every screen in a system. If the company name changes or if you are developing the system for sale, changing the name only involves changing the screen format files, and not the programs.

SCREEN DESIGN

The screen design, when properly done, should be a major part of the overall system design documentation. All fields used for input and some of those used for output will be determined as part of the screen design.

Designing a screen is mostly a matter of common sense. If the system being developed is replacing a system now implemented with paper forms, design the screens to look like the forms. This way, the person or people doing the data entry work now will suffer less of a "computer shock" and will be using the system productively sooner.

If the installation already has a data entry staff, be sure to get their opinions on the screen design. Also, in a small business, be sure to talk to the person who actually enters the data. These people can be a tremendous help in avoiding the usual pitfalls of screen design, and they can point out other design problems during the early stages. More importantly, it is these people who will have to use the system. If the person-computer interface (that is, the screen design) is faulty, difficult to follow, or even not pleasing to the eye, the system's reputation will suffer because of it.

Another point of good screen design is the amount of thought that is necessary on the part of the operator to use the system. An operator should not have to do any calculation, unless it is necessary for audit-trail checking, that is, the balancing of money fields and so forth. Even in this case, the amount of calculation should be kept to a minimum.

Ideally, the operator should not have to look up from the data they are entering. The cursor should move from field to field automatically—unless the operator does not want it that way.

There is a fine trade-off in screen design between operator productivity and operator boredom. An old data processing maxim says that if you "design a system that even a fool can use, only a fool will want to use it." Programmers, in their own peculiar brand of paranoia, sometimes believe either that 1) the operator is out to break their system, or 2) that all operators and data entry clerks are idiots. Operators (data-entry personnel and the like) are people who enjoy some challenge in their work, just as you do in yours. Your challenge, in this case, is to find the middle of the road.

There are some basic steps that you can follow in designing the screens for your system (Fig. 9-1). They follow the basic pattern for all computer activities: screens should be easy to understand, consistent, and easy to change.

First of all, decide which areas of your screens will remain constant. This includes where the titles will appear and where the error messages will appear, whether or not to use a graphic border, and so forth. The actual text displayed may change, but be sure that you determine what areas will be used, and then use them consistently. Figure 9-2 shows

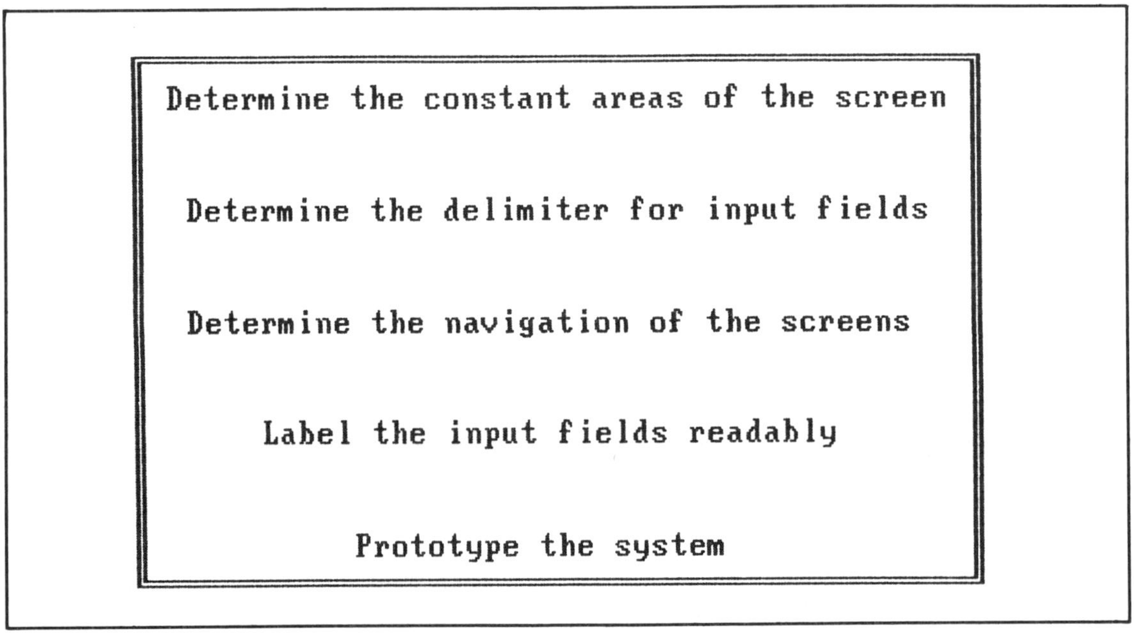

```
Determine the constant areas of the screen

Determine the delimiter for input fields

Determine the navigation of the screens

Label the input fields readably

Prototype the system
```

Fig. 9-1. The 5 steps to good screen design.

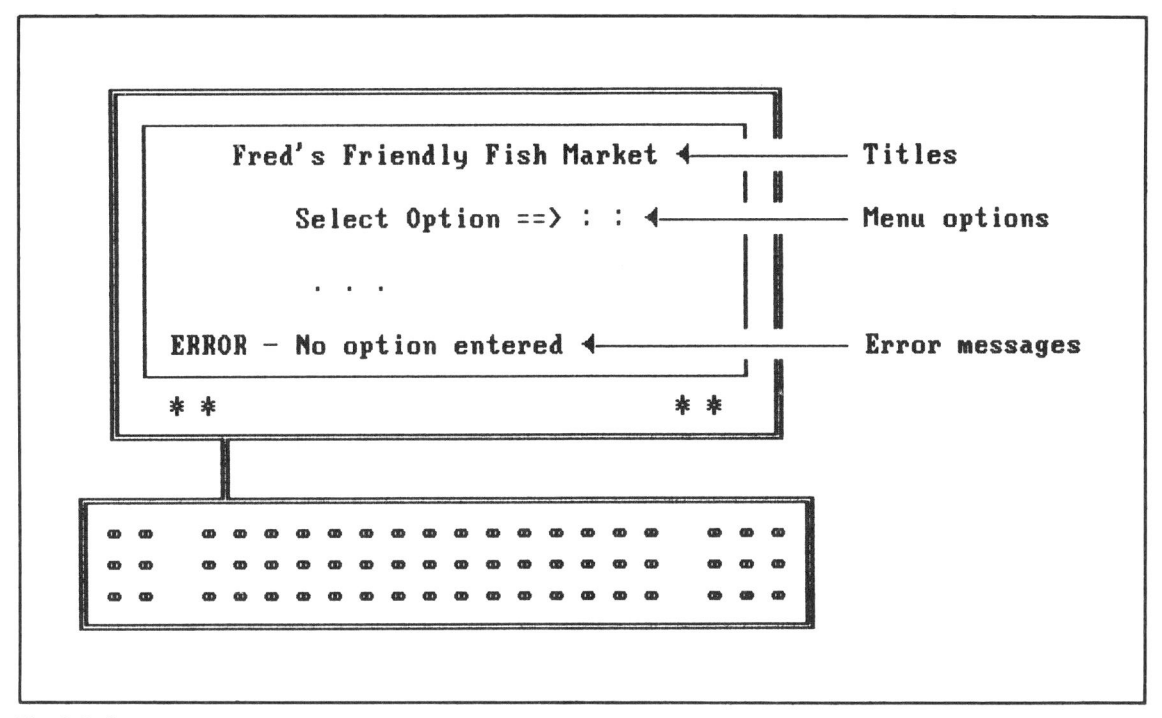

```
        ┌─────────────────────────────────┐
        │  Fred's Friendly Fish Market ←──┼──── Titles
        │                                 │
        │      Select Option ==> : : ←────┼──── Menu options
        │              . . .              │
        │  ERROR - No option entered ←────┼──── Error messages
        │  * *                      * *   │
        └─────────────────────────────────┘
```

Fig. 9-2. Constant screen areas.

the constant screen areas.

Next, determine what character or characters you will use as the delimiter of an input field. This should be readily identified by the viewer, with no explanation. As shown in Fig. 9-3, some accepted forms are a colon (:) at each side of the field, a set of arrows surrounding the field, or the use of reverse video for the input field. Color is another way of identifying fields—more on color later.

The next step is to determine how the user will move from one screen to another. This is called screen navigation and should be consistent from screen to screen. dBASE III leaves very little choice in maneuvering on the screen, and when you move past the last field on the screen, control is passed back to the program. Screen navigation also, however, includes how to exit a screen without entering any data.

For example, entering an employee's key number always retrieves the record, but when no number is entered, is the program to quit or assume that you are adding a new record? Whatever the decision, each time there is a choice of this type in the system, it should work in the same manner.

Now you are ready to start creating the detail screen. Label the input fields readably and understandably. Space limitations can sometimes force the programmer into a tight spot, and some really unbelievable abbreviations can be created. However you overcome this problem, remember to keep abbreviations consistent; if AMOUNT is abbreviated as AMT every place it is needed, the user will remember it. Replace the abbreviation only with the full word it represents.

Once you have designed the screens and menus that will be used in your system, you can present them to the user for approval. This is usually done in the form of a *prototype system*. A prototype system is the completed screens, linked together to simulate the final functional system.

What this means is that you create all of the logic necessary to display the menus, choose options, and display the detail screens. The user can then be tutored through the screens and can offer suggestions for modification. Any errors in field size, screen composition, or the general sequence of events can easily be spotted, especially as the number of people looking at the prototype increases.

The actual code that is necessary for prototyping is small, but a prototype can keep you from spending hours fixing code later. When the prototype is finished, it becomes the skeleton for the final system. Creating a prototype is also in line with structured design standards, since the uppermost levels of a hierarchy of programs are the menu programs.

USING A SCREEN FORMAT

The easiest way to develop a screen format is to create it first as a .PRG file or as a subroutine in a procedure file. This way, you can display the screen over and over until you are satisfied with its appearance and the way it works.

Once you have all of the @ . . . SAY . . . GET commands in place, you may copy them to a file with the extension .FMT. This is the standard extension for screen formats (report formats are .FRM).

The screen format may now be displayed using the command SET FORMAT TO <fmtname>. You do not need to use the file extension .FMT, since that is assumed by dBASE. Once you have set the format, the command to actually display the screen is READ, just as if you had kept the @ . . . SAY commands in your program.

Until the next SET FORMAT command is issued, each time the READ statement is encountered in your program, dBASE will display the screen format you defined. This means that you can display the screen, edit the input data, redisplay the screen with an error message, and so on, without having to repeat any @ . . . SAY commands.

Probably the easiest way to set up an understandable screen format file is to divide the

```
SET DELIMITERS OFF
SET INTENSITY ON

        Input Field:  Reverse video


SET DELIMITERS ON
SET INTENSITY OFF

        Input Field:  :Delimited by colons:


SET DELIMITERS TO "▶◀"

        Input Field:  ▶Delimited by arrows◀


SET DELIMITERS TO "‖‖"

        Input Field:  ‖Delimited by double bars‖
```

Fig. 9-3. Input field delimiters.

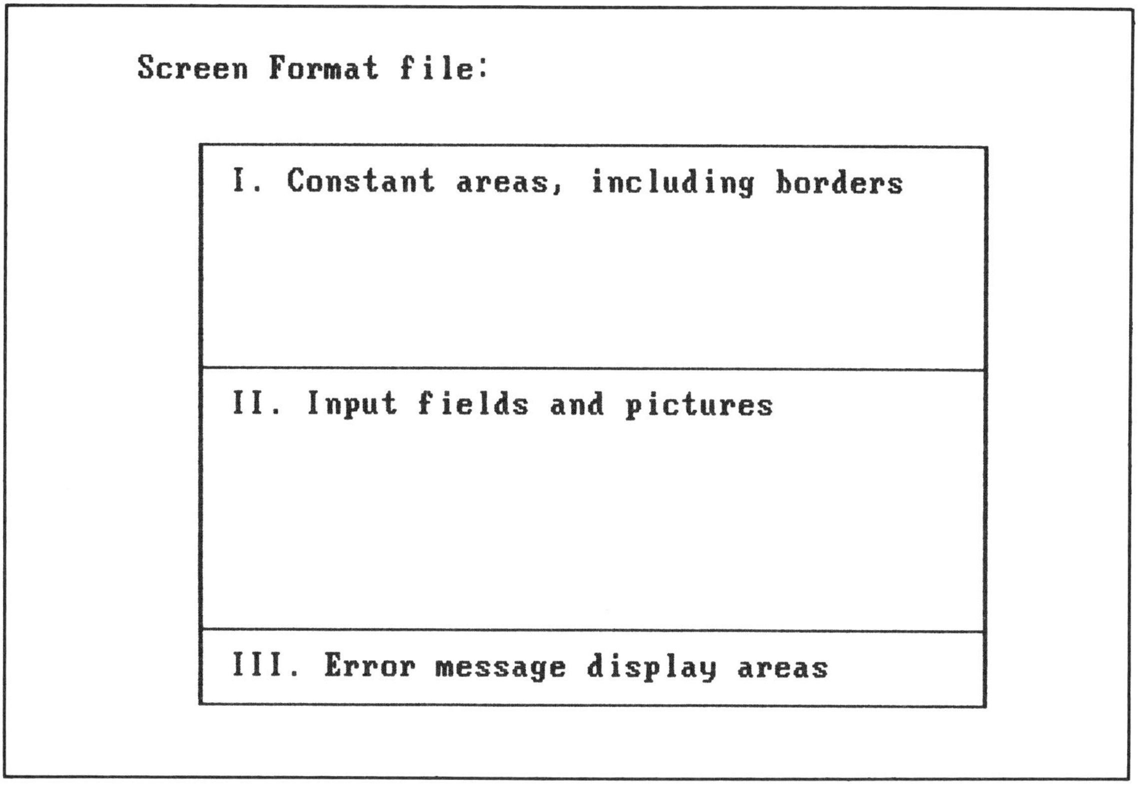

```
┌─────────────────────────────────────────────┐
│  Screen Format file:                        │
│                                             │
│    ┌─────────────────────────────────────┐  │
│    │ I. Constant areas, including borders│  │
│    │                                     │  │
│    │                                     │  │
│    ├─────────────────────────────────────┤  │
│    │ II. Input fields and pictures       │  │
│    │                                     │  │
│    │                                     │  │
│    │                                     │  │
│    ├─────────────────────────────────────┤  │
│    │ III. Error message display areas    │  │
│    │                                     │  │
│    └─────────────────────────────────────┘  │
└─────────────────────────────────────────────┘
```

Fig. 9-4. The three screen format pieces.

statements into three groups, as shown in Fig. 9-4. In the first group, place all of the @ . . . SAY commands to define the textual and constant areas of the screen, such as titles, graphic borders, and data labels.

The next section should contain all of the @ . . . GET commands for the input fields. Keeping the input data fields separate from the screen definition @ . . . SAY commands makes the modification of either group much easier. The text data on the screen may now be changed without affecting the positioning of input fields. Also, if a mistake is made, the input field will overlay the text, which will help in repositioning.

The final section contains the output fields necessary for error messages and identifiers. Since the screen attribute may not easily be changed to identify the field in error, the text error message displayed must be explicit enough to identify the exact error and its probable resolution.

It is advisable, however, to identify the field in error as well. A small (1-3 character) memory field may be defined and used in the final section of @ . . . SAY commands to contain a pointer that will identify the fields in error. A less-than sign (<) or a question mark (?) can be placed near an invalid field, by STOREing the sign to the error pointer variable that you have defined (Fig. 9-5).

Once you have issued the READ command, and the operator has filled in the fields, your program can edit the input for validity, and redisplay the screen for correction. When an edit shows incorrect data, you can STORE the pointer to the proper pointer field(s), STORE the error message to its field, and then redisplay the screen. A logical memory variable may also be set to control a DO WHILE loop, which will continuously redisplay the screen until the input data are correct. It is important, in a case like this, to give the operator some way of escaping from the entire function. This gives the operator a chance to free up the computer while looking up the correct data or to work on something else.

USING GRAPHIC BORDERS

One way to get user acceptance and enthusiasm for a system is to design screens that are interesting. A system that looks slick will almost sell itself. There are two ways to enhance screens for good looks: the use of graphic borders and the use of color.

Color is not a consideration in a system that does not have a color monitor. Most business computers are blessed with monochrome monitors, either amber or green. The system should, however, at least work on a system with a color monitor.

The way to enhance screens designed for a monochrome environment is to use borders to define the screen areas. The borders can be "drawn" using any character, but the most effective are those in the extended graphics set of the IBM PC.

The graphics characters that connect to form single or double lines have ASCII codes from X'B3' to X'DF' (179 to 223 decimal). As shown in Fig. 9-6, these codes include characters for intersections, corners, and "T" intersections in all four directions. Figure 9-7 shows some samples of graphic borders that may be created.

These characters can be entered in most editors, using an IBM PC keyboard trick: hold down the Alt-key, and type the decimal number for the character on the numeric keypad (you don't have to press the Num Lock key to do this). When you release the Alt-key, the character will be drawn at the cursor position.

The most common complaint about dBASE screens is the complexity of the @ . . . SAY . . . GET commands that make up the format. These commands can be simplified by defining all of the text information on the screen in the first set of @ . . . SAY commands. Each SAY produces one line of the screen. This way, the graphic characters and text can be adjusted to fit each other.

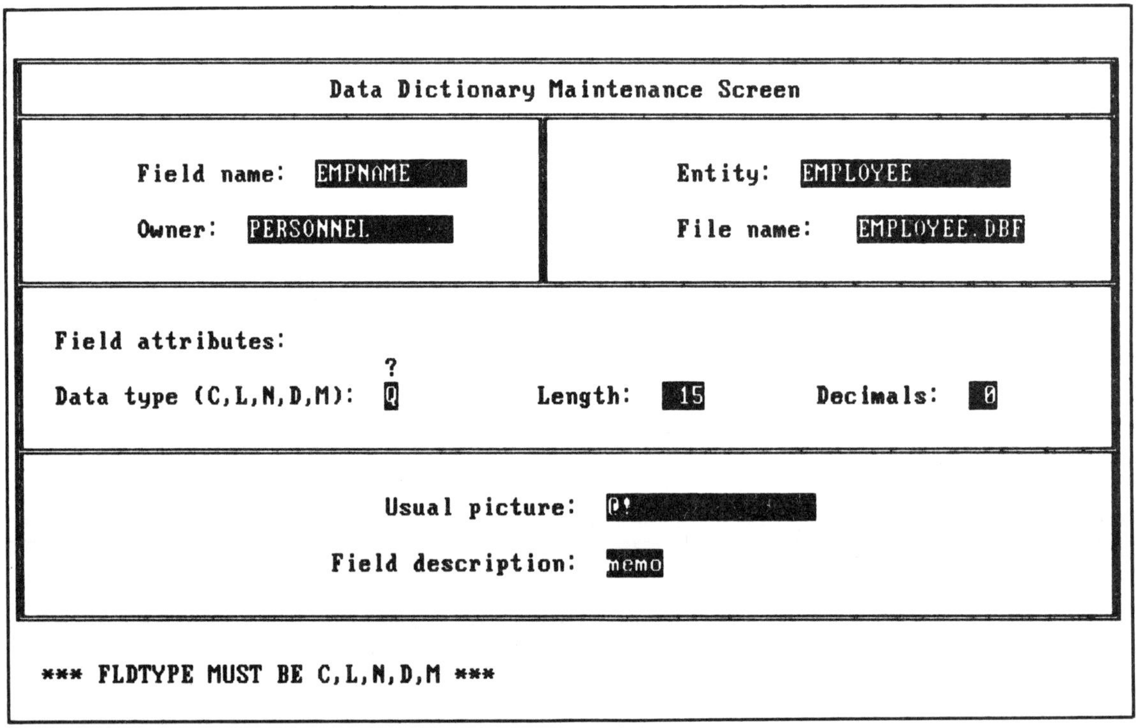

Fig. 9-5. A screen with error message and pointers.

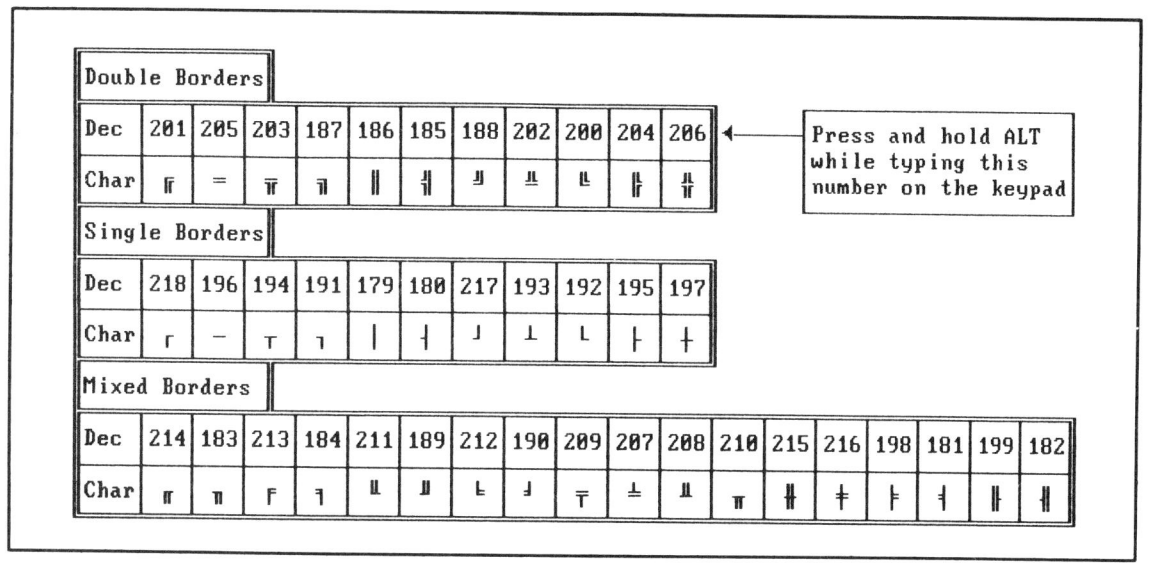

Double Borders											
Dec	201	205	203	187	186	185	188	202	200	204	206
Char	╔	═	╗	╖	╢	╣	╝	╩	╚	╠	╬

← Press and hold ALT while typing this number on the keypad

Single Borders										
Dec	218	196	194	191	179	180	217	193	192	195	197
Char	┌	─	┬	┐	│	┤	┘	┴	└	├	┼

Mixed Borders																
Dec	214	183	213	184	211	189	212	190	209	207	208	210	215	216	198	181	199	182
Char	╓	╖	╒	╕	╙	╜	╘	╛	╥	╤	╨	╧	╫	╪	╞	╡	╟	╢

Fig. 9-6. Characters for graphic borders.

Another way to make your screens stand out is to use color when writing for a system that has a color monitor. As with the other aspects of screen design, you should take a common-sense approach to the use of color. Wild and gaudy colors can make your screens look like a circus; this is to be avoided. Use color logically, by making text areas one color, input areas another, and error messages and error pointers yet another color. Too many colors will confuse the user and make the screen unreadable.

Be consistent in the use of color. If you decide to make the input fields on one screen reversed-video blue, ALL input fields should be reversed-video blue. If you suddenly switch colors the operator, either consciously or unconsciously, will be confused by the change. They may not know ex-

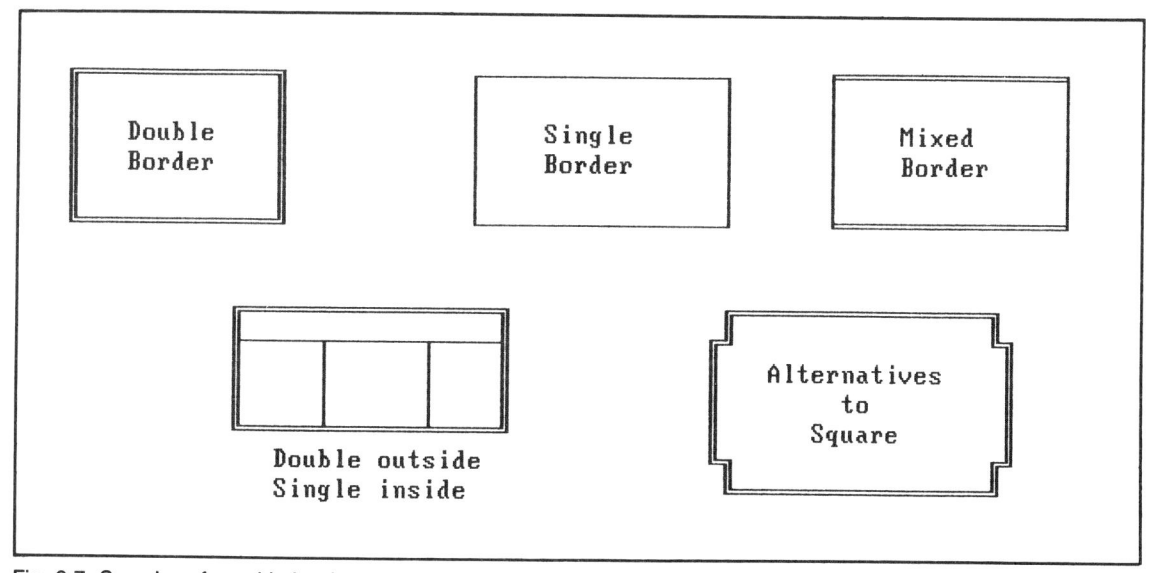

Fig. 9-7. Samples of graphic borders.

actly what is wrong—only that something IS wrong.

PROMPTING FOR INPUT

The next step in screen processing is to accept the input data from the user. In dBASE III, this is done by using an @ ... GET to place the field at the proper screen location, and using a PICTURE to assure that valid data is input.

Some input data must be edited so that incorrect data, as far as is possible, is not entered into the system. As shown in Fig. 9-8, there are three general types of editing performed: validity edits, range edits, and reasonability or relational edits.

Validity edits are global types of edits, usually aimed at the general type of data that is entered. This means making sure that numeric data is numeric, and that data, like names that must be character contain no numbers.

Validity edits can be performed for the most part by the software itself. If the PICTURE of the @ ... GET states that the input must be numbers, dBASE III will not allow other characters to be entered. This is a very effective and simple way of performing a validity edit; dates and logical fields work the same way.

Range editing is really a subset of validity editing. Certain data, such as months, must be within a specific range of values. In the case of dates, the range checking is done by dBASE automatically. Other numeric values must be tested programmatically.

Reasonability editing must be done entirely in a program, because the edits rely on other data fields. If an input field is affected by the values of other fields, those values must be tested to determine the validity of the related field. For example, the zip code of an address might not match the state entered.

Another example of reasonability editing is checking the status of the entity being processed. In a payroll system, one reasonability edit might be to see if the operator is attempting to cut a payroll check for an employee who has been ter-

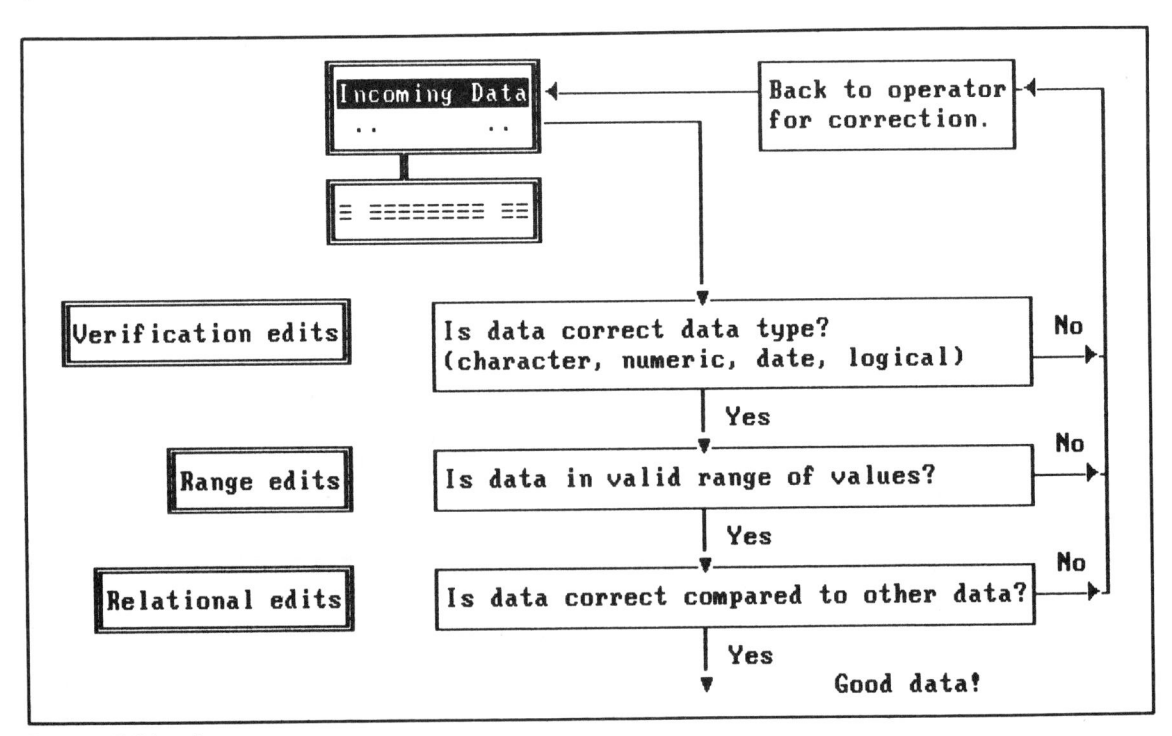

Fig. 9-8. Editing data.

minated. A good practice is to place data that can affect the input on the screen as well—this will help the operator catch this type of mistake before it is made.

The input fields should not include any data that can be calculated by the computer. An operator should not have to stop entering data to calculate an answer that can be done more quickly and accurately by your program.

One example of an unreasonable calculation can be found in some payroll-personnel systems. The operator is asked to enter both the date-of-birth of an employee AND the employee's age. In dBASE III, the age can be calculated in a single statement:

STORE INT((DATE( )—BIRTHDTE)/365.25) TO AGE

assuming, of course that BIRTHDTE is a Date field, and that the system date is current (a problem in computers that do not have a clock-calendar built in).

Once an input field has been defined on the screen, either by an @ . . . GET command directly in the program or in a screen format file, the GET must be activated. This is done by issuing the READ command. The READ will activate all GETs issued since the last READ or CLEAR GETS command.

The command READ SAVE (dBASE III vs 1.1) will allow multiple READs to be issued for one set of GETs. The SAVE keeps the READ command from clearing the GETs once they are read. Use of this feature will speed up screen processing, since the format will not have to be redrawn each time.

When the screen is entered correctly, it is important to remember to issue a CLEAR GETS to reset the system for the next screen. Otherwise, both screens may be displayed at once, if a CLEAR command is not issued. CLEAR will also CLEAR GETS.

PICTURE CLAUSES

PICTUREs are used with the @ . . . SAY . . . GET commands to format input/output data into a more readable or usable format. Dates, for example, might be stored slightly differently by some programmers if they do not use the dBASE III format.

A more common example might be the entry of character data. The operator should not have to differentiate between upper and lowercase when entering a name, unless that is important to the system. dBASE allows a PICTURE clause that will change all entered characters to uppercase, automatically. This means that you never have to change the data to uppercase in the program, and that the operator does not have to press the Caps Lock key when using your system. Figure 9-9 shows the symbols used in creating PICTUREs for input.

A good rule of thumb is to always put fields that will be used for retrieving records (such as names) into uppercase. This means that your system will not be *case-sensitive*, meaning that upper and lowercase characters must always be entered consistently. This can be overcome programmatically, if necessary, in a system that requires that the case be correct in stored data. Searching can be done using the LOWER( ) and UPPER( ) functions to mask the case-sensitivity.

As mentioned earlier PICTURE functions and templates can be used to remove some of the burden of editing from your program. By proper use of the PICTURE capabilities, the incoming data can be automatically entered in the correct data type and format, by excluding any other characters.

The numeric picture functions are: C, X, ((left parenthesis), B, and Z. These allow global editing on numeric data, where the whole number is affected.

The functions C, X, and (may only be used with numeric output (@ . . . SAY . . . PICTURE) data. The @C function displays a CR after positive numbers; the @X function displays a DB after negative numbers. These two can be used together by specifying @XC as the function. The @(function encloses negative numbers in parentheses.

The numeric functions B and Z can be used with either input or output numeric fields. The @B

67

Functions:			Symbols:	
Numeric	@C	CR after positive	9	Numbers, signs, decimals
	@X	DB after negative	#	Numbers, blanks, signs
	@(	Parentheses around negative	$	Replaces leading zeros
	@B	Left-justifies	*	Replaces leading zeros
	@Z	Blank when zero	.	Position of decimal point
			,	Inserts if digits to left
Date	@D	American date format		
	@E	European date format	A	Alphabetic only
			N	Alphanumeric
Character	@A	Alphabetic only	!	Upper case letter
	@!	Upper case only	X	Any character
	@R	Template literals not stored		

[Functions must appear first in template.]

Fig. 9-9. PICTUREs for input.

function causes the numeric data to be left-justified in the field; the @Z function displays a blank field when the value is zero.

Detailed numeric editing and formatting is done using a picture template. The template is made up of specific characters for substitution or insertion to the field. The permissible characters for numeric editing are 9, number/pound sign (#), slash (/), comma (,), period (.), dollar sign ($), and asterisk (*). The comma, period, and slash are insertion characters, meaning they will be inserted into the string at the indicated position; the other characters are substitution characters, because the data will replace them.

The $ and * characters can be used to create a "check-protected" format to display or print dollar figures. Any leading zero that is matched with an asterisk or dollar sign will be replaced by that character.

The other characters are only used in @ ... GET commands for input fields. The period is inserted for the decimal point, and the commas appear only if there are numbers to the left of their position. Figure 9-10 shows some sample numeric PICTURE strings.

Character data can also be edited and displayed using PICTURE. The alphabetic functions are A,

R, and the exclamation point (!). The @A function tells dBASE to accept only alphabetic characters in the input field; @! is a function that changes all lowercase letters to uppercase. The @R function removes the insertion characters before storing the value to a field. Figure 9-11 shows some sample character PICTURE strings.

The template characters that are used for numeric editing can also be used to edit input to character fields. The additional character template symbols are A, exclamation point (!), L, N, and X. A limits the input to only alphabetic characters in the position in the template it occupies. L accepts logical values (Y, N, T, F); N accepts alphabetics and numbers; and "X" accepts any character. The ! changes any alphabetic character to upper case, ignoring any other characters.

Characters that appear in a PICTURE string that are not template characters are placed directly into the output string, without change. This is useful in using one @ ... SAY command to place both the title and the value, especially when the positioning of the field is unclear. The PICTURE string '@R Phone number: (999)999-9999' will place both the title and the field at the specified position. In this example, the object field of the SAY must be a numeric field, because "n" is a valid

PICTURE string	Value	Result
'99999.99'	12345	12345.00
'$$$$9.99'	123.45	$$123.45
'****9.99'	123.45	**123.45
'@C'	123.45	123.45 CR
'@('	-123.45	(123.45)
'@Z'	0.00	blanks

Fig. 9-10. Sample numeric PICTURE strings.

character template symbol, and character fields are left-justified.

dBASE III SCREEN EDITOR

dBASE III version 1.1 comes with a screen format editor called SED (formerly dFORMAT). SED allows you to create a full-screen display with a few simple commands. SED also includes an on-line manual, and is menu driven.

The online manual makes the use of SED easy to learn as you are developing screens. This is most useful to professional programmers and other people who do not have the time to learn a new development tool. Unfortunately, the manual is not also repeated on paper, so that the SED is avoided by those who need examples and written direction.

The SED main menu is arranged in a horizontal hierarchical chart format. The highest level,

PICTURE string	Value	Result
'99/99/99'	"123185"	"12/18/5 "
'@R 99/99/99'	"123185"	"12/31/85"
'@!'	"peggy"	"PEGGY"
'@R (999)999-9999'	'1112223333'	"(111)222-3333"

Fig. 9-11. Sample character PICTURE strings.

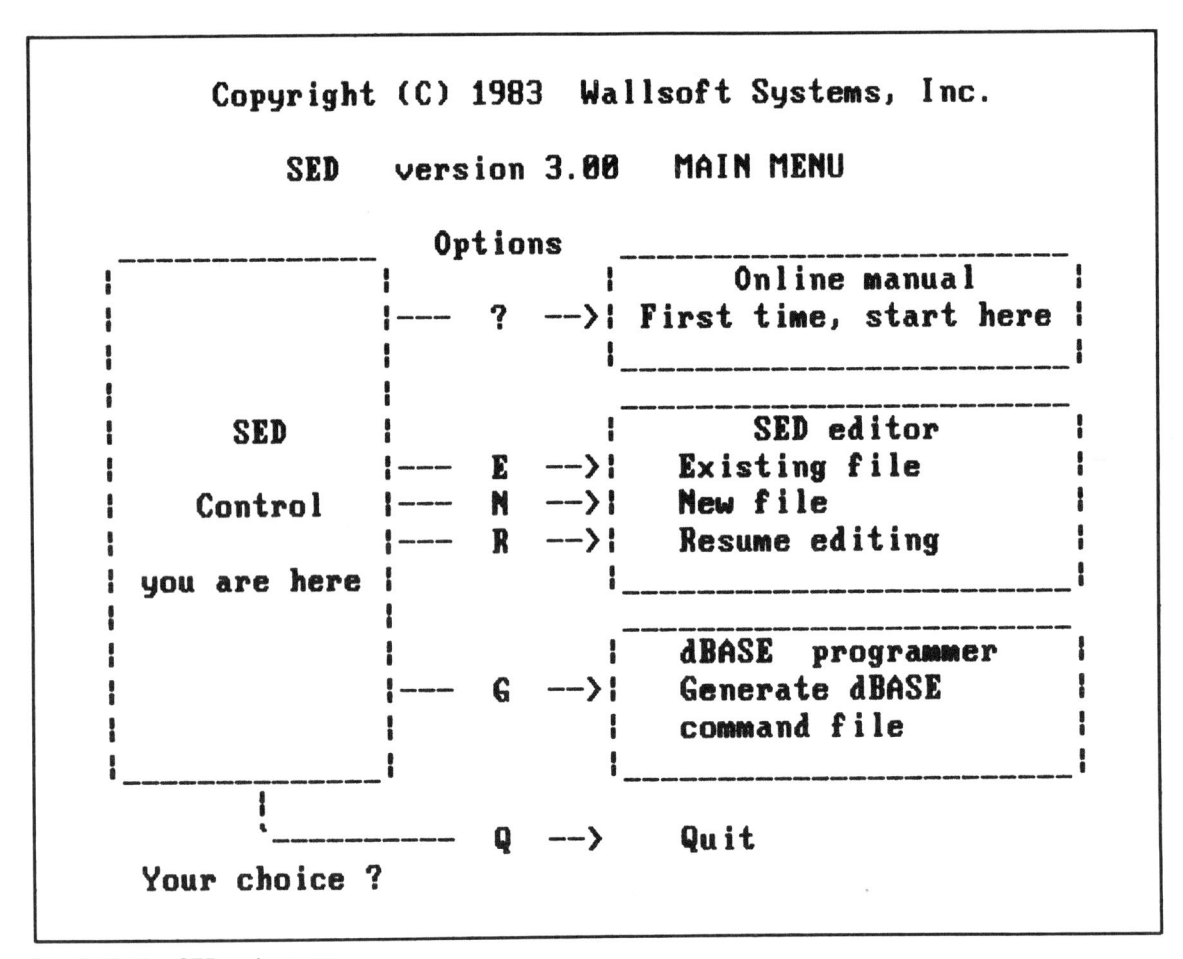

```
        Copyright (C) 1983   Wallsoft Systems, Inc.

        SED   version 3.00    MAIN MENU

                      Options
     _____          _____
    |                |        |      Online manual     |
    |                |--- ? ->| First time, start here |
    |                |        |_____|
    |                |
    |                |         _____
    |     SED        |        |      SED editor        |
    |                |--- E ->| Existing file          |
    |    Control     |--- N ->| New file               |
    |                |--- R ->| Resume editing         |
    | you are here   |        |_____|
    |                |
    |                |         _____
    |                |        | dBASE   programmer     |
    |                |--- G ->| Generate dBASE         |
    |                |        | command file           |
    |_____|        |_____|
            |
            '-------- Q -->    Quit

    Your choice ?
```

Fig. 9-12. The SED main menu.

represented by the box on the left side of the screen in Fig. 9-12, is the main menu itself. You may then choose the next action by pressing the letter on the line you wish to follow.

Two files are required to run the full implementation of SED. They are the executable file SED.EXE and the online manual and error message file SED.MSG. If SED.MSG is not on the same directory as the SED.EXE file, SED will display a temporary menu; the menu text is stored in SED.MSG as well. You can then use option D to specify where the system can find the SED.MSG file. SED can still be used without this file, but error messages will not be displayed.

It is possible to execute the SED inside dBASE III, by including these files on the same directory or disk as the dBASE overlay file (DBASE.OVL). Since SED is made to be executed independently of dBASE, you must use the RUN command to invoke it. If you include a different text or word processing editor in the CONFIG.DB file, there may not be enough room on a floppy disk for both SED files, the word processor/text editor files, and dBASE. Hard disk users do not have this problem.

To create a screen format, enter N from the main menu. SED will prompt you for a filename for the screen file you are creating—there is no default extension (suggestion: use .SCR). You must also enter a drive identifier if the screen is not to be located on the default drive.

The text can be typed in the position that you want it in. SED will figure out the position and use that in the @ . . . SAY command that will be generated. Fields can also be positioned in the same way. If a text string on the screen begins with the >, SED interprets that to mean that an output field is to be placed at that point of the screen, and that the field name follows the > (no spaces). For input fields, the < character is used.

Two other types of commands, which are identified by the first character of the line they are entered on, are used. An asterisk (*) identifies a comment line. The exclamation point (!) is used to create a named picture definition that can then be used generically throughout the screen. When the SED builds the actual program file, the correct picture will be inserted.

Picture definitions are assigned by name to an input or output field. A ! character in column 1 tells SED that a picture definition follows. The next character begins the picture name that will be used in the actual screen format. The picture function/template is then entered in quotes. Wherever SED finds the picture name in the screen format, the picture function/template will be placed in the @ . . . GET generated for that field.

One of the major drawbacks to using SED to generate screen formats is that, as with WordStar, the high-order bit in each byte is *stripped off*. This means that graphics characters used in borders can be scrambled, or changed into plain alphabetic characters (this applies to SED.EXE supplied with dBASE III version 1.1, dated 11-12-1984). Beyond this limitation, however, screens can be created using any editor and then translated using SED.

SED generates the dBASE code for the screen and places the statements in a file with a .PRG extension. The .PRG extension is used because SED will allow embedded dBASE commands within the screen definition. Square brackets ([ ]) surrounding text identify that text as a dBASE command. SED will include these in the generated file; screen formats are only permitted to contain comments and @ . . . SAY . . . GET commands.

Chapter 10
Reporting Techniques

One of the most outstanding features of dBASE III is its built-in report format generator. Reports of database information can be quickly formatted and produced without using a program. Totals, subtotals, customized headings, and subtotal labels allow a great flexibility in the interactive production of reports.

These same report formats can be used to enhance the reporting features of any system written in dBASE III. Fred's Law of Computer Reports says that most reports in a given system will be required to be in a format that cannot be generated, and those that can be generated will require special processing first, anyway. A report format, however, can be used to report on data across several open databases, and the contents of a report column can be defined as the result of calculation or concatenation.

The report format generator is designed to produce columnar reports. Line oriented reports, such as customer statements, must be programmatically produced using @ ... SAY statements or the ? command. Hybrids of these two report types do exist; for example, the customer statement might have a columnar format for the list of detailed transactions and a line format for the name, address, and totals lines.

Much of the tedium of columnar report programming can be removed from the program by using a generated report format. The generated code is also faster than the interpreted code of the program, because it is already in a compiled format and requires no interpretation. This in turn makes your programs smaller, more readable, and faster.

Report formats can be mixed with @ ... SAY commands to produce hybrid dBASE reports. The NOEJECT option keeps the printer from advancing the page before the report format is printed; the PLAIN option will stop the display of automatic headers.

PREPARING REPORT FORMATS

Report formats are created by entering the CREATE REPOrt command in the interactive dBASE mode; changes to the formats can be performed using the MODIfy REPOrt command. The format generator may only be accessed from the interactive mode.

As shown in Fig. 10-1, the first screen of the report format generator allows entry of titles and other global information that will affect the appearance of the report. This includes the line width, margins, and spacing requirements of the report. Up to five lines of report title are allowed; these lines are centered at the top of every report page.

The next screen, shown in Fig. 10-2, allows information to be entered pertaining to the production of group subtotals. This creates an automatic control break based on the contents of a database field. Each time the specified field changes value, a subtotal line will be produced to your requirements. The columns to be totaled are also specified on the group subtotal screen.

Finally, a screen is displayed to define the contents of each field of the report (Fig. 10-3). The field contents, the column heading, and the length of the output field may be defined on this screen. The display will also show a sample report line with the fields filled in as they would appear on the report.

The field contents can be defined as a total of database fields or a concatenation of character fields. In the Data Dictionary system shown in Appendix B, the Field Attributes column is actually comprised of three fields: data type, length, and decimals. The length and decimals fields, which are numeric, must be changed to character for concatenation; the conversion is performed with the STR( ) function, which is available in the report format definitions just as in a dBASE program.

dBASE stores the completed format in a file with the extension .FRM; from there, it may be invoked with the REPOrt FORM command either interactively or from within a program.

Any field from any currently open database file can be used in the report format. Those fields not in the currently selected partition can be accessed via an alias pointer, such as A − >. Most often, if multiple databases are used in generating a report format, they will be related by some shared key field. The SET RELAtion TO command will ensure that the proper database positioning is performed.

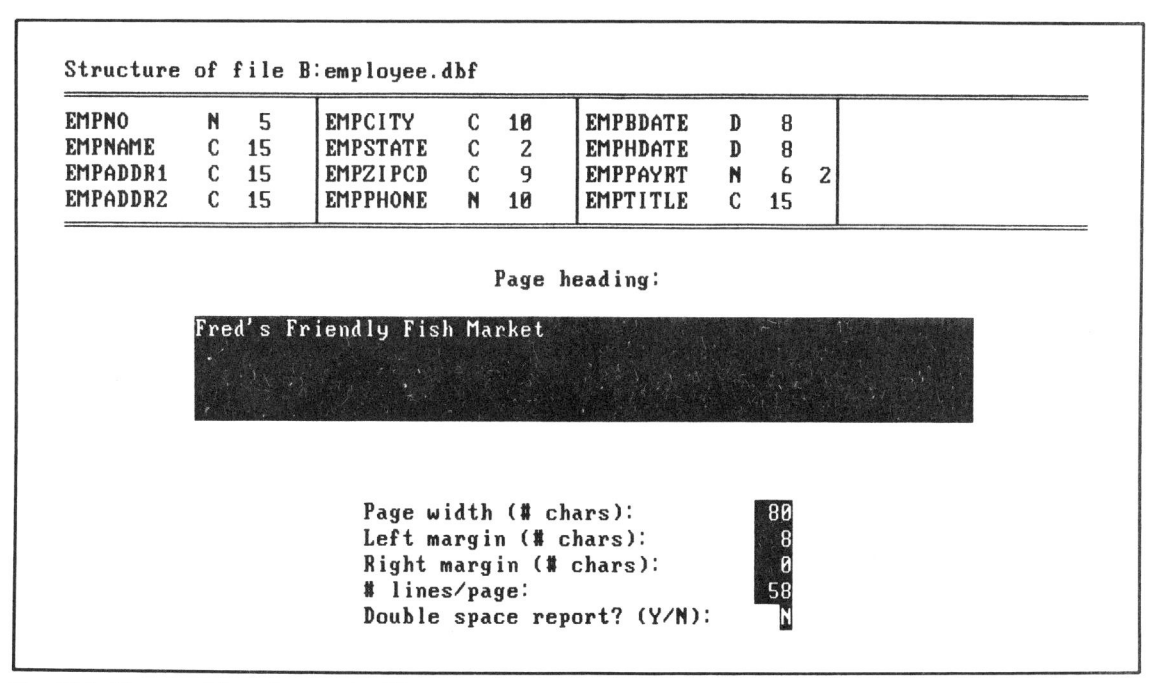

```
Structure of file B:employee.dbf

EMPNO      N   5    EMPCITY    C  10    EMPBDATE   D   8
EMPNAME    C  15    EMPSTATE   C   2    EMPHDATE   D   8
EMPADDR1   C  15    EMPZIPCD   C   9    EMPPAYRT   N   6   2
EMPADDR2   C  15    EMPPHONE   N  10    EMPTITLE   C  15


                         Page heading:

       Fred's Friendly Fish Market




                    Page width (# chars):        80
                    Left margin (# chars):        8
                    Right margin (# chars):       0
                    # lines/page:                58
                    Double space report? (Y/N):   N
```

Fig. 10-1. The report format generator title screen.

```
Structure of file B:employee.dbf
EMPNO     N  5    EMPCITY   C  10   EMPBDATE  D  8
EMPNAME   C  15   EMPSTATE  C  2    EMPHDATE  D  8
EMPADDR1  C  15   EMPZIPCD  C  9    EMPPAYRT  N  6  2
EMPADDR2  C  15   EMPPHONE  N  10   EMPTITLE  C  15
```

Group/subtotal on:

Summary report only? (Y/N): N   Eject after each group/subtotal? (Y/N): N

Group/subtotal heading:

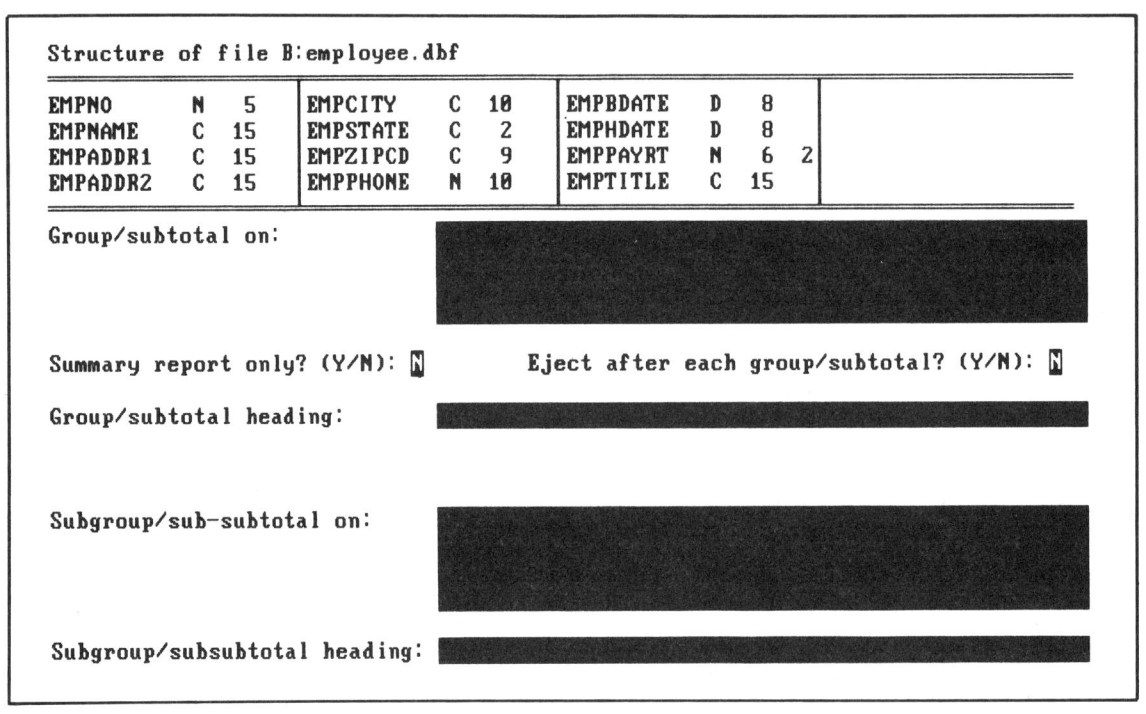

Subgroup/sub-subtotal on:

Subgroup/subsubtotal heading:

Fig. 10-2. The group/subtotal screen.

```
Structure of file B:employee.dbf
EMPNO     N  5    EMPCITY   C  10   EMPBDATE  D  8
EMPNAME   C  15   EMPSTATE  C  2    EMPHDATE  D  8
EMPADDR1  C  15   EMPZIPCD  C  9    EMPPAYRT  N  6  2
EMPADDR2  C  15   EMPPHONE  N  10   EMPTITLE  C  15
```

                                Field 1   Columns left = 72
>>>>>>>>--

Field
  contents

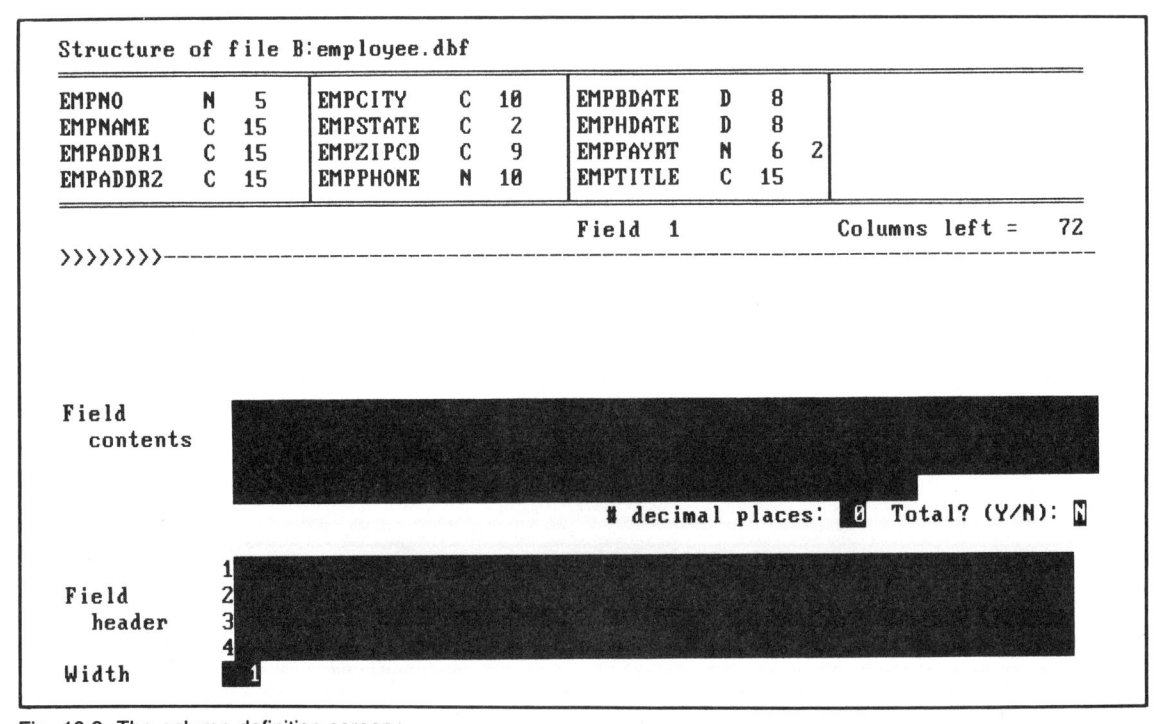

                                        # decimal places: 0 Total? (Y/N): N

          1
Field   2
  header 3
          4
Width   1

Fig. 10-3. The column definition screen.

EXTRACTING THE DATA TO REPORT

One of the overriding concerns of dBASE users is the speed at which dBASE operates. In some operations, especially when sequential database access is being performed, the programs tend to run for hours. The necessary I/O operations and arrangement of data take most of the time needed for the operation.

The reporting process, on the other hand, almost always requires that at least one database be processed sequentially. In an accounts receivable system, the program that produces the monthly account status report must sequentially process the unpaid orders, while randomly accessing the customer file.

If the dBASE program is doing calculations, database accesses, and sequential processing at the same time the report lines are being written, the printing of the report will progress at the same rate as the program—slowly. This proves very annoying to users, who are reminded of the slowness of the process each time the printer grinds across the paper.

One way of removing long processes from the sight of the users is to do the calculations and data-gathering in a separate program, called an *extract* program. The data needed for the report is accessed and calculated just as it would be in the report program, but then it is stored on a database for later printing. The report format is generated for the extract database rather than for the databases that contain the original data. Figure 10-4 shows how splitting up the task can save processing time.

This process, admittedly, takes almost as much time to complete, because there is additional disk I/O. The program can, however, be run without supervision, since there is no printing to worry about; people who leave a printer running unattended never do it twice! The extract can be the last thing done at night, and the computer left running merrily away in an empty office (for security's sake, take the keyboard with you, and turn down the glow on the monitor).

The next morning, the report can be printed from the extract database, and because most of the

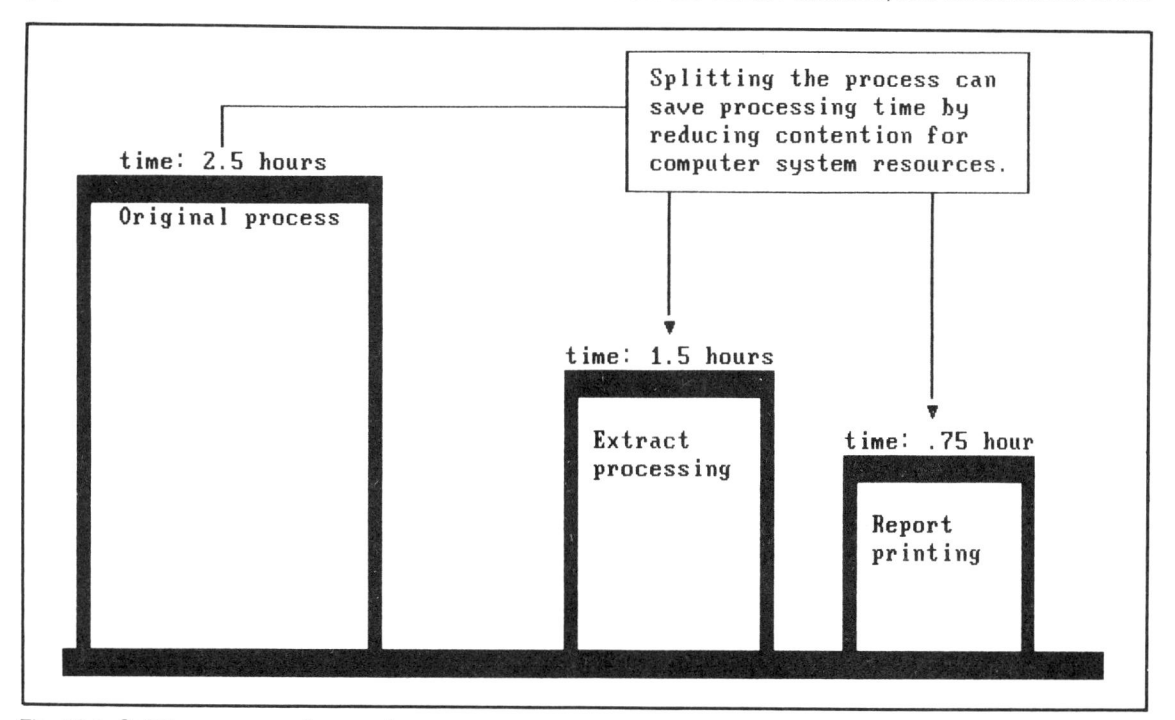

Fig. 10-4. Splitting a process for speed.

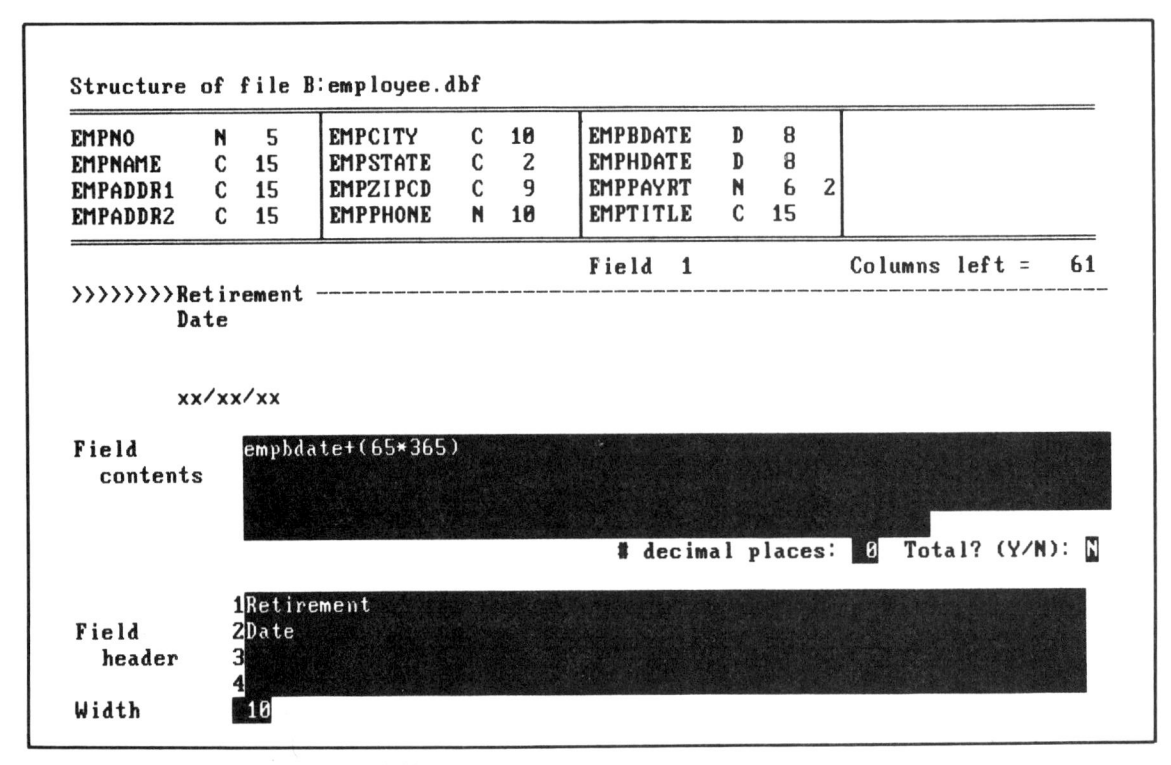

```
Structure of file B:employee.dbf
EMPNO     N  5   EMPCITY   C 10   EMPBDATE  D 8
EMPNAME   C 15   EMPSTATE  C  2   EMPHDATE  D 8
EMPADDR1  C 15   EMPZIPCD  C  9   EMPPAYRT  N 6 2
EMPADDR2  C 15   EMPPHONE  N 10   EMPTITLE  C 15
```

```
                                        Field    1          Columns left =    61
>>>>>>>>Retirement  ------------------------------------------------------------
        Date

           xx/xx/xx
Field          empbdate+(65*365)
  contents

                                           # decimal places:  0   Total? (Y/N):  N

               1Retirement
Field          2Date
  header       3
               4
Width          10
```

Fig. 10-5. Calculation in a column definition.

work has already been done, the report will be printed at the fastest speed possible.

Another way of speeding up the extract-and-report process is to leave as much of the calculations as possible to be done by the report format itself, as illustrated in Fig. 10-5. The report format file is in a compiled format, which means that the dBASE software does not have to take the time to interpret program commands.

Extract files can be stored or archived as a regular part of system recovery procedures. The report can be regenerated at any time by running the program using the archived file rather than the live one; the report can also be recreated directly from dBASE's interactive mode, using the REPOrt FORMat command and the same format generated previously.

PRINTING THE REPORT

After the data has been extracted to the database that is defined in the report format, the report can be printed. Another advantage to the extract database is that the report may be printed as many times as necessary, without rerunning the program that extracted the data.

The report format can also be changed, rearranged, or added to with a minimum of effort. In the first place, the hard work of extracting the data is already done; secondly, any data not extracted in the original program can be appended to the report just by opening the database, setting the relationship, and regenerating the report format.

Using a report format is the fastest way to produce a report. Report formats require the fewest instructions in a program because most of the work is done in the interactive mode. There are two other ways to produce reports: directly programming the report using the @ . . . SAY command, and producing the hybrid report using a report format for a part of the report and @ . . . SAY commands for other parts.

Another alternative is the use of a screen format file that contains only @ . . . SAY commands as a noncolumnar version of a report format. This type of format is not in a compiled form, so processing will be slowed down accordingly.

Directly producing the report requires programming the entire report process, including control breaks, totals, headings, page breaks, and column spacing (if any). The SET DEVIce TO PRINT routes the output of all @ . . . SAY commands to the printer instead of the SCREEN (the default).

Page breaks require the use of a memory variable as a line counter. The length of the report page must also be programmed into the process, making the entire process slightly more inflexible. Changes of paper width and form length would require program changes—which can be a cause of unexpected errors.

Fortunately, there are some steps that you can take to make program changes of this nature easily and accurately. The easiest technique for accomplishing most of the changes is to use memory variables to describe the number of lines on a page, the width of the page, the location of columns (if any), and any control codes to be sent to the printer. Storing the appropriate values into these variables at the beginning of the program that produces the report gives easy access to what would normally be numeric or character constants directly in the code. This ensures that the values need only be changed once and requires no change to statements controlling the logic of the program.

One variation of this scheme is to allow the user to change the report page length and other *pseudoconstants* themselves. The information can be stored in a "system fields" database (Chapter 11), or in a .MEM file for later retrieval. In this manner, you can devise standard names for the pseudoconstants, such as PAGELEN for the number of lines per report page. This will make coding similar functions easier, because most of the ground-work will have already been completed.

Producing a report directly from a program using @ . . . SAY commands allows the programmer to intermingle the printing operations with other logic and calculations. This will cause the printer to appear to be running more slowly, because of the extra interpretation and execution time represented by the nonprinting statements.

Depending on the requirements of the system and the users' perception, code should be arranged so that all printing is done in the same routine or at least one line right after another. Although this will not speed up the process in real terms, the perception of slowness is reduced. With a print buffer installed and a program with a low number of calculations or decision statements between I/O operations, printing may even appear continuous.

Hybrid reports are made possible with the NOEJect option of the REPOrt statement. This instructs dBASE not to send a page-feed control character to the printer before the report is printed. @ . . . SAY commands may be used before this to print in noncolumnar format at the top of the form, and the columnar report can start part way down the page. Figure 10-6 shows how this can be done.

The report format to be used in a hybrid report should be created with no titles, although subtotals and totals could be produced. The report format will place five blank lines where the title lines would appear. Furthermore, the PLAIN option should be included on the REPOrt FORMat command, to eliminate the date and time from being printed on the title lines.

Any @ . . . SAY commands that follow the REPOrt FORMat output on the same page should be positioned following the last report line. The ROW( ) function can be used after the REPOrt statement to determine the current location.

The REPOrt FORMat command does not cause a page feed at the end of printing, so either the EJECt command or an @ . . . SAY command positioned at the first line of the next page should be used to advance the printer. Figure 10-7 shows a sample hybrid report.

SETTING PRINTER FUNCTIONS

Reports produced from dBASE III can be further enhanced by using the special control codes for the printer. Most printers recognize a sequence of special characters as commands to change various printer functions: including the character

```
@ 1,1 say 'Employee overview: '+dtoc(date())
@ 5,10 say emp->empname
@ 5,50 say 'Birth date: '+dtoc(emp->empbdate)
@ 6,10 say emp->empaddr1
@ 6,50 say 'Hire date: '+dtoc(emp->emphdate)
@ 7,10 say trim(emp->empcity)+', '+emp->empstate
@ 7,50 say emp->empphone picture '@R Phone number: (999)999-9999'
@ 8,20 say emp->empzipcd picture '@R 99999-9999'
report form hybrid to print plain noeject record recno()
@ row()+1,10 say emp->emptitle
```

Fig. 10-6. Producing a hybrid report.

size, line spacing, and print style.

The printer functions used most often usually have to do with the size of the printed characters. To fit a larger amount of data on a single 8.5" × 11" page, the condensed print mode will produce characters that are 15-pitch, meaning that 15 characters will take one inch of the line. This means that 120 characters can fit on an 8-inch report line. Double-wide print, on the other hand, takes twice as much space as the normal character set of the printer. Only 40 characters will fit across a line that could accommodate 80 normal characters.

Other often-used printer functions include double-striking and emphasizing the printed characters. The double-strike function types over each line twice, making the print darker and more readable. Emphasizing a line means that the printer retypes it, but moves slightly from the original position. On a dot-matrix printer, this has the effect of "connecting the dots," and thus producing a sharper image on the paper. These functions are used when the report must be reproduced or used in a presentation. Double-strike and emphasized modes can be used together to produce high-quality printed output.

The dBASE function CHR( ) can be used to create the printer control characters. Special printer functions can be invoked by simply printing the con-

```
Employee overview: 09/02/85


    ABLE                             Birth date: 06/07/43
    111 FIRST ST                     Hire date: 05/01/63
    ONEWAY, PA                       Phone number: (714)345-6789
         17111-9090



    REVIEW      Able has shown that he can competently handle the job of
                foreman.
                He has shown initiative and imagination, tempered by common
                sense and a love of seafood.
                Recommended for promotion on 8/13/85.



    FOREMAN
```

Fig. 10-7. Sample hybrid report.

Action:	Code:
Reset the printer	CHR(27) + '@'
Condensed mode: On Off	CHR(27) + CHR(15) CHR(27) + CHR(18)
Double strike: On Off	CHR(27) + 'G' CHR(27) + 'H'
Emphasized mode: On Off	CHR(27) + 'E' CHR(27) + 'F'
Double strike/emphasize	CHR(27) + '!' + CHR(24)

Fig. 10-8. Common Epson/IBM standard printer control codes.

trol characters as if they were data fields.

For example, on the Epson line of printers, the control sequence Esc-E (the escape character followed by a capital "E") switches the printer to emphasized output. This sequence can be sent to the printer with the command:

@ 0,0 SAY CHR(27)+'E'

```
RESTORE FROM prtcodes

DISPLAY MEMORY

        ESC         pub    C    ""
        PDBLEMPH    pub    C    "!↑"
        PEMPHON     pub    C    "E"
        PEMPHOFF    pub    C    "F"
        PINIT       pub    C    "@"
        PDBLON      pub    C    "G"
        PDBLOFF     pub    C    "H"
        PCONDON     pub    C    "*"
        PCONDOFF    pub    C    "↕"
            9 variables defined,        36 bytes used
          247 variables available,    31708 bytes available
```

Fig. 10-9. Restored printer control codes.

No characters are printed by this statement; the escape code (decimal value 27) alerts the printer to the control sequence. The printer will then print everything in emphasized ('E') mode, until a control code is sent that resets the printer. If, as in the example, the position of 0,0 is used, the printer will also advance to the top of the next page unless it is already positioned there. Figure 10-8 shows some common Epson/IBM standard printer control codes.

After the report is finished, the printer should be reset. If it is not reset, the next job in or out of dBASE that uses the printer will still have those control codes set. The program should leave the printer the way it was found, because control codes set for the next report might be mutually exclusive with the previous settings, resulting in strange-looking output.

Another consideration when using the double-strike and/or emphasized modes is that each line will be printed twice for each mode, and four times if both are specified together. This will increase the length of time required to produce the report, because the printer speed will be halved or quartered. A printer that prints 140 characters per second in draft (normal) mode will be reduced to a speed of 35 characters per second when both double-strike and emphasized modes are set.

Printer control codes can also be placed in a PUBLIC memory variable or standard database field. One idea might be to store all of the possible codes in a memory variable file and to restore that file when a report is to be printed. Then all the program need do is print the appropriate control code by name or function. This will keep unnecessary constants out of the code; the code will also be transportable to any type of printer, because the memory variable values need be changed only once. If the boss ever decides to get a new printer, you will be ready. Figure 10-9 shows a restored file of printer control codes.

Chapter 11

Programming Techniques

This chapter presents a number of ideas that will enable you to develop more efficient database management systems. By applying what you learn here, you can design systems that make better use of time and better serve your clients.

File maintenance is the most time-consuming task allotted to a computer system and also the most important one. The data in the main, or master, databases, will need to be updated to reflect changing conditions of the data entity. Address and name fields may need to be changed on a file of clients or employees, for example. Other programs in the system may cause a change in condition of the entity, requiring changes to the master database of the entity.

Changing, adding, and deleting database records are the functions usually associated with file maintenance. These three types of functions cover all tasks necessary to keep the database up to date.

In dBASE, most database records are updated in *real time*, which means that when you press the Enter key from the last field on the screen, the record is immediately updated (Fig. 11-1). Real time processing is a relatively new development; microcomputers do not have problems of response time due to dozens or even hundreds of data entry clerks updating a database containing millions of records. There is no conflict among multiple users trying to access the same record.

dBASE III does not as yet function in a multiuser environment, although there is daily progress toward that goal. The problem is how to lock one record of the database when it is being updated and allow access to the other records in the database at the same time. There are some algorithms that can be used programmatically to lock a single record; one method is to place the record number of the record to be updated on another file, called a *semaphore file*. When a user tries to access a record, the program first checks the semaphore to be sure that someone else has not already retrieved it. The drawback to the semaphore method is dealing with the problems that arise when multiple users trying to access the semaphore file itself.

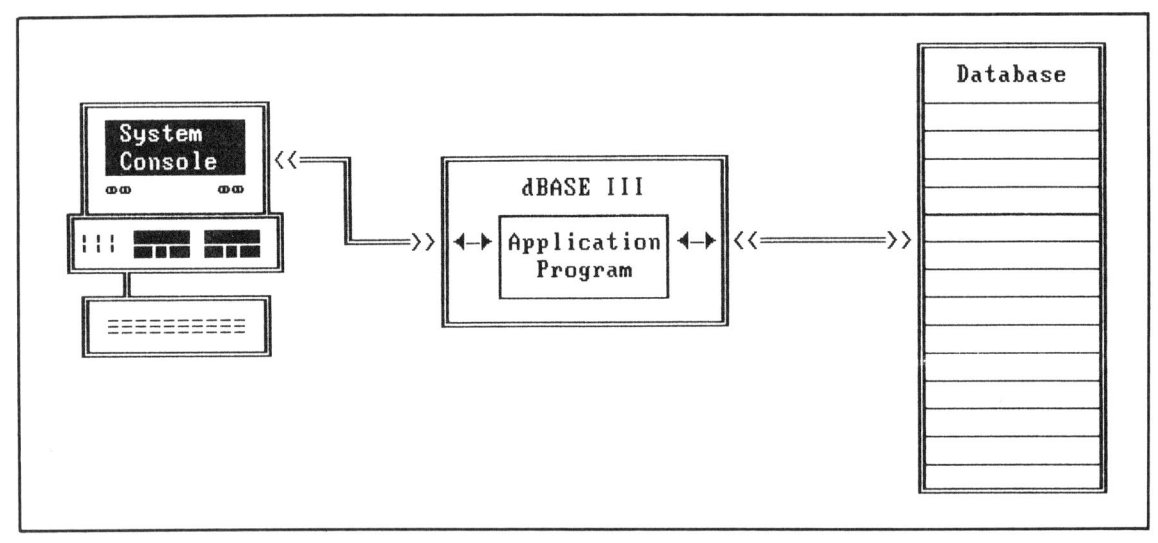

Fig. 11-1. Real-time file maintenance.

Normal "single-user" dBASE III processing is usually performed in real time; the updated data is immediately available for retrieval and further changes. All systems should have a means of updating the records in the main database, adding new records, and removing any that are incorrect. These functions can be performed in a relatively simple and reusable routine by making dBASE do most of the work.

A screen format is used for the data entry screen, while another is used for the initial access to the file maintenance functions. The first screen requests the key of the record to be changed or deleted. If ADD is entered, a new record is added to the end of the database with APPEnd BLANK, a key assigned, and an empty screen displayed for the new data. If an existing key is entered on the first screen, the record is retrieved, and the current contents displayed. The record can be changed by overtyping the fields with their new contents, or it can be deleted by entering a Y in the delete indicator field.

Deleted records are not removed from a database file until a PACK command is issued. This feature enables the use of the dBASE unseen field to indicate that the record has been deleted and also allows the implementation of an "undelete" function. The RECALL statement removes the asterisk from the unseen field, making the record visible to dBASE again. Deleted records are maintained in index files, so the record will be fully available immediately after the RECALL.

Sometimes, however, real-time processing can be a burden. Leaving some work for another, "end-of-the-day" program can allow faster access during peak usage times. For example, if up-to-the-second data is not required from the system, the file maintenance functions are not necessary for the bulk of processing done during the workday. The actual file updating can be performed at a later time.

The reason for using nonreal-time processing on a microcomputer system is not because of response time but because of access. The very reason real-time applications work so well on a microcomputer is because there are not multiple terminals; it is ironic that the reason for sometimes not using real-time processing is because there is only one terminal. This creates an information bottleneck, right at the keyboard of the computer.

If the stored data is needed on an instant's notice, access to inquiry functions has to be a top priority. Any functions that slow or inconvenience this process should be performed when the data is not needed instantly. This is especially necessary on systems on which the users are performing customer service inquiries. If the machine is not available for two hours, because someone is printing a report or doing some other processing, the user will become frustrated; the person using the computer will be yelled at; the customer will get another vendor, and the programmer will be blamed.

There are several solutions to this kind of bottleneck; proper planning will eliminate it before it occurs. Sometimes, however, a bottleneck will not become apparent until after the system has been used for a while. That's when it's time to split the process into several steps, performing as much of the function as possible in a noninteractive program.

One method of splitting the process is to produce a file in the first subprocess that will identify the requested function to the second subprocess. Each record in this new file will cause the second part of the original process to be invoked at a later, more convenient time. Several different functions can be identified, each with its own programs and procedures. This type of file is called a *transaction file*, and it is the main feature of noninteractive processing.

As shown in Fig. 11-2, the transaction file will be used as a guide in updating the master database; this type of processing is sometimes called *batch processing*. This comes from the practice, in data processing's earlier days, of gathering a certain number of cards in a group for auditing or verification purposes. Since card-dropping is not a major source of fear these days, actual "batching" has been dispensed with—but the term lives on.

For example, Fred's Fish Market has an accounts receivable system in which customer's orders are stored on a database and later used to print statements and to report the status of the accounts. The account balancing could be performed in real time for each order or payment entry, but it would take a few minutes longer for each entry. As the size of the order database grows, so does the length of the response time.

Rather than process each order or payment in

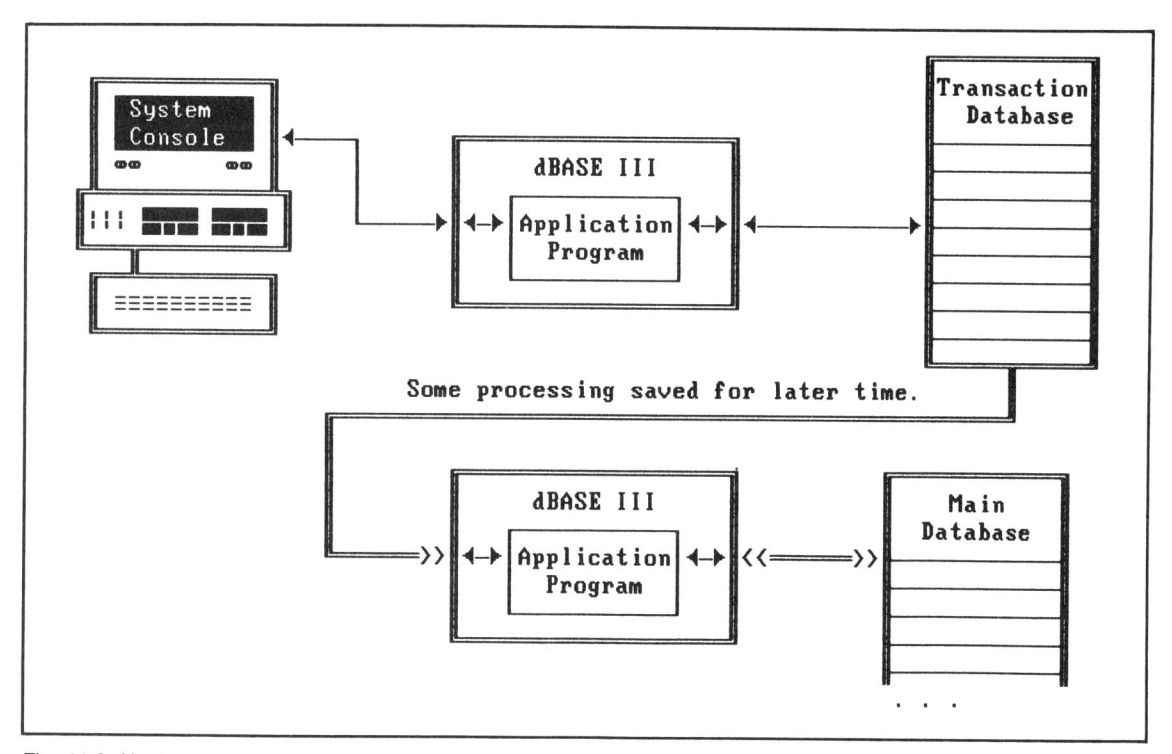

Fig. 11-2. Noninteractive ("batch") processing.

real time, Fred decided to run that process monthly, just before the statements are produced. This way the statements can show the results of the account balancing, especially the amounts over 30, 60, and 90 days overdue. The process of balancing the accounts takes about two hours when done noninteractively, while it can take five or ten minutes to perform each time in real time.

Of course, some account balancing must be done in real-time; one of the most usual questions a customer asks is "how much do I owe you?" This is easily solved by placing a running total balance directly on the customer file, and updating it as necessary. The true balancing is done later, when the computer is not needed for other, more critical tasks.

So when impatient customers call to find out their balances, Fred can look up the balances instantly, and not leave them hanging on the phone waiting for the computer.

USING ARRAYS

Most programming languages include two ways of structuring data items. One is the record structure, which is the same as a dBASE database structure; the second is the array, a group of data items that are the same length and data type. Items in an array are referenced by subscripts, and each item is referred to as an element of the array.

The first item in the array is referenced as "array-name (1)," which means "the first element of array-name." dBASE III does not have an array data structure built into the language, but as usual, there is a way to create a structure that can be used for the same purpose.

The main purpose of an array is to keep some tabular data that can be used in processing. For example, a program that converts a Gregorian date to a Julian date needs to determine the number of days in each month. An array containing these values might be called DAYS__IN__MONTH and the values referenced as DAYS__IN__MONTH (1), and so forth.

There are two parts to an array—the data elements and the positional indicator, or subscript. Implementing a single array in dBASE requires building two arrays, one to store the positioning data and the other to store the values to be retrieved.

In dBASE III character strings can be used as arrays through the use of the functions AT( ) and SUBSTR( ). The positioning data are stored in one character variable, and the values to be retrieved are stored into a second character variable and aligned to the positioning data.

As shown in Fig. 11-3, the AT( ) function can then be used to find where a character string appears in the positioning array, and the SUBSTR( ) function can be used to retrieve the corresponding value. For example, the number of days in each month can be placed underneath the first two letters of the month name in the positioning array. The CMONTH( ) function can be used to get the month name for a date, then the positioning of that name in the positioning string is found with the AT( ) function. The SUBSTR( ) function is then used to get the two characters in the values string at the same position as the name in the positioning string. The VAL( ) function changes the characters to a numeric data type, and the number of days is available. Figure 11-4 shows how this procedure can be coded.

Another example of the use of an array will be presented in the next chapter as a part of the SOUNDEX algorithm.

CREATING DYNAMIC FILENAMES

The dBASE III programming language has a feature that allows it to use the actual value of memory variables in programs. This is not a usual practice, since it can lead to self-modifying programs—a structured programming no-no.

When the dBASE interpreter finds a memory variable name preceded by an ampersand (&), the interpreter inserts the value of the variable at that spot in the statement. This allows use of variable information in creating dynamic values for filenames. The technical term for this feature is *macro substitution*, and the &<variable name> is called a *macro*.

Macro substitution can be used to create backup files for archival purposes directly from

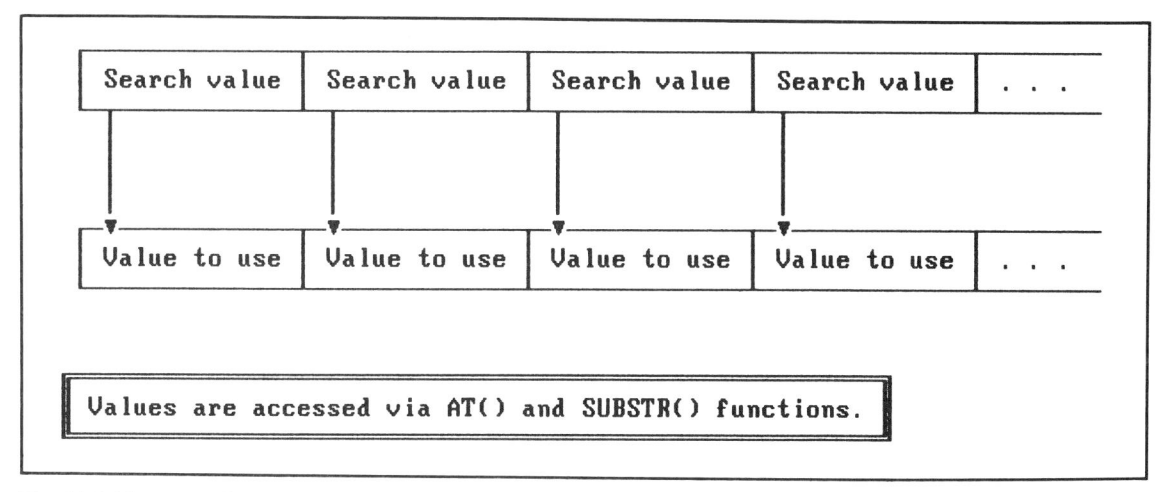

```
┌─────────────────────────────────────────────────────────────────────┐
│  ┌──────────────┬──────────────┬──────────────┬──────────────┬─────┐│
│  │ Search value │ Search value │ Search value │ Search value │ ... ││
│  └──────┬───────┴──────┬───────┴──────┬───────┴──────┬───────┴─────┘│
│         │              │              │              │              │
│         ▼              ▼              ▼              ▼              │
│  ┌──────────────┬──────────────┬──────────────┬──────────────┬─────┐│
│  │ Value to use │ Value to use │ Value to use │ Value to use │ ... ││
│  └──────────────┴──────────────┴──────────────┴──────────────┴─────┘│
│                                                                     │
│  ┌───────────────────────────────────────────────────────────────┐  │
│  │  Values are accessed via AT() and SUBSTR() functions.         │  │
│  └───────────────────────────────────────────────────────────────┘  │
└─────────────────────────────────────────────────────────────────────┘
```

Fig. 11-3. The array data structure.

your program. The system date and/or time can be used to create unique filenames for databases or SDF files (see Chapter 3).

Any value can be placed in a memory variable and then used as a macro. It is possible to place dBASE statements into a character variable and then use the macro substitution feature to execute it. If the macro has a null value, nothing happens; when an executable statement is placed in the variable, the statement is executed whenever the macro is encountered by the interpreter.

Using macros to store statements or partial statements and then substituting the macro for a program statement creates a self-modifying pro-

```
STORE SPACE(10) TO dtefld
STORE
 'JanuaryFebruaryMarchAprilMayJuneJulyAugustSeptemberOctoberNovemberDecember'
   TO monthnm
STORE
 '31      28      31     30    31 30 31 31     30       31       30       31     '
   TO monthdays
STORE 'y' to logopt
DO WHILE logopt = 'y'
  CLEAR
  @ 10,10 SAY 'Enter date here:' GET dtefld PICTURE '99/99/9999'
  READ
  STORE CTOD(dtefld) TO dtefld2
  STORE AT(CMONTH(dtefld2),monthnm) TO numpos
  STORE VAL(SUBSTR(monthdays,numpos,2)) TO numdays
  STORE VAL(SUBSTR(monthdays,(AT(CMONTH(dtefld2),monthnm)),2)) TO numdays2
  @ 15,10 SAY numdays
  @ 17,10 SAY numdays2
  ACCEPT 'Do again? ' TO logopt
ENDDO
CLOSE DATABASES
RETURN
```

Fig. 11-4. Finding the number of days in a month.

gram. For example, the following statement:

IF &test EOF( )

can take on different meanings depending on the current value of "test". If "test" contains no value, the statement is interpreted as:

IF EOF( )

If "test" contains the string ".NOT.", the statement becomes:

IF .NOT. EOF( )

Or the statement can be completely changed by storing another comparison in "test". If "test" contains "DATE( ) > CTOD('12/31/1985') .AND. .NOT.", the statement would become:

IF DATE( ) > CTOD('12/31/1985') .AND. .NOT. EOF( )

This kind of coding is unreadable and a real mess to try to debug. Self-modifying code should be avoided at all costs. A good rule to program by is to always assign the result of a macro substitution to a variable. This is useful and does not cause self-modification to occur.

ADDING STANDARD FIELDS TO A SYSTEM

Just as CONFIG.DB can set up a customized dBASE III environment, you can design into your system a standard configuration for information that changes rarely but is needed as a constant in calculations.

One example of this type of information is the percentage of state sales tax. This figure may change twice in a decade and even more rarely in most cases.

Another type of data that can be stored in this system parameters database are dates with significant meaning for the function—for example, start and end dates for monthly processing. The number of days to hold old data records may also be stored here; after a certain number of days, unneeded records are stored to an archive database. If the main database becomes a problem because of size, the number of days can be adjusted easily. Figure 11-5 shows such a configuration database.

Rather than coding the literal value directly in the code, it can be stored on a configuration database and introduced as a global memory variable. This means that when your state legislature decides to raise the sales tax, you do not have to scramble around trying to find all occurrences in which the literal percentage is included in a calculation.

Another method of storing overall system values from session to session is to store the values into memory variables, and use the SAVE command to save them to a .MEM file. The values can be restored at the beginning of each program where they are needed. This has the added feature of not

```
Structure for database : B:SYSPARM.DBF
Number of data records :        1
Date of last update    : 04/13/85
Field  Field name  Type      Width    Dec
    1  STATETAX    Numeric      5      3    [state sales tax]
    2  ARCHDAYS    Numeric      3           [number of days before archive]
    3  LSTSDTE     Date         8           [last statement start date]
    4  LSTEDTE     Date         8           [last statement end date]
    5  MRPTDTE     Date         8           [last monthly report date]
    6  DCODATE     Date         8           [date for discounts]
    7  STOREFC     Numeric      5      3    [finance charge percent]
** Total **                    46
```

Fig. 11-5. The configuration database.

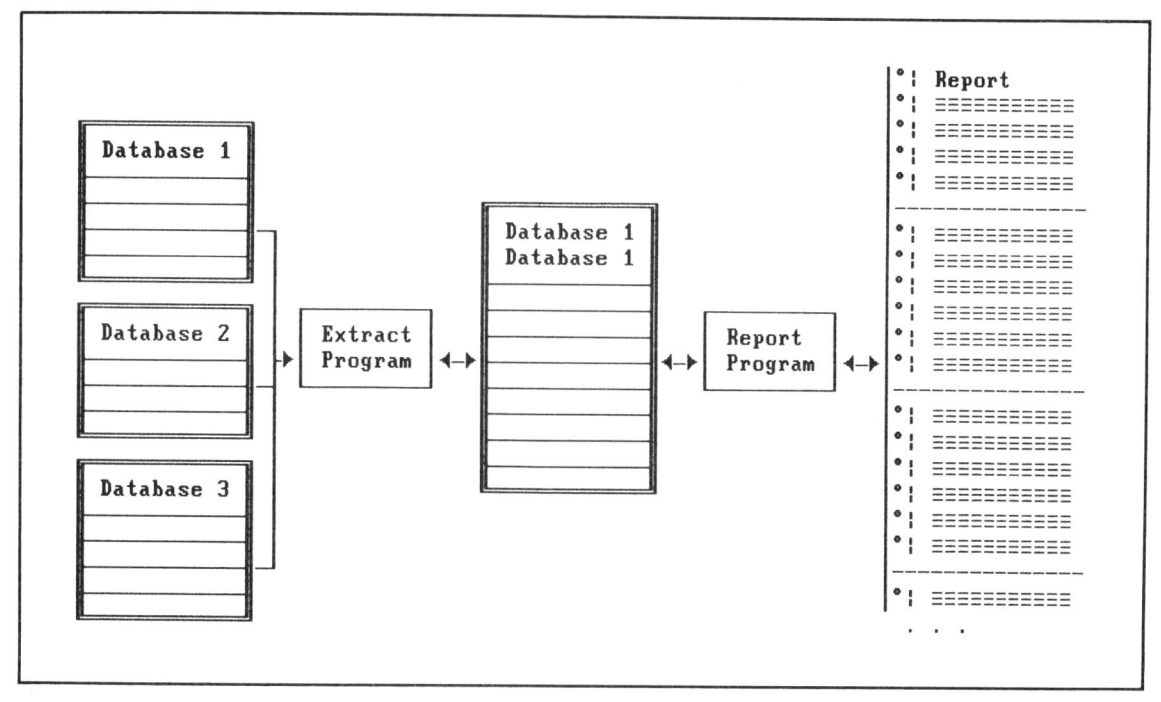

Fig. 11-6. The extract process.

allowing changes to the variables, because any new values will not be saved until a SAVE command is issued. The memory variable file can be restored many times without saving; the original values will still be intact.

EXTRACTING NEEDED DATA

Reporting is not the only function of a system that can benefit from the technique of extracting data from several files and producing a new file of combined data. Extract files can be used for other types of processes also.

The new file can contain data in exactly the same format as the "parent" databases, or calculations and conversions can be performed on the extracted data. Calculations can also be split between programs, because extracting data assumes there are two parts to the process, the extract program and the main function program. Figure 11-6 illustrates the extract process.

Installations with more than one computer can also benefit from data extracts. The extracted files can be copied onto a floppy diskette and transported between computers for inquiry or report purposes. The most difficult part of learning the extract process is to believe that two programs performing a single function can sometimes run faster than one program that performs the same function all at one time. To convince yourself, remember that the extract program does most of the necessary I/O operations, while the main program does the major part of the calculations. If the extract file is properly designed, the main process will execute faster because of the rearrangement.

The extraction technique should be used anytime the existing database structure is compromised. This usually occurs when a program, when using the normal structure, breaks the limitations of dBASE; the system can also reach *breakpoint*, meaning that the processing for a time period takes more time than the period contains. The process may require that more than fifteen files be open or the speed with which the data is accessed may be too slow for real-time processing.

The extraction technique requires that the main process, the one the data will be extracted for, be

87

examined for clues to the data structure that will accommodate the needs of the program and the user. Once this structure is determined, it is turned into a dBASE database and used to store the extracted data.

The extract program is written in such a way that the limitations broken by the main process are not also broken by the extract program. This can be done in several ways, such as storing record numbers and closing databases when not needed to avoid having too many files open at once. The extract program, because it has been removed from the main process, can include techniques that could not have been used in that program. This "divide to conquer" strategy is often used in data processing.

SPEEDING UP THE PROCESS

Most of the techniques outlined in this book have the goal of speeding up the execution of a dBASE III system. These techniques include extracting report data (Chapter 10), indexing (Chapter 6), and noninteractive processing (this chapter). Figure 11-7 summarizes the techniques that can be used to speed up processing.

Speeding up a process is an exercise in trial-and-error problem solving. The major bottleneck to avoid is the sequential processing of databases, which can greatly slow a system. Sequential processing is sometimes necessary, but it can be done in dBASE accidentally, simply by using the wrong command. For example, the command:

TOTAL ON custnum FIELDS orderamt FOR custnum = '310'

will cause the entire database to be sequentially processed, no matter how many 310 records are on it. Since the database must be indexed on the field used in the ON clause of TOTAL, the following sequence could be used instead:

STORE '310' TO savenum
SEEK savenum
TOTAL ON custnum FIELDS orderamt WHILE custnum = savenum

This will cause the database to be processed sequentially, but only for those records that have a custnum of 310. When the field custnum changes,

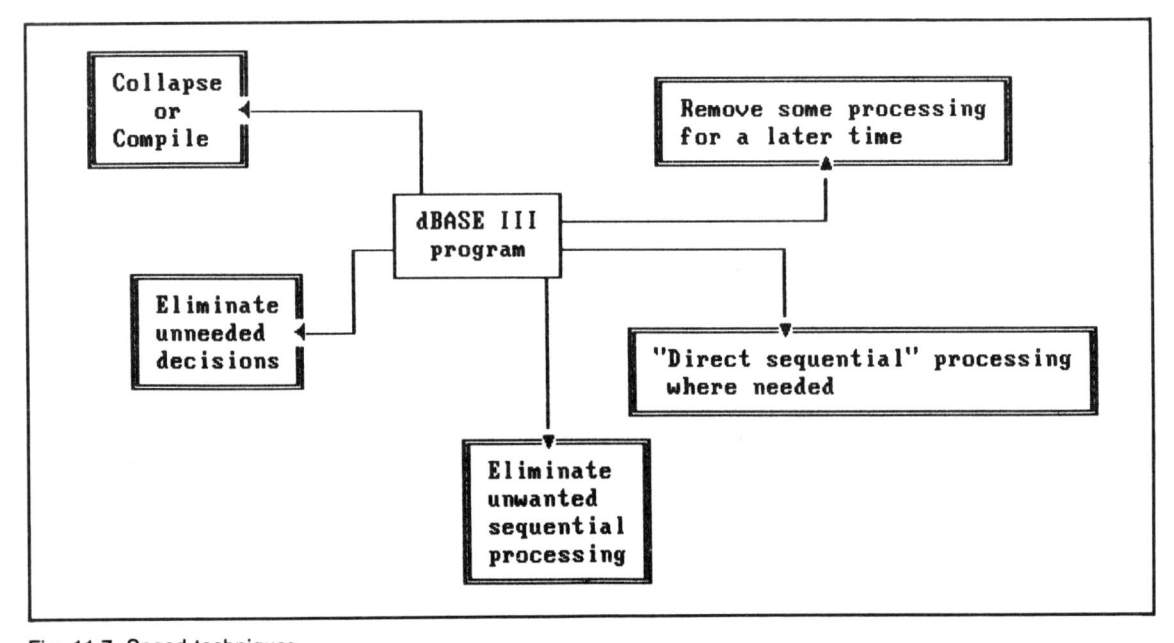

Fig. 11-7. Speed techniques.

the TOTAL command stops processing. This eliminates all of the time wasted by dBASE in reading a record to determine if the custnum is 310 before proceeding to the next record.

The functions that soak up most of a system's speed are sequential database access, program file loading, and decision statements, in that order. Any time one of these can be eliminated, the process will be faster. Processes such as indexing and sorting should never be done in real-time programs, because of the large amounts of time and I/O that are required. Speeding up the process requires a common-sense approach to the problem and a little patience.

Chapter 12
Fred Discovers SOUNDEX

The activity of programming is one of continuous learning. Not only does computer hardware become obsolete before it is in the hands of the consumer, but the software is constantly changing as well. New releases of dBASE III, for example, usually mean a few new commands and changes in the execution of existing commands.

This constant shifting of the environment is one of the reasons that computer programs must be designed to be flexible. In structured or modular programming, new additions to the language can usually be integrated into the system with little trouble.

THE PROGRAMMER AND NEW IDEAS

This is, however, only a part of the programmer's learning burden. A good programmer is constantly on the lookout for new, faster, more flexible ways of writing processes. This may mean learning to program in a different language, so that systems in dBASE can be augmented be external routines. It may also mean looking for little tricks that other programmers use to write their processes and modifying them for your own use. Figure 12-1 shows the programmer's tool chest, the resources that are available to enable him to write better systems.

The most common way of learning new processes is to try new variations of programs that you have already written. The ability to take several different, seemingly unrelated commands and meld them into a useful programming technique is central to the programming task. The discovery of a new technique often begins with the words "I wonder what happens if I do THIS?"

Programming is most often compared with the process of problem solving in general. This can lead to a semantic trap: a problem that is solved no longer exists. A program, in contrast, is an evolving solution to an ongoing problem; programs must be modified if a shift in the environment demands it. Programs should also be modified when their use changes, or when you discover a better way of performing a process that makes the system faster, more flexible, or more accurate.

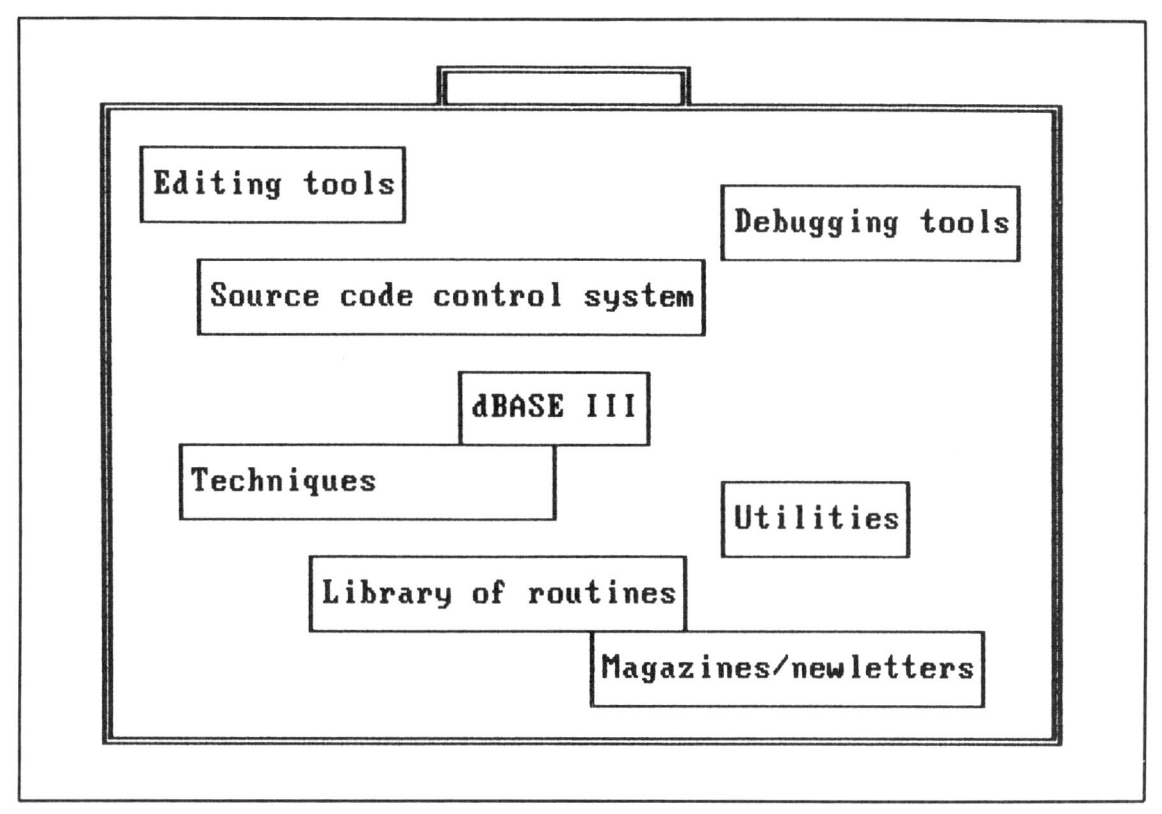

Fig. 12-1. The programmer's toolchest.

Books, magazines, and user-group newsletters contain an endless wealth of information on new techniques and products. You can find out tricks used by other dBASE programmers to write programs, solve various problems, and get their systems to work. This network of information also provides support, and the people involved will help you with any problems.

Fred has discovered several techniques that have made his programs better and increased the speed of his system. Some techniques, however, he could not see a need for; one was a way of performing phonetic searches on names in a database. Fred could not think of a possible use that he might have for it.

Fred, however, is nothing if not diligent; he clips the articles he finds new techniques in and saves them in a file drawer. Many professional programmers store techniques for future reference. When a programmer runs into a situation where one of the saved techniques will be useful, the techniques are right at hand or at least available.

Fred stored the phonetic look-up thing in his file and then went off to the local fire station for the regular weekly volunteer firemen's meeting.

THE DISPATCHER'S DILEMMA

After the meeting, Fred talked to the fire dispatcher, Eagle-beak Hawkins. E.B. told Fred about the problems he was having with the fire dispatch system in use at the fire station. The system uses a card file that contains the name of the street, the cross streets, and the closest fire hydrant to each corner. (Fred could have written a dBASE system to handle this, but it would have been too slow for responding to a fire call.)

The problem with receiving a phone call from a person who may be out of breath or over-excited is that the name of a street can be blurted out, with no chance of checking the correct spelling. An

91

algorithm that can find a phonetic spelling of the street name would speed up the process, and make the system more accurate. E.B. could use a personal computer to retrieve the possible street names while taking the information and finding the needed street and hydrant data in the card file.

Fred stared off into space for a moment. Didn't he see something about phonetic look-ups in a recent magazine article? He turned to E.B. and said "I think I know of something that could help." He rushed back to the Fish market, and looked in the drawer of programming techniques. There it was right on top, the SOUNDEX algorithm.

The solution is to give groups of consonants that sound alike like numbers, forget the vowels, and save the resulting value on the database as a field. The SOUNDEX algorithm was first discussed in a magazine article in 1965 and later modifications have made it extremely useful in many data processing systems.

HOW SOUNDEX WORKS

The SOUNDEX routine groups consonants together by their sound, as shown in Fig. 12-2. The consonant is assigned a number, which can be used to build a string that identifies the word or name by sound. Comparisons of the SOUNDEX code for differently spelled words will show that the words sound alike.

The first step in translating a word into its SOUNDEX code is to replace the letters with their corresponding numbers (see Fig. 12-2). The first character can be left out of this process, because most often the first letter of a name or word is known. Leaving the first letter of the word as the first character in the SOUNDEX code will also make the phonetic look-ups faster, because there will be fewer choices.

Once the name or word is translated into the SOUNDEX numbers, duplicate codes are reduced to single codes. This is because in a phonetic lookup, double and single consonants have the same sound and might be misspelled.

The final step is to remove the code for vowels (0), and the resulting string is the SOUNDEX code. The code can almost always be reduced to four

SOUNDEX Group	Letters
1	B, P, F, V
2	C, G, J, K, Q, S, X, Z
3	D, T
4	L
5	M, N
6	R
0	A, E, I, O, U, W, Y, H

Fig. 12-2. The SOUNDEX groupings.

```
   String:      HAMMITT                    [string to be SOUNDEXed]

                H055033                    [translated to SOUNDEX codes]

                H0503                      [duplicates removed]

   SOUNDEX:     H53                        [zeros removed]




   HAMMETT   HAMID   HAMOT    HEMMAT
   HAMIT     HANET   HAMMYTT  HEMID        all have same SOUNDEX as HAMMITT
   HAMID     HOMED   HIMIT    HIMMOD
```

Fig. 12-3. The SOUNDEX translation process.

characters because most phonetic "mistakes" occur at the end of a word. If two words yield the same four-character SOUNDEX code, it is a fairly safe bet that they sound alike. Figure 12-3 shows the SOUNDEX translation process.

Fred looked at his Employee database. The addition of a SOUNDEX routine could help in finding an employee's record when the exact spelling of the name cannot be remembered. Before executing the routine, however, the normal search methods should be used, because a SOUNDEX search may result in more than one match.

The SOUNDEX code for each employee name is placed into a new database field, and the database is indexed by this code. If a match is not found on name, the SET INDEX TO command can be used to change to the SOUNDEX index, and a new search started by translating the name to be found into its SOUNDEX code.

SOUNDEX IN dBASE III

After Fred learned the process of creating a SOUNDEX code, he examined the statements available in dBASE III that can help produce it. First, letters from the input field Name must be translated into SOUNDEX codes.

Fred created a positioning array containing all of the consonants by storing the string to a memory variable. In a second memory variable, he placed the corresponding SOUNDEX codes for the letters. Now the SOUNDEX code of a consonant can be retrieved by determining the position of the consonant in the first string; the SOUNDEX code is the number retrieved from the second string at the same position. Figure 12-4 shows the process used to access the SOUNDEX code.

Vowels do not have to appear in the positioning string, because they all have a value of zero, although they could be placed in the string with corresponding zeros. The nice thing about programming is that there are several ways of doing any one function. If the string requested in an AT( ) function is not found in the target string, AT( ) returns a zero value; the "$" operation could also be used to determine if the character exists in the positioning string.

As each character is translated, the SOUNDEX code is appended to the end of the character string that will hold the code. This is done by concatenating the character to be appended to the rest of the string. The first character is not translated, but moved intact to the SOUNDEX code string. Figure 12-5 shows the code used to translate the string.

The next step is to strip out consecutive duplicate values from the translated string. The

```
STORE 'BPFVCGJKQSXZDTLMNRA' TO SNXLETS

STORE '11112222222233455560' TO SNXNUMS

. . .

DO WHILE (I <= LEN(DBSNDIN)) .AND. (SUBSTR(DBSNDIN,I,1) # ' ')

   STORE AT(SUBSTR(DBSNDIN,I,1),SNXLETS) TO SNDLOC
        [finds the location of the letter in the letter string]
. . .

   STORE DBSNDTMP + SUBSTR(SNXNUMS,SNDLOC,1) TO DBSNDTMP
   [adds the corresponding number in the number string to code string]

   STORE (I + 1) TO I

ENDDO
```

Fig. 12-4. Accessing the SOUNDEX code.

```
STORE 'BPFVCGJKQSXZDTLMNRA' TO SNXLETS
STORE '11112222222233455560' TO SNXNUMS

STORE 0 TO SNDLOC
STORE SPACE(1) TO SNDTHIS, SNDNEXT
STORE 2 TO I

STORE SUBSTR(DBSNDIN,1,1) TO DBSNDTMP, DBSNDTM2, DBSNDOUT

DO WHILE (I <= LEN(DBSNDIN)) .AND. (SUBSTR(DBSNDIN,I,1) # ' ')

   STORE AT(SUBSTR(DBSNDIN,I,1),SNXLETS) TO SNDLOC

   IF SNDLOC = 0
     STORE LEN(SNXLETS) TO SNDLOC
   ENDIF

   STORE DBSNDTMP + SUBSTR(SNXNUMS,SNDLOC,1) TO DBSNDTMP
   STORE (I + 1) TO I

ENDDO
. . .
```

Fig. 12-5. Translating the string.

```
   . . .

   STORE 2 TO I

   DO WHILE (I <= (LEN(DBSNDTMP) - 1))

      STORE SUBSTR(DBSNDTMP,I,1) TO SNDTHIS
      STORE SUBSTR(DBSNDTMP,(I+1),1) TO SNDNEXT

      IF SNDTHIS # SNDNEXT
         STORE DBSNDTM2 + SUBSTR(DBSNDTMP,I,1) TO DBSNDTM2
      ENDIF

      STORE (I + 1) TO I

   ENDDO

   . . .
```

Fig. 12-6. Stripping the duplicate codes.

```
   . . .

   STORE 2 TO I

   DO WHILE (I <= LEN(DBSNDTM2))

      STORE SUBSTR(DBSNDTM2,I,1) TO SNDTHIS

      IF SNDTHIS # '0'
         STORE DBSNDOUT + SUBSTR(DBSNDTM2,I,1) TO DBSNDOUT
      ENDIF

      STORE (I + 1) TO I

   ENDDO

   . . .
```

Fig. 12-7. Stripping the zeros.

```
    . . .

    IF LEN(DBSNDOUT) > 4

        STORE SUBSTR(DBSNDOUT,1,4) TO DBSNDOUT

    ENDIF

    RETURN
```

Fig. 12-8. Truncating the result.

string is examined for two identical codes positioned next to each other, using the SUBSTR( ) function. This process can also start in the second position of the string, because the first position is a letter and will not be duplicated. Figure 12-6 shows the process used to strip the duplicate codes.

The new code value is stored into a new string character by character, but only if the current code does not equal the next code. When this process was finished, Fred repeated the logic to strip out codes of zero, by just changing the "IF" statement. This removes the vowels from the code and results in the full SOUNDEX code for the name. Figure 12-7 shows how the zeros are stripped.

The final step in creating the SOUNDEX code is to shorten the result to four characters, if it is not already four characters or shorter. Figure 12-8 shows how the result is truncated.

The SOUNDEX code can now be placed on the database (Fred wrote a special one-time program to SOUNDEX his employee's names) and used as an index field. When a name is entered for an inquiry function, and the name that was entered does not exist on the database, the entered name can be SOUNDEXed and its code used to locate names that sound alike.

Fred also created a database for looking up the street names at the fire dispatcher's office. Now, when E.B. hears someone say ". . . on Howl" street, he can just enter "HOWL," and he will see a list of the streets with names that sound like HOWL, such as Howell Street, where Fred's Fish Market is located. If more than one choice appears, he can question the caller further; thus response to a fire call becomes more accurate because of dBASE III and SOUNDEX.

Chapter 13
Beyond dBASE III

dBASE III operations become more efficient when everything is at the user's fingertips. The programmer will often find that he must make sure that his client can use other programs from within dBASE III, can export data to other programs, can import data from other programs, and can get help when it is needed.

EXECUTING OTHER PROGRAMS

dBASE III must be loaded into the memory of a computer to be executed; both dBASE III and the PC-DOS operating systems are programs, and a computer can only execute programs that reside in RAM memory. The minimum PC memory requirement for dBASE III is 256 kilobytes of RAM. dBASE itself only uses about 192K, but the PC-DOS operating system also takes up room in RAM. Sidekick and other memory-resident programs also take up some memory, reducing the space available to dBASE III to store record buffers and so forth.

In systems with less than 320K of RAM memory, it is impossible to execute a DOS command or any other program from inside the dBASE III system. The message "Insufficient memory" appears, and that is that. This occurs because dBASE creates a "subcopy" of DOS, which uses the remaining unallocated memory. This *command shell*, as it's called, also requires an extra 7K of RAM memory.

The MAXMEM parameter of the CONFIG.DB file sets a limit on the amount of memory that dBASE will retain when a command shell is invoked. As indicated in Fig. 13-1, MAXMEM does not limit the memory that dBASE will use; any memory above this limit will be over-written by the command shell and the memory used to execute a program in that copy of PC-DOS. dBASE III freezes right where it is when the new command shell is invoked because it is the new copy of DOS that has control.

PC-DOS allows two ways of starting a command shell. First, the PC-DOS COMMAND command loads a new copy of the command processor (COMMAND.COM). If a /P is a parameter to this command, the command shell becomes permanent;

97

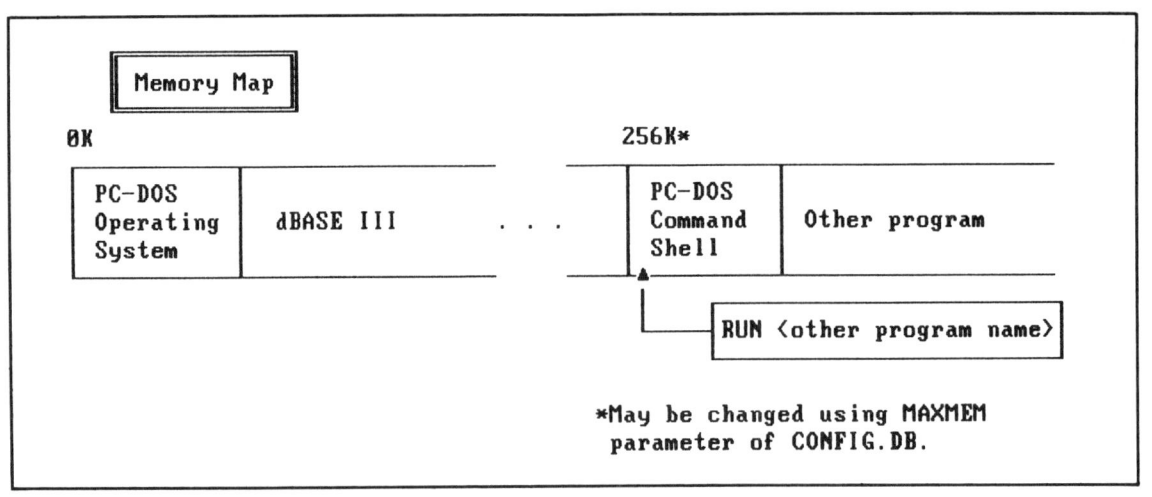

```
┌─────────────────────────────────────────────────────────────────┐
│         ┌──────────────┐                                        │
│         │ Memory Map   │                                        │
│         └──────────────┘                                        │
│    0K                              256K*                        │
│    ───────────────────────────────────────────────────────      │
│    ┌─────────┐                     ┌─────────┐                  │
│    │ PC-DOS  │                     │ PC-DOS  │                  │
│    │Operating│  dBASE III   . . .  │ Command │  Other program   │
│    │ System  │                     │  Shell  │                  │
│    └─────────┘                     └─────────┘                  │
│                                         ▲                       │
│                                         └──┤RUN <other program name>│
│                                                                 │
│                              *May be changed using MAXMEM       │
│                              parameter of CONFIG.DB.            │
└─────────────────────────────────────────────────────────────────┘
```

Fig. 13-1. Executing subtasks.

otherwise, the EXIT command will end the command shell and return to wherever the computer was when the shell was loaded. A /C parameter passed to COMMAND will cause the shell to be loaded for one command only, with this command also passed as a parameter.

This last example is the method that dBASE uses to execute programs externally with the RUN or ! commands. The command is passed to a temporary command shell, which is exited upon completion of the subtask.

You can also operate in PC-DOS directly from dBASE, given enough memory. The COMMAND command can be used in a RUN/! command in the same way as any other DOS command. The initial command shell is started as if with the /C option, but then a new command shell is started inside the first, where you may execute other programs or DOS commands. The amount of memory available for DOS operations will be any memory above the MAXMEM limit (default 256K) set in CONFIG.DB. The EXIT command ends the second command shell, which also ends the first command shell because it was started for one command only. dBASE resumes operations immediately thereafter.

EXPORTING DATA TO OTHER PROGRAMS

A major concern of most people buying software for their PC or their company's PC is how well the new software will interact with other existing software. Can the files it creates be read by other programs, or can files created by another program be brought into the new software in a usable format?

Fortunately, dBASE III has several ways of exporting and importing data. The SDF parameter of the COPY TO and APPEnd FROM statements tells dBASE that the file that is the object of the statement is in Standard Data Format. This means that the data is in standard ASCII characters, and the values are placed on the SDF record in the same order that the fields appear on the database. The format of the COPY command is:

COPY TO <filename> [SDF][DELimited [WITH <character/BLANK>]]

If the DELimited parameter is omitted, dBASE creates a file in sequential file format, with each field value defined to be the same length as its corresponding database field. Memo fields are not copied to the SDF file.

The DELimited parameter means that the outgoing data values will be separated by commas, and the character fields will be enclosed in quotation marks ("). The WITH option of DELimited allows you to choose your own delimiters, which surround each character string, for character values. DELImited WITH BLANK tells dBASE to separate the values by one space, with no commas or character delimiters. DELImited and DELImited WITH " are functionally equivalent. Figure 13-2 shows some sample SDF and DELImited output.

Date fields are stored in the SDF file in the format YYYYMMDD, the same way they are internally stored in a dBASE database. Programs receiving this data must recognize not only the order of the fields, but their format as well; this is because the new file is not a dBASE database. The external programs cannot take advantage of the database management features of dBASE III.

If no parameters are specified, the output file will be a dBASE database file. For SDF output, the entire filename must be entered, including an extension of your choice.

IMPORTING DATA FROM OTHER PROGRAMS

The APPEnd FROM command is used to move data in the other direction; values from an SDF file are copied into database fields. Each line of the SDF is added to the end of the database as a new record. SDFs are ASCII text files, which means that each line ends with a carriage return/line feed code (hexadecimal values X'0D0A').

The values may be in any of the formats produced by the COPY TO command—the same parameters (SDF and DELImited WITH) are used in the APPEnd FROM statement. The format of the APPEnd statement is:

APPEnd FROM <filename> [SDF];
   [DELImited [WITH <character/BLANK>]]

```
COPY TO <filename> SDF yields this output file:

    X       1.00xxxxx19851231xxxxxFxxxxx
    XX    123.45yyyyy19540104yyyyyTyyyyy
    XXX    -9.00zzzzz19431231zzzzzFzzzzz

COPY TO <filename> DELIMITED yields this output file:

    "X",1.00,"xxxxx",19851231,"xxxxx",f,"xxxxx"
    "XX",123.45,"yyyyy",19540104,"yyyyy",t,"yyyyy"
    "XXX",-9.00,"zzzzz",19431231,"zzzzz",f,"zzzzz"

COPY TO <filename> DELIMITED WITH BLANK yields this output file:

    X 1.00 xxxxx 19851231 xxxxx f xxxxx
    XX 123.45 yyyyy 19540104 yyyyy t yyyyy
    XXX -9.00 zzzzz 19431231 zzzzz f zzzzz

COPY TO <filename> DELIMITED WITH - yields this output file:

    -X-,1.00,-xxxxx-,19851231,-xxxxx-,f,-xxxxx-
    -XX-,123.45,-yyyyy-,19540104,-yyyyy-,t,-yyyyy-
    -XXX-,-9.00,-zzzzz-,19431231,-zzzzz-,f,-zzzzz-
```

Fig. 13-2. SDF and DELImited output.

Any file produced in one of these formats can be imported to a dBASE III database. The database must be CREAted with fields that are large enough to handle the largest incoming data value for that field. The easiest way of importing the values is to produce the file in a standard sequential file format; this means that each field value is contained in the same number of characters as the dBASE database field.

The DELImited option may be used to import varying-length data, because the data values are delimited by commas. The receiving database field must be large enough to accommodate the largest incoming value for each field. Fields are placed on the sequential records in the same order they exist on the database.

THE STACK DATABASE

The ability to import and export database field values yields a quick and easy technique for passing values to an external program. The programming language used to create the external program (probably) has the ability to read standard ASCII text files; dBASE has the ability to create them.

The program receiving the incoming data passed from dBASE must be able to interpret the data being passed. An entire database can be written to an SDF file and then read by the external program. This method, however, requires that every character be written, which wastes disk space and response time if only one field needs to be passed. One way of getting around any of these problems is to stack the data field to be passed into a unique database.

The method involves creating a dBASE database that contains one field—a character-type field that is large enough to contain the data to be transmitted and/or received. The data to be passed can either be placed into this database and then copied to an SDF, or the FIELDS parameter of the COPY command can be used to restrict output to only the chosen field. This kind of a file is called a FIFO (First In, First Out) stack, because the values are retrieved in entry-order.

The external program then reads the file, processes the data, and places the results in a new file.

This file is then copied back into dBASE with the APPEnd FROM SDF command. The database receiving the results can be created in the same format as the results; the stack database could also be used as a receiving field.

For example, if an external program is used to translate all of the Employee names on the Employee database into SOUNDEX codes, you would first create the stack database for receiving the codes; it would have one field, four characters long. The next step is to COPY the names from the Employee database to an external file with the command:

COPY FIELDS empname TO soundex.inp SDF

Then the RUN/! command is used to execute the external SOUNDEX program. This program translates each line of the input file, each containing an employee name, to its SOUNDEX code. The codes are then written to the second file in the same order as they existed in the first file. Figure 13-3 shows the code that accomplishes this.

When the external program finishes, dBASE will process the statement following the RUN, which should be something like:

USE stack
APPEND FROM soundex.out SDF

The database STACK will now contain the SOUNDEX codes for all of the names on the Employee database. These can be reinserted into the database (provided a field was created to hold them) by transferring each one-field record on the stack database to the corresponding record in the Employee database.

ADDING A HELP FUNCTION TO YOUR OWN SYSTEM

"Users never read manuals" is an old programmer's saying. Most people who use computers have the attitude that the system should be so easy that everything will be obvious, so why read the manual? This leads to the user's not consulting the manual at the times when it should be consulted,

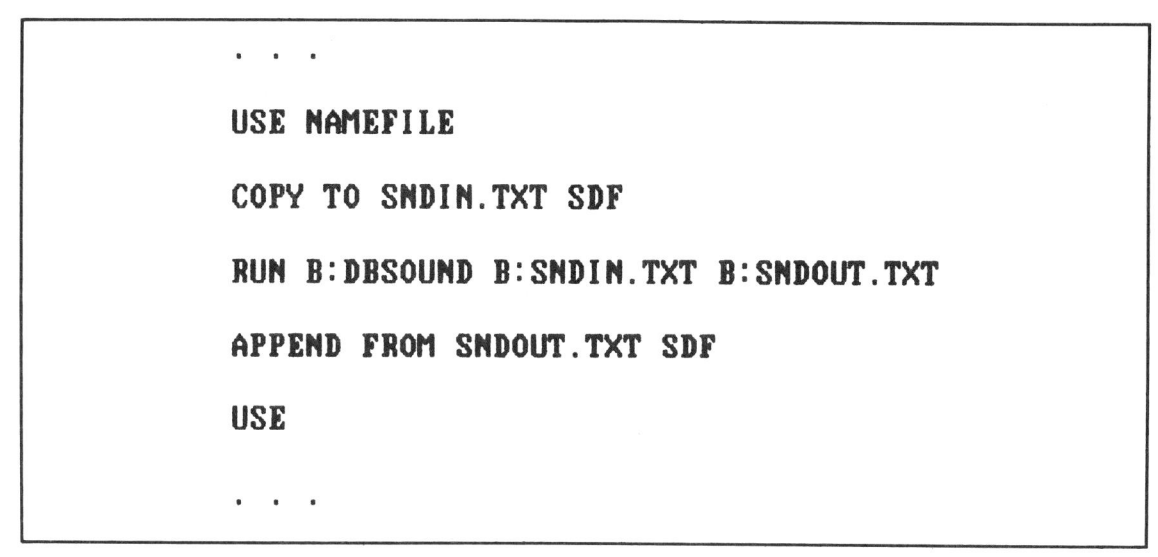

```
. . .

USE NAMEFILE

COPY TO SNDIN.TXT SDF

RUN B:DBSOUND B:SNDIN.TXT B:SNDOUT.TXT

APPEND FROM SNDOUT.TXT SDF

USE

. . .
```

Fig. 13-3. Using the Stack database.

because it is unfamiliar and inconvenient to use.

Many existing software systems, especially those produced by large companies, include their own online reference. For example, dBASE III has not only an online reference manual, but also has a subsystem that allows the user to enter commands via a menu while viewing information about the function (the ASSIST feature).

Help functions can also be added to an application system written in dBASE III by creating the proper screens and programs. These would be called whenever the user requests Help. The Help function, if you include one in a system, should clearly, simply, and accurately point the user in the proper direction. Figure 13-4 shows the various types of Help systems that can be created.

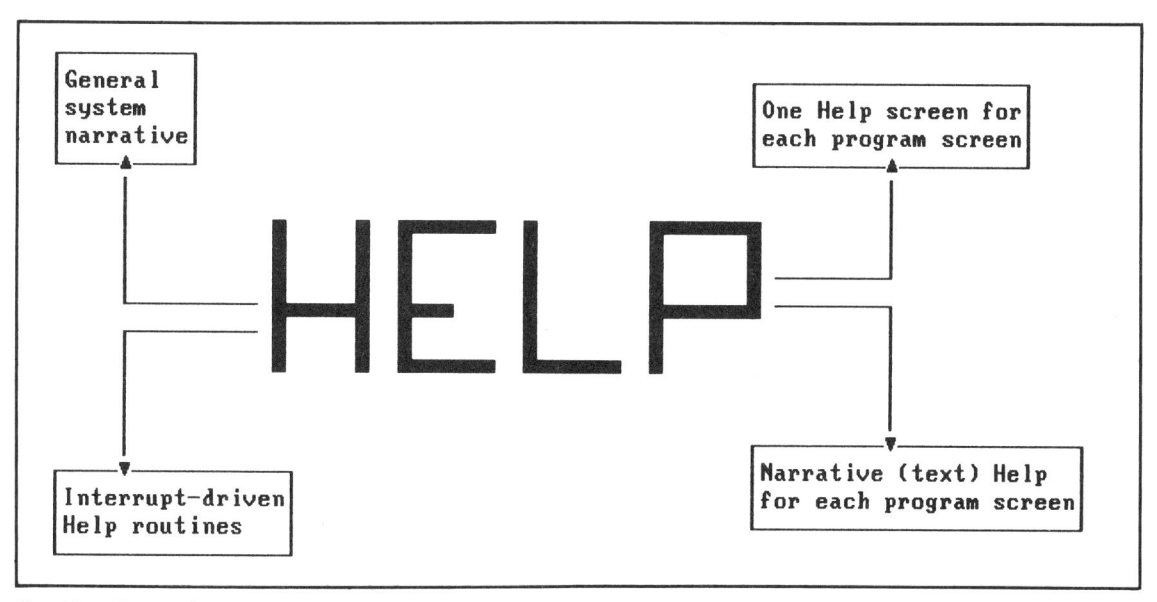

Fig. 13-4. Types of Help system.

There are several types of online reference. The first type is a narrative that describes the overall function of the system. This is usually included in separate system documentation, either on paper or in a disk file. This file can, if short enough, be written to the screen for the user's reference. The disadvantage of using a single Help narrative is that users often have specific questions, and a generalized narrative will only aggravate them.

Another method of providing aid to system users is to have a reference screen for each screen in the system. This can be a more detailed reference, explaining each field and its expected contents. Information of this type can be stored in screen formats or in TEXT/ENDTEXT sections in a dBASE program.

Help information can also be placed directly on any screen. This type of Help usually describes the keys used for navigation on the screen and the methods of navigation from this screen to others. The disadvantage of placing Help information directly on the screen is that it can make the screen look cluttered, less readable, and distracting. Only small amounts of information should be placed directly on a data entry screen.

Any of the Help function types can be implemented in a system written in dBASE III. There are many different methods through which they can be used; the main considerations in deciding the best way are the needs of the user, the convenience of the Help system, and dBASE's limitations on file access.

A Help system should be instantly available to a user, usually by pressing a single key. This is not always possible in dBASE, depending on the design of the Help system that is implemented. The Help system, as a last resort, could be made into a system function and accessed from the main menu like any other function. This is most inconvenient to the user, who must exit the function wherein they have a question to access the Help system.

A function key can be set in CONFIG.DB to execute dBASE programs or external programs. Enough information must be made available to these programs so that they can determine the exact location of the user in the system. This will work with an external program or with a dBASE .PRG but not with other methods. Setting a function key also requires that a special CONFIG.DB file be provided when the application is requested.

A less convenient method is to have the user type in a screen field that indicates to the program that Help access is desired. The field would appear in an out-of-the-way place on the screen, in a lower corner for example. The user would enter a "Y" in the field if he or she wanted to view the Help information.

If a screen field is needed to access Help in the system, another alternative to the Y or N type of field is to use a Memo field. This would require the creation of a Help database, keyed by the screen name; a memo field on that database would contain the Help narrative for that screen.

The TEXT and ENDTEXT commands of dBASE III could be used to type Help information to the screen as needed. This method will not raise the number of open files, but it is slower and requires that the Help coding be incorporated directly in a dBASE program.

One method that can be used by more advanced programmers is to create a resident external program that would be started before entering dBASE III. The Help screens can be coded in this program, which must be written in a language that can access the PC-DOS interrupt table.

All PC-DOS functions, including keyboard input, are performed by creating an interrupt, which executes the appropriate operating system code to perform that function. The locations or vectors of the interrupt routines are stored in a table called the interrupt vector table at the very beginning of memory. If a new address is placed in the table for the keyboard interrupt (the ninth vector in the jump table), PC-DOS will transfer control to the routine at that location, whatever it is. The Help program would be written to steal this interrupt from PC-DOS by saving the address stored there and placing its own address in the table. After establishing itself in memory, another PC-DOS interrupt is used to have the program terminate but still stay resident in memory. When dBASE is loaded, it would be placed in memory "above" the resident program's location. Figure 13-5 illustrates this procedure.

The program would test for a particular sequence of keys, for example, Alt-H (for Help), to be pressed. When any key is pressed, the Help routine would get control because of the changed interrupt vector; any keystrokes other than Alt-H, however, would be passed along to the normal interrupt handler, which is why the vector was saved. The program, upon receiving an Alt-H, would display a Help system menu, and the user could look up the answer to any question they might have. When execution finishes, normal processing is resumed.

Almost all Help functions involve either needing enough memory to run an external program or having another database file open. Applications systems that approach the limits of dBASE should use a Help method that does not cause the limits to be breached.

The most important thing to remember about a Help system is that it will need to be updated as the system is changed. This is a task usually delayed to the last possible second, and then forgotten. Just as updating the comments in a program is important for maintainability, so updating the Help messages is vital to usability.

IMPLEMENTING SECURITY

The question of data security is an extremely controversial topic in the data processing industry. Most companies go way overboard in checking and double-checking the access passwords of their own employees, thereby reducing productive time; these same companies are routinely worked over by pirates or saboteurs.

To set the record straight: the media in recent years has used the word *hacker* to describe a computer pirate or saboteur. This is a misnomer, and like the term *user-friendly*, makes long-time programmers wince. There are several varieties of computer literate mentalities; most are usually harmless, like hackers, who follow the path of programming down to the very bottom and then follow the path of the hardware back up to the computer

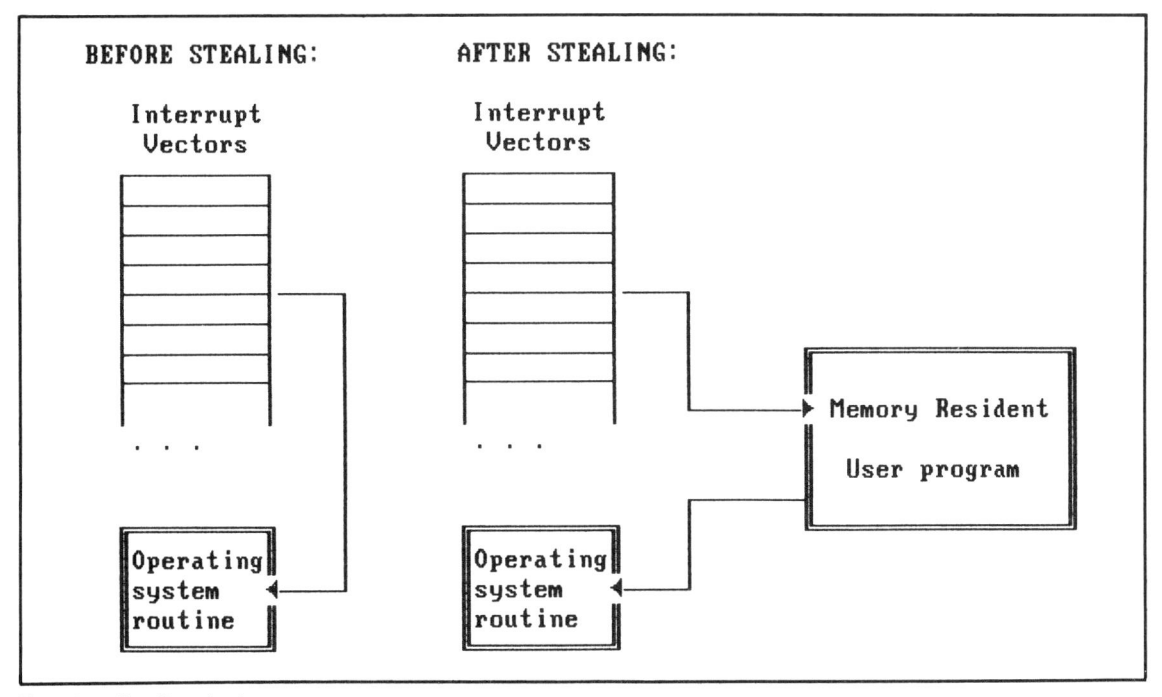

Fig. 13-5. Stealing the interrupt.

system. They may relate with computers to the exclusion of all else, including human contacts.

Illegal activities are carried out by *pirates* or *saboteurs*. A pirate is someone who takes something from someone else and then sells it or uses it for his/her own profit. One example of this is copying software without license to do so; another is stealing credit card numbers, access numbers, passwords, and so on. A saboteur is someone who physically damages or attempts to physically damage a computer installation. The damage may be to hardware via explosion, fire, or tampering; scrambling, modifying, or erasing data is another example of physical damage, even though invisible to the naked eye.

Most companies err in the direction of paranoia when it comes to security. Protecting your computer and data investment should be looked at logically and rationally. Just as a door's lock is useless if the lock is stronger than the door itself, so is over-protecting data from prying eyes when the computer itself can be stolen.

There are several myths about computer security that must be dispelled:

Myth One: The Pirates Are Out To Get Me. A myth because your installation is probably not all that interesting to anyone but you. A pirate needs a challenge and a goal to become interested in your system, and over-securing it is one way of calling attention to yourself.

Myth Two: My Employees Are Out To Get Me. Why hire them in the first place, if you can't trust them? Probably 95 percent of all employee-caused damage is accidental; having plenty of backup copies will insure you against accidents. Virtually all intentional damage is to data or software, which the backup copies will also cover. Embezzlement, fraud, and other misuse is the responsibility of the company and can be detected with the proper audit trails.

Myth Three: A Modem Will Give Pirates Access To All My Stuff. This is true only if you leave your computer in the answer mode, only if your computer is switched on, and only if your software allows remote access. The solution: rest easy—unplug the modem when it is not in use.

Myth Four: My Data Is Safe With Brand-X Security Program. No way: as any locksmith will tell you, the lock that cannot be picked has not yet been made; some are more difficult than others. This is the same for data security—too much is silly. Sufficient knowledge is all that is needed to break any security system.

As illustrated in Fig. 13-6 the basic priorities of installation security are the following: physical security of the programs and data, ensured by adequate backup with copies maintained off-site; physical security of the computer equipment by taking reasonable precautions against theft, fire, water, and other fatal catastrophes; and, finally, precautions against fraud, such as audit trails, operator passwords, and casual supervision. The degree of the implementation of security should be included in the design of the system; physical security and insurance for the computer equipment are the responsibility of their owner.

Operator codes and passwords can also be enhanced by using a secondary password based on the employee's own knowledge. For example, after ascertaining the operator code and password, the system could then ask for the operator to enter his or her mother's maiden name. This would be (presumably) only known to the operator and his or her family, and would prevent unauthorized use of a valid password. This method can be further enhanced by using as many as five questions one of which is picked at random each time the operator enters the system.

Programmers should have an understanding of what types of information and totals will be required in an audit trail. As shown in Fig. 13-7, the types of information used in audit trails usually falls into three categories: control data, selected totals of data items, and logs.

Control data in an audit trail usually consist of the number of database records, the highest key field assigned, and the dates and times of the last update to the file. These values can be tracked day by day; they show the physical activity against the file. The control values that are calculated or stored by the functions that cause them to change can be checked against the values on the database itself;

Type:	Method:	Guards against:
Physical security	Hardware backup	Fire, theft, natural disaster
	Software backup	Accidental erasure
	Data backup	Accidental erasure, vandalism
Data security	Audit trails	Embezzlement, fraud
	Limited access	Sabotage, vandalism
	Supervision	Espionage

Fig. 13-6. Security considerations.

dBASE places the number of records and the date/time of the last update directly in the database header area.

Totals of selected data fields can be stored, compared against the values for previous days, and cross-checked for accuracy. This type of audit trail tracks the correctness of the data contained in the system. Totals from any data entry performed during a single day, for example, are added to the previous day's totals; the values on the database can then be totaled and balanced. Discrepancies in the totals can indicate program bugs—or they can be the symptoms of deliberate embezzlement.

An activity log is a file that shows, in detail, exactly what operations were performed on a system during a given time period. The operator performing those activities can be identified by an operator identification code. This is another reason passwords are important—the audit trail should reflect accurately the use to which the system is put and who put it to that use. Allowing operators to swap passwords and code or allowing use of the same code and password by several employees all the time can lead to misunderstandings, hard feel-

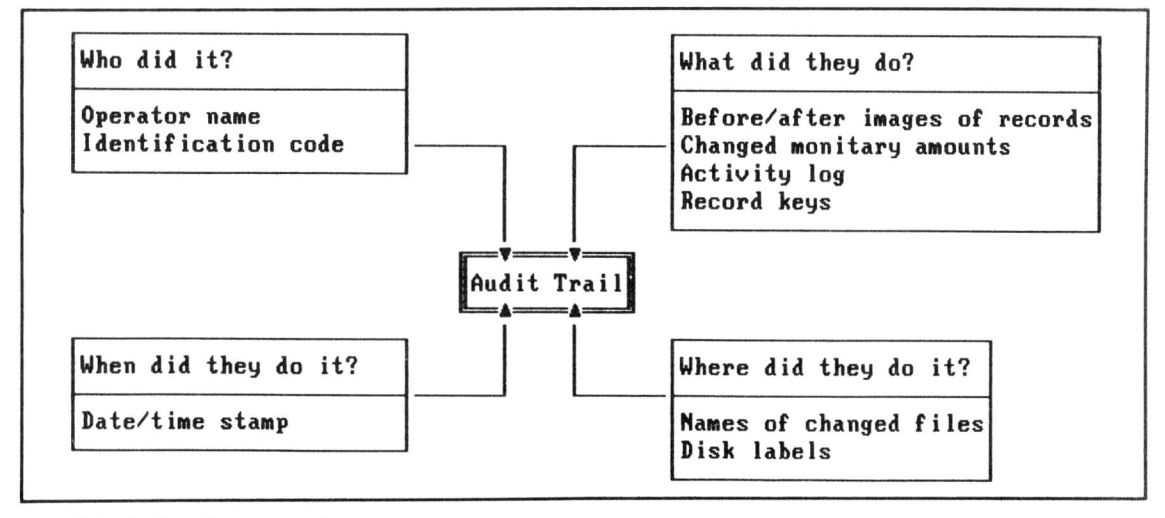

Fig. 13-7. Audit trail components.

ings, and untraceable sabotage.

Another security technique lies in the operations of PC-DOS itself. Files can be created with special attributes that do not allow the file to be changed or even seen in the disk directory. These attributes can only be set by the operating system, which means that you must write a program in assembly language or some other language; there are several freeware programs available that can change the file attributes.

The *read-only* or *protect* attribute can be used to make .PRG files unchangeable. This will reduce the possibility of accidental erasure or modification, thus eliminating two common system bugs.

dBASE III can access files with the *hidden* attribute. They do not appear on DOS directory displays, and most DOS commands will not work with hidden files. A hidden database file, however, can be USEd and accessed in dBASE like any other database. In conjunction with compilation, the database filenames will be unavailable to any but the most determined pirates.

The use of the protected and hidden file attributes will not stop a determined pirate; it will just make the task slightly more difficult. This method is actually a low-key approach; a real pirate already knows how to deal with hidden files, so there is no challenge. The major advantage to using hidden and/or read-only files is that they will prevent unintentional modification to the system by the users.

Chapter 14
Technical Techniques

There are a number of ways to make dBASE III function more quickly. This chapter outlines some ways of creating a faster, more efficient system.

"COLLAPSING" PROGRAMS FOR FASTER EXECUTION

One of the major drawbacks of an interpreted language like dBASE III is the length of time that is taken by the interpreter to look up the command in its library, check for correct syntax, and so forth.

One way of helping dBASE run faster is to make the interpreter run faster. The execution time of the interpreter can be shortened by giving the interpreter less work to do by using the shortest form of commands, removing extra blank spaces and tab characters, and joining continued lines.

As shown in Fig. 14-1, most command keywords can be shortened to four characters. Most keywords in dBASE are already less than four characters, but REPLACE, STORE, APPEND, PROCEDURE, and RETURN are very common statements. When a command is shortened, the interpreter can stop working on it as soon as it reaches the space following it. This means that up to six extra characters are bypassed on every long keyword, which means a savings in response time.

Tab characters should be removed. The interpreter skips over them, anyway, and they just take up unnecessary disk storage.

Continuation lines should be combined into a single line. Again, this is the same action the dBASE interpreter takes, so you are relieving the interpreter of a time-consuming function.

The savings realized from this are cumulative. In the first place, the file takes less time to load from disk. This means that the operator does not have to wait as long for the procedure file to be loaded after selecting a menu option. Any small change in this regard is instantly noticed and slowness here is one of the main sticky points in selling a system. Everyone expects instantaneous response from the computer—only you as the programmer know how much work is really happening inside.

Secondly, in reducing the size of the procedure

Normal dBASE III code:	Collapsed code:

SET ALTERNATE TO buglog.txt
USE employee INDEX empnox
FIND &enumb
IF .NOT. (EOF() .OR. BOF())
   SET ALTERNATE ON
   ? employee->empno+' retrieved.'
   SET ALTERNATE OFF
ENDIF
REPLACE empname WITH enamein
SET ALTERNATE ON
? employee->empno+' updated.'
SET ALTERNATE OFF
	SET ALTE TO buglog.txt
	USE employee INDE empnox
	FIND &enumb
	IF .NOT. (EOF() .OR. BOF())
	   SET ALTE ON
	   ? employee->empno+' retrieved.'
	   SET ALTE OFF
	ENDI
	REPL empname WITH enamein
	SET ALTE ON
	? employee->empno+' updated.'
	SET ALTE OFF

Fig. 14-1. Collapsed code with its uncollapsed counterpart.

and program files you are saving space on the floppy disk or hard disk, which can be used for data or other programs. The original "source code" programs can be stored on floppy disk or other backup medium. The collapsed programs can also be made read only by setting the file attribute so that it cannot be accidentally modified. Collapsed code is extremely difficult to read, and even well-intentioned modifications can easily go astray.

COMPILATION

In general terms, compilation is the process of translating a computer language into a different form. As indicated in Fig. 14-2, the new program created by a compilation is in a language that the machine can directly recognize and execute—*machine language*.

The dBASE III software has no compiler built into it. The interpreter resolves one statement at a time, calling in a library of machine-code programs to get the process done. A compiler would preinterpret the dBASE code, bringing all of the machine-language routines together in a way that would perform the same process outlined by the original code.

There are a few compilers available for dBASE III, which will be discussed in Section IV. Compilers often require that a library of routines, called a *run-time library*, also be present on the disk when a compiled program is executed. This library contains routines external to the program, which are called so often that their addition to the compiled program would make it incredibly (and unusably) large.

Compiled programs have several advantages, not the least of which is speed. The *lag-time* that the interpreter uses to translate a dBASE statement in a .PRG file is small, but it accumulates quickly. The cumulative effect of the removal of this lag-time can result in processes that execute up to twenty times faster.

Another advantage to the compilation process is that changes to the source code do not change the executable program until the compilation is again performed. This means that changes can be bench-checked through the normal dBASE interpreter before the user sees the changes.

There are several drawbacks to using dBASE compilers. Most of the compilers do not support all the features of dBASE III; the interactive commands such as EDIT or APPEnd are usually the first to be traded off for speed and compiler size. Another drawback is how the use of the compiled code is licensed; there may be a fee required by the company who makes the compiler or a license fee for the use and copying of the run-time library that must accompany the programs. You may even find your own code copyrighted by someone else!

USING SUBDIRECTORIES

Floppy disks and hard disks contain directories of all files contained on the disk, which include their names and locations. Viewing a directory of a hard disk, especially when there are a lot of files present, can be almost impossible without some other-tool written for the purpose. There is also a limit to the number of files that can be contained in a disk directory.

Subdirectories were added to the features of PC-DOS because of the advent of large-format media, like hard disks. They provide the microcomputer user with the means to more effectively manage files stored on these devices. The subdirectory is a file, and as such it appears in the main directory of the disk. The subdirectory, however, contains the names and locations of other files, which do not appear on the main directory. Files are added to this directory when the particular subdirectory is chosen as the currently active path. Each of the subdirectories is also limited in the number of files it can contain, but further directories can be created within a subdirectory.

The PC-DOS commands MKDIR, RMDIR, and CHDIR are used to create, delete, and manage subdirectories. The PATH command can be used to set the sequence that directories are searched for command (.COM) or executable (.EXE) files. The current directory is searched first, and then those listed in the PATH.

Data files cannot be searched for in this way, because the full specification of the dataset, including the subdirectory name (if any), must be included when a dataset is allocated to a program. If the program does not specify the directory path of the file, it is assumed to be on the currently set directory. The CHDIR (abbreviated "CD") command is used to set the current directory. There are utilities available from several sources that do allow PATH-type searches for data files. Figure 14-3 shows the commands that change directory paths.

The dBASE SET PATH command creates a search path for dBASE to use in finding any dBASE files, including .PRG files. dBASE will place the named directory path or paths at the end of the directory chain specified by CHDIR before dBASE was started. This only applies to files that already

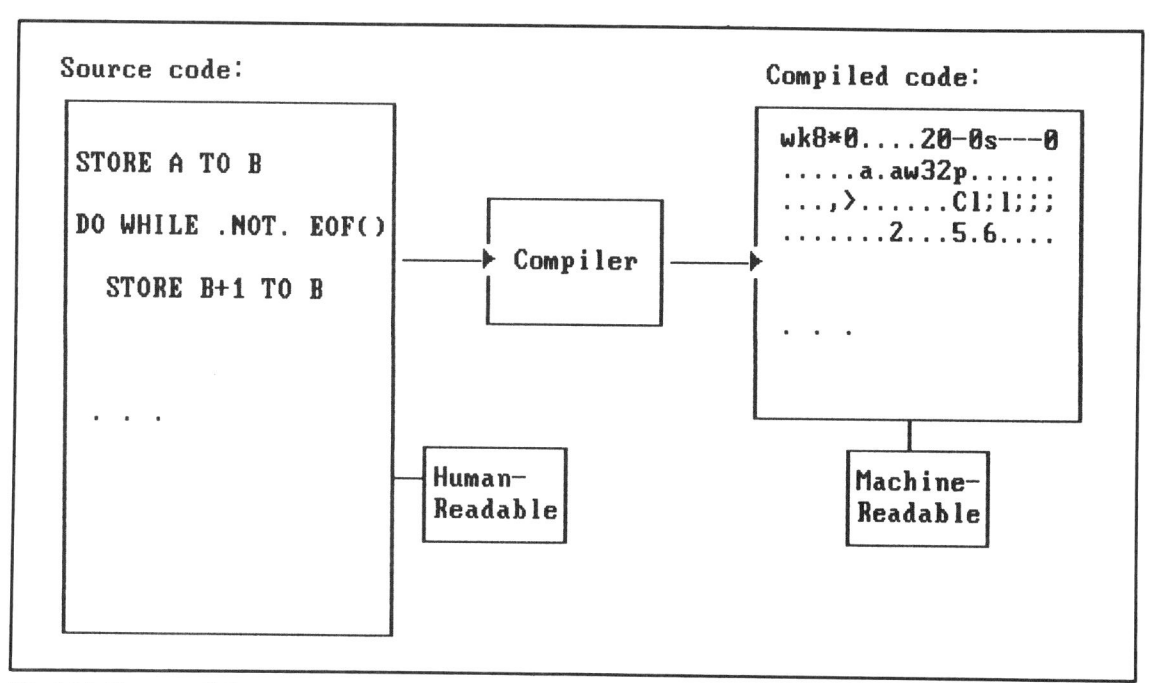

Fig. 14-2. The compilation process.

```
┌─────────────────────────────────────────────────────────────────┐
│  ┌───────────────────────────────────────────────────────────┐  │
│  │ PC-DOS command:                                           │  │
│  ├───────────────────────────────────────────────────────────┤  │
│  │ CHDIR or CD -- changes current directory at system level  │  │
│  ├───────────────────────────────────────────────────────────┤  │
│  │ Syntax: CD <path>                                         │  │
│  └───────────────────────────────────────────────────────────┘  │
│                                                                 │
│  ┌───────────────────────────────────────────────────────────┐  │
│  │ dBASE III command:                                        │  │
│  ├───────────────────────────────────────────────────────────┤  │
│  │ SET PATH TO -- gives new search path for dBASE. Directory │  │
│  │                specified must be within currently set     │  │
│  │                system directory.                          │  │
│  ├───────────────────────────────────────────────────────────┤  │
│  │ Syntax: SET PATH TO <path>                                │  │
│  └───────────────────────────────────────────────────────────┘  │
└─────────────────────────────────────────────────────────────────┘
```

Fig. 14-3. Commands that change directory paths.

exist; if a file is to be created on a subdirectory, the entire specification must be used.

Subdirectories can be used to organize the files necessary to a dBASE system into logical groups. A subdirectory could be created for each system, which would include further subdirectories for data, program, and format files. The SET PATH command can be used to set individual search paths for each function or system. Figure 14-4 shows one method of directory organization.

When a large number of subdirectories are used, the person operating the system may easily forget the current directory path. One method of reducing this confusion is to use the PC-DOS PROMPT command to generate a system prompt that shows not just the currently-logged disk drive, but also the currently-set directory path. The following command, either entered directly or placed in an AUTOEXEC.BAT file, will cause this to happen:

PROMPT PG

After this command is issued, PC-DOS will place the directory path at the > prompt, instead of just the current drive letter.

The dBASE DIR command ignores the SET PATH and displays only the files in the current directory. This can be overriden by using the subdirectory paths in the command or using the PC-DOS DIR command.

The most common method of organizing dBASE files using subdirectories on a hard disk is to place the dBASE software into its own directory and place all application files in further subdirectories. The highest level should contain all of the dBASE functions necessary to system operation, such as the CONFIG.DB file and the dBASE software. Any external editors used should also be placed in this directory.

As shown in Fig. 14-5, each application system can then be placed in a subdirectory within the directory containing the dBASE system software. This method also requires that the highest program in the application system hierarchy must also be placed on the highest directory because the SET PATH for that system would be included in that program.

Subdirectories to group the various dBASE file types can be created within the application system. Programs and procedures can be placed in one

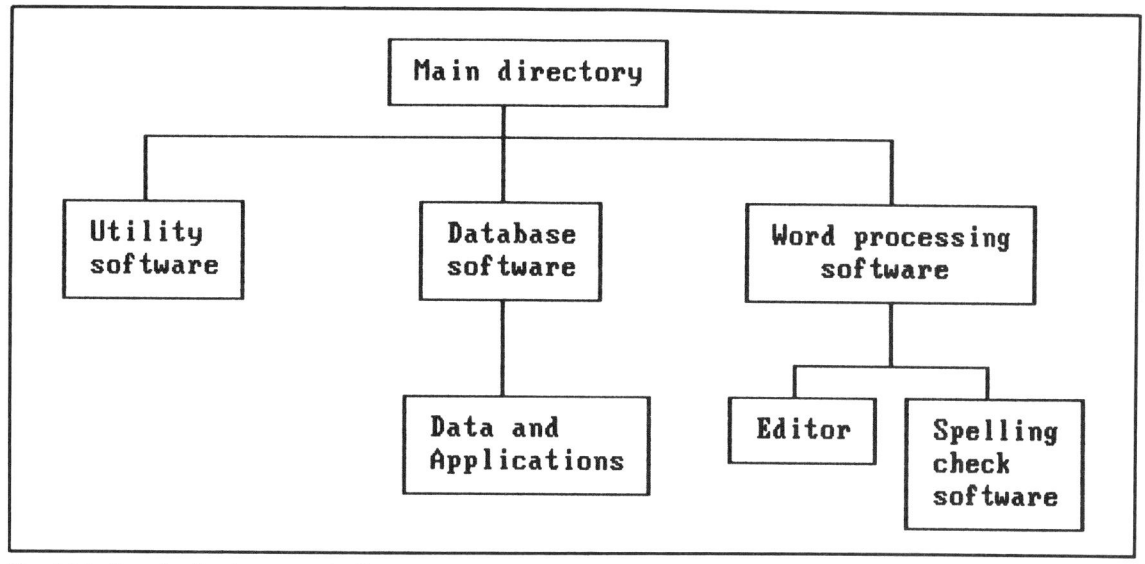

Fig. 14-4. Sample directory organization.

directory; database, index, and memo-field files can be placed in a second, while screen and report formats can be placed in still another subdirectory. This will facilitate moving the files to and from floppy disk for backup and recovery purposes; programmers also use subdirectories on floppy disks to organize these files.

dBASE III must be installed to a hard disk with a special procedure. This is a part of the copy-protection feature used with dBASE, and allows the dBASE user greater flexibility in managing their system. Once installed on a hard disk, the original dBASE disk is useless unless dBASE is deinstalled. The installation can be routed to a subdirectory

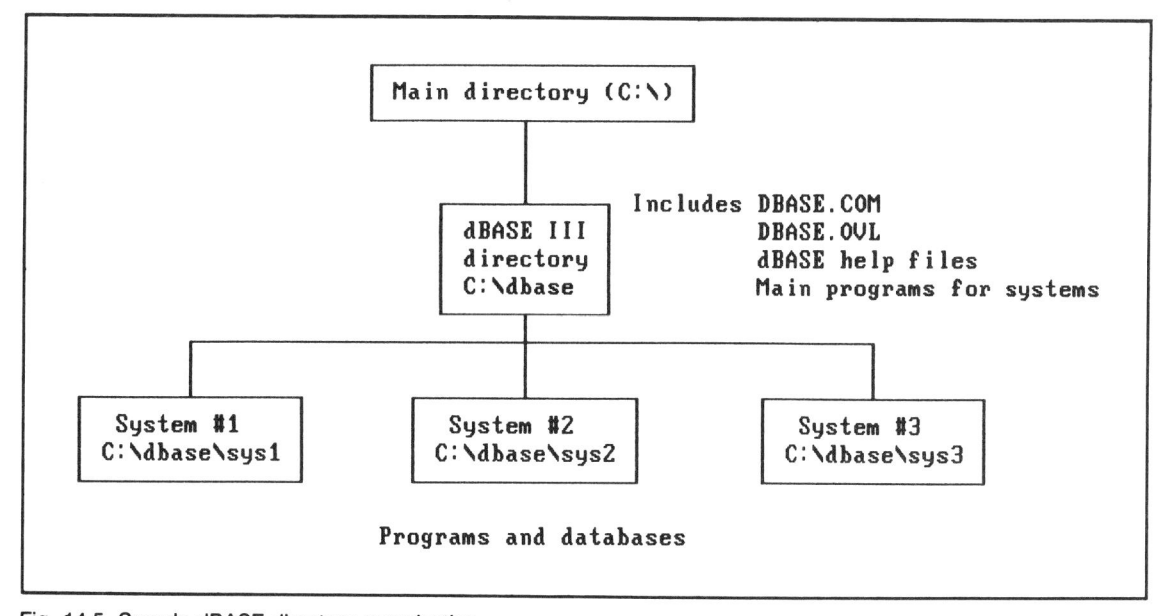

Fig. 14-5. Sample dBASE directory organization.

111

very easily, but the installed files cannot then be copied. This means that before each backup of the hard disk's files, the dBASE software must be deinstalled back to the original system disk. When a hard-disk recovery is performed, dBASE must be reinstalled.

SPOOLING AND CACHING

There are utilities available that will speed up the operation of dBASE III or allow the computer to be used for other purposes while peripheral operations (like printing) are taking place. There are two general types of program that fit this pattern: the *print spool* utility, and the *disk cache*.

Spool is an acronym borrowed from mainframe computer programming. It stands for *Simultaneous Peripheral Operations On Line*; the meaning is that while some I/O operation is performed, the computer is available for other uses. Both print spooling and disk caching utilities are variations of the spool technique.

A print spooling utility reserves an area of RAM memory, called a *buffer*, for printed output. The size of the area can be specified by the programmer, so that fine-tuning is possible as you balance the amount of memory taken against the speed desired. There is also a hardware device, called a print buffer, that performs this same function. The print buffer contains its own RAM memory, so that "main" memory is not used. Some printers have a small (2K to 8K) buffer memory built into them.

Print spooling software and/or print buffering hardware will cause printed lines to be placed in the reserved memory, instead of allowing them to be sent directly to the printer. This operation is much faster than normal printing, because there is no time spent waiting for the printer to finish a line. The transfer of print lines from one area of memory (dBASE III) to another (the spool or buffer) takes much less time; the printer proceeds at its normal speed while the buffer/spool memory fills up with print lines.

If a print buffer or spool is completely filled, the system will wait for more of the lines that are stored there to be sent to the printer and then continue. A print spool large enough to contain the entire report or file being printed will allow almost immediate use of the computer for other functions.

A disk cache is a buffer for records read from disk. Instead of reading each record or sector individually, the entire track is placed in memory. If the next record requested is on the stored track, no disk I/O need be performed.

Disk caching programs can also be tailored to fit your system needs by adjusting the amount of memory used by the cache. In application programs where there is a lot of disk I/O, disk caching can increase the speed at which these operations are performed. The effect of this is to decrease the amount of time the program takes to execute, sometimes by as much as 50 percent. This is really only effective for "disk-bound" operations, where most of the execution time can be traced to disk I/O operations. Programs that do little or no disk I/O will realize little, if any, increase in speed.

The major disadvantage to the use of print spooling and disk caching software is that more of the computer's memory is taken by these programs. External print buffers do not affect the amount of internal memory used, because they contain their own memory. Hardware print buffers, however, can only be adjusted by replacing the device; the usual rule for external print buffers is the bigger, the better.

Finding the correct "balance point" between the amount of memory used and the time savings realized is a process of trial-and-error; there is no real way to do more than "guesstimate" the affect of a change on a program until it is tried. There is no doubt, though, that for most application systems these utilities will speed up the process, dramatically.

Chapter 15
dBASE III Hardware and System Considerations

One of the problems facing the business planner is that of the hardware needs of both the present and the future. The growth of computerization has lead to the realization that there must be storage space for the data. One of the symptoms of this is the race to provide more and more storage space for less and less cost.

The most common microcomputer storage device in use is the 5.25-inch floppy disk drive. Use of this device as a storage medium has its disadvantages. The latest trends seem to indicate that, more and more, the floppy disk is becoming a medium for storing archival copies of software and data files.

The major disadvantage to a floppy disk, at least for business users, is its limited storage capacity. At the time of the microcomputer's inception, nobody thought that they would complain about having only 360K to work with. Now floppy disks can store over two megabytes of storage, but only if the proper drive is purchased and installed. Disks produced on such drives cannot usually be read by any other drives, making portability between machines impractical if not impossible.

Assuming an average dBASE database consists of ten fields, the entire record being 100 characters long (101 characters, counting the unseen field). The largest number of records that would fit on a single floppy disk, with no other files on the disk, can be computed:

```
  362496  (number of bytes on a floppy disk)
-     35  (dBASE header and extra bytes)
-    320  (field descriptions)

= 362141  (number of remaining bytes)
```

The number of remaining bytes or characters can be divided by the record size (101) to yield the total number of database records that can be contained on a single, empty floppy disk. The result is 3585 (and change). Business databases easily can and frequently do exceed this limit.

As shown in Fig. 15-1, data storage is only one part of the system configuration. Devices used for

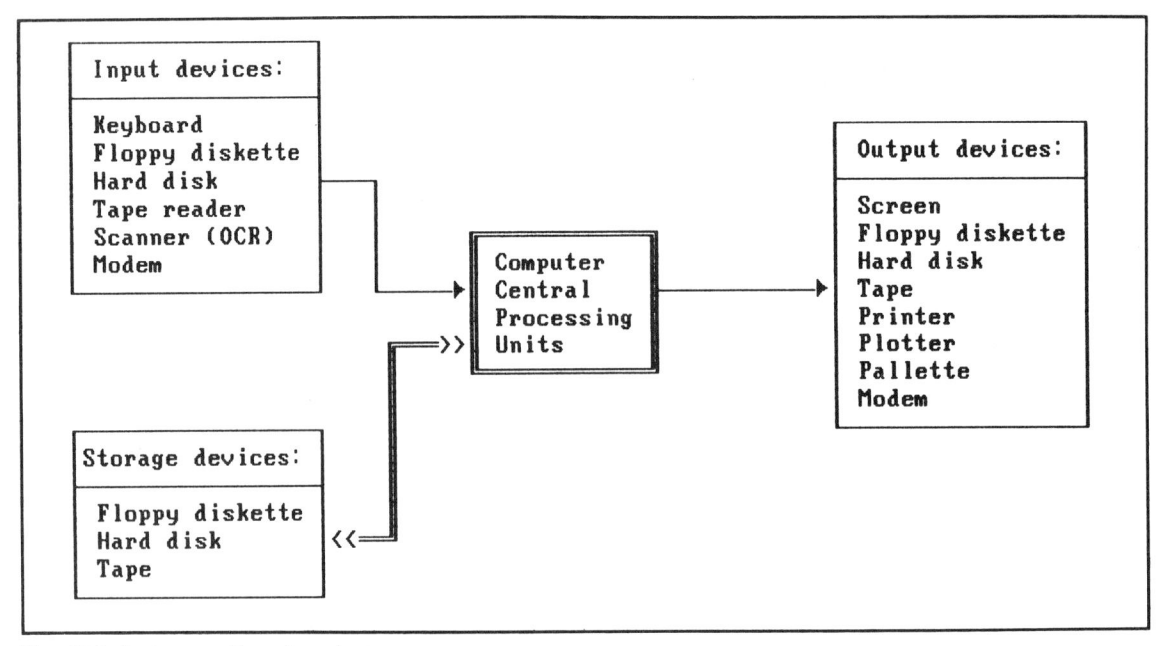

```
┌─────────────────────────────────────────────────────────────────────┐
│  ┌─────────────────────┐                                            │
│  │ Input devices:      │                     ┌─────────────────────┐│
│  │ Keyboard            │                     │ Output devices:     ││
│  │ Floppy diskette     │                     │ Screen              ││
│  │ Hard disk           │                     │ Floppy diskette     ││
│  │ Tape reader         │    ┌──────────┐     │ Hard disk           ││
│  │ Scanner (OCR)       │    │ Computer │     │ Tape                ││
│  │ Modem               │───▶│ Central  │────▶│ Printer             ││
│  └─────────────────────┘    │Processing│     │ Plotter             ││
│                        =≫ │ Units    │     │ Pallette            ││
│                             └──────────┘     │ Modem               ││
│  ┌─────────────────────┐                     └─────────────────────┘│
│  │ Storage devices:    │                                            │
│  │ Floppy diskette     │ ≪=                                        │
│  │ Hard disk           │                                            │
│  │ Tape                │                                            │
│  └─────────────────────┘                                            │
└─────────────────────────────────────────────────────────────────────┘
```

Fig. 15-1. System configuration chart.

input and output operations also have their limitations and possibilities.

Entering data via the computer keyboard is the usual method of getting data into a database. This method may prove impractical for some applications, however. A company installing a new system may already have most of the data necessary for the system stored in some other form, perhaps in paper files. Reentering the data via the keyboard may be too time-consuming and not cost-effective.

If the data is already available in a computerized format, it is possible to transfer that data to the storage of the microcomputer by several means. The computers can be joined by some form of telecommunications network, and the data can be transferred directly from one computer to another. This is usually the fastest method of transfer, even if some form of error-checking is used to verify the transmission.

Data files can also be transferred via some common medium. Most IBM-compatible and semicompatible computers use the same type of floppy drive, so that data can be transferred on one or more floppy disks. This usually does not involve any change to the data file itself; it can be simply copied to another floppy disk, or hard disk.

Nine-track computer tape drives are now available for microcomputers; this enables an IBM PC to read a tape created on a mainframe IBM computer, although there is a small conversion that must take place. Mainframe computers generally use a different code for the arrangement of bits than do microcomputers. Microcomputers (usually) use the American Standard Code for Information Interchange, or ASCII (pronounced "ASK-ee"); mainframes (usually) use IBM's Extended Binary Coded Decimal Interchange Code, or EBCDIC (pronounced "EB-sid-dik"). The translation process, however, is (usually) a function of most mainframe operating systems.

Transferring data from paper files to a database is probably the most time-consuming activity in the implementation of a computer system. The paper files must be translated into a data entry format and then entered one at a time. This can discourage companies with large paper files from entering the information that can help them run their business.

Optical character readers, collectively known as OCRs, have been in existence for a long time; earlier machines of this type were large, inaccurate, and could only read characters printed in a special character set.

Recently, optical scanners have become available for use with microcomputers. These range from full-page copiers to a device with a hand-held scanner and guide ruler. If large quantities of paper information must be transcribed, an optical scanner might be the answer.

HARD DISKS

The present-day solution to the storage space crisis is the direct access storage device (DASD, pronounced "DAZ-dee"). DASDs have been used on mainframe computer systems since the late 1960s. Their main advantage is access speed; the rotating disk moves the data past magnetic heads floating scant microns above the surface (about half the width of a single particle of cigarette smoke). Their speed makes the DASDs excellent devices for storing data to be retrieved by large online networks.

The second advantage of DASD is the amount of data that can be stored on a single device. The limit is now approaching several gigabytes (1024 megabytes equal one gigabyte); new research is leading to storage in the terabyte (1024 gigabytes equal one terabyte) range.

The average size of a microcomputer DASD is about ten (10) megabytes. Microcomputer DASDs are usually referred to as hard disks. The speed of the hard disk increases the apparent speed of dBASE, because the I/O functions now move about 20 times faster than with a floppy disk. This usually is the reason for using a hard disk, but the storage space is another advantage.

The hard disk gives the microcomputer user the room to store databases and other files, using much more space than is available on a floppy disk. dBASE itself can be installed on the hard disk, making the wait time for the initial dBASE entry much faster.

Some business applications of dBASE III systems could cause even 10 megabytes to be too limiting. Hard disks do exist with capacities up to about 800 megabytes; the astute business planner has to ask, "Is this only postponing the inevitable?"

Eventually, some large-capacity, portable storage medium will be needed, although the need may not become apparent for years.

One answer to this need is the removable hard disk, sometimes called a cartridge hard disk. The ten megabyte disk, which is built into a fixed disk drive, is instead inside a cartridge, which can be inserted into a cartridge hard disk drive and used in the same way. The advantage is that the disk may then be removed, copied onto another cartridge, or stored off site for archival and backup purposes. There is now only a limit on the size of the database itself—10 megabytes. When used in conjunction with computers like the IBM PC/XT or COMPAQ Plus that have built-in hard disk drives, the storage available becomes limitless.

Data and programs stored on hard disks must be copied for backup purposes. The contents of the disk can be copied to a series of floppy disks or copied to a tape cartridge drive designed for the purpose. Many of these devices are available, and usually prove to be much faster and less expensive than floppy disk backup.

FUTURE DEVICES

New innovations in technology are constantly in progress, producing larger and larger amounts of space on a single device. This trend has been continuing since the early days of commercial computer use; the trend in microcomputer DASD storage has been to provide larger amounts of storage and faster access times in smaller packages.

Very few installations plan for future innovations in system hardware configuration. The thought is that "once the system is running, it will run forever." This myth, coupled with the impossibility of predicting change, can cause serious problems in the small computer installation. The day on which these problems will happen can be predicted—it will be the day that the storage requirements of the system exceed available storage space.

The latest trends in DASD storage technology have lead to such devices as the removable-cartridge hard disk, tape cartridge drives that are accessed as if they were disks, and bubble memory that behaves like a hard disk drive. These devices all have their good and bad points, and are merely serving to whet the appetite of the microcomputer industry.

The advent of the laser video disk has brought a whole new reassessment of information storage. Almost a gigabyte of storage can be placed on a blank video disk that costs about $20. The problem in developing the laser disk as a computer medium was the technology needed to write the data to the laser disk. This problem has been overcome, and soon large storage capacities will be available for competitive prices.

Laser disk drives are sometimes called WORM drives for "Write Once, Read Mainly." The data, encoded as dots burned onto the surface of the disk, cannot be erased. This is not a major disadvantage, however; the disks contain enough storage that a file can be rewritten at another place on the medium, rather than overwritten. The relatively inexpensive disks can be purchased in any quantities needed.

A system planner must recognize the trends in data storage technologies, calculate the system storage growth, and then loosely predict the dates when new storage will be needed. New equipment should only be considered when the savings realized by its use are greater than the cost of purchase and conversion.

FILE HANDLING AND RECOVERY

One of the most important functions of any system is one that is not part of the business function being performed. All files used in the system, including both programs and data, must be copied and stored to provide duplicate files that will be available if the originals are lost or tampered with. System recovery usually comes under the function of system security, but is in itself a critical process. Even if no other security measures are implemented in an application system, file backup and recovery must be.

The main point of file recovery is to take copies of the data files and bring them up to date (Fig. 15-2). This must be done as quickly as possible; in small businesses, where the computer is not critical, as much as a week can elapse before the system is fully recovered. The more critical that computer processing and the stored data are to your business, the more quickly you must be able to recover them.

There are two ways that files can become unusable: either through physical damage to the recording medium, or through modification to the

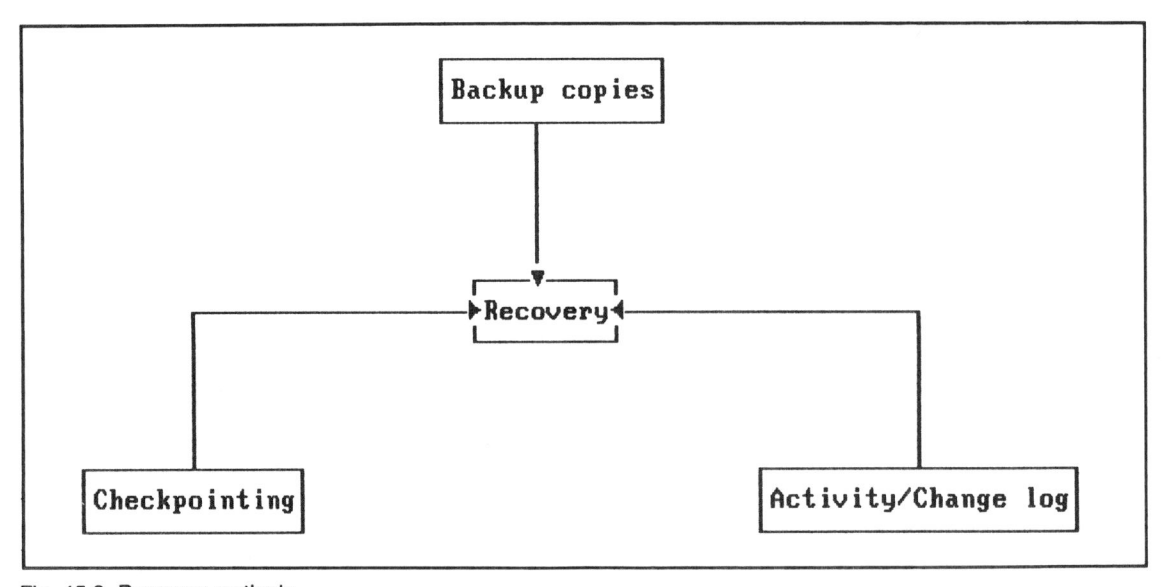

Fig. 15-2. Recovery methods.

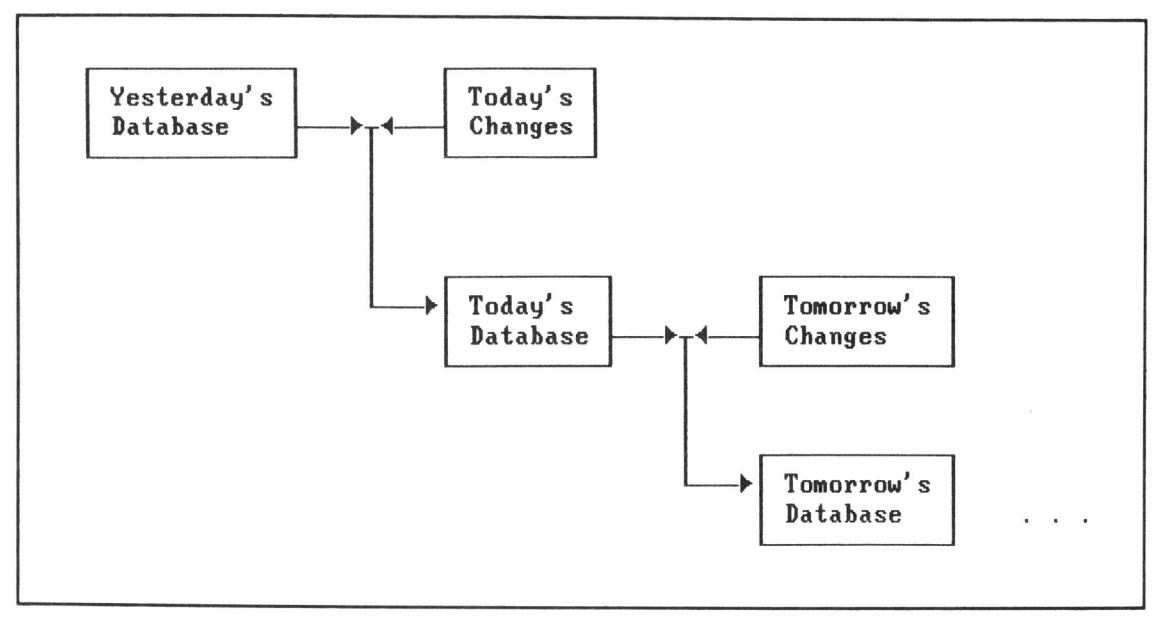

```
┌─────────────┐      ┌─────────┐
│ Yesterday's │─────▶├◀─────── │ Today's │
│  Database   │      │ Changes │
└─────────────┘      └────┬────┘
                          │
                          ▼
                    ┌──────────┐      ┌───────────┐
                    │ Today's  │─────▶├◀──────── │Tomorrow's │
                    │ Database │      │  Changes  │
                    └──────────┘      └─────┬─────┘
                                            │
                                            ▼
                                      ┌───────────┐
                                      │Tomorrow's │   . . .
                                      │ Database  │
                                      └───────────┘
```

Fig. 15-3. Grandfather—father—son recovery.

file itself, including deletion. These disasters can also happen to the directory where the file information is stored; the system can no longer find the files, although they may still be intact.

Physically damaged disks that still contain intact information can be read using certain utilities made for that purpose. There are several utility packages of this type on the market, most notably The Norton Utilities by Peter Norton. These utilities search out ASCII text information on the disk, skipping over the damaged areas. Utilities such as these, although necessary for hard disk users, are only necessary when inadequate backup procedures are used.

The basic rule of recovery is that any time a file is changed, a copy should be made and stored in a safe place. This copy can then be used to replace a damaged or deleted file. Creating a backup copy each and every time a change is made, however, is not always practical.

Most system planners make daily copies of files that are changed during the course of the day, monthly copies for files used in end-of-month processing, and copies of all other files on an as needed basis. Using this method alone, there will never be more than one day's work to recover, which is acceptable to businesses with small amounts of daily activity.

Up-to-the-minute recovery can be performed by writing a description of each database change to a file, which is called an *activity log* or *change log*. This becomes a record of the system's activity between the times when backup copies are created. This log can then be printed and used by an operator to redo all of the activity; the file could also be input to a program that performs the same tasks.

The activity log should also be copied on a daily basis at the same time that the backup copies of the data files are made. The full-day's change log can be used to recreate a data file from the previous day's copy. This recovery method is known as *grandfather-father-son* recovery, because files several days old can be used to recover the current database, if the change logs are available (Fig. 15-3).

Ideally, two copies should be made of every file. One copy is stored close to the computer site, so that it can be immediately available if needed. The second copy should be stored away from the computer site in the event of a local disaster. The nearest that off-site backup copies should be stored is in a detached building near the computer site;

they should be available on less than one hour's notice, depending on the critical nature of the installation. The off-site backup site should never be so close that the same disaster could overcome all backup copies.

The process of recovering the company's database in the event of natural or man-made disasters should be a part of the overall computer plan of the company. Any application systems that are created should conform to the plan; using the same method for all recovery will ensure that recovery will be as fast and easy as possible. Standard recovery programs or procedures can be used to recover files in all application systems. The recovery procedures should also be stored with the off-site backup copies, especially if they include computer procedures on disk.

Floppy disk is not the only medium for storing backup copies. The procedure of copying all hard disk files onto a series of floppy disks is time-consuming and expensive. Streaming tape backup units can be used to store the entire contents of a hard disk onto a tape cartridge, which can be stored in less space and with less expense than a comparable number of floppy disks.

Removable 10-megabyte cartridge hard disks can be copied in the same way as other hard disks. If two cartridge drives are available on a system, however, a backup copy can be made on another removable cartridge. In the event of damage to the original cartridge, the data on the backup cartridge would then be immediately usable; no recovery procedure is necessary other than changing the cartridge and redoing any activity that occurred after the copy was made.

In an application system that combines both interactive and noninteractive (batch) processing, a temporary backup should be created after the interactive processes are completed and before the batch processes are executed. This will ensure that activities performed during the day will not be lost due to a power outage or other natural occurrence while the computer is running unattended. This copy can be erased after the batch processing has completed, but only after another, more permanent backup copy is created.

Application programs that are executed noninteractively can also keep up-to-the-minute logs of activity against the databases. This will ease recovery in case an application program causes a file to be lost. Changes that have occurred in batch processing can be applied to the prebatch "temporary" copy to bring the files up to the place that they were prior to the program that caused the problem. Once that program is fixed or the problem solved, the processing can then be continued from that point.

Checkpoint-restart is another method of recovery that is used to restart a program that failed during its execution without executing the entire program again. This is most useful when a program takes a long time to run; if a program that normally executes for three hours fails in the last 15 minutes, it will not be necessary to rerun the entire task. The disadvantage to this method is that it will increase the amount of I/O operations performed by the pro-

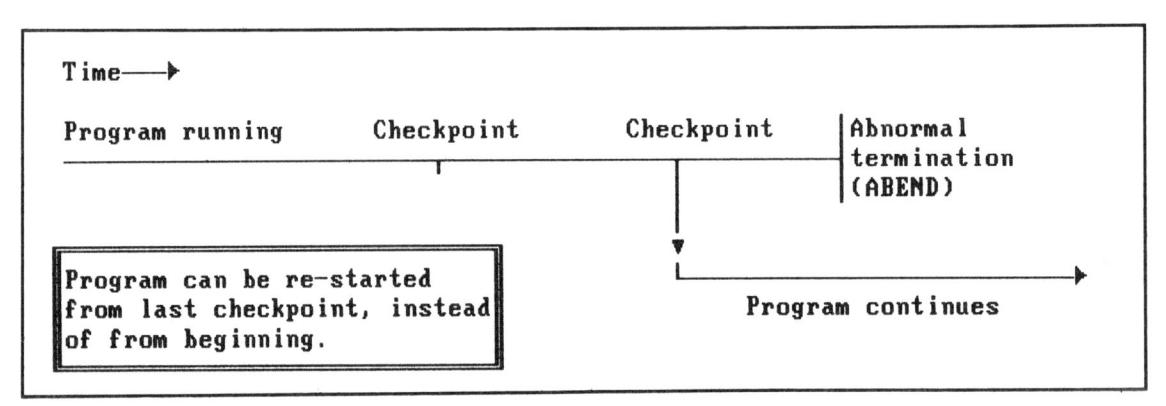

Fig. 15-4. Checkpoint restart.

gram, thus making it take still longer.

As illustrated in Fig. 15-4, at certain intervals in a program, a snapshot or *checkpoint* of the values of all system variables and file positions is created and placed on an external file. If the program fails at a later point, the values can be recovered from this file and the process continued from that point.

dBASE systems cannot take full advantage of this method without making copies of the databases at each checkpoint, which would be impractical for most applications. This is because dBASE updates the database records directly, and the prior values are overwritten. If a checkpoint is taken at each sequentially-processed record, including the before- and after-images of the current records in all open databases, checkpoint recovery is possible. These values could be stored in memory variables, and then stored in a .MEM file using the SAVE command.

Chapter 16
dBASE III File Structures

The dBASE programmer has little reason for knowing the physical internal structure of a database or index file, other than curiosity. dBASE III performs all of the operations necessary to retrieve and replace records, so that the dBASE user has no real need to know the file structure.

What can be realized from studying the physical structure of a dBASE file is the knowledge that dBASE in not performing a magical function. There are reasons that dBASE behaves in the manner it does, mostly dependent on the file organization. The techniques used by dBASE III in file storage and retrieval can be applied to other applications, even those written in dBASE.

THE STRUCTURE OF A DATABASE FILE

A dBASE database file is divided into three main areas: the header, the field descriptions, and the data. The information stored in the header and the field descriptions is what makes dBASE tick; this describes the data stored in the data area and provides other information so that dBASE can perform the operations it does.

As shown in Fig. 16-1, the database header area contains general information about the database. This information includes the number of data records contained on the database, the date of the last update to the database, the length of each data record, and an indicator that specifies whether or not a memo field exists on the database. The header also contains a pointer to the first record in the data area.

The field that stores the number of records on the database is a 32-bit number, which is where the dBASE specification of a "1,000,000,000" record limit comes from. This may be the largest number that can fit into a 32-bit binary field, but that many records, depending on their size, would be beyond the storage capacities of most machines.

32-bit numbers work like other binary numbers used in computer processing. As shown in Fig. 16-2, the data is stored with the bytes in reverse order; that is, the leftmost byte of the number contains the rightmost two hexadecimal digits.

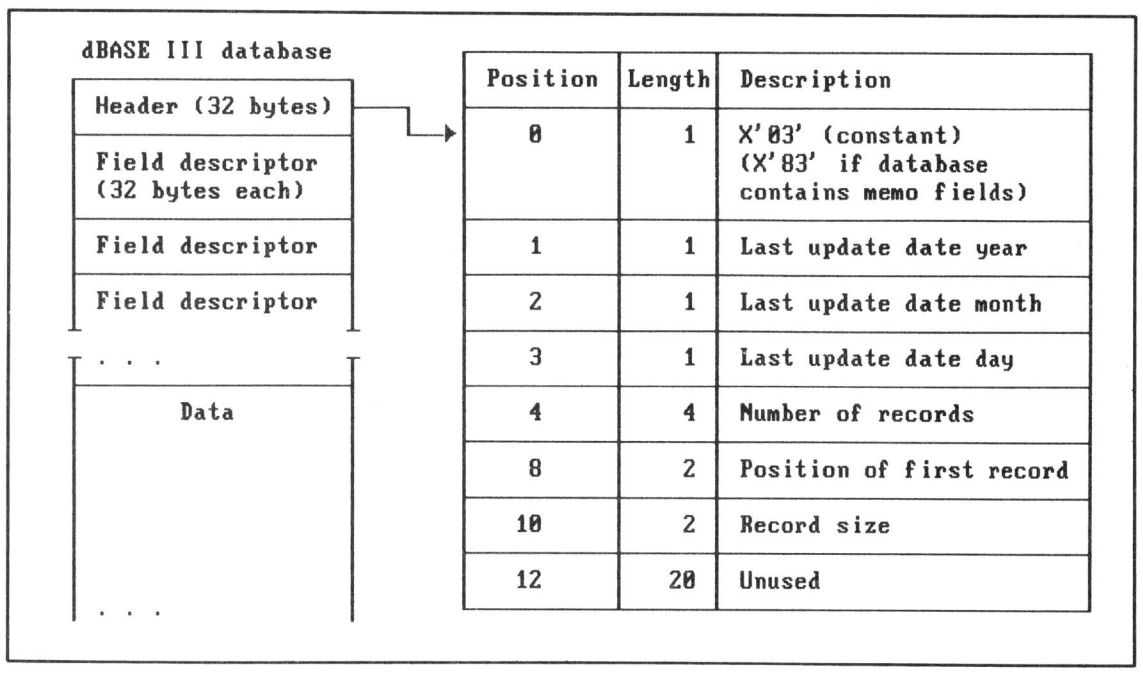

```
dBASE III database
┌─────────────────────────┐
│ Header (32 bytes)       │
├─────────────────────────┤
│ Field descriptor        │
│ (32 bytes each)         │
├─────────────────────────┤
│ Field descriptor        │
├─────────────────────────┤
│ Field descriptor        │
├─────────────────────────┤
│ ...                     │
│                         │
│ Data                    │
│                         │
│ ...                     │
└─────────────────────────┘
```

Position	Length	Description
0	1	X'03' (constant) (X'83' if database contains memo fields)
1	1	Last update date year
2	1	Last update date month
3	1	Last update date day
4	4	Number of records
8	2	Position of first record
10	2	Record size
12	20	Unused

Fig. 16-1. The database header structure.

The date of last update contained in the header is also stored in binary; one byte each is allocated to year, month, and day. Other numbers on the database header are in the "normal" low byte-high byte 16-bit binary format. The first character of the header indicates whether or not there is a memo field contained in this database, so that dBASE can prepare for its access. Finally, there is a large area of the header that is not used; this is reversed for use by dBASE at a later date.

As indicated in Fig. 16-3, each field on the database is represented by an entry in the field description area. Each entry is 32 characters long and contains all information necessary for dBASE III to recognize and work with the data in that field. Included are the field name, its length, the number

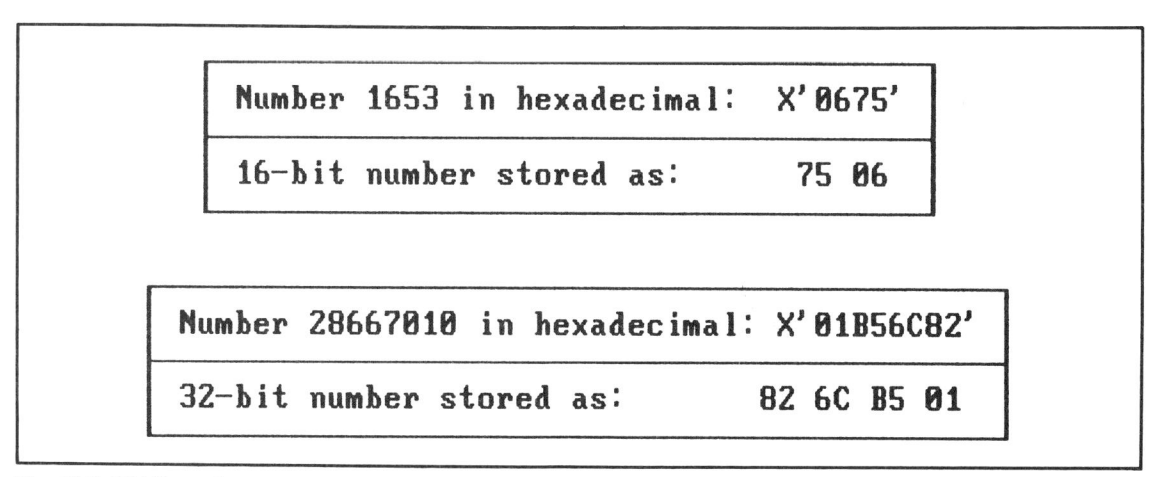

```
Number 1653 in hexadecimal:    X'0675'
16-bit number stored as:       75 06

Number 28667010 in hexadecimal: X'01B56C82'
32-bit number stored as:        82 6C B5 01
```

Fig. 16-2. 32-bit numbers.

121

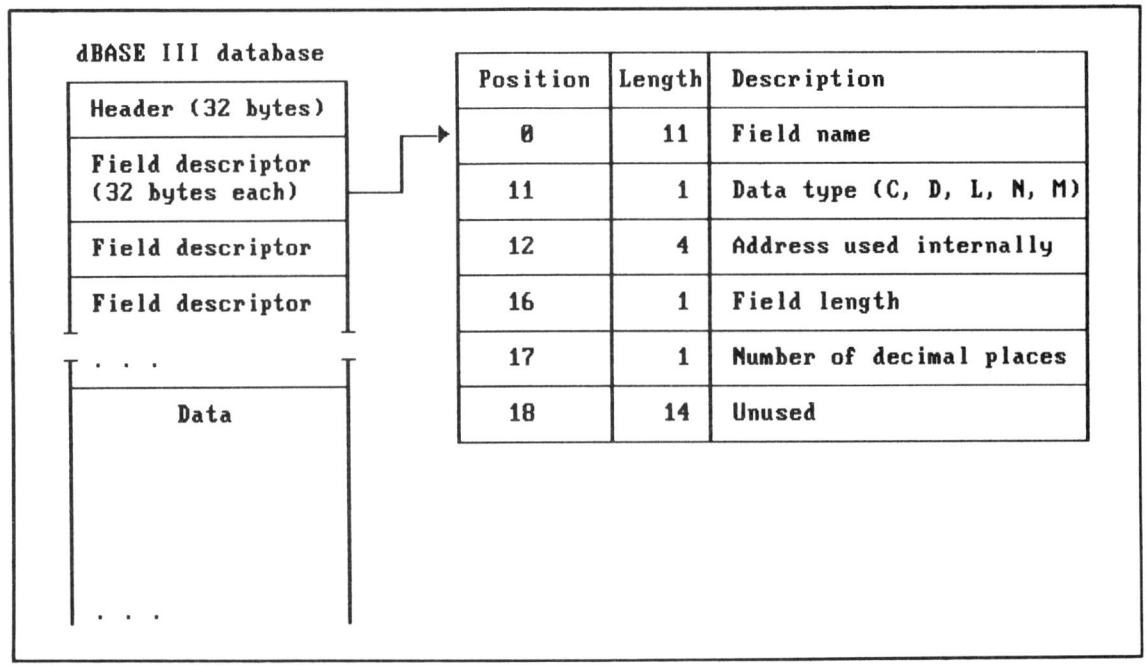

```
dBASE III database
┌─────────────────────────┐
│  Header (32 bytes)      │
├─────────────────────────┤
│  Field descriptor       │
│  (32 bytes each)        │
├─────────────────────────┤
│  Field descriptor       │
├─────────────────────────┤
│  Field descriptor       │
├─────────────────────────┤
│        . . .            │
├─────────────────────────┤
│         Data            │
│                         │
│        . . .            │
└─────────────────────────┘
```

Position	Length	Description
0	11	Field name
11	1	Data type (C, D, L, N, M)
12	4	Address used internally
16	1	Field length
17	1	Number of decimal places
18	14	Unused

Fig. 16-3. The field description structure.

of decimal places, and the data type. There is also a large area reserved for future expansion and a field that is an internal memory pointer to a dBASE buffer. This last field can only be deciphered and used by dBASE III.

The data area of the database contains all of the data records in the order they were placed on the file. There are no special codes between records, because the record length is available from the header area. Each record contains one more character than the field descriptions allow for, the unseen deletion indicator; this field is accounted for in the header's record length field.

As indicated in Fig. 6-4, each field in the data area is stored as a character string. The number of characters is defined by the field length; there are no varying-length fields nor is there any compression performed to rid the file of unneeded blanks. Character and numeric fields are stored as they are viewed; numeric fields contain blanks in place of leading zeros.

Date fields are stored as character strings in the format YYYYMMDD. The four-digit year is also used in a slightly different manner; the first position can represent one or two digits, depending on the year. If a date with five positions of year is placed in a Date field, the first position of the stored field will contain a hexadecimal code that represents the first two digits. Dates with four digits of year or less will be stored in character-string format.

Logical fields contain the value that was placed into them by the full-screen operation or REPLace command used to store the value. The values Y, y, T, and t represent true or on switches; N, n, F, and f represent false or off values. These values are also redisplayed during full-screen operations.

Memo fields use ten characters of storage on the record. This area is used to store a pointer into the memo field file (.DBT) that is associated with the database being accessed.

THE STRUCTURE OF AN INDEX

The dBASE III index file is a structure called a B+ tree. This is a hierarchical tree structure that contains the keys of each record that is in the database and the associated record number. Each place where the tree branches is called a node; the highest node in the structure is called the root node. The B in B+ tree stands for Binary—each node point has two and only two hierarchical paths leading to the next lower level of the tree.

Each node contains a key value. During a SEEK or FIND operation, the node value is compared to the value of the key being sought. The relationship of this key value to the node key is determined. If the value being searched for is greater than the node key one path is followed; otherwise the second path is followed. As shown in Fig. 16-5, the paths eventually lead to the lowest level, which contains the keys of all database records, and their record numbers.

The search continues through the nodes of the tree until the matching lowest-level node, called a *leaf node*, is reached. The record number is then used to quickly retrieve the database record. The number of searches necessary to reach the correct leaf is very small; most keys can be found in three index accesses (the system's, not yours).

The leaf nodes also form a sequential index to the database, so that sequential processing in index order is possible. This is what allows the technique of direct-sequential access to be used; the first key can be found via a SEEK or FIND index search, and then the database can be sequentially processed in key value order.

Index problems with dBASE III versions 1.0 and 1.1 have been discovered by many dBASE users. The problem as of this writing seems to be with index keys whose length is not an even multiple of four characters long. dBASE allocates its index keys in groups of four characters; keys that have less than four characters or are not an even multiple of four characters will not replace information in the remaining characters allocated.

For example, an Employee database might be indexed by Social Security Number. This field is nine characters long; however, dBASE will allocate a twelve character key area to contain the value.

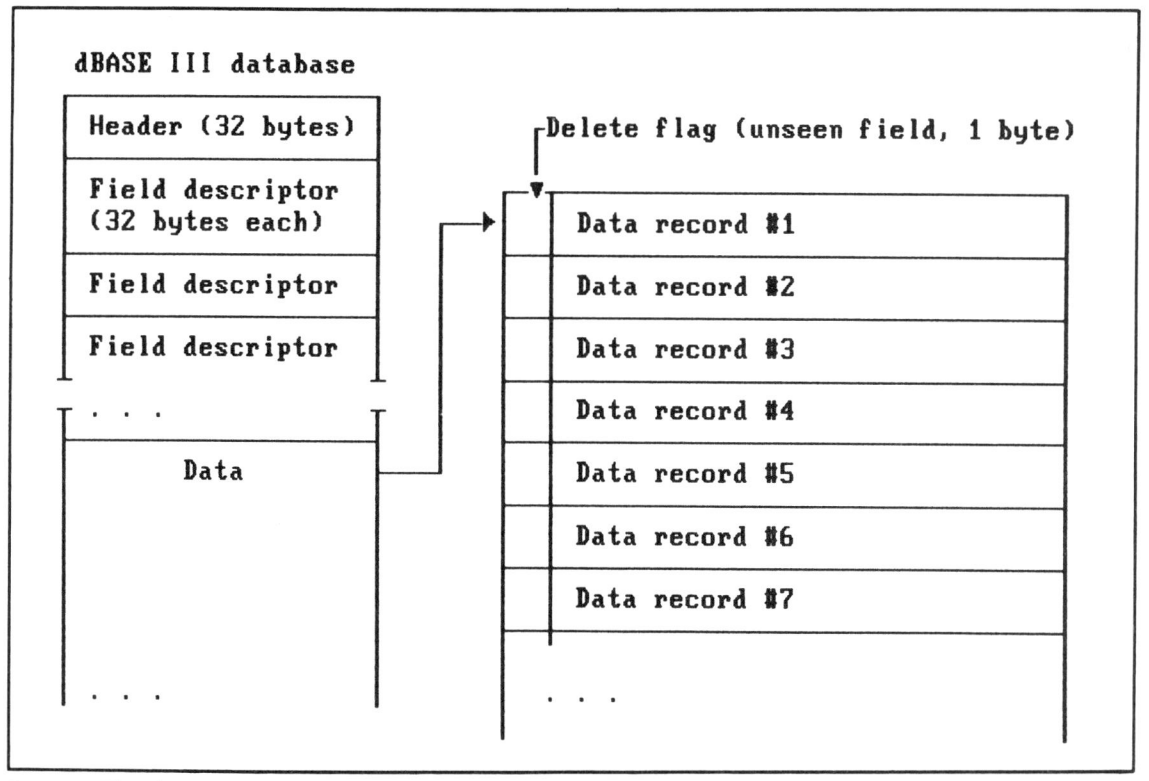

Fig. 16-4. The data structure.

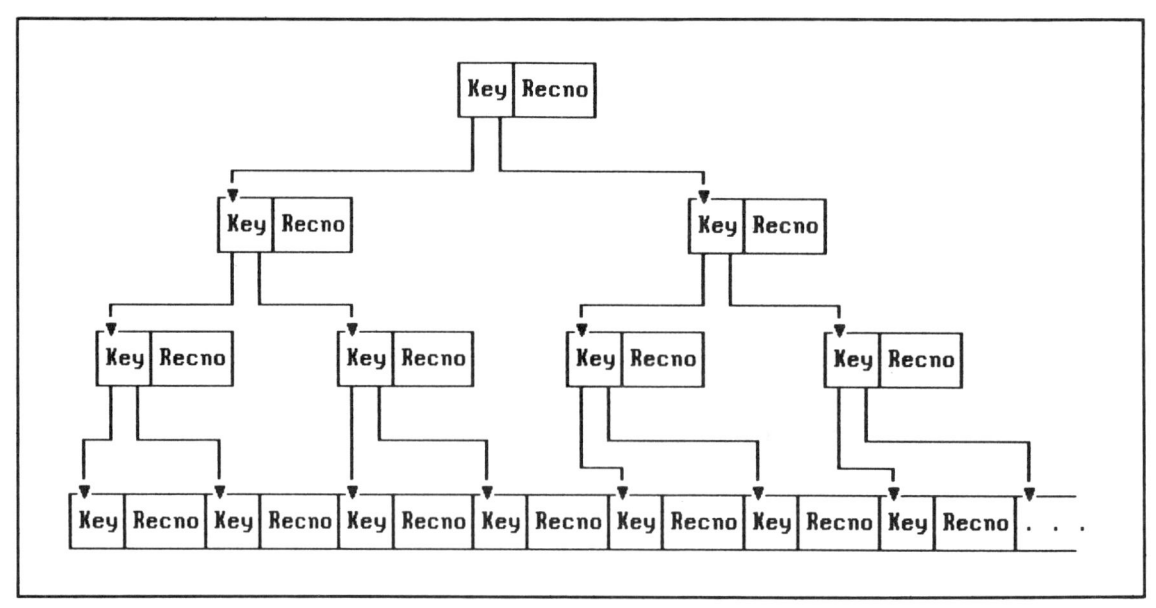

Fig. 16-5. The tree index structure.

The remaining three bytes are not cleared, so that any information existing in this area previously is still present in those three characters. The message "ILLEGAL OPERATION" may result from this, with no apparent reason. This also applies to concatenated keys, formed by joining more than one field as the index key. The overall key length must be a multiple of four to avoid this problem.

The problem described above may not even happen to you in your system. The easiest "workaround" if this problem does occur is to make the index an even multiple of four bytes by adding a SPACE(n) to the key value, where n is the number of characters needed to make up an even multiple of four.

Chapter 17
Fred, Inc.

The growth of Fred's company has created more and more uses for his computer and dBASE III. The applications systems he has created are still performing their functions, and he has decided to purchase another computer, perhaps two. His expertise has increased, due to the amount of time he has spent with the computer; Fred has even learned a traditional programming language, Pascal. His dBASE III programming experiences have lead him further into the world of programming.

REEXAMINING A SYSTEM FOR EFFICIENCY

Fred is now taking a look at the systems he has written, because of the planned purchase. He wants to consolidate and document his "computer plan of action," before the new machines are swept into the everyday grind. The planning that goes into this plan, Fred knows, will greatly enhance his position in the future. After all, he thought, proper planning and design made my application systems work. That same design and planning effort, applied to the overall computer plan, will work just as well.

When Fred considered his system in terms of the rules presented in Fig. 17-1, the first efficiency problem he noticed is the use of the dBASE SOUNDEX program. The number of looping decisions causes the code to take much more time than necessary. Fred decides to move the SOUNDEX algorithm to an external Pascal program. Even with the necessary passing of the data to and from the external program, the SOUNDEX routine executes in less than half the time used by the dBASE routine.

Fred has noticed that the amount of space used by the dBASE procedure files is excessive; he has found that his ten-megabyte hard disk really has a limited quantity of storage available. Ten megs seemed like so much room, at the time! Collapsing the programs and procedures, after they have been debugged, retrieves 50 percent or more of the disk space used by the procedure files.

Fred has also decided on the type of Help system he will use in his systems. Each procedure file will contain a single routine that will handle the

```
┌─────────────────────────────────────────────────────────┐
│  1. Remove unnecessary decisions                        │
│  2. Remove unnecessary function calls                   │
│  3. Eliminate unwanted sequential processing            │
│  4. Collapse or compile programs                        │
│  5. Split processes for non-interactive processing      │
│  6. Reduce I/O operations where possible                │
└─────────────────────────────────────────────────────────┘
```

Fig. 17-1. General rules for speeding up the process.

Help functions. This procedure, shown in Fig. 17-2, is placed at the end of the procedure file, where it can be called when needed.

The Help procedure, shown in Fig. 17-3, contains text Help information for each screen and/or function in the entire procedure file. If the user wants to access this information, he or she enters a Y in a logical field displayed on the screen. The function will interrogate this field, and if a Y has been entered (true), the Help procedure is called. A value is passed to the Help routine that indicates which text is to be displayed.

Some security, Fred realized, is needed in his company because of its growth. It is not always possible to hire only the most loyal or the most honest people, but deliberate sabotage to Fred's systems is highly unlikely. Beside the fact that the information would only be of use to another computerized fish market, Fred has a very vicious watch-lobster. The probability of accidents occurring to the data files, however, increases with the number of people with access to them.

He implements a system of passwords and operator identification codes to ensure that the people who use the machine have a right to do so. Audit trails, in the form of activity logs, will also aid in discovering the cause of accidents and their effects on the system.

Fred realizes that there is no secure way to preserve passwords and operator IDs on a database; he settles for changing the file attribute on that database to hidden and protected. This way, a new operator cannot be added to the system unless the

```
STORE .N. TO SHELP

SET FORMAT TO screen1
STORE 'screen1' to screen1
. . .
STORE .T. TO notdone
DO WHILE notdone
   READ SAVE
   . . .
   IF SHELP
      DO helpproc WITH screen1
   ELSE
      STORE .F. TO notdone
   ENDIF
   . . .
ENDDO
. . .
```

Fig. 17-2. Accessing text help.

```
PROCEDURE HELP
PARAMETERS scrname
DO CASE
    CASE scrname = 'screen1'
        TEXT
        <help information for screen1 goes here>
        ENDTEXT
    CASE scrname = 'screen2'
        TEXT
        <help information for screen2 goes here>
        ENDTEXT
    CASE scrname = 'screen3'
        . . .
    OTHERWISE
        TEXT
        No help available for this screen.
        Notify programmer.
        ENDTEXT
ENDCASE
WAIT
CLEAR
RETURN
```

Fig. 17-3. The Help procedure.

file is unprotected, and the person performing the change knows the name of the database where this information is stored. Like the security system Fred just installed at his house, it will not stop a real pro, but it sure will stop anyone less!

There are several print spooling and disk caching utilities that Fred has been looking at. None of them affect the actual coding of the programs, so the decision on their purchase can be deferred until later. The amount of I/O operations that Fred's systems have is not large enough to need such time-savers, although they may be needed in the future.

After Fred completes the fine-tuning of his existing applications, he uses his experience with them as the basis for his company's computer plan of action.

A COMPUTER PLAN OF ACTION

Using his existing systems as a model, Fred is ready to develop his computer plan of action as outlined in Fig. 17-4. This plan will guide the future computer applications of the company, allowing for growth and new technology. As more and more systems are added to the data processing functions, the planning performed now, at the beginning, will provide a uniform and maintainable structure for the future.

The computer plan of action should be flexible enough to allow for innovation, but firm enough to reduce or eliminate redundant data, duplicated effort, and incompatibilities. Just as the process of system design is a process of evolution, the computer plan of action should grow and change with the company it is supporting.

The first step is to define the purpose of the plan. This can be a narrative that explains the types of computer application covered by the plan. Some computer-assisted techniques can be used by anyone with access to one of the company's computers; the computer can help individuals to "work smarter." The computer plan of action should never limit the actions of this type of user, as long as those actions benefit the company.

On the other hand, applications written by a user or other software developer should not be recognized as a company standard unless those applications conform to the plan. If this rule is compromised even once, the plan will have been rendered useless; in such a case, it would have to be rewritten to include the new situation.

Some companies see this as an excuse to limit the software that their employees use. In a large company, this is perhaps understandable; there are so many software packages on the market that no information center or problem desk could possibly know all of them. Passive limitations are made by "approving" only certain packages and providing assistance only on those packages. Also, large companies use a large number of microcomputers that must all interact with each other and possibly with a mainframe as well. These interactions must be standardized simply for efficiency.

The computer plan of action is meant to lend continuity and conformity to a computer system. If one of Fred's employees needs to learn how to operate a new application, he or she will rest assured that the screen navigation, Help, and

---

```
A Computer Plan of Action

I.   Purpose and scope

II.  Current configuration
        A. Hardware
        B. Software

III. Security
        A. Physical
        B. Software
        C. Requirements for audit trails

IV.  Required development documentation
        A. Design documents
        B. Data Dictionary requirements
        C. Programming standards/guidelines/suggestions

V.   Considerations for growth
        A. Storage requirements
        B. Computing hardware
```

Fig. 17-4. The outline for the computer plan of action.

security functions are all standardized. Standardization of these functions will drastically reduce the time that the employees spend in learning the new system.

The standards set forth in the plan can be as detailed or as vague as the planner wants to make them. If the plan is too detailed, identifying specific software packages and methods, the applications created will be stiff and unyielding where flexibility is desired. Application systems will take longer to develop, and a multitude of exceptions will occur. A plan that is not detailed enough, however, will lead to total loss of control; information that could be vital to the company may be missed because two different applications could not share data due to incompatibility.

The accepted design methodology should also be standardized throughout the company. This can also be either vague or detailed in scope; if the policy is too detailed it will lead to decreased efficiency and lack of innovation. A design methodology that is too detailed will also result in the programmer spending as little time as possible designing the application—and then spending that time after the application has been written! If the accepted design methods are too vague, the result will also be reduced design time—"honor system" designs never seem to get done.

The solution is the Seven Step Method, outlined in Chapter 5. Each of the seven steps requires that a written document be produced, including the problem definition/feasibility study, the output definition, the input definition, and the detailed design of the process. Coding yields the programs themselves as documentation, along with questions raised during walk-throughs of the programs and their resolution. Testing and evaluating a new application produces the testing document, which compares expected results against the actual results achieved.

The formats for these documents should not be specified in the computer plan of action. These documents will take the form and style of the individual designer/programmer. Control is maintained over the design process by not allowing the design to proceed to the next step until the document for the current step is finished. The persons that review the design should examine it carefully to be sure that all the requirements for that step of the design are complete. These requirements can be specified in the plan in a general way. Format of the design documents is not important—the content is!

Other standards that should be set forth in the plan are the use of a data dictionary, if one is available; the location of the backup copies of data and programs; and the use of a library of generic procedures that perform common functions, such as date conversions or SOUNDEX routines. These standards will keep designers and programmers from reinventing the wheel.

General goals of design and standardized functions make up two parts of the computer plan of action. The final part should be predictions for the future, a picture of how the system might look in ten years. This can be extrapolated from existing information by studying the growth-rate of data files and records. This can be used as an estimate of the future hardware and software needs of the system and a guide for the purchase of new machines and/or programs. Tentative solutions for predicted problems may also be recommended.

Now, armed with a computer plan of action and backed by good design techniques and good software, Fred is ready to take on the world of big-time data processing.

Chapter 18
Report Writers

dBASE II and dBASE III feature easy ways to generate reports. dBASE II uses questions to prompt the user for the format of the report. dBASE III contains a menu driven system to create the report format, using the CREAte REPOrt command. Both methods are equally effective in producing reports. dBASE III has made it easier and more visual, which makes it easier to see what you will create.

The first part of this chapter discusses the report creation process in dBASE II and dBASE III. Later, you will see how to create the same report and others using QuickReport by Fox and Geller.

dBASE II AND III REPORT COMMANDS

The database structure found in Fig. 18-1 was used for the reports shown in this section. The data was entered through the normal dBASE commands. The database used for the reports is a sample customer file containing the customer's name, state, date when they became a customer, the amount of merchandise sold to the customer in 1985 and 1984, the amount owed, and the customer's credit limit.

When you are producing a report, the most important item to control is how the output data looks. A report-writer should let you decide which fields to include on the report, what order they will appear in, the width of each field when printed, and the column title. You can also create fields that are the results of calculations using other fields. Another important capability is that of totaling and subtotaling. With dBASE II and dBASE III, you can control all of these options and more.

Figure 18-2 shows the report that was produced by dBASE III. This report can be produced by dBASE II or dBASE III though the methods used to create the format are very different. Many aspects of the report can be controlled: the field CUST_SINCE does not appear in the report. The fields on the report are in a different order than the fields on the database. The column headers are different than the field names as well. Certain fields are totaled in the report, while others are not. Each field is subtotaled by STATE. The last field on the

131

```
. USE CUSTOMER
. DISPLAY STRUCTURE
Structure for database : C:CUSTOMER.dbf
Number of data records :        1
Date of last update    : 08/31/85
Field  Field name  Type        Width    Dec
    1  NAME        Character     15
    2  STATE       Character      2
    3  CUST_SINCE  Character      4
    4  SOLD_1985   Numeric        6
    5  SOLD_1984   Numeric        6
    6  AMT_OWED    Numeric        6
    7  CREDIT      Numeric        6
** Total **                      46
```

Fig. 18-1. A sample dBASE customer Database.

```
                    CUSTOMER REPORT FOR ABC COMPANY
                         PERIOD ENDING 12/31/85

CUSTOMER NAME   SALES FOR   SALES FOR  CREDIT LIMIT  AMOUNT    CREDIT
                YEAR ENDING YEAR ENDING              OWED     AVAILABLE
                   1985        1984


** STATE CA
O'CONNELL         20152        1576        5000      22728     -17728
** Subtotal **
                  20152        1576                  22728


** STATE CT
BOYD                  0           0           0          0          0
DSSWARE INC.       5342      143521           0     148863    -148863
HAYDEN            17563        6745        5000       2300       2700
RINALDI            5252        2314        1500       1500          0
SZEWCZAK            231        2415        1000        500        500
ZARETSKY          32574       14352       15000          0      15000
** Subtotal **
                  60962      169347                 153163


** STATE MA
BROWN             18363       23626       35000      30000       5000
ELIZABANN          2525           0        3000       2000       1000
STAMERIS-CASEY     3521        6352        3500       3000        500
** Subtotal **
                  24409       29978                  35000

*** Total ***
                 105523      200901                 210891
```

Fig. 18-2. A sample dBASE customer Report.

report is the result of a calculation involving two other fields.

Creating a report in dBASE II is a matter of answering a series of questions. As shown in Fig. 18-3, you should first tell dBASE the name of the database to be reported; this one is called CUSTOMER. The second line starts the REPORT sequence. The sequence in Fig. 18-3 creates a report format, also named CUSTOMER. You are given the options to change the left margin, the number of lines per page, and the page width. In this report, the default values are accepted.

To enter a page heading, you would answer the question affirmatively and then type the heading at the prompt. Entering a semicolon (;) in the title indicates that the line will be split at that point.

This series of questions lets you specify how to space the report; you are also prompted to indicate which numeric fields, if any, are to be totaled. dBASE II allows one level of subtotals, which are also known as *control breaks* because each time the specified field changes, a "break" in processing occurs and a subtotal is created.

A summary report means that only the totals would be printed. You can also start each subtotal on a new page by ejecting the page after each subtotal. The subtotal heading is text that will precede each subtotal line.

Once these "housekeeping" functions are taken care of, the user specifies the fields to be printed on the report. dBASE II asks you for the field width necessary to contain the data and the field description/column title. You can also tell dBASE II the field name you want on the report. The field contents and titles are entered for each field on the report, in the order you want them. The last entry in Fig. 18-3 is for a calculated field. This is a field that is not on the database; the value can be calculated by performing operations on fields that do exist on the database.

When you enter a blank field width, dBASE II assumes you are finished and produces the report format. Later you can rerun the report to the printer or to the screen again. If you make any mistakes, or want to make changes in the report format, you will be disappointed. You can make changes by editing the .FRM file, using the dBASE editor or any text or word processor.

Creating a report format file in dBASE III is quite simple; it is as if you simply type in your answers without the questions.

dBASE III includes some needed improvements to the report creation process, as it gives you added flexibility. After you create a report format, you can make all the changes you want. dBASE III also gives you the added flexibility of two different subtotal fields. These changes are extremely important for creating complex reports. Many times after you create a report, you may realize that you have left out a field or that one field is too close to another. dBASE III lets you easily change the report format by following the steps used to create the report. The command to do this is MODIfy REPOrt.

Figure 18-4 shows the first screen that is displayed when the dBASE III command CREAte REPOrt is entered. The fields in the current database can be displayed by pressing function key F1 when you are using any of the menus. Many times, you might forget the exact field name as you begin to create your report format. Without this feature, you would have to leave the report generator and display the database structure.

In each of the multiple screens in the sequence, you may move the cursor anywhere on the screen that is used for an input field. When you move to any subsequent screen, you can go back to a previous screen by simply pressing the up arrow key several times, or by using the PgUp key.

The first screen allows you to enter a four line heading that will appear at the top of each page on the report. You can also enter the page width, margins, lines per page, and the spacing to be used for the report (double or single). This is very similar to dBASE II, except in menu form. Once you finish one screen, the next screen appears.

Figure 18-5 shows the totals report screen. This screen prompts you to enter the field name to be subtotaled along with the subtotal heading, whether or not the report is to be a summary-only report, and whether or not each new group is to appear on a separate page. You can also enter a sub-subtotal

```
. USE CUSTOMER
. REPORT FORM CUSTOMER
ENTER OPTIONS, M=LEFT MARGIN, L=LINES/PAGE, W=PAGE WIDTH
PAGE HEADING? (Y/N) Y
ENTER PAGE HEADING: CUSTOMER REPORT FOR ABC COMPANY;PERIOD ENDING 12/31/85
DOUBLE SPACE REPORT? (Y/N) N
ARE TOTALS REQUIRED? (Y/N) Y
SUBTOTALS IN REPORT? (Y/N) Y
ENTER SUBTOTALS FIELD: STATE
SUMMARY REPORT ONLY? (Y/N) N
EJECT PAGE AFTER SUBTOTALS? (Y/N) N
ENTER SUBTOTAL HEADING: STATE IS
COL     WIDTH,CONTENTS
001     20,NAME
ENTER HEADING: CUSTOMER NAME
002     15,SOLD:1985
ENTER HEADING: SALES FOR;YEAR ENDING;1985
ARE TOTALS REQUIRED? (Y/N) Y
003     15,SOLD:1984
ENTER HEADING: SALES FOR;YEAR ENDING;1984
ARE TOTALS REQUIRED? (Y/N) Y
004     15,CREDIT
ENTER HEADING: CREDIT LIMIT
ARE TOTALS REQUIRED? (Y/N) Y
SUBTOTALS IN REPORT? (Y/N) Y
ENTER SUBTOTALS FIELD: STATE
SUMMARY REPORT ONLY? (Y/N) N
EJECT PAGE AFTER SUBTOTALS? (Y/N) N
ENTER SUBTOTAL HEADING: STATE IS
COL     WIDTH,CONTENTS
001     20,NAME
ENTER HEADING: CUSTOMER NAME
002     15,SOLD:1985
ENTER HEADING: SALES FOR;YEAR ENDING;1985
ARE TOTALS REQUIRED? (Y/N) Y
003     15,SOLD:1984
ENTER HEADING: SALES FOR;YEAR ENDING;1984
ARE TOTALS REQUIRED? (Y/N) Y
004     15,CREDIT
ENTER HEADING: CREDIT LIMIT
ARE TOTALS REQUIRED? (Y/N) N
005     8,AMT:OWED
ENTER HEADING: AMOUNT;OWED
ARE TOTALS REQUIRED? (Y/N) Y
006     7,CREDIT-AMT:OWED
ENTER HEADING: CREDIT;AVAILABLE
ARE TOTALS REQUIRED? (Y/N) N
007
```

Fig. 18-3. The dBASE II Report sequence.

```
Structure of file C:CUSTOMER.dbf
NAME       C  15    SOLD_1984  N  6
STATE      C   2    AMT_OWED   N  6
CUST_SINCE C   4    CREDIT     N  6
SOLD_1985  N   6
```

Page heading:

```
CUSTOMER REPORT FOR ABC COMPANY
      PERIOD ENDING 12/31/85
```

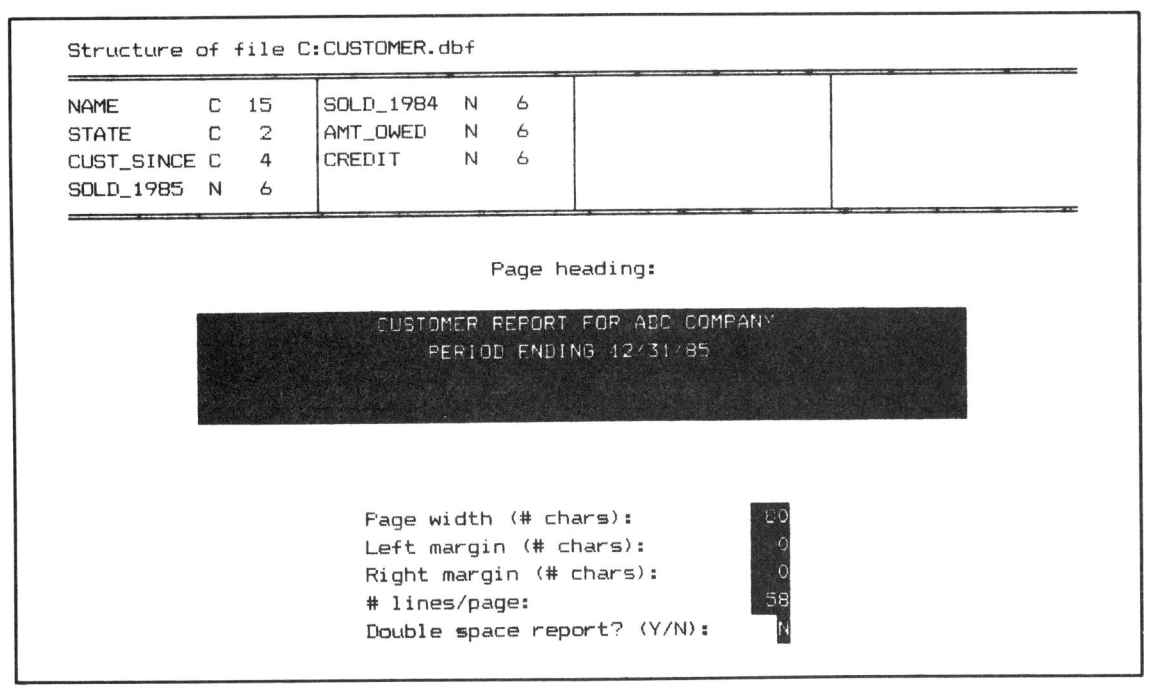

```
Page width (# chars):         80
Left margin (# chars):         0
Right margin (# chars):        0
# lines/page:                 58
Double space report? (Y/N):    N
```

Fig. 18-4. The dBASE III main report screen.

```
Structure of file C:CUSTOMER.dbf
NAME       C  15    SOLD_1984  N  6
STATE      C   2    AMT_OWED   N  6
CUST_SINCE C   4    CREDIT     N  6
SOLD_1985  N   6
```

Group/subtotal on: STATE

Summary report only? (Y/N): N   Eject after each group/subtotal? (Y/N): N

Group/subtotal heading: STATE IS

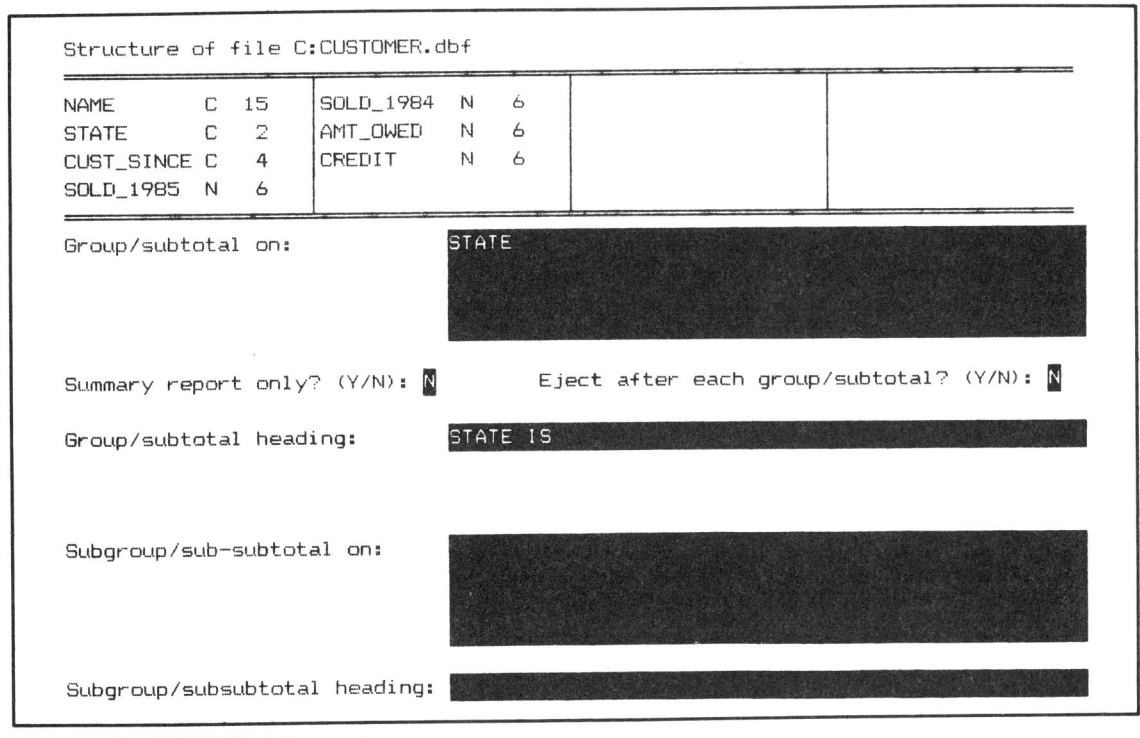

Subgroup/sub-subtotal on:

Subgroup/subsubtotal heading:

Fig. 18-5. The dBASE III totals report screen.

or second-level control break. This screen tells dBASE to create subtotals every time the value of those fields change. If you do not choose to total any fields as you select each field for the report, the breaks will occur without any values being calculated. The subtotal heading, however, will be printed.

After you have completed the dBASE III "housekeeping" menus, you then complete a screen for each of the fields that are to appear on the report. You can move between screens by using the arrow keys or the PgUp/PgDn keys. Fields can be inserted or deleted by using the standard dBASE III insert and delete key combinations (Ctrl-N and Ctrl-T).

Figure 18-6 shows the last in a sequence of six screens. Just under the field names is a visual display of how the data will look. All six fields have been defined. Based on the margins, dBASE III can tell that there are still 10 columns left in which to print data. The field headings are shown first, followed by the approximate position of the fields in the report. The Xs define a character field, while #s depict a numeric field that will be totaled. The 9s indicate a numeric field that will not be totaled.

Each field is defined in the same way. First the field name or calculation is entered in the contents box. If the field is numeric, the number of decimal places can be specified and an indicator set to show whether or not totals are wanted for that field. The field header can be up to four lines of eighty (80) characters each. The width is automatically adjusted to the database field width or the longest line in the field header, whichever is longer. You can adjust the field length if you want to make it longer or shorter.

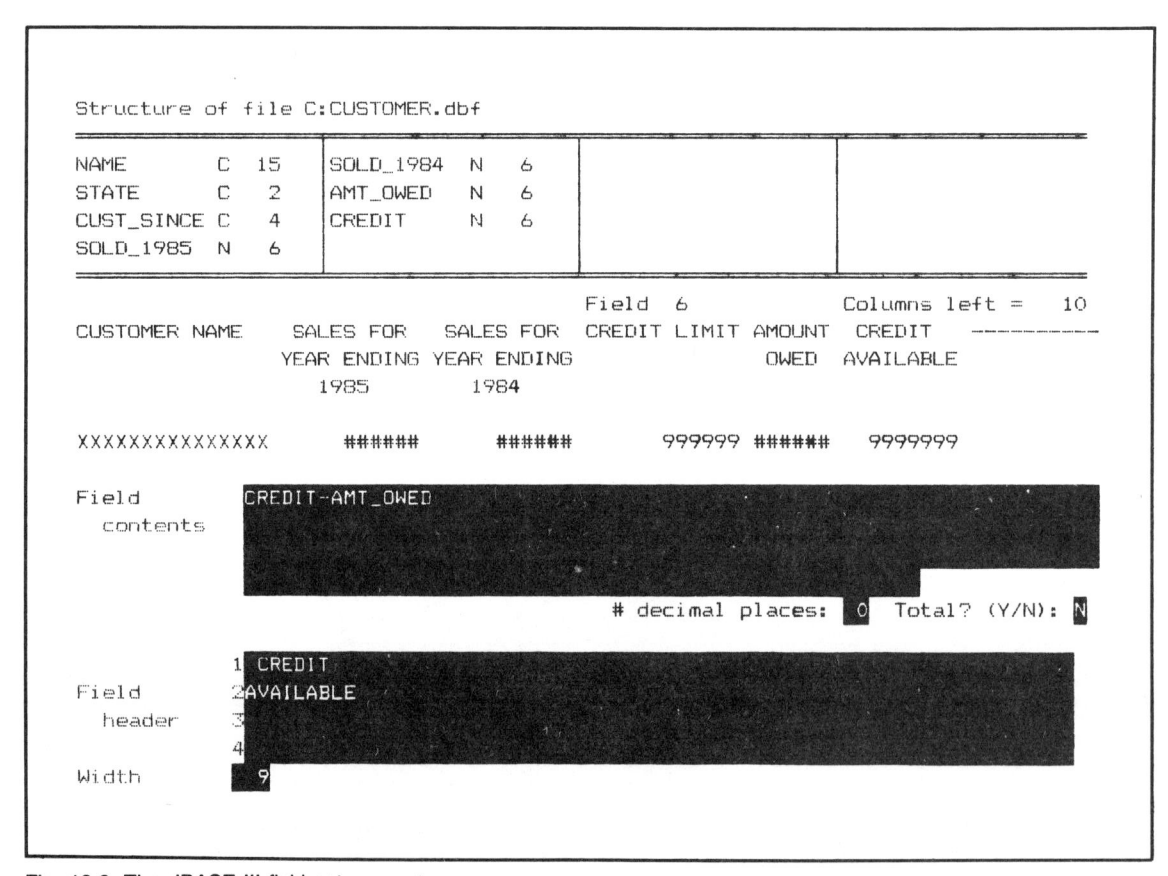

Fig. 18-6. The dBASE III field entry report screen.

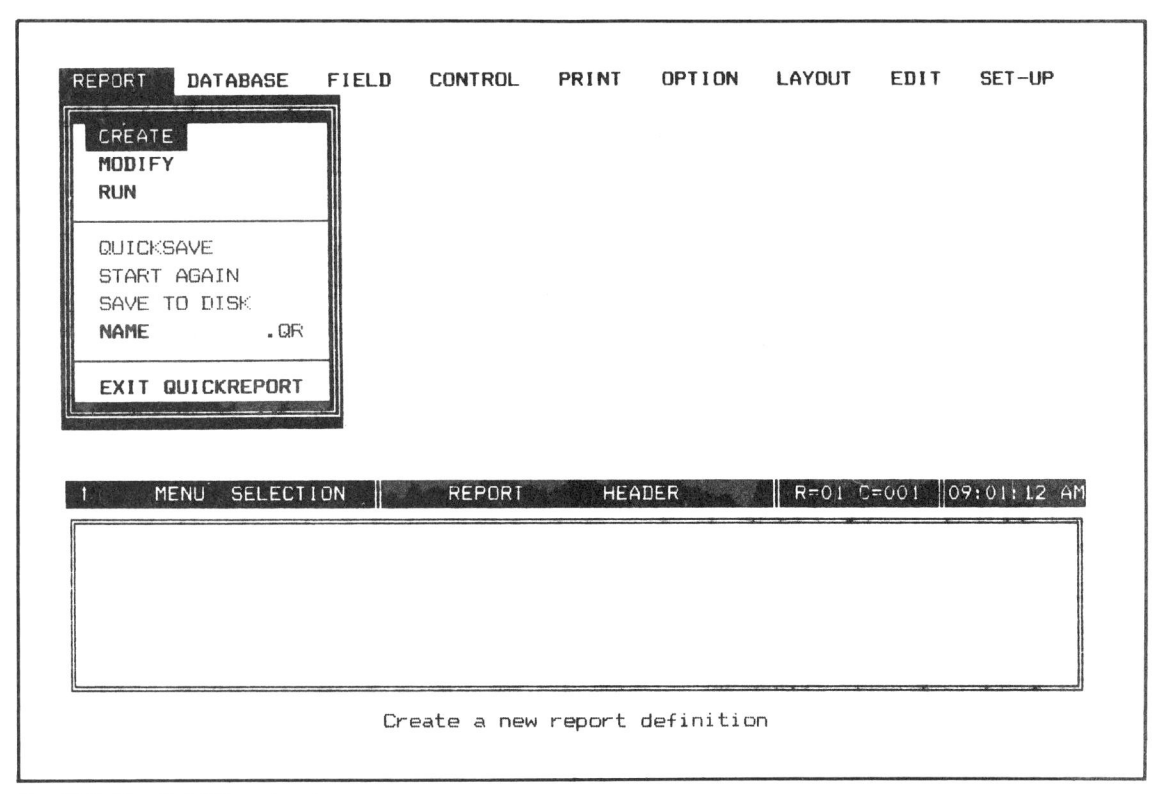

Fig. 18-7. The QuickReport main screen.

Once a field is entered, a new field contents screen is displayed and the previous entries shown in the "visual aid" line.

This is how you create dBASE II and dBASE III report formats. The dBASE III format is much easier to produce and much more powerful than the dBASE II format. There are serious deficiencies in the dBASE report commands that can be addressed by a peripheral product. When you are working with one file, it is usually adequate to use the dBASE report writer. dBASE II offers no way to link multiple files without programming the report directly or using the JOIN command. dBASE III lets you report on files linked together by SET RELAtion. This way data from a second or third file can be easily added to the report format. The commands in dBASE III are simple but require an extra step aside from the REPORT command.

dBASE reports are line-oriented, meaning that data records are displayed across a printed line. A report form, such as an invoice with multiple items, cannot be produced. QuickReport will allow you to do this, and much more.

QUICKREPORT

There is a product by Fox and Geller, called QuickReport, that adds even more power and simplicity to the dBASE reporting process. QuickReport uses pull-down menus and complete prompting, providing an even more sophisticated interface than dBASE III alone. If you have enough RAM memory, it can even be called from within dBASE in place of the dBASE REPORT command, by using the RUN/! command.

When you run QuickReport, the first screen is presented with the Report menu automatically pulled down (Fig. 18-7). *Pull down menus* allow you to choose from menus that are vertically oriented instead of horizontally oriented. The menus remain hidden until you pull them down. These menus are considered easier to use than full-screen menus or those that are horizontally oriented.

You first set your hardware defaults by moving the menu selector to the Set-Up choice at the far right of the screen; this menu allows you to define your hardware configuration, including file paths and printer drivers. The different menus are selected by moving the cursor across the top of the screen. QuickReport uses the box at the bottom of the screen to display the possible choices, which makes it simple to complete the menu. The only menus you can "pull-down" when you first enter QuickReport are the "Report" and the "Set-Up" menus. The hardware selections can be saved or changed at any time. When you enter QuickReport, the previously saved Set-Up entries are retrieved.

The Report menu lets you create, modify, or print a report. It also controls the file commands, such as saving and retrieving report forms, starting over with a blank form, naming your form, and the option for leaving QuickReport.

There are two separate processes involved in printing a report. Once you create or modify a report form, it must be saved before you can use it to print. Once you run a report, it must be retrieved again with the Modify choice before you can make changes.

You choose Create to begin to create the report form; QuickReport automatically guides you through the necessary steps to create a report. Figure 18-8 shows the Database choice. This lets you select the databases that will be used to make up the report. When you choose Select Input File, all databases found in the current disk directory are shown in the box at the bottom of the screen. This lets you visually select the database by moving the cursor within the box. When you press Enter, the chosen file is selected as the primary database. You can also select multiple databases by a process known as linking. This lets you easily combine fields from several databases to create complex reports.

Once you select the database, the fields are shown in a box as shown in Fig. 18-8. If you are only selecting a few fields from the database, you can select them individually. If you are going to use most or all of the fields you can choose Select All. This simply limits the number of fields that will be shown in future displays. If you have a database of a hundred fields and are working only with a few, it is easier to select the ones you need; only those fields will appear in the box.

When you have selected your database files and fields, you are ready to begin creating your report. The process of describing your report to QuickReport is well-designed; you alternate between the "blackboard," where you describe the report, and the pull down menu screens, where you select special functions, such as field formatting, sort order, control breaks (subtotaling), and other functions.

Figure 18-9 shows a blank blackboard. The blackboard is divided into five sections. The Report Header section is used for items that appear before the entire report on a separate page. A memo, cover page, title section, the date, or anything else that you place in this section will appear on a single page preceding the report.

The Page Header appears at the top of each page. Titles and column (field) headers are defined in this section. The Report Body is the most important section. All the text and fields that make up the report go in the Report Body. You can produce everything from a simple report, such as the one shown in the dBASE Report command overview, to complex forms that can be customized for any business.

The Page Footer section is used for totals at the end of each page and/or other items such as page numbers or footnotes. This differs from subtotals, which are placed in the report body through a separate process, which will be discussed later in this chapter. The Report Footer is used for grand-totals and other items that only appear once at the end of a report. Text and data can appear in this section. The field names are shown in the box at the bottom of the page.

QuickReport features an excellent set of on-line help menus. They are *context sensitive*, which means that when you press a certain key, QuickReport knows where you are and offers you help for that

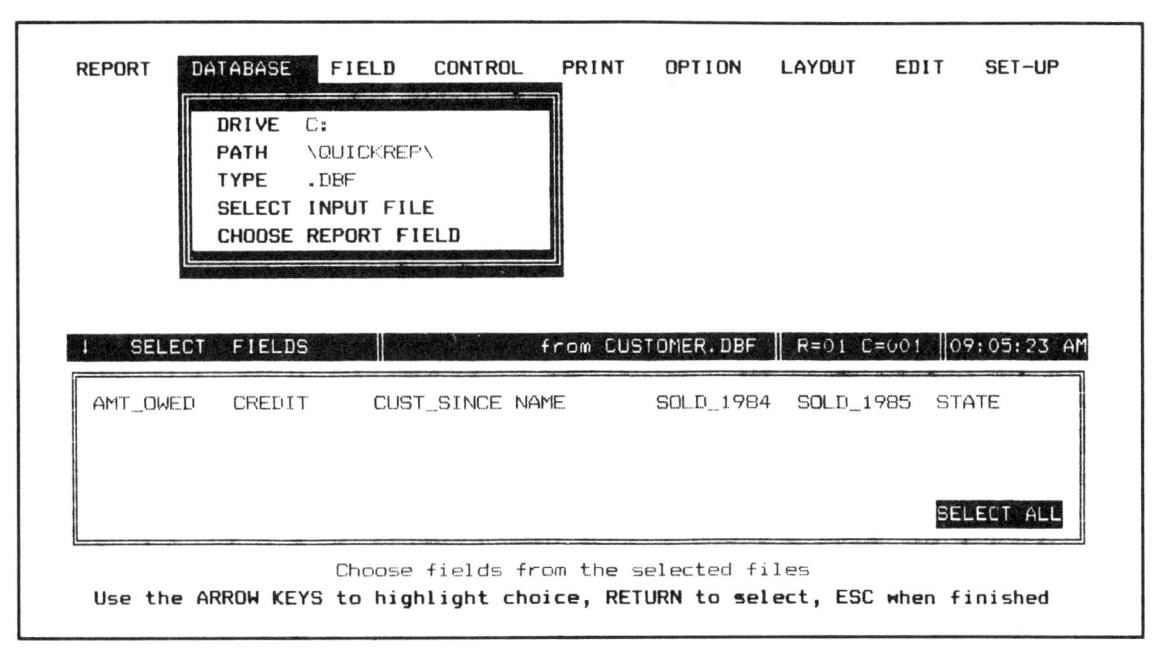

Fig. 18-8. The QuickReport Database Menu screen.

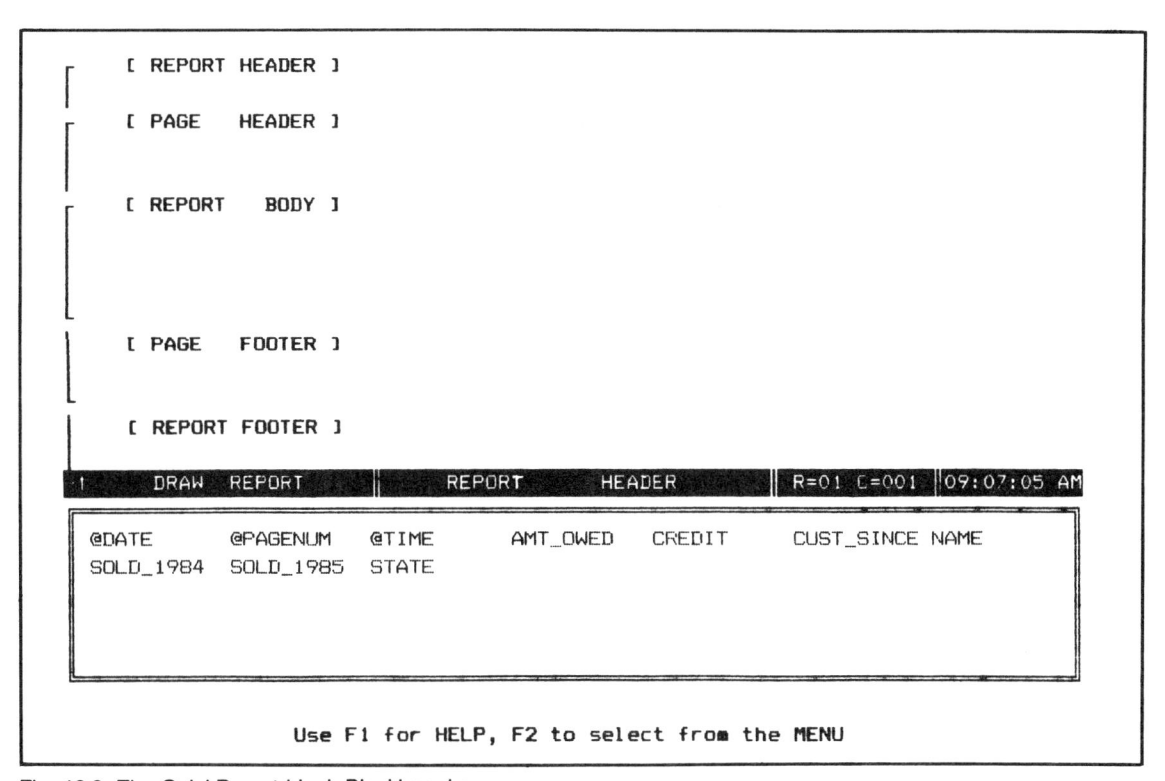

Fig. 18-9. The QuickReport blank Blackboard screen.

139

screen or function. The help screen for the blackboard is shown in Fig. 18-10.

The main report header and column headers are entered first, in much the same way as when you are working with the dBASE report commands. You do not have to enter the headers first, but it makes the most sense. It is much easier to align the data fields in the report after you enter the column headers.

The titles and column headers are entered just as you want to see them appear in the report. Whatever way you space them on the screen will be the way that they are printed out.

As you type in the various areas, the header line disappears. The lines on the left side of the page as well as a description in the status line tell you which section you are working in.

Once you have entered the headers for each page, you may begin to enter the fields that will appear in the report. Figure 18-11 shows a report in progress. The headers have been typed in, and the first three fields have already been defined. The fourth field is in the process of being defined.

Defining the report fields is simple with QuickReport. First, you move the cursor to the place in the Report Body section where you want the field to appear. Next, you press the Get key, which is function key F5. This places the cursor in the box at the bottom of the screen where you can move between the fields and select the field that you want. The fields that are highlighted have already been included in the report. After you have highlighted the field you want, such as Credit in Fig. 18-11, you simply press Enter and the field is placed in the report.

The length of the field determines the alignment and maximum field width in the report. As you can see in Fig. 18-11, the Name field has a longer band than the Sold__1985 and Sold__1984 fields, both of which appear identical in name

```
                    ┌──────────────┐
                    │  BLACKBOARD  │
                    └──────────────┘

  Using the BLACKBOARD is analogous to using a word processor. ANYTHING TYPED on
  the BLACKBOARD will appear in the SAME RELATIVE LOCATION on the report. The
  first time the BLACKBOARD is used, it contains the names of SECTIONS found in a
  typical report. The left hand border shows the dimensions of these sections.

  ⌈     [REPORT HEADER]            Appears ONCE at the beginning of the report.
  |                                Can contain TEXT or the fields @DATE and @TIME.
  ⌈     [PAGE    HEADER]           Appears at the TOP OF EVERY PAGE. Can contain
  |                                TEXT or ANY FIELD.
  ⌈     [REPORT   BODY]            Appears EVERY TIME A RECORD IS READ. Can contain
  ⌊                                TEXT or ANY FIELD.
  ⌈     [PAGE    FOOTER]           Appears at the BOTTOM OF EVERY PAGE. Can contain
  ⌊                                TEXT or ANY FIELD.
  ⌈     [REPORT FOOTER]            Appears ONCE at the END OF THE REPORT. Can
  ⌊                                contain TEXT or ANY FIELD.
                                                                 continued . . .


        Press RETURN for more HELP, F1 for a list of HELP TOPICS, ESC to exit
```

Fig. 18-10. The QuickReport Blackboard Help screen.

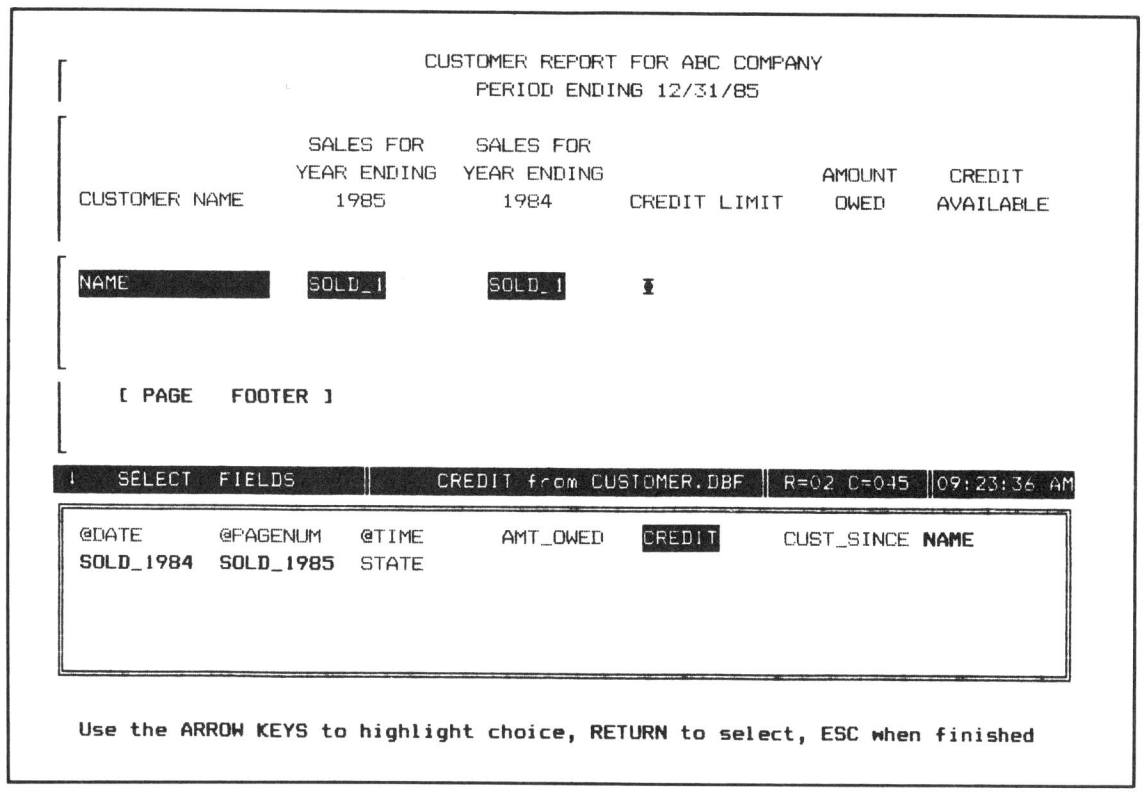

```
┌─────────────────────────────────────────────────────────────────────────┐
│                      CUSTOMER REPORT FOR ABC COMPANY                    │
│ ┌                      PERIOD ENDING 12/31/85                            │
│ ┌                                                                       │
│                SALES FOR    SALES FOR                                   │
│                YEAR ENDING  YEAR ENDING              AMOUNT    CREDIT   │
│  CUSTOMER NAME    1985         1984    CREDIT LIMIT   OWED    AVAILABLE │
│ ┌                                                                       │
│  [NAME        ]  [SOLD_1]    [SOLD_1]       I                           │
│ ┌                                                                       │
│                                                                         │
│       [ PAGE    FOOTER ]                                                │
│ ┌                                                                       │
│ ┌─ SELECT  FIELDS ──────── CREDIT from CUSTOMER.DBF ── R=02 C=045 ─ 09:23:36 AM ─┐
│ │ @DATE       @PAGENUM    @TIME      AMT_OWED    CREDIT     CUST_SINCE  NAME     │
│ │ SOLD_1984   SOLD_1985   STATE                                                  │
│ │                                                                                │
│ │                                                                                │
│ └────────────────────────────────────────────────────────────────────────────────┘
│                                                                         │
│  Use the ARROW KEYS to highlight choice, RETURN to select, ESC when finished │
└─────────────────────────────────────────────────────────────────────────┘
```

Fig. 18-11. The QuickReport Blackboard screen.

because of the field width (four characters). Figure 18-12 shows how to change the field width on the report.

You can switch between the blackboard and the menu selection screen with a single key. The menu selection screen is where you add the details to your reports. Figure 18-12 shows the screen with the Field menu pulled down. A new field is being defined called Avail, and it is being defined as a calculation. When a name is typed in the Name field that does not appear on the database, QuickReport assumes it is a new field created by a calculation.

The formula for any calculated field is typed in the center of the screen above the field box. You cannot just type in the field names; QuickReport always lets you select the fields by pressing the Get key. You can then move the cursor to the field that you want, press Enter, and it appears in the formula you are creating. When you are through, the new field is added to the existing fields. You still must add it to the report at the place where you want it to appear.

Other items in the field menu let you choose the type of formula you want to create. Fields that are simply mathematical relations of other fields are entered as in Fig. 18-12. Other formulas must be selected from the Field menu. Many dBASE III functions are displayed on the menu when you choose the -more- option. As you choose the functions, they will appear on the formula line. When you are done, you can add the new variable to the report. A variable must be created before you can make it into a formula.

This process allows you to create subtotal and total fields for the report. You will need a second variable for each field you wish to total or subtotal. One variable can be used for totals and subtotals for the same field.

The control menu pulls down to reveal options to describe the Sort Order, Break Groups, and Ex-

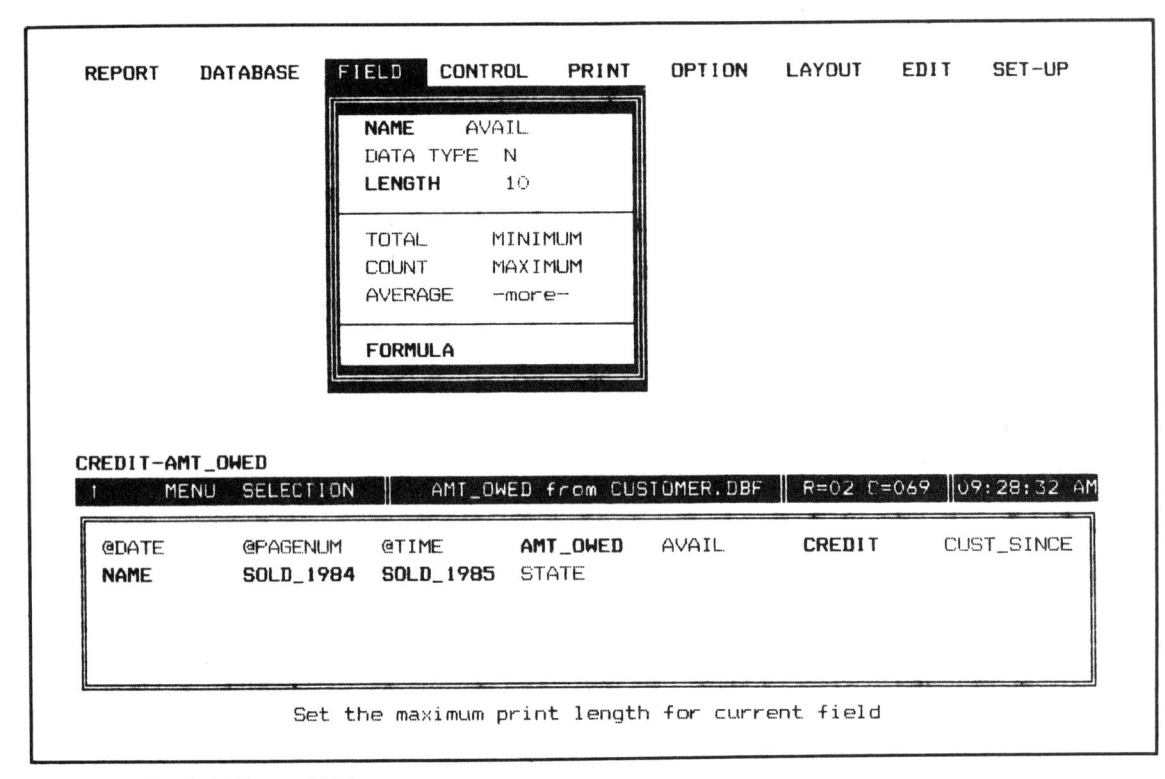

```
    REPORT    DATABASE    FIELD    CONTROL    PRINT    OPTION    LAYOUT    EDIT    SET-UP
                          NAME      AVAIL
                          DATA TYPE  N
                          LENGTH    10

                          TOTAL     MINIMUM
                          COUNT     MAXIMUM
                          AVERAGE   -more-

                          FORMULA

 CREDIT-AMT_OWED
 │   1    MENU  SELECTION  │ AMT_OWED from CUSTOMER.DBF │ R=02 C=069 │ 09:28:32 AM

   @DATE       @PAGENUM    @TIME       AMT_OWED    AVAIL      CREDIT      CUST_SINCE
   NAME        SOLD_1984   SOLD_1985   STATE


                    Set the maximum print length for current field
```

Fig. 18-12. The QuickReport Field menu.

tract Criteria. The Sort Order allows you to specify a sort key for QuickReport to index the database file by. You can have up to 16 levels of sorting.

The Break Groups will create new headers on the blackboard around the first and last line of the report body. The control breaks are listed in order from major to minor, each having a header section and footer section. If you had three different breaks, COMPANY, DEPARTMENT, and NAME, with each record containing a date and payroll amount, the report body would appear like this:

```
COMPANY HEADER
   DEPARTMENT HEADER
      NAME HEADER
         Date Payroll
      NAME FOOTER
   DEPARTMENT FOOTER
COMPANY FOOTER
```

You could then place any text or fields in each header or footer line. You would probably have some type of header with the field name in each header line, while the footer line might contain some type of description or total formula for that field. Up to sixteen levels of control breaks may be specified.

The criteria selection lets you decide, much like the dBASE REPOrt command, which records you want to select. You can include or exclude any combination of records.

A final report description is shown in Fig. 18-13. The headers appear first in the headers section. The Report Body section shows the Break Header, which specifies that the only field to break on is STATE. This was described in the Control menu. The text "STATE HEADER" is replaced with "STATE IS" and the field STATE. Only the first two characters of state are shown because it is a two character field. Each time a new state is read from the database the report lines for that state

```
                    CUSTOMER REPORT FOR ABC COMPANY
                         PERIOD ENDING 12/31/85

                    SALES FOR    SALES FOR
                   YEAR ENDING  YEAR ENDING               AMOUNT      CREDIT
   CUSTOMER NAME      1985         1984     CREDIT LIMIT   OWED      AVAILABLE

       STATE IS ST
   NAME                SOLD_1       SOLD_1       CREDIT       AMT_OW   AVAIL

     Subtotal:       TOTAL85      TOTAL84                   TOTALAMT

    [ PAGE    FOOTER ]

     GrandTotal:     TOTAL85      TOTAL84                   TOTALAMT
  1    DRAW   REPORT            STATE       FOOTER       R=01 C=004  09:56:33 AM

   @DATE      @PAGENUM    @TIME      AMT_OWED   AVAIL      CREDIT       NAME
   SOLD_1984  SOLD_1985   STATE      TOTAL84    TOTAL85    TOTALAMT
```

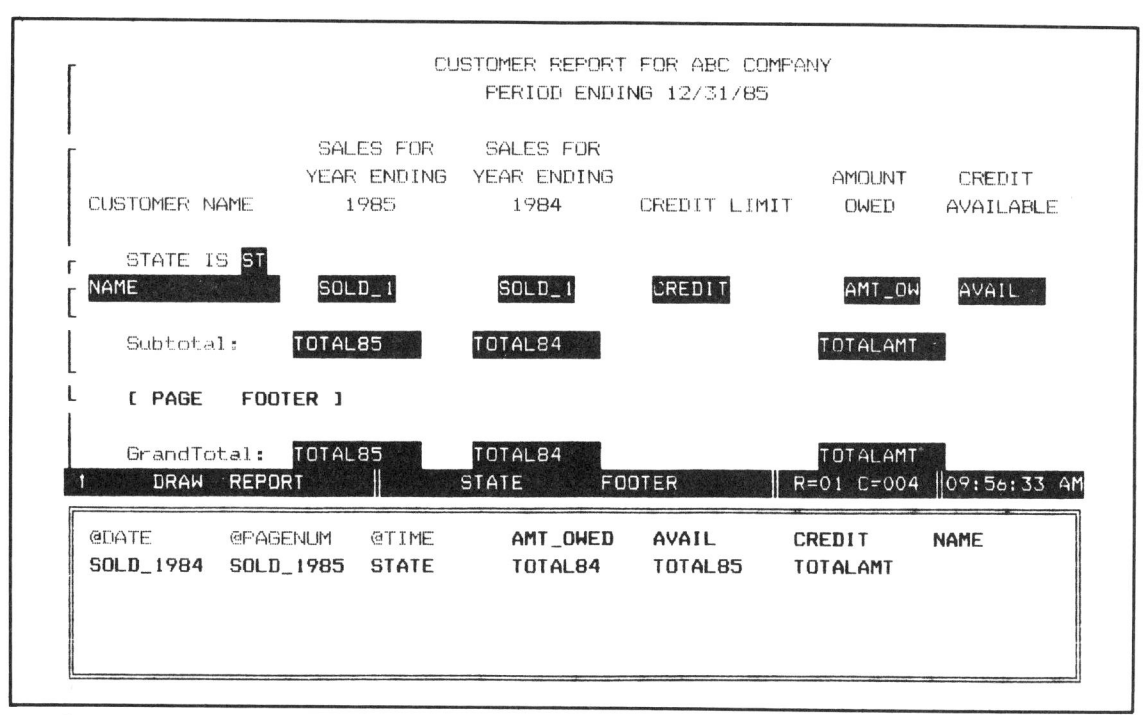

Fig. 18-13. The QuickReport Final description.

```
                    CUSTOMER REPORT FOR ABC COMPANY
                         PERIOD ENDING 12/31/85

                    SALES FOR    SALES FOR
                   YEAR ENDING  YEAR ENDING               AMOUNT      CREDIT
   CUSTOMER NAME      1985         1984     CREDIT LIMIT   OWED      AVAILABLE

       STATE IS CA
   O'CONNELL          20152         1576        5000       22728      -17728
     Subtotal:        20152         1576                   22728

       STATE IS CT
   BOYD                   0            0           0           0           0
   DSSWARE INC.        5342       143521           0      148863     -148863
   HAYDEN             17563         6745        5000        2300        2700
   RINALDI             5252         2314        1500        1500           0
   SZEWCZAK             231         2415        1000         500         500
   ZARETSKY           32574        14352       15000           0       15000
     Subtotal:        60962       169347                  153163

       STATE IS MA
   BROWN              18363        23626       35000       30000        5000
   ELIZABANN           2525            0        3000        2000        1000
   STAMERIS-CASEY      3521         6352       35000        3000       32000
     Subtotal:        24409        29978                   35000


     GrandTotal:     105523       200901                  210891
```

Fig. 18-14. The QuickReport Report.

will be preceded by "STATE IS".

The six fields in the report appear below the subtotal header, with the subtotal footer following the fields. This footer will print subtotals for three different fields. SOLD__1985, SOLD__1984, and AMT__OWED. These three fields were selected with the Field menu, and will be preceded by the text Subtotal:.

After the break footer is the Report Footer. This includes the text "Grand Total" and totals for the three fields that were subtotaled. The same field is used to contain the subtotals and totals.

The final report generated from this code is shown in Fig. 18-14. This is just about the same report as generated with dBASE. For this type of report, QuickReport was easier to use but actually

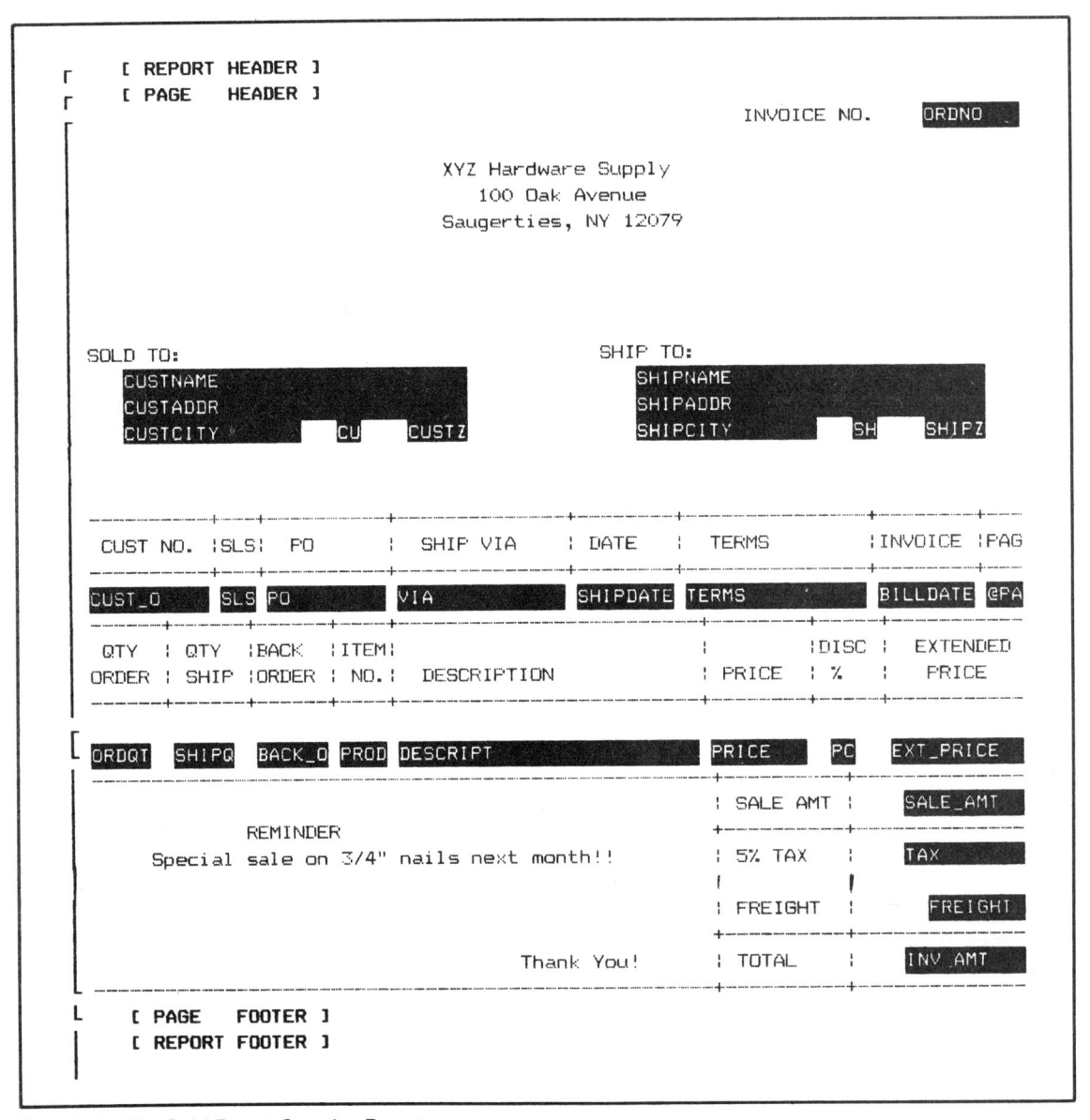

Fig. 18-15. The QuickReport Complex Report.

took a little longer to create. Its true power lies in its ability to create more complex reports.

The first complex task would be to add formatting control to the report. This defines how numbers look, including the number of decimals, and also how zeros, negative numbers, and large numbers would appear. It would let you control dollar signs and fill characters to handle check protection, like the dBASE PICTURE strings used with @ . . . SAY. The Option menu allows the user to handle these with ease. Simply choose a field and format it.

The true power of QuickReport shines when you need nonstandard reports that look like forms instead of lists of numbers with a few headers and totals.

QuickReport lets you create perfect forms as well as adding lines to the report for clarity and expression. Figure 18-15 shows a complex form from the QuickReport sample library. The entire form is created in the Report Body section, because each page is an entire invoice. There is no need for page headers as the report contains its own headers. Each form will be printed on one page.

The interesting thing about this report is that is uses multiple files. The information that is needed for the middle of the Invoice file comes from several files. Through a simple process known as *linking*, you can create reports that use many different files. You must have a common key field known as a lookup (or search) field. This is standard with dBASE relational database technology. This report would take the Sold To and Ship To data from one database. The CUST_O (customer order) line each would be filled with one piece of data. The detail lines of the report (ORDQT through EXT _Price) would produce one line of output for each line in the file that matches the invoice number. If there were ten records in the file, the detail section of the report would contain ten records.

QuickReport can probably take care of all of your reporting needs. It is fun to use and easy to learn. The only drawback is the documentation. It is for the most part well-done, although the advanced section is skimpy. There are plenty of diagrams and pictures. The documentation is photo reduced instead of typeset. It is in extremely small type and is very difficult to read. A magnifying glass would help you learn QuickReport. Other than that, this is the best of Fox & Geller's products; it is the most advanced and useful. This is one product that we strongly recommend. It is an excellent supplement to dBASE.

Chapter 19
Screen and Program Generators

Screen and program generators are still in their functional infancy. They exist, but still at rudimentary levels. A screen generator should let you create a screen format that looks exactly like your screen would look. It should create the dBASE code to let you enter, validate, and display data. You should be able to precisely control placement of text and data fields. You should be able to create computational fields for output as well as format data fields.

The more closely the screen you create resembles the screen that the user sees when displayed from dBASE, the better the package. The dBASE code it generates should be compatible with dBASE II or dBASE III. The code produced must allow easy customization and use few (if any) undocumented tricks. You should be able to create any screen that you can create with dBASE in less time and with less effort.

Beyond screen generators are program generators. A screen generator by definition only generates the dBASE code to handle the input and display of the screen, that is, the @ . . . SAY . . . GET commands. A program generator creates the code for an entire system, which may include displaying, adding, editing, and deleting data. It may also include code to sort, search, select, and produce reports from the data.

There are several screen editors and program generators on the market. The market was dominated for the first year by one program; QuickCode by Fox & Geller, the leading dBASE add-on producer. Later, Ashton-Tate bought the rights to the Screen Editor, a program written by WallSoft Systems to create screens and generate limited amounts of code. With dBASE III, both these products were improved. Until late 1985 these remained the best products. A new product called FlashCode by Software Bottling Company was released in August of 1985 and is sure to be a hit. Screen Editor, FlashCode, and QuickCode III will all be discussed in this chapter. Each package has its own set of pros and cons.

Screen Editor is only a screen generator. It produces simple screens easily and lets you create code "around" the generated code to build your system. FlashCode and QuickCode III both are full program and screen generators. Both let you generate just the screen or a complete dBASE system. There is a version of QuickCode III called QuickCode, which works with dBASE II.

FlashCode has a marvelous screen generator. It creates dBASE II or dBASE III code from a single program. It features a simple-to-use graphics drawing tablet and excellent control of color. Several innovative menus control the field definition to a fine degree. It uses pop-up and pull-down technology to provide a very modern user interface to create screens.

QuickCode III generates slightly easier programs and lets you control which modules you want generated. QuickCode also makes it easier to customize your programs. As you read the reviews of the various programs, you can decide which is best for you.

SCREEN EDITOR

The first thing you may notice as you read your dBASE manual is that there is a screen generator quietly hidden in the documentation. Actually, it is hidden on the dBASE III utility disk. The documentation only mentions it. The documentation for the screen editor is on the disk as well. WallSoft Systems, a company that makes an excellent debugging tool described in a later chapter, is the author of this screen generator. It is simply called SED. When you run SED you see the menu in Fig. 19-1.

The Screen Editor has few options. You can edit or create a new file or generate a dBASE program. Much like the report writers, you enter your screen format on a blank screen following a few rules that concern areas such as what the name of your fields are, how wide they are, and what data

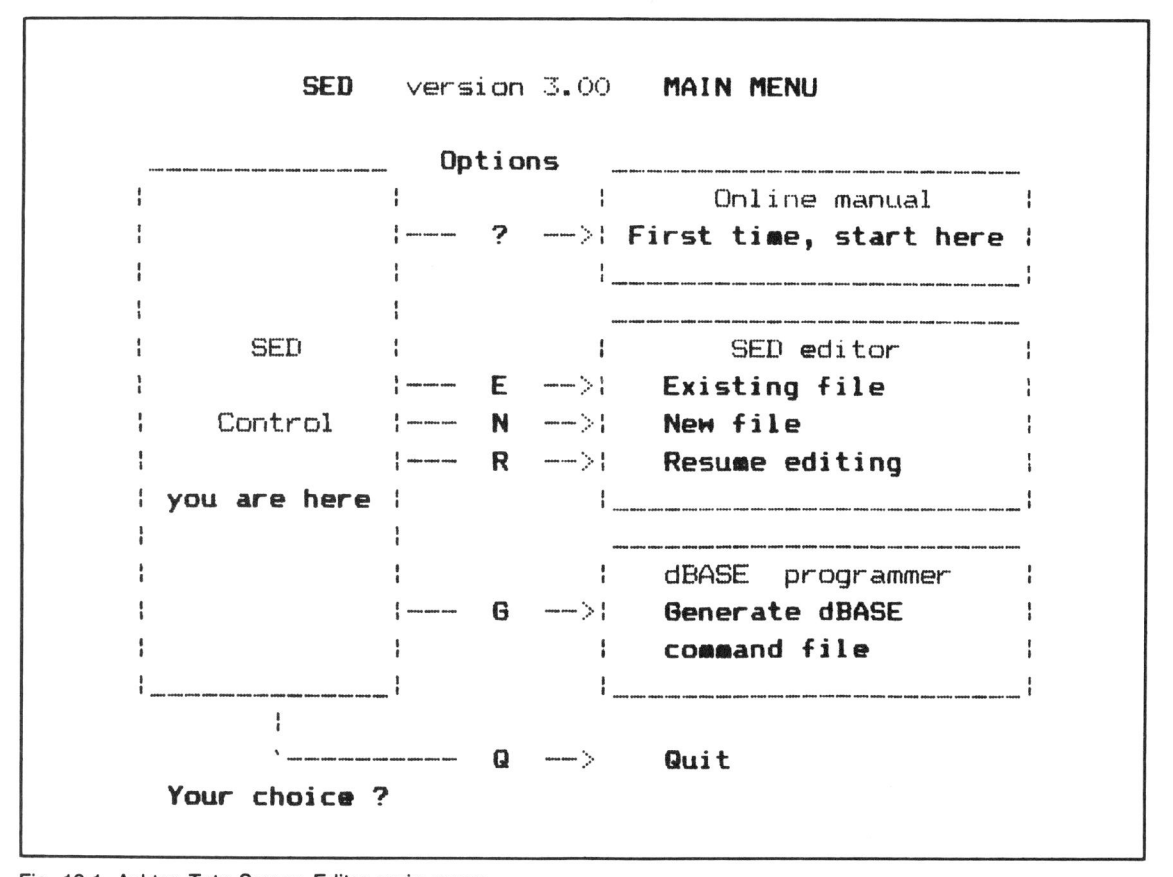

```
           SED    version 3.00    MAIN MENU

    _____       Options    _____
    |              |   |        |   Online manual           |
    |              |---- ? --->| First time, start here    |
    |              |   |        |_____|
    |              |   |
    |     SED      |   |         _____
    |              |   |        |   SED editor              |
    |              |---- E --->| Existing file             |
    |   Control    |---- N --->| New file                  |
    |              |---- R --->| Resume editing            |
    | you are here |   |        |_____|
    |              |   |
    |              |   |         _____
    |              |   |        | dBASE   programmer        |
    |              |---- G --->| Generate dBASE            |
    |              |   |        | command file             |
    |_____|   |        |_____|
            |
            `_____-- Q -->   Quit
     Your choice ?
```

Fig. 19-1. Ashton-Tate Screen Editor main menu.

type they are. The simplest way to explain how the Screen Editor works is to show a sample help screen. Figure 19-2 shows the first help screen that you see.

The concept behind a screen editor is that there has to be a way to enter text and data fields. There also should be a way to further define those fields in terms of size and formatting. SED handles all of these problems simply.

Figure 19-2 shows the traditional way that SED works. You type into a blank data entry form. SED produces dBASE code, and the code can then be integrated within your dBASE program.

SED uses a variety of symbols to describe the attributes of the data fields. In Fig. 19-2, you can see that the less than (<) sign is used to denote a field.

Figure 19-3 shows the screen that might have been used to input the data that was used in the examples in the previous chapter. Fields that do not begin with any special characters are text fields, and would be displayed with the @ . . . SAY commands. These include field headers such as NAME, STATE, and CUSTOMER SINCE. The field names that are on the database are preceded by the < symbol. When Screen Editor sees this, it creates the code with the @ . . . GET command.

You can format the field entry by using the ! character directly after the field name. In Fig. 19-3 the NAME field is defined as !"AAAAAAAAAAAAAAA". This means that only alphabetic characters are allowed, and it will be fifteen characters wide when displayed. The definition of CREDIT is !"999999". This identifies a numeric field 6 digits long.

The last field in the example, CREDIT AVAILABLE, uses a > in front of the field. This denotes a display only (or output) field. dBASE will only generate the @ . . . SAY command, because it is not a database variable. The field name is not a field name are all but a calculation. This is how SED lets you input formulas for display fields.

In this simple example, you can see how easy it is to describe a screen to SED. When you return to the main menu shown in Fig. 19-1 and press G, the dBASE command file is generated as shown in Fig. 19-4.

SED documents the code with a single comment indicating the program name. The @ . . . SAY . . . GET positions are generated in precisely the same locations as the fields are typed on the SED screen. Picture clauses are used to describe the field attributes. Once this code is generated, it can easily be incorporated into your dBASE program.

When this code is run from dBASE it produces the simple screen shown in Fig. 19-5. SED does not perform any validation or range checking, but this can easily be added. SED only generates the screen display portion of your code. This is the job of a screen editor and generator. Going beyond these simple functions would require a program generator, as described in the next sections.

One final advanced feature of SED is its ability to let you place dBASE code directly into the SED

```
You type a template        SED writes dBASE commands        dBASE runs
------------------                                          ------------------
: Data entry form :                                         : Data entry form :
:                 :         @ 1,2 SAY "Data entry form"     :                 :
: Name            :         @ 3,2 SAY "Name"                : Name            :
: <name           :         @ 4,2 GET name                  : :             : :
:                 :         @ 6,2 SAY "Age"                 :                 :
: Age <age        :         @ 6,6 GET age                   : Age :   :       :
: Sex <sex        :         @ 7,2 SAY "Sex"                 : Sex : :         :
:_____:         @ 7,6 GET sex                   :_____:
```

Fig. 19-2. Ashton-Tate Screen Editor Help menu.

```
    NAME:    <NAME!"AAAAAAAAAAAAAAA"

    STATE:       <STATE!"AA"

    CUSTOMER SINCE: <CUST_SINCE!"9999"

    SALES:       1985                        1984

           <SOLD_1985!"999999"      <SOLD_1984!"999999"

    AMOUNT OWED:     <AMT_OWED!"999999"

    CREDIT:          <CREDIT!"999999"

    CREDIT AVAILABLE:    >AMT_OWED-CREDIT!"999999
```

Fig. 19-3. Screen Editor entry code.

screen. When the dBASE program is generated, the dBASE code will be added to the generated code. This way you can generate more than just the screen with the SED editor. Figure 19-6 shows one of the SED help menus. It shows how the dBASE code can be added into the SED screen. The bracket characters are used to contain the dBASE code. Comments can be coded into the SED screen

```
* CARY.PRG
@ 4,4 SAY "NAME:"
@ 4,12 GET NAME PICTURE "AAAAAAAAAAAAAAA"
@ 6,4 SAY "STATE:"
@ 6,15 GET STATE PICTURE "AA"
@ 8,4 SAY "CUSTOMER SINCE:"
@ 8,21 GET CUST_SINCE PICTURE "9999"
@ 10,4 SAY "SALES:      1985                        1984"
@ 12,13 GET SOLD_1985 PICTURE "999999"
@ 12,39 GET SOLD_1984 PICTURE "999999"
@ 14,4 SAY "AMOUNT OWED:"
@ 14,20 GET AMT_OWED PICTURE "999999"
@ 16,4 SAY "CREDIT:"
@ 16,20 GET CREDIT PICTURE "999999"
@ 18,4 SAY "CREDIT AVAILABLE:"
@ 18,24 SAY AMT_OWED-CREDIT PICTURE "999999
```

Fig. 19-4. dBASE Code generated by SED.

```
       NAME:     ████████████████

       STATE:    ███

       CUSTOMER SINCE:  ██████

       SALES:     1985                    1984

                        ██████              ██████

       AMOUNT OWED:     ██████

       CREDIT:          ██████

       CREDIT AVAILABLE:      0
```

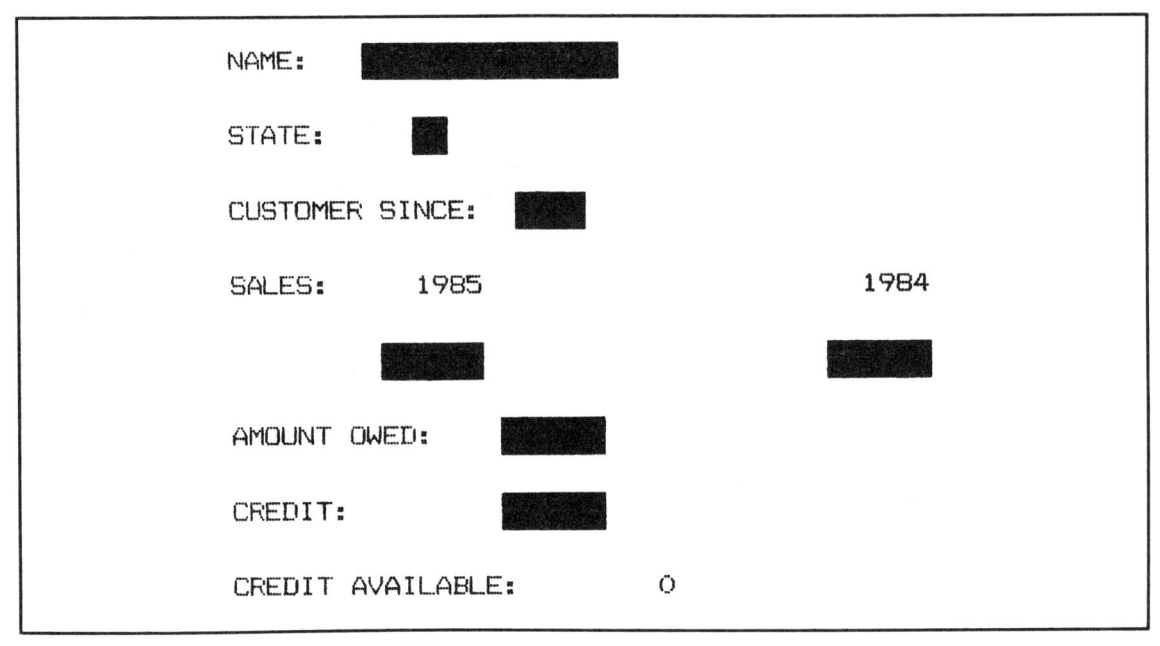

Fig. 19-5. dBASE Screen generated by SED.

by starting a line with an asterisk.

A feature of dBASE III that addressed the problem of boring screens was the capability to draw graphic borders around screens. SED features block commands that let you place lines and boxes around any portion of the screen. These lines are copied into the @ . . . SAY commands when SED generates the dBASE code.

This is a quick review of the most important features of the simple screen editor that comes with dBASE. As new products are placed on the market, they become better and better. The newest of these is FlashCode. The next section will thoroughly describe FlashCode and its amazing abilities.

```
 ----------------------------------
 :* open data base, add record    :        * open data base, add record
 : [USE namefile]  [APPEND BLANK] :        USE namefile
 : [CLEAR]                        :        APPEND BLANK
 :                                :        CLEAR
 :    Enter client's name         :        @ 4,4 SAY ."Enter client's name"
 :    <c_name                     :        @ 5,4 GET c_name
 :                                :
 :    Enter client's address      :        @ 7,4 SAY  "Enter client's address"
 :    <address                    :        @ 8,4 GET address
 :                                :        * read new data, close file
 :* read new data, close file     :        READ
 : [READ] [USE]                   :        USE
 :_____:
```

Fig. 19-6. SED Help Menu example of advanced features.

FLASHCODE

When you first start FlashCode you notice something exciting about it right away. As shown in Fig. 19-7, the main logo is flashy, and if you have a color monitor, it is colorful. FlashCode was designed by a company called The Software Bottling Company of New York. Rumor has it that its name came from its first location, next to the Pepsi bottling plant in Purchase, New York. Wherever it came from, Software Bottling Company is fairly well-known for its earlier product Screen Sculptor, a program generator that creates BASIC or PASCAL code from an excellent screen editor.

Software Bottling Company has a lot of experience in the field of program generators; they have transcribed their Screen Sculptor program nicely to become FlashCode for dBASE II and dBASE III. The program evolved and improved as a result of spending over a year on the market as Screen Sculptor. It is surprising that they did not name the dBASE version "Screen Sculptor for dBASE," but even with an unknown name this program is expected to sell very well.

FlashCode is written in assembly language and Turbo Pascal for optimum speed and flexibility. It uses wonderful monochrome graphics to present its user interface. If you have a color monitor, it uses colors correctly. Many packages present you with a dazzling array of colors that only confuse the user; FlashCode and Screen Sculptor do not. The people at Software Bottling Company are very skilled at contemporary screen design.

The package uses the latest technology of pop-up and pull-down menus like other best-selling products. These types of menus are the simplest to use and can be the most flexible to program.

The FlashCode documentation is well written and produced. It is nicely typeset and only falls short in a few areas. It assumes you have used dBASE beyond the novice level. This is unfortunate, because in some cases, the program is far easier to use than the manual describes. The manual also suffers as most manuals do, from a lack of screen photographs. There are brilliant screens as well as an excellent on-line help facility, and none of these are apparent from reading the manual. This does not hurt the program, however, because it stands by itself.

Fig. 19-7. FlashCode startup screen.

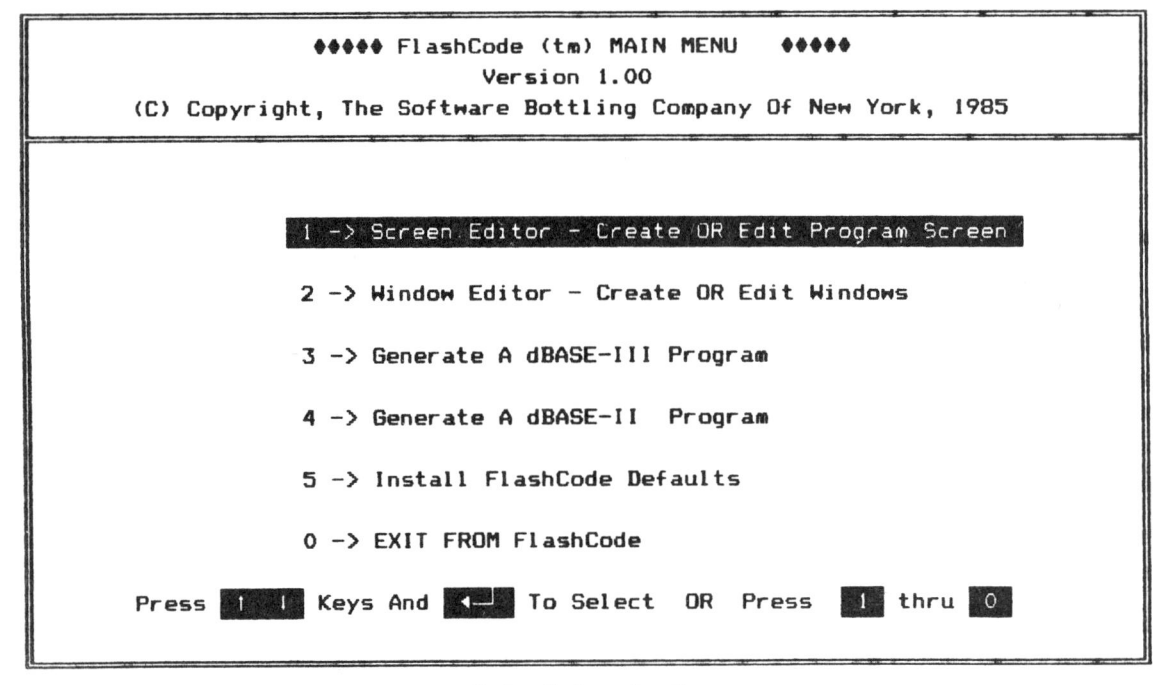

```
┌─────────────────────────────────────────────────────────────────┐
│              ♦♦♦♦♦ FlashCode (tm) MAIN MENU   ♦♦♦♦♦             │
│                         Version 1.00                            │
│        (C) Copyright, The Software Bottling Company Of New York, 1985  │
├─────────────────────────────────────────────────────────────────┤
│                                                                 │
│                                                                 │
│           ▌1 -> Screen Editor - Create OR Edit Program Screen▐  │
│                                                                 │
│            2 -> Window Editor - Create OR Edit Windows          │
│                                                                 │
│            3 -> Generate A dBASE-III Program                    │
│                                                                 │
│            4 -> Generate A dBASE-II  Program                    │
│                                                                 │
│            5 -> Install FlashCode Defaults                      │
│                                                                 │
│            0 -> EXIT FROM FlashCode                             │
│                                                                 │
│        Press ▌↑↓▐ Keys And ▌◄┘▐ To Select  OR  Press ▌1▐ thru ▌0▐│
│                                                                 │
└─────────────────────────────────────────────────────────────────┘
                          Data Drive is C:
```

Fig. 19-8. FlashCode main menu.

FlashCode is actually three programs in one. It is an excellent screen generator; in fact, it is the best on the market. It does not let you create better screens than any other programs; it just makes it radically easier to create a screen. You can control all of the features from simple menus. Choices are rarely left to the user without explicit and logical instructions. The screen generator lets you create text and graphics to highlight the screen. Lines, boxes, and graphics characters are easily selected from menus. Its ability to let you choose different colors at the character level allows you to create some amazing screens.

FlashCode can create the generated screens with normal dBASE code. It can also use a memory-resident program called Flashup to instantly display your screens. This saves the @ ... SAY commands and the relatively slow speed at which they are drawn on the screen.

FlashCode is also a program generator. It can generate just the code to run the screen you create or it can generate an entire program. The generated program handles all of the screen input/output, including adding, changing, and deleting records. It creates a module for displaying the data, and lets you see the data many ways, such as by record number or by any field's content. FlashCode also creates a utility menu to let you index, select, or pack the database. You can customize the code generated by FlashCode or use pieces of it in your own programs. FlashCode even has a "runtime" version so that other people who do not own the package can use your generated code.

Finally, FlashCode is also a window and menu generator. FlashCode can create pop-up windows and menus that you can add to your dBASE code to add value to your systems. This feature will be described in detail in Chapter 24.

Figure 19-8 shows the FlashCode Main Menu. There are six choices. These let you create a screen or a window, generate the dBASE program, and configure or exit FlashCode. The main menu acts as the traffic cop that controls the major functions of the program.

Choosing 1 places you into the Screen Editor. When you enter the Screen Editor, you are presented with a blank screen. Like most screen editors, you can type your field names and text anywhere on the screen. Figure 19-9 shows the screen after an example has been entered.

The text is entered anywhere on the screen. Fields are entered by pressing the F4 key the number of times that corresponds to the length you want the field to be. Later, you can further define a field by bringing up another menu and choosing the defaults.

This is a rather simple screen. Actually, screens really can't be very complicated. You have text, fields and their attributes, and graphics. Graphics include color added to the screen, attributes such as flashing text, lines, boxes, and filled-in backgrounds. Later, you will see how to create screens with graphics; FlashCode's greatest attribute is its ability to create screens with color and monochrome graphics.

When working in a screen editor it is important to be able to add, insert, or delete lines or to move text around on the screen. FlashCode has all of these features. The easiest way to remember the FlashCode functions is to press the standard help key, which is function key F1. The Screen Editor help screen is displayed as shown in Fig. 19-10.

The context sensitive help screens are an integral part of FlashCode. The help screen in Fig. 19-10 describes the function key codes and other key combinations necessary to operate the Screen Editor.

Using the simple function keys, you can copy, move, insert, or delete line of the screen. You can "paint" any portion of the screen any color you select from the color selection menu. This menu, chosen by pressing the F8 function key, lets you change the background color and the foreground text color, and to control whether or not the text is blinking.

Another important key is the F2 function key.

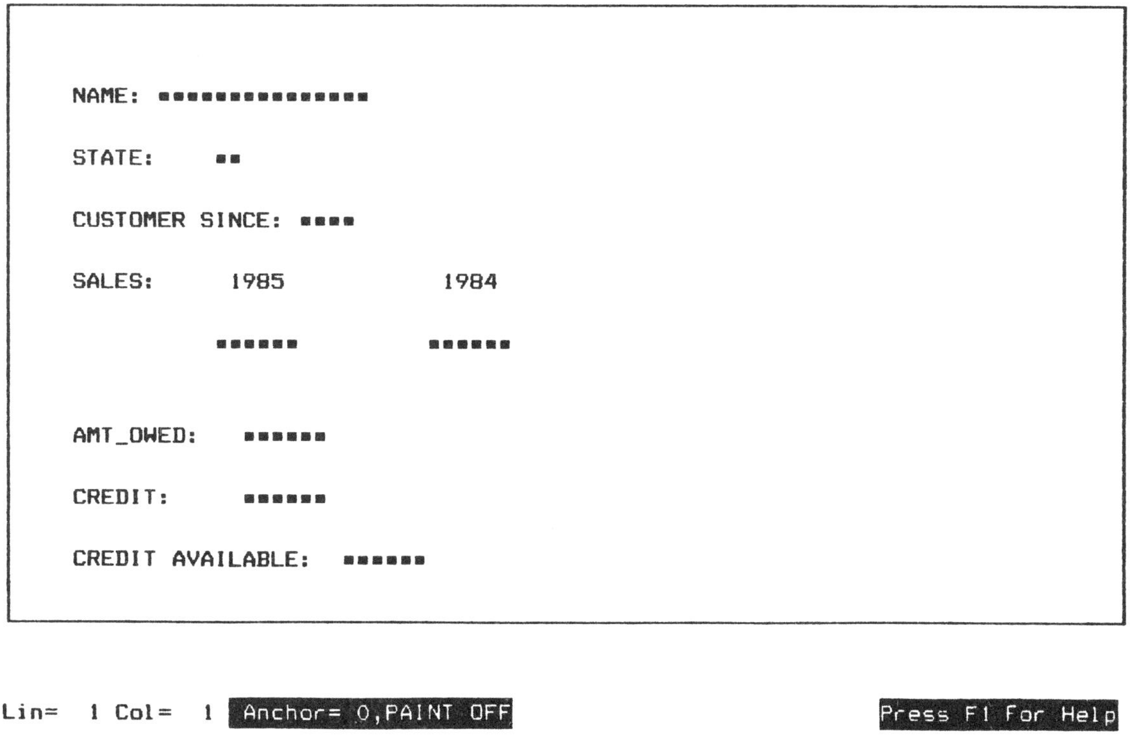

```
    NAME:    ■■■■■■■■■■■■■■

    STATE:   ■■

    CUSTOMER SINCE: ■■■■

    SALES:       1985           1984

                 ■■■■■■         ■■■■■■


    AMT_OWED:    ■■■■■■

    CREDIT:      ■■■■■■

    CREDIT AVAILABLE:  ■■■■■■
```

Lin= 1 Col= 1 `Anchor= 0,PAINT OFF`   `Press F1 For Help`

Fig. 19-9. FlashCode screen editor.

153

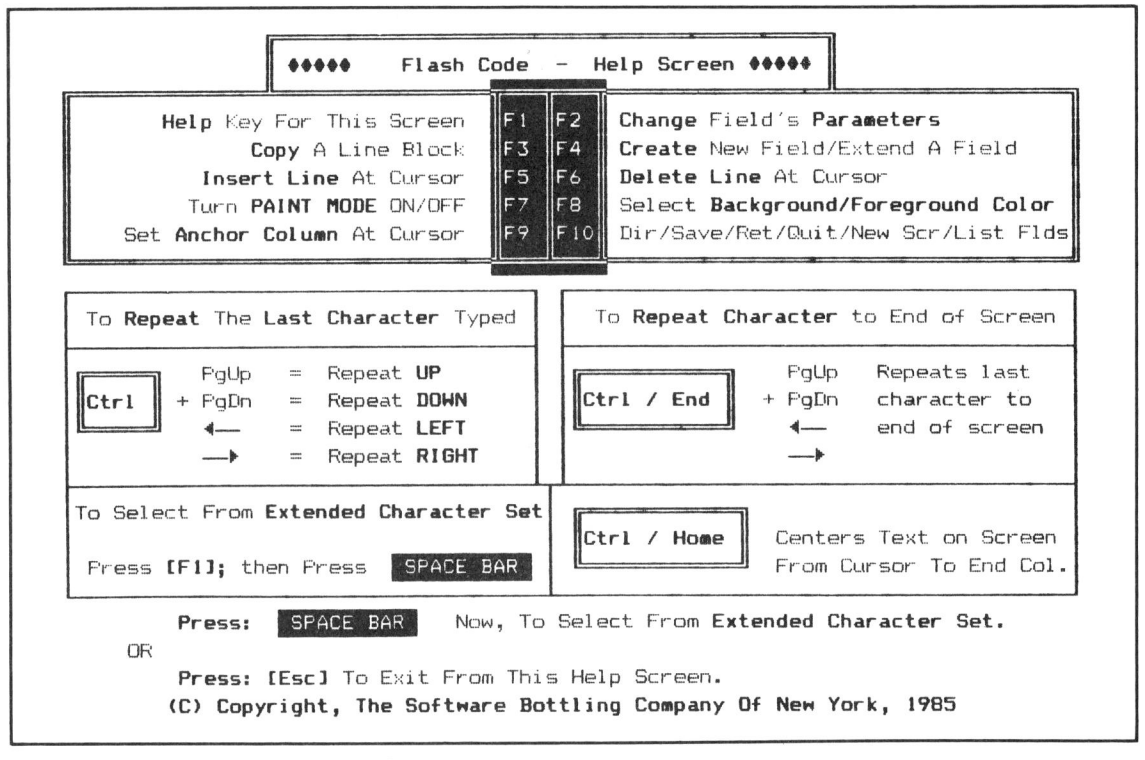

```
╔══════════════════════════════════════════════════════════════════╗
║              ♦♦♦♦♦  Flash Code  -  Help Screen  ♦♦♦♦♦            ║
║  ┌─────────────────────────────────┬──┬──┬──────────────────────┐║
║  │     Help Key For This Screen    │F1│F2│ Change Field's Parameters
║  │            Copy A Line Block    │F3│F4│ Create New Field/Extend A Field
║  │          Insert Line At Cursor  │F5│F6│ Delete Line At Cursor
║  │       Turn PAINT MODE ON/OFF    │F7│F8│ Select Background/Foreground Color
║  │     Set Anchor Column At Cursor │F9│F10│Dir/Save/Ret/Quit/New Scr/List Flds
║  └─────────────────────────────────┴──┴──┴──────────────────────┘║
║  ┌──────────────────────────────────┐ ┌────────────────────────────┐
║  │ To Repeat The Last Character Typed│ │ To Repeat Character to End of Screen
║  │ ┌────┐   PgUp  =  Repeat UP       │ │ ┌──────────┐  PgUp    Repeats last
║  │ │Ctrl│ + PgDn  =  Repeat DOWN     │ │ │Ctrl / End│+ PgDn    character to
║  │ └────┘   ←     =  Repeat LEFT     │ │ └──────────┘  ←       end of screen
║  │          →     =  Repeat RIGHT    │ │               →
║  ├──────────────────────────────────┤ ├────────────────────────────┤
║  │ To Select From Extended Character Set│ │┌───────────┐ Centers Text on Screen
║  │ Press [F1]; then Press  SPACE BAR │ ││Ctrl / Home│ From Cursor To End Col.
║  └──────────────────────────────────┘ └────────────────────────────┘
║       Press:  SPACE BAR   Now, To Select From Extended Character Set.
║    OR
║       Press: [Esc] To Exit From This Help Screen.
║       (C) Copyright, The Software Bottling Company Of New York, 1985
╚══════════════════════════════════════════════════════════════════╝
```

Fig. 19-10. FlashCode screen editor Help screen.

This key displays the menu on which you can specify how a field will be defined. On the screen you only define the length of the field. Everything else is defined "behind" the scenes. The big advantage to this is that the screen appears exactly as it will look when generated; you do not have to design your screen around the formatting options.

Figure 19-11 shows the FlashCode Field Parameter screen. From this screen you can move from area to area defining the field's attributes. The screen displayed is for the last field on the screen in Fig. 19-9. The field that is called Credit Available is being described. The top of the screen describes the line, column, and length of the field. The entire screen line is then displayed with arrows pointing to the field being described. If there were other fields on the line, they would be shown without the arrows. You can move from field to field by pressing the PgUp and PgDn keys. The highlighted areas of the screen change accordingly as you move from field to field.

A complete set of help screens is always available to help you understand how to use this menu. The first item to fill in is the Sequence #. This determines in what order the cursor will move from field to field. If you change the present setting, the other fields would be reordered to accommodate the change, if necessary.

If you have many fields that are the same, you can create one set of parameters and then copy the parameters into other fields. This is useful, especially when you have many numeric fields that are almost the same and you want to only make slight adjustments.

The variable name is very important to FlashCode because it is used in all the dBASE code that is generated. FlashCode places the letter X in front of all the variable names when it generates the code in order to make it easier for FlashCode. You don't have to worry about this unless you are modifying the code.

You then can answer a series of menu fill-ins

to determine what the variable attributes will be. A file variable means that it will be in the dBASE database. A search variable means that you can later display it using a value or range of values in a search program generated by FlashCode.

The field can be defined as a display-only field, or as a field that can be entered with the @ ... GET command. When you define the data type (memo fields are not supported, but can be defined as display-only; the code can be modified later) you are defining it in case you want FlashCode to create the database for you.

If your field is defined as numeric, you can further define it by including the number of decimals, range checking numbers, picture formatting symbols, and an initial value. If the field is to be calculated, the formula can be entered at the bottom of the screen. Any valid dBASE formula can be coded in that area.

Once the text and graphics are placed on the screen, the fields are defined, and the screen looks just the way you want it, it is time to generate the screen.

From the main menu, you can choose to generate a dBASE II or dBASE III program. You do not have to generate a program; once you save the screen, you can write your own code and call the screen. It is, however, easier to start from something than to start from scratch.

Figure 19-12 shows the screen that appears when you generate a dBASE program. There are four options to choose. You can convert up to ten screens into a single program at one time. The screens would be displayed one at a time when the program is generated and run. The name that the program is to be called is also specified here.

Once the programs are named the serious choices are made. With FlashCode there are two ways to create the programs and screens. One way is to produce the standard dBASE code such as every other program generates. The other uses a memory resident routine called "Flashup," which

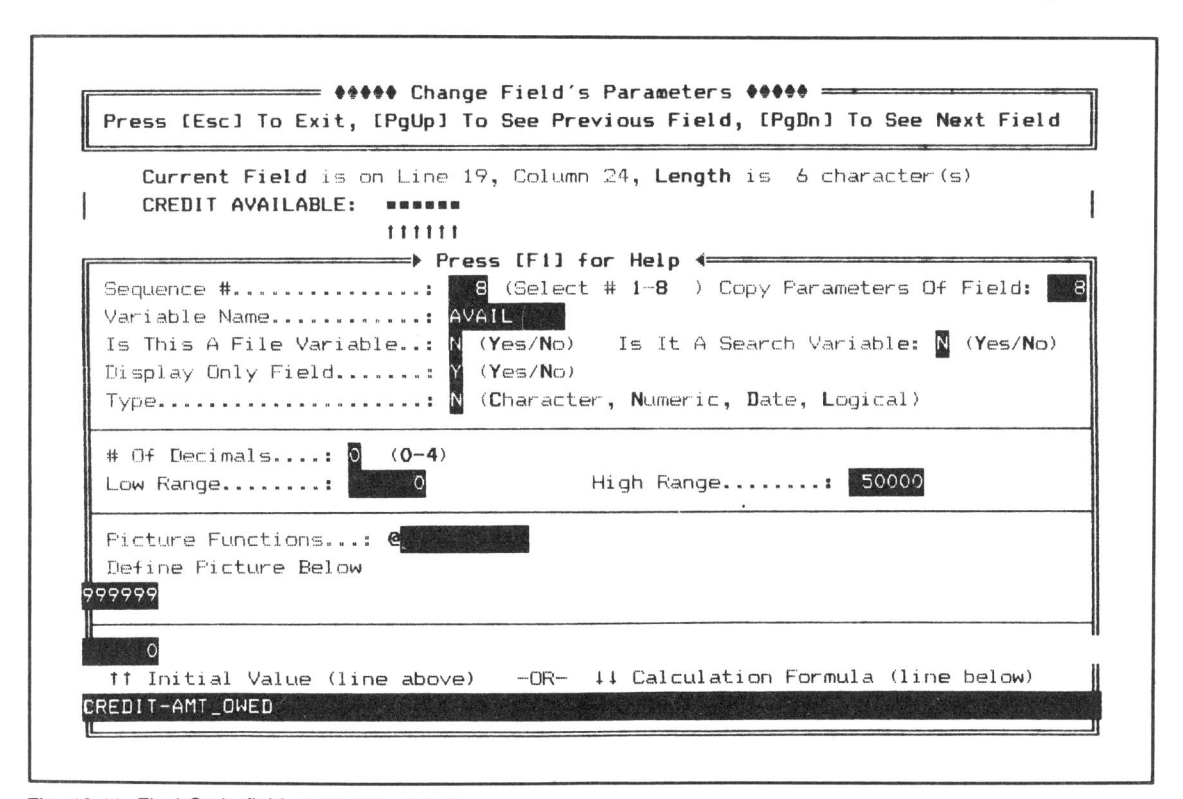

Fig. 19-11. FlashCode field parameter screen.

```
**** Generate dBASE-III (tm) Program ****
(C) Copyright, The Software Bottling Company Of New York, 1985
```

1. Enter the names of the Screen Files you want converted into a program: C:CUSTOMER   C:

   Default Disk Drive: C

2. Enter the Name of the Program you wish to generate: C:CUSTOMER.PRG

3. Select one of the following for the generated program : B
   - Flash Up Screens
   - & Pop-Up Menus
   - Standard DBASE-III Display Screens (Using @ SAY)

4. Select one of the following : B
   - Full Database Program
   - Screen Input Program

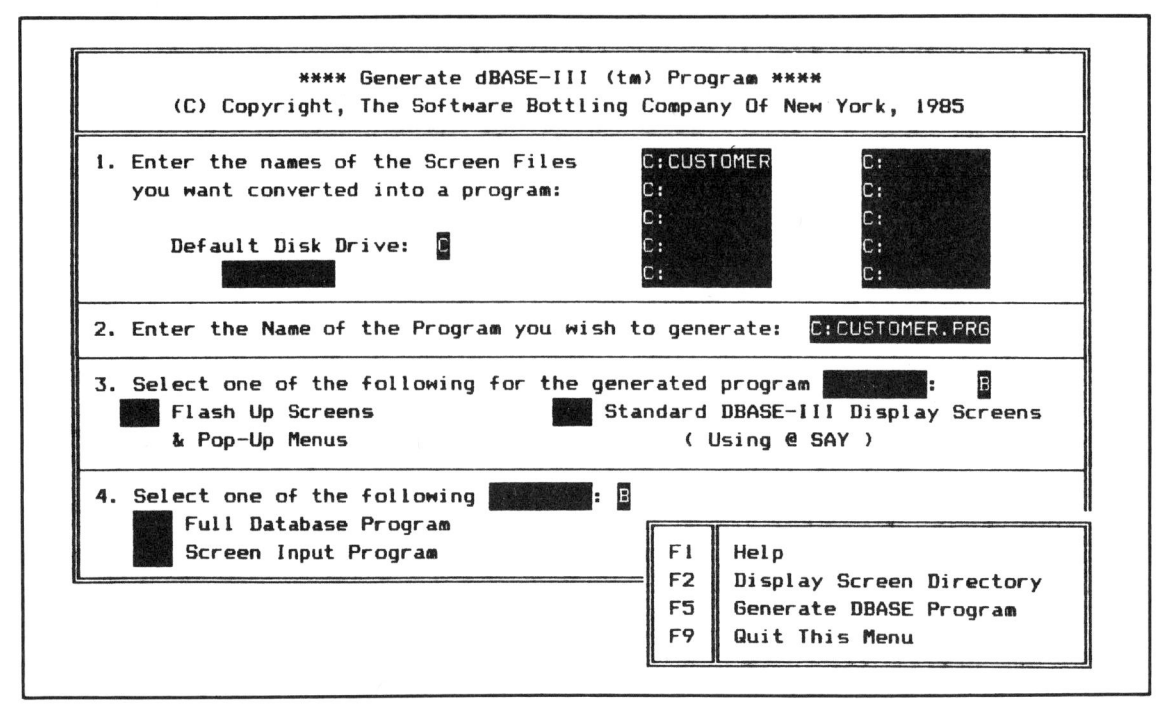

F1	Help
F2	Display Screen Directory
F5	Generate DBASE Program
F9	Quit This Menu

Fig. 19-12. FlashCode dBASE generate screen.

is actually where FlashCode got its name. Sometimes, you may want to create standard dBASE code, such as when other people who are unfamiliar with FlashCode need to see your programs. But when you decide to produce this kind of screen, the FlashCode program takes only about 3K and sits in the background, ready to display your screens instantly.

The code to activate a flashup screen will be discussed later. It simply replaces the @ . . . SAY commands with a simple call to invoke Flashup and display a certain screen. One line of code is all that it takes.

The last item to chose is whether you want just the screen generated or a complete system. The complete system may or may not be the type of system you would like. It is described later in this section. Either way, the dBASE code is available for you to customize as you see fit. It is not overly complicated code; anyone who has worked seriously with dBASE for a few months and understands how to program should have no trouble customizing the code.

As the code is generated for dBASE, the current directory is searched for the database. If it is not found, it is created. If it is found you are asked if you want to recreate it or leave it alone. You are also asked to select an index for later use in indexing the data.

Once the screen is filled in, you can generate the program. In the following comparison the "screen-only" program has been generated in two different ways—with and without FlashCode. The entire program without FlashCode is shown and is called CUSTOMER.PRG. The major difference between the two versions is found where the screen is displayed; the differences are marked and boxed on the printout in Fig. 19-13.

Figure 19-13 shows that the differences are minimal. The first box shows that a variable called FLASH is set to CHR(145). This is how FlashCode calls up a screen. The code is:

?? CHR(145) + "S.<screenname>.SCR/"

By setting a memory variable to CHR(145), the call

```
*  -- CUSTOMER.PRG
*  -- Procedures Generated By FlashCode V1.00 on 09/01/1985 - 19:52:45
*  -- (C) Copyright 1985, The Software Bottling Company Of New York
*  -- This Program may not be used without the above Copyright Notice
*
*
*  -- Screen Input Program For CUSTOMER --
*
CLEAR
SET TALK OFF
SET ECHO OFF                                          ──────  FLASH = CHR(145)
@ 24,0 SAY "Initializing Variables"
*  -- C:CUSTOMER
PUBLIC XNAME,XSTATE,XCUST_SINC,XSOLD_1985,XSOLD_1984,XAMT_OWED,XCREDIT,XAVAIL
XNAME = SPACE(15)
XSTATE = SPACE(2)
XCUST_SINC = SPACE(4)
XSOLD_1985 = 0
XSOLD_1984 = 0
XAMT_OWED = 0
XCREDIT = 0
XAVAIL = 0
@ 24,0
ScrnNumFL = 1
MaxScrnFL = 1

DO WHILE .T.
  *  -- DISPLAY SCREEN --
  DO CASE
  CASE ScrnNumFL=1
    *  -- Screen Display C:CUSTOMER.SCR
    SET COLOR TO 15/0,15/0
    CLEAR
@ 4,11 SAY "NAME:"
@ 6,11 SAY "STATE:"
@ 8,11 SAY "CUSTOMER SINCE:"                    *  -- Screen Display C:CUSTOMER.SCR
@ 10,11 SAY "SALES:     1985"                   SET COLOR TO 15/0,15/0
@ 10,37 SAY "1984"          ──────              CLEAR
@ 15,11 SAY "AMT_OWED:"                         ?? FLASH+"S.C:CUSTOMER.SCR/"
@ 17,11 SAY "CREDIT:"                           SET COLOR TO 15/0,0/7
@ 19,11 SAY "CREDIT AVAILABLE:"
SET COLOR TO 15/0,0/7
  ENDCASE
  @ 0,0 SAY "SCREEN #"+STR(ScrnNumFL,2)
  *  -- Do Calculations For All Fields --
  *  -- From Screen C:CUSTOMER --
  XAVAIL = XCREDIT-XAMT_OWED

  *  -- Get Data Input --
  @ 24,0 SAY "Enter or Re-Enter Information"
  DO CASE
  *  -- From Screen C:CUSTOMER --
  CASE ScrnNumFL=1
    SET COLOR TO 15/0,15/0
    @ 4,17 GET XNAME PICT "XXXXXXXXXXXXXXX"
    @ 6,21 GET XSTATE PICT "XX"
    @ 8,27 GET XCUST_SINC PICT "XXXX"
    @ 12,21 GET XSOLD_1985 PICT "999999"
    @ 12,36 GET XSOLD_1984 PICT "999999"
    @ 15,23 GET XAMT_OWED PICT "999999"
    @ 17,23 GET XCREDIT PICT "999999"
    @ 19,30 SAY XAVAIL PICT "999999"
  ENDCASE
```

Fig. 19-13. FlashCode dBASE code. (Continued on page 158.)

```
  READ
  SET COLOR TO 15/0, 0/7
  @ 24,0 SAY "Edit Calculations OR Press 'PgDn' To Exit."
  * -- Re-Do Calculations For All Fields and Re-Display --
  DO CASE
  * -- From Screen C:CUSTOMER --
  CASE ScrnNumFL=1
    SET COLOR TO 15/0,15/0
    XAVAIL = XCREDIT-XAMT_OWED
    @ 19,30 SAY XAVAIL PICT "999999"
  ENDCASE
  READ
  SET COLOR TO 15/0, 0/7

  @ 24,0
  @ 23,80 CLEAR
  WAIT
  ScrnNumFL = ScrnNumFL+1
  IF ScrnNumFL > MaxScrnFL
    ScrnNumFL = 1
  ENDIF
ENDDO
************************************************************************
*    The following section is provided by FlashCode for use in programs with   *
*  a .DBF file.  It is not needed in the "Screen Only" program but is helpfull *
*  nevertheless.                                                               *
************************************************************************
* -- RETRIEVE data from a file section --
* -- From Screen C:CUSTOMER --
XNAME = NAME
XSTATE = STATE
XCUST_SINC = CUST_SINC
XSOLD_1985 = SOLD_1985
XSOLD_1984 = SOLD_1984
XAMT_OWED = AMT_OWED
XCREDIT = CREDIT

* -- REPLACE data in a file section --
* -- From Screen C:CUSTOMER --
  REPLACE NAME WITH XNAME,STATE WITH XSTATE,CUST_SINC WITH XCUST_SINC
  REPLACE SOLD_1985 WITH XSOLD_1985,SOLD_1984 WITH XSOLD_1984
  REPLACE AMT_OWED WITH XAMT_OWED,CREDIT WITH XCREDIT
```

to bring up the screen is shortened to:

?? FLASH + "S.<screenname>,SCR/"

This code displays the screen named in <screenname>. The second box shows the @ ... SAY statements replaced by the call to Flashup. This is the only difference between a Flashup program and a traditional dBASE program. The screens are displayed instantly rather than being drawn by a series of commands. The real difference shows up when you are displaying complex screens with graphics, colors, and a lot of text. One call can replace many @ ... SAY commands.

The second phase of FlashCode is the complete system it generates. This is what determines how good a program generator it is. FlashCode generates a very rigid menu based system to help you use your dBASE program.

Rather than examining much of the code, I will present some of the different screens that FlashCode presents to give you better understanding of how FlashCode creates the different screens.

When you first run any program generated with FlashCode you will see the menu shown in Fig. 19-14. This gives you the ability to handle record manipulation including adding, displaying, changing, and deleting records. You can add reports that have already been defined into a reporting menu and run these reports. Finally, you can perform some database maintenance, including looking at the structure, indexing, and packing the data.

Figure 19-15 shows the effect of running the add program and adding a record. After the data is entered into the record, any calculated fields are calculated and the results displayed. This is an added feature over most generators. Most generators do not recalculate the field unless you redisplay the record.

Software Bottling Company decided for some unknown reason to complicate their record addition process by putting in not one but two safety checks. This is probably the biggest deficiency in their generation process. Figure 19-15 shows a pop-up menu that appears when you add a record. In the nonFlashup version it appears as a prompt line. You are forced to decide if you want to make changes in the record before leaving it or if you are ready to leave it. They also call leaving the record Quit, which leaves the user thinking they are going to exit the program.

If you move the menu bar to Edit, you can then retype or change your entries. If you move the menu bar to Quit, another menu or prompt line is displayed that asks you if you want to save the record. This is fine if you tend to make mistakes on every record. If you want to quickly enter the records one after the other, it is a nuisance.

Fortunately, you can quickly remove the offending code and enter one record after another. A more generally accepted way to end the addition process is to enter a blank first field, which in this case is NAME.

In the chapter that covers miscellaneous topics, FlashCode is again covered because of its windowing ability. There, the creation of dBASE code for windowing is discussed in greater detail.

Figure 19-16 shows the result of pressing 2 from the main menu shown in Fig. 19-14. This lets

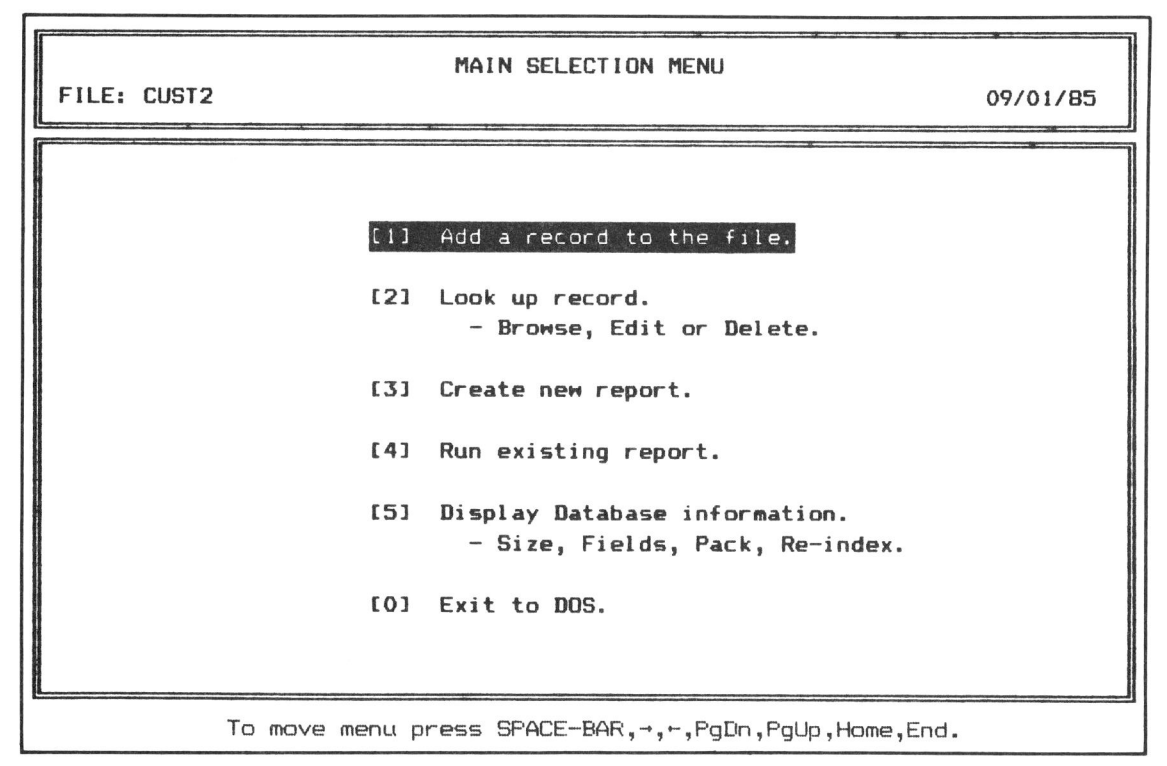

```
╔══════════════════════════════════════════════════════════════╗
║                    MAIN SELECTION MENU                       ║
║ FILE: CUST2                                        09/01/85  ║
╠══════════════════════════════════════════════════════════════╣
║                                                              ║
║                                                              ║
║              [1]  Add a record to the file.                  ║
║                                                              ║
║              [2]  Look up record.                            ║
║                    - Browse, Edit or Delete.                 ║
║                                                              ║
║              [3]  Create new report.                         ║
║                                                              ║
║              [4]  Run existing report.                       ║
║                                                              ║
║              [5]  Display Database information.              ║
║                    - Size, Fields, Pack, Re-index.           ║
║                                                              ║
║              [0]  Exit to DOS.                               ║
║                                                              ║
║         To move menu press SPACE-BAR,→,←,PgDn,PgUp,Home,End. ║
╚══════════════════════════════════════════════════════════════╝
```

Fig. 19-14. FlashCode Generated main menu.

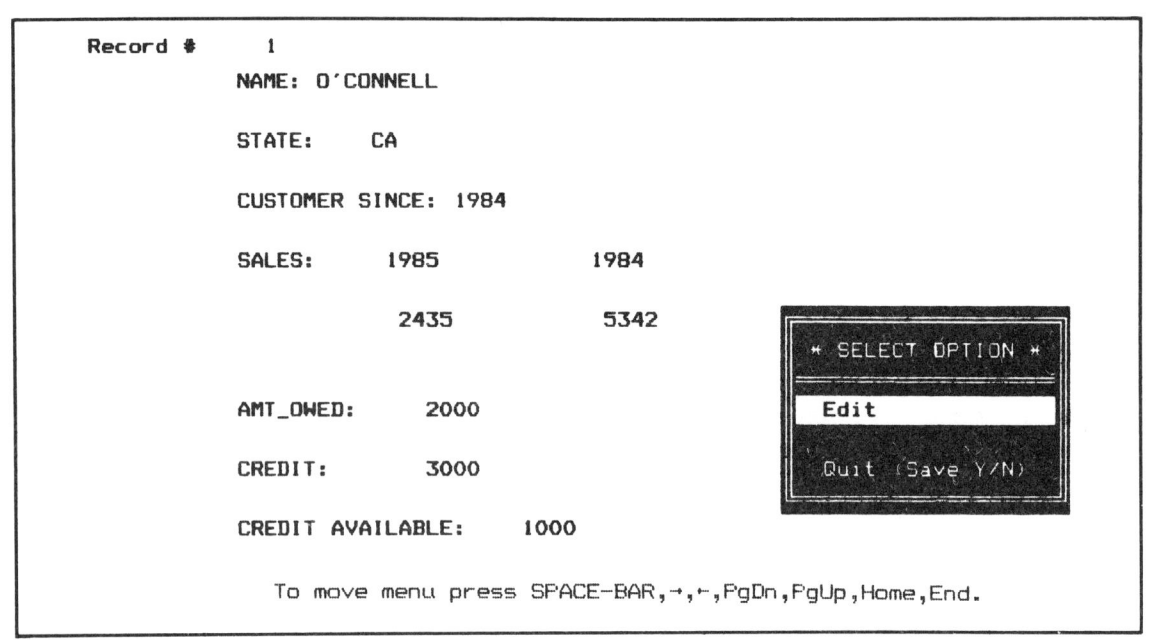

```
        Record #    1
                    NAME: O'CONNELL

                    STATE:    CA

                    CUSTOMER SINCE: 1984

                    SALES:    1985          1984

                              2435          5342
                                                        ┌─────────────────────┐
                                                        │  * SELECT OPTION *  │
                                                        ├─────────────────────┤
                    AMT_OWED:     2000                  │  Edit               │
                                                        │                     │
                    CREDIT:       3000                  │  Quit (Save Y/N)    │
                                                        └─────────────────────┘
                    CREDIT AVAILABLE:    1000

                To move menu press SPACE-BAR,→,←,PgDn,PgUp,Home,End.
```

Fig. 19-15. FlashCode Add screen with choice.

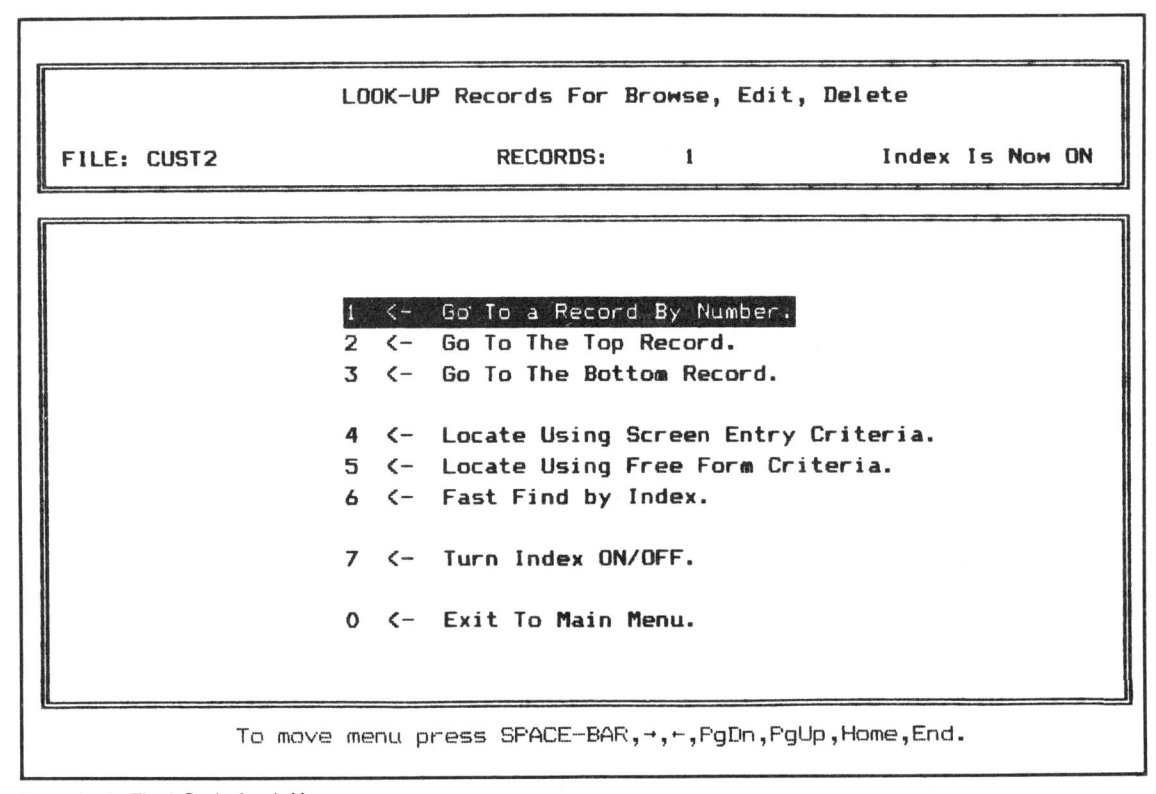

```
┌──────────────────────────────────────────────────────────────────┐
│              LOOK-UP Records For Browse, Edit, Delete            │
│                                                                  │
│  FILE: CUST2              RECORDS:    1         Index Is Now ON  │
└──────────────────────────────────────────────────────────────────┘
┌──────────────────────────────────────────────────────────────────┐
│                                                                  │
│                                                                  │
│                                                                  │
│              1  <-  Go To a Record By Number.                    │
│              2  <-  Go To The Top Record.                        │
│              3  <-  Go To The Bottom Record.                     │
│                                                                  │
│              4  <-  Locate Using Screen Entry Criteria.          │
│              5  <-  Locate Using Free Form Criteria.             │
│              6  <-  Fast Find by Index.                          │
│                                                                  │
│              7  <-  Turn Index ON/OFF.                           │
│                                                                  │
│              0  <-  Exit To Main Menu.                           │
│                                                                  │
│                                                                  │
└──────────────────────────────────────────────────────────────────┘
         To move menu press SPACE-BAR,→,←,PgDn,PgUp,Home,End.
```

Fig. 19-16. FlashCode Look Up menu.

you find and then edit, browse, or delete a record. As you can see, the choices include finding a record by number or by any field value. You can also find a record with or without the index.

The last menu that is automatically generated is the "housekeeping" menu. As shown in Fig. 19-17, it lets you see your database structure and allows you to reindex or pack the database. When you generate programs with FlashCode, seven files are created. They start with the program name and include the following suffixes:

programname.FLD—	A file that stores the database fields defined
programname.DBF—	The name of the dBASE database
programname.PRG—	The main menu, which calls the other programs
programname.PRC—	A procedure file called from the main menu
programname.BAT—	A batch file that calls Flashup and dBASE
programname.PUB—	A file that contains all the memory variables
programname.NDX—	The database index file

The .PRG file contains only the code to display the menu in Fig. 19-14. The code calls many procedures that are stored in the .PRC file. These procedures handle the various functions that make up the program.

The color and graphics that make FlashCode's screen generator second to none have already been mentioned. An excellent example appears on the demo disk. Figure 19-18 shows the example. Unfortunately, it appears in black and white. If the figure was in color, you would see the various colors that make up this screen, including the excellent choice of a red masthead on a blue background.

The lines that appear within the screen are

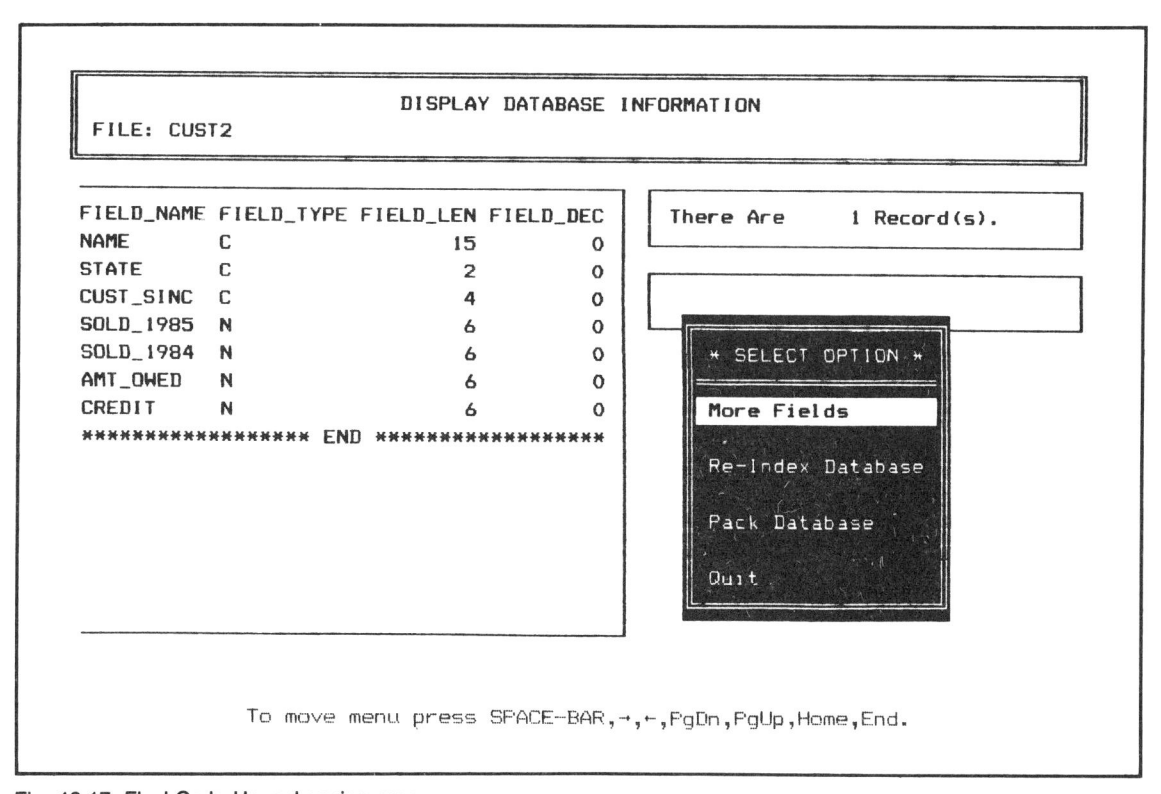

Fig. 19-17. FlashCode Housekeeping menu.

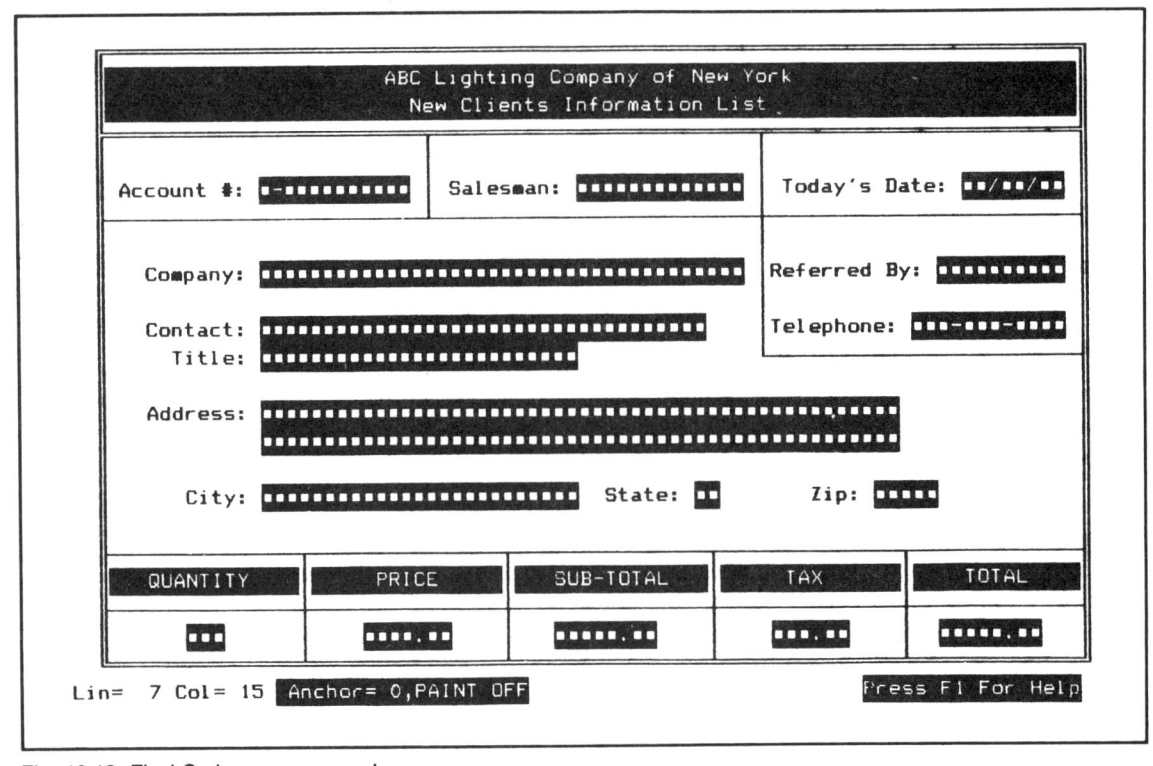

Fig. 19-18. FlashCode screen example.

created with the FlashCode graphics generator. Other packages require you to learn sixty different key combinations that create the various graphics characters; FlashCode lets you bring up a menu of all the different graphics characters. They are arranged in the most logical order for use. This graphic menu screen appears in Fig. 19-19. You place the cursor in the place you want the graphic character to appear on the Screen Editor screen. F1-spacebar brings up the graphics screen as shown in Fig. 19-19. You then place the cursor on the graphics symbol you want to select, press the Enter key; and the character appears on the Screen Editor screen. Then, by using the Ctrl key and the arrows, you can repeat the character as many times as necessary to create boxes, underlines or any figure you can imagine.

FlashCode is a truly remarkable product. It is brand-new, technologically state-of-the-art, and actually fun to use. Except for the strange logic used in adding records, it is very well thought-out. It is a product that is a real value for its price and will add to your productivity. The windowing capabilities, described in a later chapter, make it an even more amazing product. Whether you have simple program needs or are writing complex systems, FlashCode is an excellent choice.

QUICKCODE III

QuickCode III is the most powerful of the programs reviewed in this chapter. Though it's slightly harder to use because of its use of numerous key combinations to select choices, it offers greater flexibility and can create more complicated programs. These advanced features will be discussed in this section. Rather than making the generation process flashy, QuickCode III makes it powerful, easily creating programs that can access many screens, menus, and files. It can create complicated systems; of course, the more complicated the system, the higher the learning curve.

QuickCode was the predecessor of QuickCode III. This program enjoyed prominence during the dBASE II days. It began as an add on to the CP/M version of dBASE and then was rewritten for the MS-DOS version. QuickCode III is the Fox and Geller entry into the dBASE program generator market. It is very similar in many ways to FlashCode, but in some ways it is completely different. It is not as fancy or flashy, and it is somewhat harder to learn and operate.

The biggest drawback to QuickCode III is documentation that is overly wordy and tends to skip important concepts. It is written in very small print, and like most manuals, it lacks adequate diagrams and pictures. The advantage is that Fox and Geller started in this business many years ago and understand program generators very well.

The code that QuickCode III generates is extremely clean and logical. Anyone who has written a program in dBASE can understand the code. They use very traditional methods to display their screens and menus. Instead of using one large procedure file, they place each function in a separate module. From a customization standpoint, it is easier to customize this type of modular code.

There are a number of other factors that make QuickCode III a powerful package. It allows you to tie multiple files together, though the method is slightly cumbersome and confusing to anyone but an experienced dBASE programmer.

Menus that replace the automatically generated main menu in the program can be defined. These types of enhancements make QuickCode III a product worth considering.

The QuickCode III main menu appears in Fig. 19-20. The QuickCode III main menu provides you with options to create, change, and rename screens. You can also import a text file and save it as a QuickCode III screen. Various options also let you customize your screen settings including which keys perform what tasks and what special symbols will mean to the user. Normally the semicolon (;)

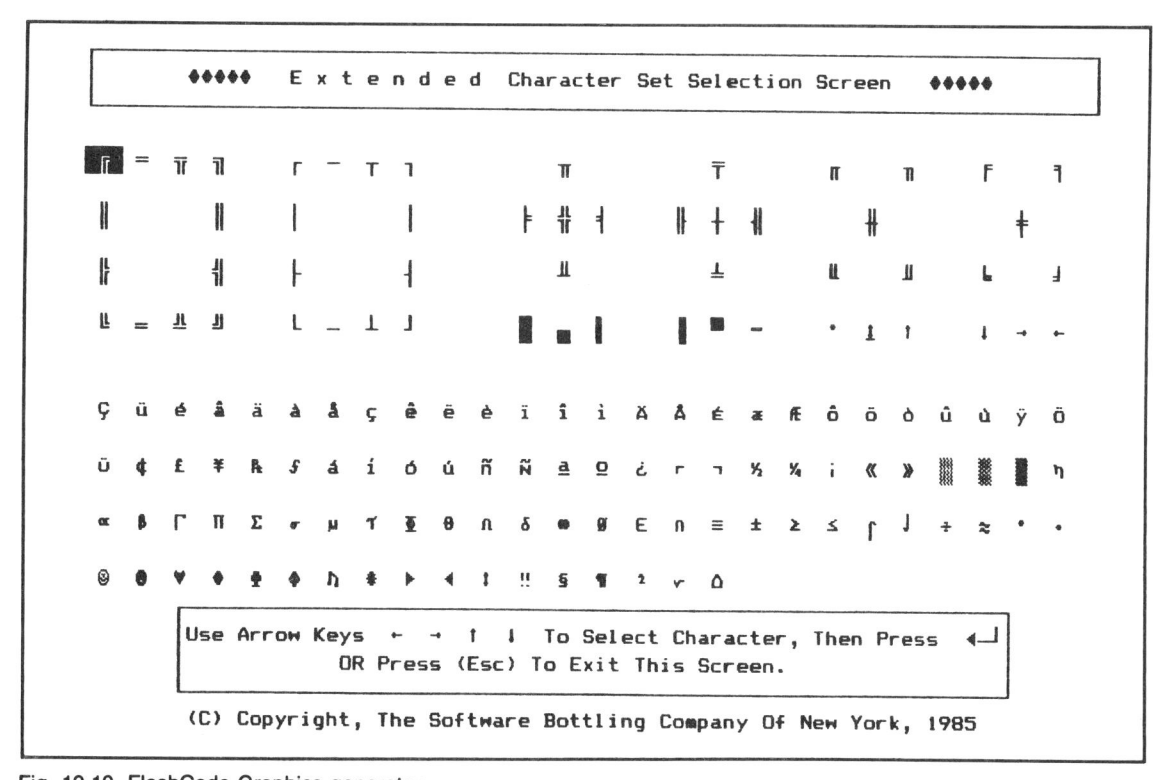

Fig. 19-19. FlashCode Graphics generator.

163

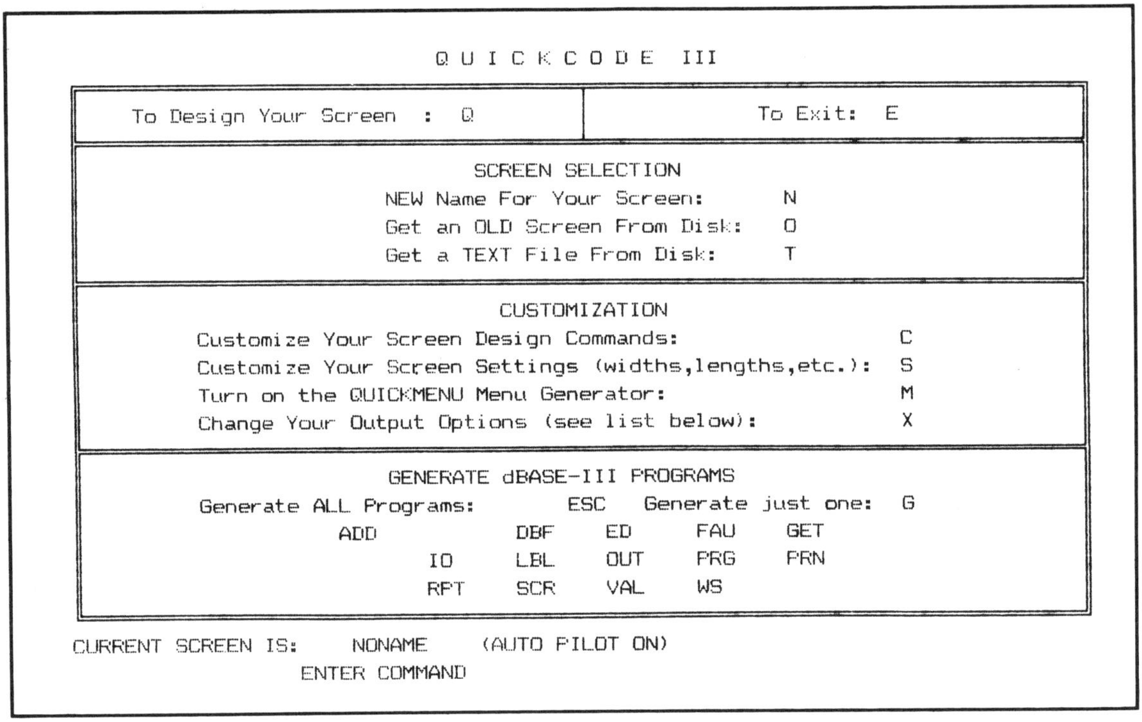

```
                    Q U I C K C O D E  III
  ┌─────────────────────────────────────┬─────────────────────────┐
  │ To Design Your Screen :  Q          │        To Exit:  E      │
  ├─────────────────────────────────────┴─────────────────────────┤
  │                        SCREEN SELECTION                       │
  │           NEW Name For Your Screen:         N                 │
  │           Get an OLD Screen From Disk:      O                 │
  │           Get a TEXT File From Disk:        T                 │
  ├───────────────────────────────────────────────────────────────┤
  │                         CUSTOMIZATION                         │
  │      Customize Your Screen Design Commands:            C      │
  │      Customize Your Screen Settings (widths,lengths,etc.): S  │
  │      Turn on the QUICKMENU Menu Generator:             M      │
  │      Change Your Output Options (see list below):      X      │
  ├───────────────────────────────────────────────────────────────┤
  │                  GENERATE dBASE-III PROGRAMS                  │
  │        Generate ALL Programs:   ESC  Generate just one:  G    │
  │           ADD          DBF     ED     FAU     GET             │
  │            IO          LBL     OUT    PRG     PRN             │
  │           RPT          SCR     VAL    WS                      │
  └───────────────────────────────────────────────────────────────┘
  CURRENT SCREEN IS:   NONAME      (AUTO PILOT ON)
             ENTER COMMAND
```

Fig. 19-20. QuickCode III main menu.

character precedes a field in the screen drawing mode. You can change this to anything you desire if that is easier for you. This screen is also used to decide what programs you want to generate from your screens.

There are a number of programs that you can generate. Figure 19-21 lists the many types of program that you can create. For example, if you aren't using WordStar, there is no need to create a file that can be used by the MailMerge facility. You probably always want to create the programs to add, edit, and get a value. This is the screen that lets you select the various programs to be generated. This is an example of QuickCode III's increased flexibility over other generators: you can select precisely the modules that suit your needs.

When you enter the QuickScreen screen editor you are presented with a blank work area, as with most screen generators. Here you can type text, fields, or graphics such as boxes, lines or other characters. Color is not a part of this package.

The screen in Fig. 19-22 shows that, like the Ashton-Tate/WallSoft SED, special symbols are used to define the various types of fields including edit fields and display only. A suffix is used to show the type of field. The # denotes an integer. The > delimits the field width. This screen shows that most screen editors work in approximately the same way, letting you create the screen as it will look and then generating dBASE code to produce it.

There is another way to define your fields. You can use the field definition screen shown in Fig. 19-23. This menu is called from QuickScreen and is used to set the field attributes and even to link files by a common field.

The first column is the field number. The second column contains the various field names that have been defined. MQ_MODE appears at the top of the screen and is used to name the screen when it is displayed.

Next comes the type of field, followed by the length of the field, and an indication telling whether the field is a database field or a display field. A default value to appear when the field is first displayed

```
            QUICKCODE III PROGRAMS TO GENERATE
  ┌─────────────────────────────────┬─────────────────────────────────┐
  │       PROGRAM         OUTPUT    │      PROGRAM          OUTPUT    │
  ├─────────────────────────────────┼─────────────────────────────────┤
  │                                 │                                 │
  │  1- ADD TO FILE       (.ADD) Y  │  14- SCREEN DEFINITION (.SCR) Y │
  │  2- SET BANK SWITCH   (.BSW) N  │  15- VALIDATE ENTRY    (.VAL) Y │
  │  3- DATABASE FILE     (.DBF) Y  │  16- WORDSTAR CONNECTION (.WS) Y│
  │  4- EDIT FILE         (.ED ) Y  │                                 │
  │  5- SET DEFAULTS      (.FAU) Y  │                                 │
  │  6- GET FROM FILE     (.GET) Y  │                                 │
  │  7- SET UP INDEX      (.GO ) N  │                                 │
  │  8- I/O SCREEN        (.IO ) Y  │                                 │
  │  9- LABELS/FORMS      (.LBL) Y  │                                 │
  │ 10- OUTPUT SCREEN     (.OUT) Y  │                                 │
  │ 11- MAIN MENU PROGRAM (.PRG) Y  │                                 │
  │ 12- SCREEN IMAGE      (.PRN) Y  │                                 │
  │ 13- RUN REPORT        (.RPT) Y  │                                 │
  │                                 │                                 │
  └─────────────────────────────────┴─────────────────────────────────┘
              ( S = SAVE,   E = EXIT,   Q = QUICKSCREEN MODE )
   ENTER # TO CHANGE:
```

Fig. 19-21. QuickCode III program list.

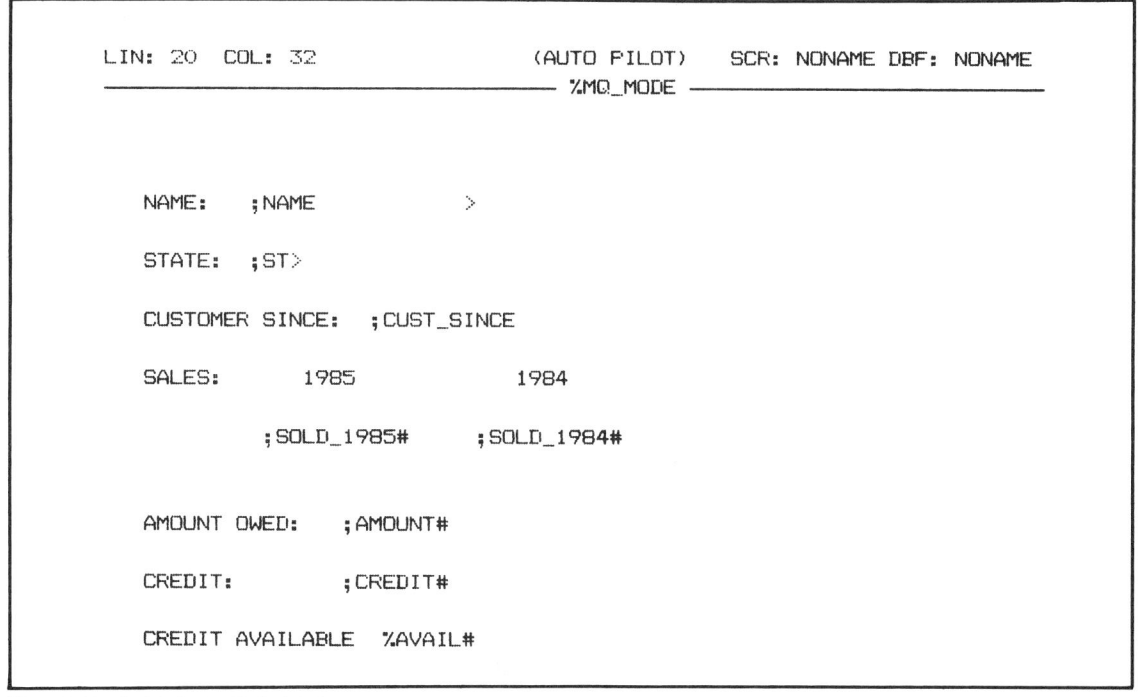

```
   LIN: 20  COL: 32              (AUTO PILOT)  SCR: NONAME DBF: NONAME
   ─────────────────────────────── %MQ_MODE ───────────────────────────



       NAME:    ;NAME               >

       STATE:   ;ST>

       CUSTOMER SINCE:  ;CUST_SINCE

       SALES:       1985            1984

                 ;SOLD_1985#     ;SOLD_1984#


       AMOUNT OWED:    ;AMOUNT#

       CREDIT:         ;CREDIT#

       CREDIT AVAILABLE   %AVAIL#
```

Fig. 19-22. QuickCode III QuickScreen.

```
    #  FIELDNAME   T LEN F DEFAULT   MINIMUM    MAXIMUM    ERROR MESSAGE   VAL  ER
    0  MQ_MODE     C 7     *NONE*    *NONE*     *NONE*     *NONE*           *    3
    1  NAME        C 15  F *NONE*    *NONE*     *NONE*     *NONE*           *    0
    2  ST          C 2   F *NONE*    *NONE*     *NONE*     *NONE*           *    0
    3  CUST_SINC   C 4   F *NONE*    *NONE*     *NONE*     *NONE*           *    0
    4  SOLD_1985   I 6   F 0         *NONE*     *NONE*     *NONE*           *    0
    5  SOLD_1984   I 6   F 0         *NONE*     *NONE*     *NONE*           *    0
    6  AMOUNT      I 6   F 0         *NONE*     *NONE*     *NONE*           *    0
    7  CREDIT      I 6   F 0         0          5000       *NONE*           *    0
    8  AVAIL       I 6     0         *NONE*     *NONE*     *NONE*           *    3


    #  FIELDNAME   T LEN F SHOW                 COMPUTATION                      ER
    0  MQ_MODE     C 7     YES    *NONE*                                          3
    1  NAME        C 15  F YES    *NONE*                                          0
    2  ST          C 2   F YES    *NONE*                                          0
    3  CUST_SINC   C 4   F YES    *NONE*                                          0
    4  SOLD_1985   I 6   F YES    *NONE*                                          0
    5  SOLD_1984   I 6   F YES    *NONE*                                          0
    6  AMOUNT      I 6   F YES    *NONE*                                          0
    7  CREDIT      I 6   F YES    *NONE*                                          0
    8  AVAIL       I 6     YES    CREDIT-AMOUNT                                   3
```

Fig. 19-23. QuickCode III Field menu.

comes next. The range checking feature occupies the next two columns, allowing range-type editing of the input value. The Error Message column is used to enter a message when there is an error in the input. QuickCode III will display a generic error message if none is provided.

There are several types of validation checking that can be performed. The asterisk indicates the minimum/maximum checking known as range checking. If you place an L in this column, you can use the minimum and maximum fields for a list of values. Up to 22 total characters can be entered. The last type of validation is file checking. Using this method, you can search other files for valid entries.

The ER field is an error code. Anything other than 0 or 3 indicates an error in creating the screen. The 3 indicates a display only field and is not an error. The screen at the bottom of Fig. 19-23 lets you decide whether or not the field should appear on the data form. Sometimes, if the field is only used for calculation, you may not want to show it on the data entry form.

The next field is the Computation field. This field shows that the field AVAIL is to be equal to the field CREDIT minus the field AMOUNT.

The field menu controls many of the fields' attributes and is very important in the generation of the program. Although it is not fancy, it is straightforward and allows you to see all of the fields at one time.

Once you have created the screen, it is time to generate the program. The screen in Fig. 19-21 shows the different programs that will be generated. Fig. 19-24 shows the generation process in progress. As each program is generated, the asterisk moves from start to end. Any errors are reported immediately.

The screen system that is generated is simple and concise. Fig. 19-25 shows the standard main menu that is generated by QuickCode III. You can replace it with your own menu by creating a menu

```
                    QUICKCODE III Program Generation
┌─────────────────────────────────────┬──────────────────────────────────┐
│ Screen/Page:    customer.SCR        │ Number of Errors:                │
├─────────────────────────────────────┴──────────────────────────────────┤
│                                                                         │
├──────────────────────────┬──────────────────┬────────┬────────┬────────┤
│ Generating:              │ Name:            │ Start: │ End:   │ Errors:│
│    Database File         │ customer.DBF     │        │   *    │        │
│    Main Menu Program     │ customer.PRG     │        │   *    │        │
│    Input/Output Screen   │ customer.IO      │        │   *    │        │
│    Output Only Screen    │ customer.OUT     │        │   *    │        │
│    Add Program           │ customer.ADD     │        │   *    │        │
│    Edit Program          │ customer.ED      │        │   *    │        │
│    Get Program           │ customer.GET     │        │   *    │        │
│    Default Program       │ customer.FAU     │   *    │        │        │
│    Validation Program    │                  │        │        │        │
│    Report Program        │                  │        │        │        │
│    WordStar Program      │                  │        │        │        │
│    Label Program         │                  │        │        │        │
│    Jumbo File Mgt        │                  │        │        │        │
│    Index Database        │                  │        │        │        │
│    Screen Image          │                  │        │        │        │
└──────────────────────────┴──────────────────┴────────┴────────┴────────┘
```

Fig. 19-24. QuickCode III Generator menu.

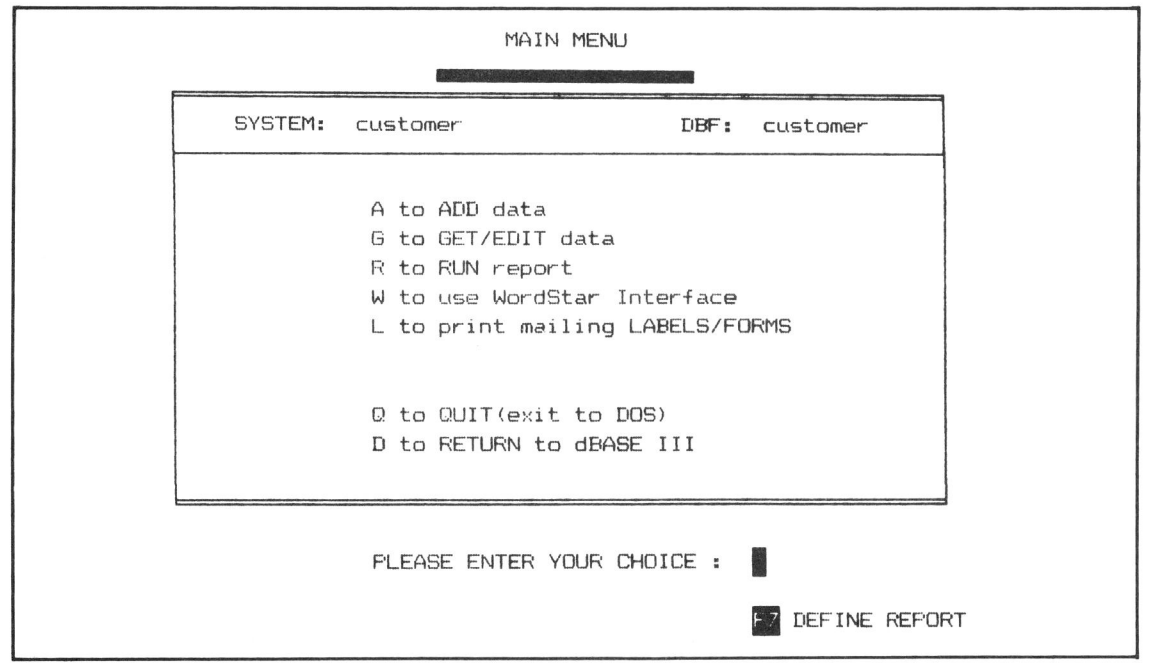

```
                              MAIN MENU
                         ▄▄▄▄▄▄▄▄▄▄▄▄▄▄▄▄

        SYSTEM:   customer              DBF:   customer
       ┌──────────────────────────────────────────────────┐
       │                                                  │
       │           A to ADD data                          │
       │           G to GET/EDIT data                     │
       │           R to RUN report                        │
       │           W to use WordStar Interface            │
       │           L to print mailing LABELS/FORMS        │
       │                                                  │
       │                                                  │
       │           Q to QUIT(exit to DOS)                 │
       │           D to RETURN to dBASE III               │
       │                                                  │
       └──────────────────────────────────────────────────┘

              PLEASE ENTER YOUR CHOICE :   ▇

                                        ▐F-7▌ DEFINE REPORT
```

Fig. 19-25. QuickCode III Generated main menu.

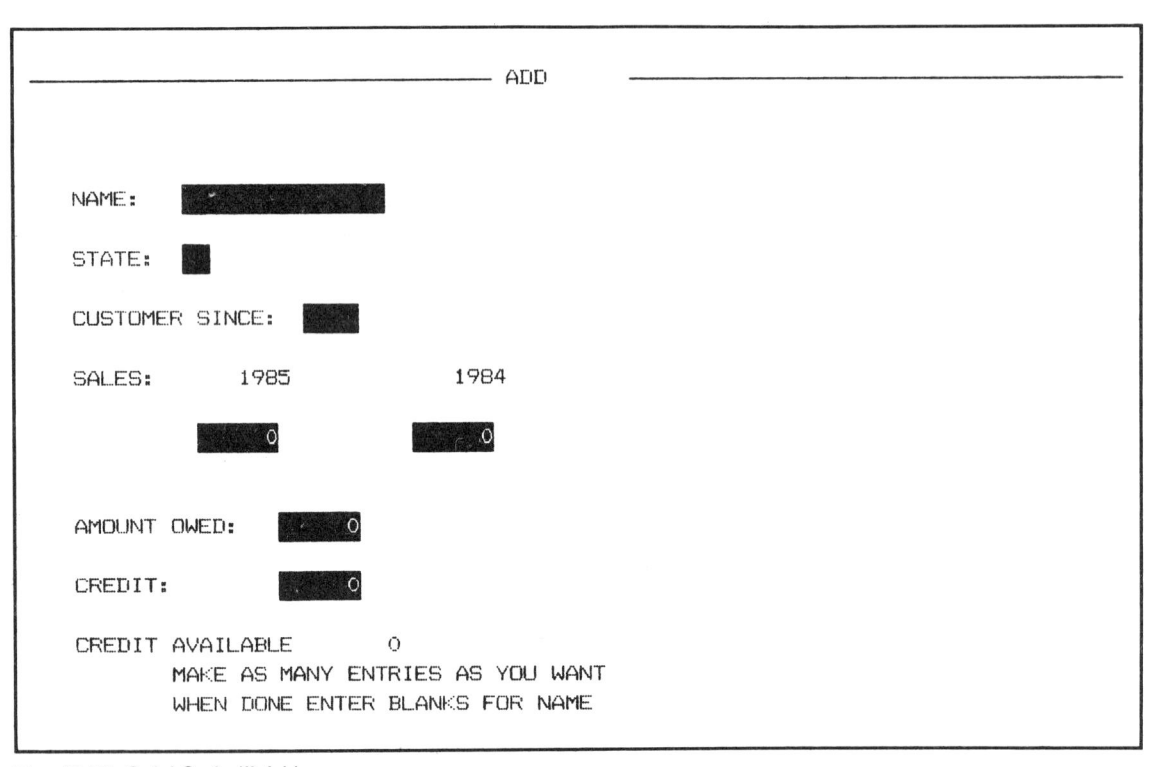

Fig. 19-26. QuickCode III Add screen.

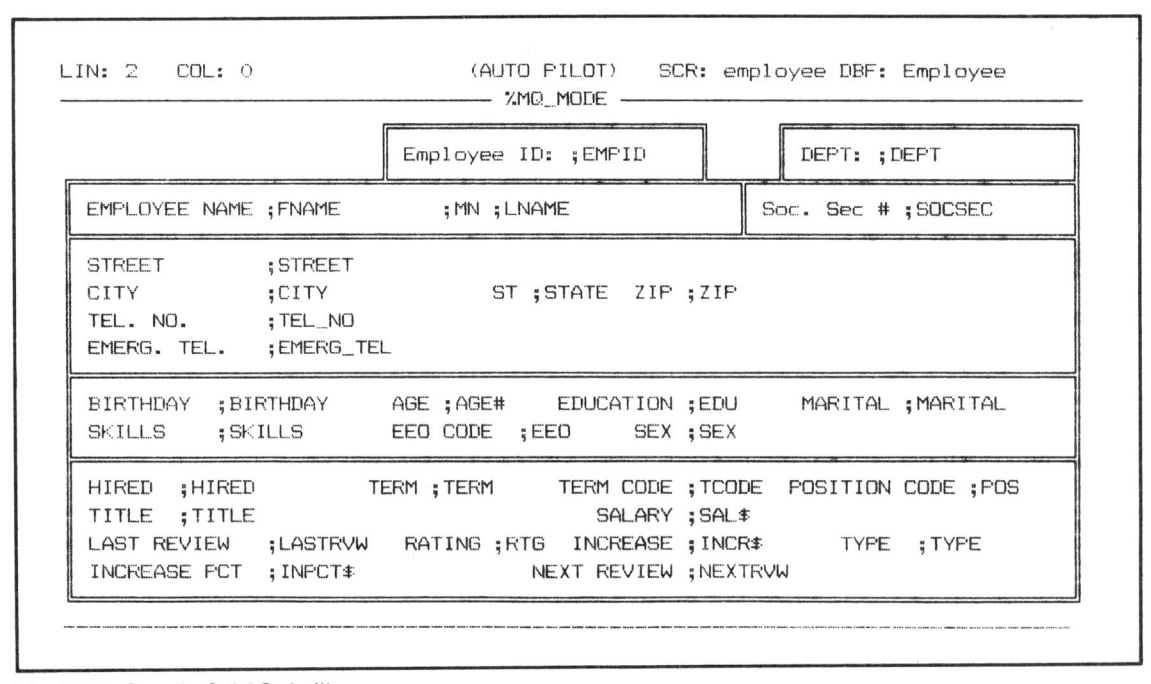

Fig. 19-27. Sample QuickCode III screen.

168

with QuickMenu, the menu generator part of QuickCode III.

The menu has the standard add data option, along with the get/edit option, which includes changing, displaying, and deleting the record. There are many ways to retrieve the record before deleting, changing, or displaying it.

Another option lets you run formerly-created reports, to create a WordStar-MailMerge file, and to print mailing labels. You can easily customize the code to make any part of the menu system perform as you want.

Another difference between FlashCode and QuickCode III is the way that adding records is handled. QuickCode III assumes that every record you enter is correct. When you are done entering records, you would simply enter a blank for the first field. Figure 19-26 shows the QuickCode III sample add screen. The message at the bottom of the screen is standard with QuickCode III.

As you can see from the two previous sections, FlashCode and QuickCode III are very similar in what they do and very dissimilar in how they do it. A final look at a complicated screen created with QuickCode III shows you the complexity of the screens you can create. Figure 19-27 is from the EMPLOYEE system that comes with QuickCode III.

Whatever your program and screen generation needs are, FlashCode and QuickCode III are two of the best programs available. Every serious dBASE user should have at least one of these fine programs.

Chapter 20
Debugging Tools

There are two types of errors that can be made in any program: syntax errors and logic errors. Syntax errors are errors in computer grammer or a failure to adhere to the standards of punctuation and rules for the particular language. This type of error includes unmatched parentheses or quotation marks, missed closing statements (ENDIF, ENDDO, ENDCASE), unknown or illegal field names (too long, or containing invalid special characters), and invalid function names (spelled wrong or having incorrect parameters).

Logic errors occur when the program does not work the way you expected it would. This means that the programmer is at fault, not the computer. Many times, programs contain code that is in the wrong place or possibly code that should be inside a loop but is placed outside the loop by mistake. No computer program can tell you if you have logic errors. You only find those when you run the program. Syntax errors are easily corrected, when you can find them. Most programs just stop working, leaving the user or the programmer to guess what might be wrong. Hopefully, through a short series of display statements or by trial and error, the offending code can be found and changed.

dFLOW

Today, with the help of debugging tools, this process can be dramatically shortened. In particular, there is one relatively new product that stands above the rest: dFlow by WallSoft Systems. This is the company that wrote the SED screen editor for dBASE almost three years ago; Ashton-Tate liked it so much that they give it away with dBASE. SED was the best package of its type three years ago. dFlow is the best of its type today, because it is comprised of several different types of debugging tools. Users are quickly finding that dFlow can also be used to document the flow and logic of their programs.

Debugging tools provide the user with a quick way to check their dBASE program for errors. Although this is not the only function of a debugging tool, it is the main one. There are many types of errors that need to be checked for. Many of these are the type of errors that occur when using DO WHILEs, CASE statements, and IF-THEN-ELSE conditions. These are the most common errors and the hardest to spot in large programs. DO WHILEs must have ENDDOs, CASE statements must have ENDCASE statements, and IF-THEN-ELSEs must have ENDIFs. When you write programs that nest these statements in even small quantities, even the best dBASE experts need help to debug the programs.

Other types of errors include calls to modules that don't exist, functions that are spelled or used incorrectly, labels without matching quotes, unmatched parentheses in mathematical expressions, and even variable names that are illegal, too long, or misspelled. A package that can perform this service and document the locations of the errors in your code would be an excellent package.

There is more to debugging than just finding errors. Documenting the code is also very important. Loops, IF-THEN-ELSEs, and CASE statements are an integral part of any program. When the dBASE programmer is checking for logic errors, there needs to be a way to tell what loop you are in and whether the IF-THEN-ELSE you are checking is in the "then" part or the "else" part.

Many days have been spent by dBASE programmers in "lining" the code. This means drawing lines from the DO WHILE to the ENDDO, from the IF to the ENDIF, and from the DO CASE to the ENDCASE. dFlow does all this in seconds without any intervention by the user.

dFlow already sounds like a great package, but there's more! dFLOW also cross-references your program's variables. It produces a listing of your program and shows every variable you created and each line where it is used. There are programs that do only this type of cross-referencing, and they cost more than dFLOW!

dFLOW does still more wonderful things! Suppose you have eight modules. Module 1 calls modules 2, 3, and 4. Module 2 calls modules 5 and 6. Module 3 calls modules 6 and 7. Finally module 4 calls modules 5 and 7. With dFlow, you need only give it the name of module 1. dFlow figures out that module 1 calls other modules and that the other modules call still other modules. When it is done, you can have cross-reference listings for each in-

```
  dFLOW 3.08b     (Copyright (C) MCMLXXXV, WallSoft Systems, Inc.)
          Your dBASE program file:A:CUSTADD.PRG

  ┌────────────┤ FLOW ANALYSIS ├──────────┐  ┌───────────┤ DOCUMENTATION ├─────────┐
  │                                       │  │                                     │
  │  D   Diagram program flow             │  │  V   Variables concordance          │
  │  L   Line numbering                   │  │  M   Modules cross-reference        │
  │  C   Controls only (IF, DO WHILE, etc.)│ │                                     │
  │  E   Error messages only (no program listing)│                                 │
  │                                       │  │                                     │
  └───────────────────────────────────────┘  └─────────────────────────────────────┘


  ┌────────────────┤ OUTPUT ├────────────┐   ┌─────────────┤ ACTION ├──────────────┐
  │                                       │  │   ┌─────────────────────────┐       │
  │  S   Screen                           │  │   │ RETURN when ready       │       │
  │  P   Printer                          │  │   └─────────────────────────┘       │
  │  F   File                             │  │     A   Analyze another program     │
  │                                       │  │     F1  Help                        │
  │                                       │  │     Q   Quit dFLOW                  │
  └───────────────────────────────────────┘  └─────────────────────────────────────┘
```

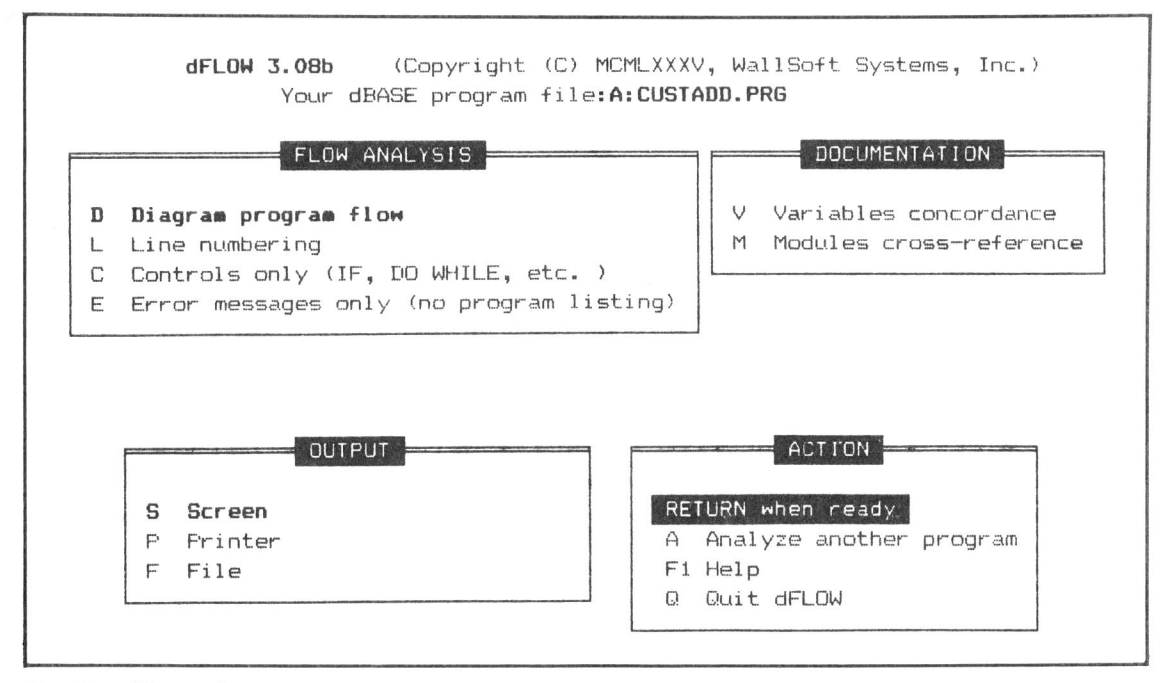

Fig. 20-1. dFlow main menu.

```
dFLOW 3.08b                    CUSTREM              Sep 02, 1985
- Module CUSTREM
   1 ***********************************
   2 *                                  *
   3 *              1.3                 *
   4 *        FREDS FISH MARKET         *
   5 *    CUSTOMER REMOVAL PROGRAM      *
   6 *           CUSTREM.PRG            *
   7 *                                  *
   8 ***********************************
   9 USE CUSTOMER INDEX CUSTOMER
  10 STORE 'T' TO MORECUST
  11 STORE '     ' TO CSN
  12 CLEAR
  13 DO WHILE MORECUST = 'T'
  14 W       @ 1,20 SAY 'FREDS FRIENDLY FISH MARKET'
  15 W       @ 3,20 SAY '     CUSTOMER REMOVAL     '
  16 W       @ 7,18 SAY 'CUSTOMER NUMBER: ' GET CSN PICTURE '#####'
  17 W       READ
  18 W       IF CSN = '     '
  19 W    T     PACK
  20 W    T     USE
  21 W    T     CLEAR
  22 W    T     RETURN
  23 W       ELSE
  24 W    F     FIND &CSN
  25 W    F     IF .NOT. (EOF() .OR. BOF())
  26 W    F  T     @  9,15 SAY 'COMPANY:       '   GET COMP
  27 W    F  T     @ 10,15 SAY 'LAST NAME:     '   GET LNAME
  28 W    F  T     @ 11,15 SAY 'FIRST NAME:    '   GET FNAME
  29 W    F  T     @ 13,15 SAY 'ADDRESS:       '   GET ADDR
  30 W    F  T     @ 14,15 SAY 'CITY:          '   GET CITY
  31 W    F  T     @ 16,15 SAY 'STATE:         '   GET ST
  32 W    F  T     @ 16,35 SAY 'ZIP: '             GET ZIP
  33 W    F  T     @ 18,15 SAY 'PHONE NUMBER: '    GET PHONE
  34 W    F  T     @ 20,15 SAY 'DISCOUNT:      '   GET DIS
  35 W    F  T     CLEAR GETS
  36 W    F  T     STORE ' ' TO DELCON
  37 W    F  T     @ 5,15 SAY 'ENTER "D" TO CONFIRM DELETE ===> ' GET DELCON
  38 W    F  T     READ
  39 W    F  T     IF UPPER(DELCON) = 'D'
  40 W    F  T  T     DELETE
  41 W    F  T  T     CLEAR
  42 W    F  T  T     @ 5,15 SAY '    *** CUSTOMER DELETED ***
  43 W    F  T     ELSE
  44 W    F  T  F     CLEAR
  45 W    F  T  F     @ 5,15 SAY '   *** CUSTOMER NOT DELETED ***
  46 W    F  T     ENDIF
  47 W    F  T     STORE '     ' TO CSN
  48 W    F     ELSE
  49 W    F  F     ? CHR(7)
  50 W    F  F     CLEAR
  51 W    F  F     @ 5,15 SAY '*** CUSTOMER NUMBER NOT FOUND ***'
  52 W    F     ENDIF
  53 W       ENDIF
  54 ENDDO              ++ End of program ++  dFLOW found no errors.
              ** END OF ANALYSIS **
```

Fig. 20-2. dFlow program listing.

dividual module and a global cross-reference of all the variables in the system and what modules they are found in.

dFlow can also display a complete module flowchart and then print out a table of contents if your program listing extends through several pages.

Figure 20-1 shows the dFlow main menu. dFlow lets you select the type of processing you want and where the output should go. It also lets you select the main module name from your disk. Everything you can select is all on one menu. It is one of the easiest pieces of software to operate you will ever use. The manual is well-produced and totally unnecessary.

The menu is divided into four sections: Flow Analysis, Documentation, Output, and Action. Flow Analysis lets you produce a listing of your code. There are options that are toggled on and off by pressing the first letter of the option. They are highlighted to show when they are on. The Flow Analysis and Documentation portions will be shown in detail in this chapter.

The Output section lets you control where you want the results produced by dFlow to be sent. You can choose the screen, printer, or an ASCII file. Each is automatically paged correctly for the device it is being sent to.

The Action section lets you run dFlow, choose another program to analyze, get on-line help or return to DOS.

Figure 20-2 shows a dBASE program that was checked with dFlow. The options Diagram program flow, and Line numbering were turned on. The program is automatically indented to make the loops and IF-THEN-ELSEs stand out.

The program is line numbered from 1 to 54. Most importantly, the DO WHILE loop is clearly marked with Ws connecting the DO WHILE and the ENDDO. Each IF-THEN-ELSE is connected by a series of Ts and Fs, indicating whether the program is in a "then" (true) state or an "else" (false) state.

The program is marked with the version of

```
dFLOW 3.08b                        CUSTREM           Sep 02, 1985

- Module CUSTREM
   1  ****************************************
   2  *                                       *
   3  *                1.3                    *
   4  *         FREDS FISH MARKET             *
   5  *      CUSTOMER REMOVAL PROGRAM         *
   6  *            CUSTREM.PRG                *
   7  *                                       *
   8  ****************************************
  13  DO WHILE MORECUST = 'T'
  18      IF CSN = '        '
  22          RETURN
  23      ELSE
  25          IF .NOT. (EOF() .OR. BOF())
  39              IF UPPER(DELCON) = 'D'
  43              ELSE
  46              ENDIF
  48          ELSE
  52          ENDIF
  53      ENDIF
  54  ENDDO                  ++ End of program ++   dFLOW found no errors.
                        ** END OF ANALYSIS **
```

Fig. 20-3. dFlow control listing.

```
                              A:CUSTADD.PRG

  - Module A:CUSTADD.PRG * dFLOW found no errors.

       VARIABLES: LOCAL CONCORDANCE FOR CUSTADD
   Variable      Line number in file
   --------      -----------------------
   ADDR:         46
   ADR:          16    29    46    53
   CITY:         46
   CMP:          13    26    46    50
   COMP:         46
   CSN:          12    25    36    41    46    49
   CTY:          17    30    46    54
   CUSTN:        46
   DIS:          46
   DS:           21    34    46    58
   FNAME:        46
   FNM:          15    28    46    52
   LNAME:        46
   LNM:          14    27    46    51
   MORECUST:     11    22
   PHN:          20    33    46    57
   PHONE:        46
   ST:           46
   STT:          18    31    46    55
   ZIP:          46
   ZP:           19    32    46    56
```

Fig. 20-4. dFlow variable cross reference.

dFlow, the date, and the name of the program being analyzed. The page number is also added to each page. There were no errors in the program or they would have been indicated as well.

The next type of run was Controls Only. This lists all the loops and logical constructs without the processing code in between. Figure 20-3 shows the results.

The line numbers make it easy to see where the control statements occur. This is used for debugging large programs when the number of Ds and ENDDOs match but the logic still doesn't work.

Documentation is an important part of any program. The variables that store data play a key role in documenting a system. When you are debugging logic flow, often it is important to see where certain variables are used in order to understand how values are changed and computed as a program runs.

Figure 20-4 shows the cross reference listing of a customer program. There are 21 variables used in the program. The variable CSN is used the most, six times in various lines. This type of listing is very valuable as your programs become larger and contain more variables. The dFlow literature calls this list a *variable concordance*.

Figure 20-5 shows the screen displays for one of Fred's systems. dFlow was only told of the program MAIN.PRG. It found the rest by itself. dFlow was asked to analyze MAIN every possible way. The result was a fifteen page program that contained analysis for every individual module, a complete flowchart as shown in Fig. 20-5, variable cross reference listings for each module, a global variable listing as shown in Fig. 20-6, and a table of contents for the entire document.

The first screen dump in Fig. 20-5 is an overall view of the four modules that MAIN calls. To view the second screen dump, you simply move the cursor to the CUSTOMER box and press the Enter key. Instantly, the second screen dump appears. The cursor could be moved to other boxes, but none of the modules calls any further modules. These screen dumps were produced by simply pressing the Shift and PrtSc keys. You can also send the output to the printer and get a line diagram as shown in Fig. 20-8.

dFlow also produced the global cross-reference chart as shown in Fig. 20-6. This describes every variable in the entire system and the modules they were found in. You can then look at the individual module cross-reference listings for further detail.

The final pages that dFlow produced were the table of contents for each system. The various procedures are listed, along with the page of the dFlow report that contains the individual cross-reference listings, the module flowcharts, and the global concordance pages.

Figure 20-8 is the printed flowchart for CUSTOMER. When dFlow prints the flowchart, it adds descriptive labels telling what the diagram is.

The most amazing thing about this software is that you barely have to operate it. The preceding figures were generated only by telling dFlow to analyze the module MAIN. dFlow did all the work of cross-referencing the module flow. dFlow was

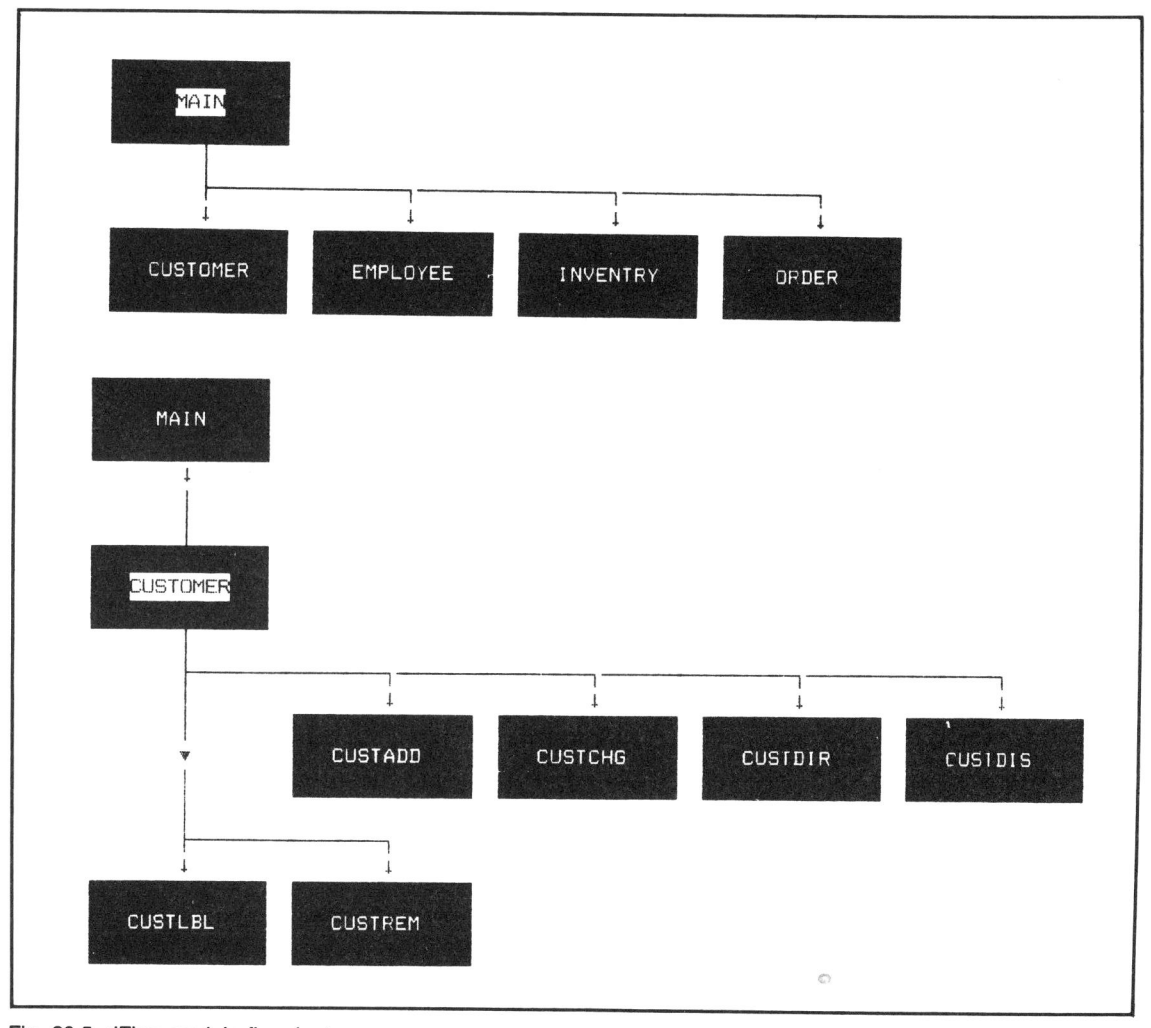

Fig. 20-5. dFlow module flowcharts.

```
             VARIABLES: GLOBAL CONCORDANCE

Variable  occurs in Modules
--------            -------
A1                  CUSTLBL CUSTLBLF
A2                  CUSTLBL CUSTLBLF
A3                  CUSTLBL CUSTLBLF
ADDR                CUSTADD CUSTCHG CUSTDIR CUSTDIS CUSTLBLF CUSTREM
ADR                 CUSTADD
ANS                 CUSTLBLA
B1                  CUSTLBL CUSTLBLF
B2                  CUSTLBL CUSTLBLF
B3                  CUSTLBL CUSTLBLF
C1                  CUSTLBL CUSTLBLF
C2                  CUSTLBL CUSTLBLF
C3                  CUSTLBL CUSTLBLF
CITY                CUSTADD CUSTCHG CUSTDIR CUSTDIS CUSTLBLF CUSTREM
CMP                 CUSTADD
COMP                CUSTADD CUSTCHG CUSTDIR CUSTDIS CUSTLBLF CUSTREM
COUNT               CUSTLBLA
CSN                 CUSTADD CUSTCHG CUSTDIS CUSTREM
CTY                 CUSTADD
CUSTEXIT            CUSTOMER
CUSTN               CUSTADD CUSTDIR
D1                  CUSTLBL CUSTLBLF
D2                  CUSTLBL CUSTLBLF
D3                  CUSTLBL CUSTLBLF
DELCON              CUSTREM
DIS                 CUSTADD CUSTCHG CUSTDIR CUSTDIS CUSTREM
DS                  CUSTADD
FNAME               CUSTADD CUSTCHG CUSTDIR CUSTDIS CUSTLBLF CUSTREM
FNM                 CUSTADD
LBLCNT              CUSTLBL CUSTLBLF
LINECNT             CUSTDIR
LNAME               CUSTADD CUSTCHG CUSTDIR CUSTDIS CUSTLBLF CUSTREM
LNM                 CUSTADD
MOREANS             CUSTDIR CUSTLBL
MORECUST            CUSTADD CUSTCHG CUSTDIS CUSTREM
OPTION              CUSTDIR CUSTLBL CUSTOMER
PHN                 CUSTADD
PHONE               CUSTADD CUSTCHG CUSTDIR CUSTDIS CUSTREM
RESP                CUSTDIS
ST                  CUSTADD CUSTCHG CUSTDIR CUSTDIS CUSTLBLF CUSTREM
STT                 CUSTADD
ZIP                 CUSTADD CUSTCHG CUSTDIR CUSTDIS CUSTLBLF CUSTREM
ZP                  CUSTADD

             Cross-reference for system CUSTOMER follows.
```

Fig. 20-6. dFlow global cross references.

tested with a system that once took 2.5 days to cross-reference. It was a large consulting job that lasted over a year. The finished system contained almost one hundred thousand lines of code and well over two hundred modules. Although earlier versions of dFlow had problems with this system, the latest version had no problems and completely documented the system in under an hour. Unfor-

```
          System CUSTOMER                            23:59
                                 CONTENTS
                                 --------

                                              Local      Module
Procedure       Module                        Concordance Cross-reference
---------       ------                        ----------- ---------------
CUSTADD                                            2          11
CUSTCHG                                            3          11
CUSTDIR                                            7          11
CUSTDIS                                            5          12
CUSTLBL                                            6          12
CUSTLBLA                                           8          12
CUSTLBLF                                           9          13
CUSTOMER                                           1          13
CUSTREM                                            4          13
Global Concordance                    10
```

Fig. 20-7. dFlow output table of contents.

tunately, it also discovered numerous as-yet undiscovered errors—and the system has been running for over a year!

When documenting large systems, dFlow has a scroll feature that lets you move back and forth between screens as easily as looking at a computer listing.

As you have seen in this chapter, dFlow is the complete debugging tool for dBASE. If you are looking for a cross reference program, syntax checker, and module flowcharter, dFlow helps you do it with ease.

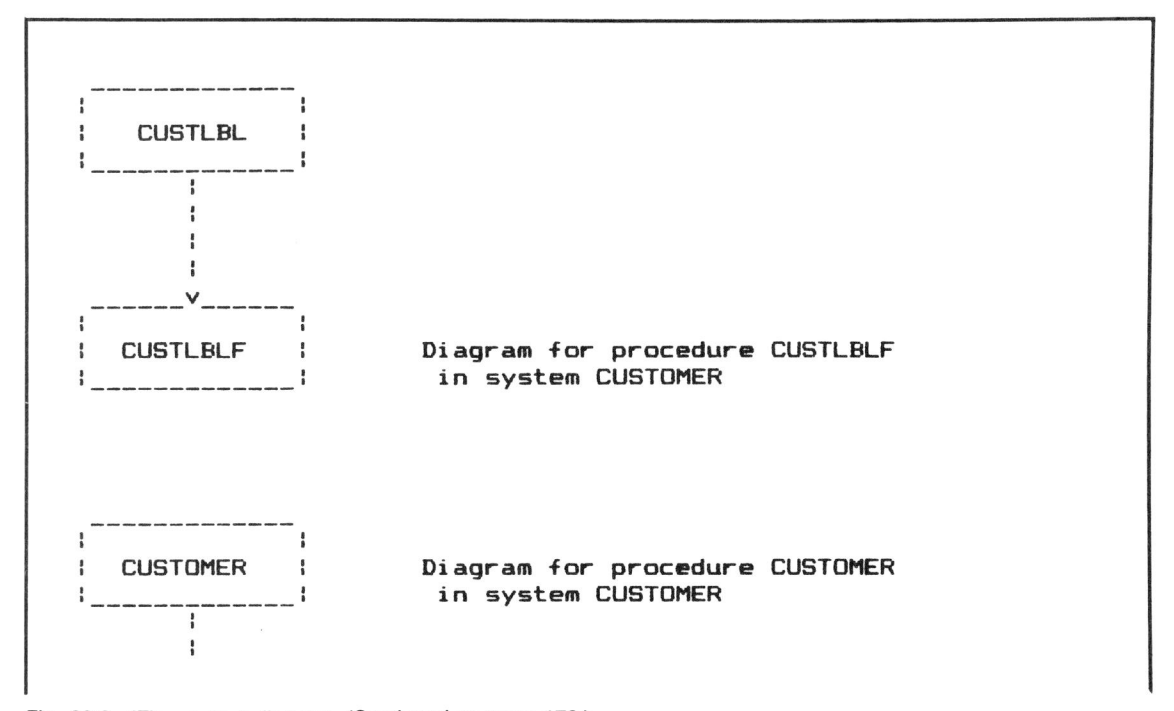

```
       ---------------
       !             !
       !  CUSTLBL    !
       !             !
       ---------------
              !
              !
              !
          ----v------
       ---------------
       !             !
       !  CUSTLBLF   !         Diagram for procedure CUSTLBLF
       !             !             in system CUSTOMER
       ---------------




       ---------------
       !             !
       !  CUSTOMER   !         Diagram for procedure CUSTOMER
       !             !             in system CUSTOMER
       ---------------
              !
              !
```

Fig. 20-8. dFlow output diagram. (Continued on page 178.)

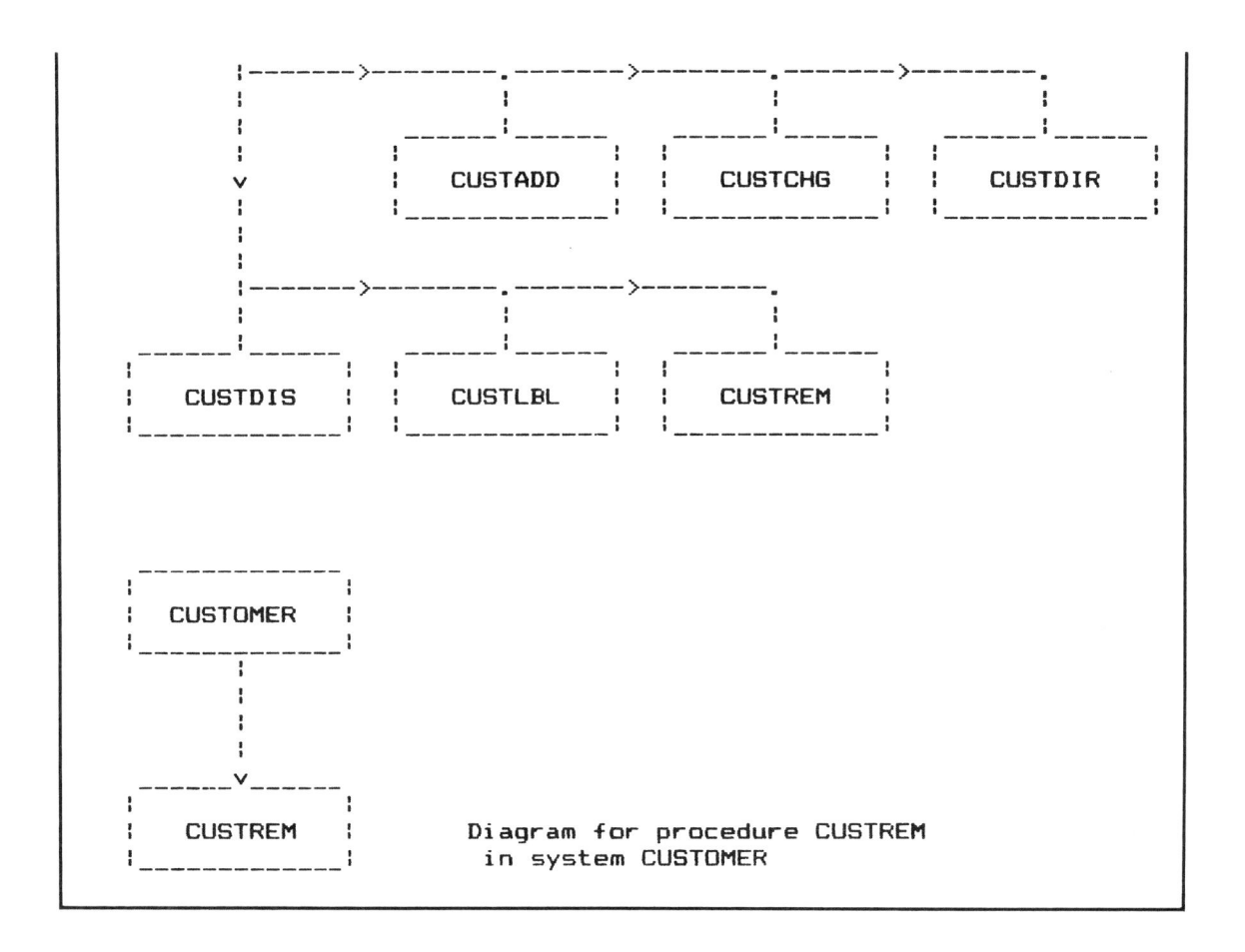

Diagram for procedure CUSTREM in system CUSTOMER

Chapter 21
dBASE Compilers

Compilers, as described in Chapter 14, can add a lot to the speed and ease of running a dBASE program. The major advantage is the speed with which the program will run. The second advantage is the fact that you do not need dBASE to run the program once it is compiled.

Compilers simply add a two-step process to executing your dBASE code. First, you compile the dBASE program, creating an *object module*. This is a set of machine code instructions that calls many subroutines to perform functions such as reads, writes, and branches. Your program is then linked or made into a *load module* that can be run on its own. Some load modules require that an extra file, called a *run-time library*, also be on the disk.

Once this simple process is completed, the program is ready to run. Since compilers by nature only translate the program from an application language into a machine language, the reviews in this chapter will only address the highlights of what each compiler does best.

THE CLIPPER COMPILER

The first compiler is Clipper, by Nantucket Software. This is a true compiler that produces 8088 machine code. Once you have produced a Clipper program, it can run all by itself.

Clipper does not use the standard dBASE index files. If you are running both dBASE III and a Clipper version, you will need two sets of indexes.

Clipper contains many new commands that are not included in dBASE III. Clipper lets you use line 0 at the top of the screen so that your program screens can be a little larger. New functions include:

FIELDNAME(n)—Tells you the fieldname of the "Nth" field in the database

IF(exp1,exp2,exp3)—Evaluates expression 1; if it is true, it executes expression 2, or if not, it executes expression 3

INKEY( )—Returns the value of the key that was pressed

LASTKEY( )—Returns the value of the last key pressed

LASTREC( )—Returns the number of records in a file

PROCLINE( )—Returns the source code line number of the current program

PROCNAME( )—Returns the name of the current program

REPLICATE(exp1,exp2)—The first expression (a characters string) is repeated exp2 number of times

STR(exp,length,decimals)—Used to line up decimals

TYPE( )—Returns the data type of a memory variable

Some of these functions are invaluable to writing complex programs.

There are other advantages to Clipper besides these functions. For example:

	Clipper	dBASE III
Variables	64,000	256
Fields	1,024	128
Files Open	250	15
Relations open	1 parent	1 parent
	Unlimited children	1 child

Clipper also lets you call separately compiled or non-dBASE programs from within the program.

Memo fields have been enhanced so that you can use memo fields as memory variables. Scientific notation has also been added, along with extended use of macros in such places as DO WHILE loops. Context sensitive help is also available to add to your program.

There are a few commands that Clipper does not support. Most of these are the interactive commands of dBASE and are generally not used in compiled programs. All of the missing functions can be implemented through other means.

Using Clipper is simple too. To compile the program, simply type "Clipper programname". Your program name will be compiled to a module called programname.OBJ. To link the program, you must enter a series of commands after running either the standard DOS Link command or the Clipper version of PLink86.

Either way, CLIPPER runs the linker and your load module is created. If you have never used a compiler before, it just adds a few steps to creating dBASE III programs. If you are familiar with the power of compilers, you will find that it is worth the wait.

WORDTECH dBIII COMPILER

dBIII Compiler is by WordTech Systems. It features enhancements to dBASE III, including new commands such as:

CLEAR KEY which clears the type ahead buffer

DOSINT which allows values to be sent and retrieved from DOS interrupt vectors

IN to poll system ports

INKEY to capture the key that was pressed

OUT to give programmable control to output devices

SET DBF TO to specify different directories for data

SET FORMFEED to turn on or off automatic printer formfeeds

SET NDX TO to specify different directories for indexes

Macro substitution is also allowed in loops.

With very few differences, dBIII is identical to Clipper. dBIII is not a true compiler, as you need a run-time library on the disk. Its features are not quite as extensive as Clipper's, but it is from a company that has been in the compiler business for a long time.

Depending on your timing, the newest versions of both Clipper and dBIII should be carefully examined before any buying decisions are made. They will continue to duel in this market for many years to come.

Chapter 22
Other Software Programs

dBASE III can be used productively in conjunction with a number of types of programs. Some make it easier to program in dBASE III, while others add to its power and versatility.

dBASE AND TEXT EDITORS

dBASE II was well known for having a very poor editor for modifying dBASE programs. When you typed MODIFY COMMAND and specified the program name, you were presented with a text editor that made creating your programs about as much fun as debugging them at 2:00 in the morning.

dBASE III improved the text editor a great deal and made it so that editing your program simply required you to learn another text editor. It behaves as text editors should when using a 16-bit computer. The PgUp and PgDn keys work the way they are meant to, and you only have to memorize a limited number of control key sequences to operate the program.

When you type MODIFY COMMAND and specify the program name in dBASE III, the dBASE III text editor retrieves your program, and you can begin editing. After you save your program, you can run it again to see the effect of any changes you have made.

You can also use your favorite text editor to modify your dBASE code. dBASE II forced you to quit dBASE and run your favorite editor or word processor separately to edit your program. After you had finished making changes and saved your dBASE code, you would have to leave the editor, load dBASE again and then run your program. The time consumed by leaving one program and then running another was greater than the time spent running and debugging the program.

dBASE III lets you "attach" your favorite text editor automatically to dBASE III. When you type MODIFY COMMAND your editor is automatically run without leaving dBASE. You must have the editor on the dBASE III System Disk #2 along with PC-DOS (at least COMMAND.COM). This is easy on a hard disk, but it is somewhat limiting on a floppy-disk system.

The secret to this is the CONFIG.DB file. Essentially it is a simple ASCII file in which you list the special parameters you want set (the list is found on page B-1 of your dBASE III manual), including function key values, default SET command switches (on or off), and hardware configurations.

To change the name of your word processor to WordStar (for example), you would code "TEDIT = WS.COM" in CONFIG.DB. dBASE would automatically call WordStar when you type MODIFY COMMAND. The changes take effect the next time you enter dBASE III.

You can also call your editor through the dBASE III system interface using the RUN command. To load WordStar you would type the dBASE command:

RUN WS.COM

If you are looking for a good text editor to use with dBASE III, consider the IBM Personal Editor; it fits the dBASE environment, takes up little memory and disk space, and offers a full range of features. It has been used for development programming for several years with a high degree of success.

If you are using dBASE II, you still have the problem of needing a good text editor while dBASE is running. In the section called "Running dBASE Concurrently with Other Software," two packages that will allow this capability are discussed. These products can be used to run dBASE in one part of your computer's available memory and also run Personal Editor (or any editor that will fit) in whatever memory you have left. You save the time it takes to leave dBASE and run your editor; you can instantly flip back and forth between dBASE and your editor to debug programs more easily.

dBASE AND 1-2-3

There are times when you may be interacting with other people who are using Lotus 1-2-3, or you may be using it and have a need to use data stored in a dBASE database. You will need to translate dBASE II or III files into Lotus 1-2-3 format. You may also have to transfer information from a Lotus 1-2-3 spreadsheet into dBASE II or III.

The easiest way to move data between 1-2-3 and dBASE is to use the 1-2-3 Translate program. Figure 22-1 displays the first screen of the Lotus translate facility for 1-2-3 version 2.0. This will automatically transfer data from 1-2-3 to dBASE II or dBASE III or from dBASE II or dBASE III to 1-2-3.

To use the Lotus version 2 Translate utility, move the cursor to the appropriate item to translate from. Select the item and press the Enter key. The screen then lets you choose the type of file you will be translating. The screen then changes, as shown in Fig. 22-2, to ask for the type of file you want your file to become.

You will then be asked a few specific questions such as "Do you want to translate an entire worksheet or just a specified range?" After answering the questions and specifying the source and target drive, the process begins.

The utility for 1-2-3 version 1A is very similar except that there are fewer choices. To use this utility, move the cursor to the appropriate menu item and press the Enter key. The only two items that pertain to dBASE are DBF to WKS and WKS to DBF. After selecting the direction of the transfer, 1-2-3 will ask you where the source data is found. Specify the drive, and 1-2-3 will show you a list of the dBASE or 1-2-3 files on the disk. Select the file by moving the cursor to each file you wish to translate and press the space bar. When you are done press the Enter key. You will then be asked where you want the translated items to go. Specify the drive and the process begins.

Lotus translates the files completely from the dBASE file format into the 1-2-3 file format. Unfortunately, this is not true of most other translate utilities. Older versions of 1-2-3 will only translate to dBASE II. You will have to use a CSV format to work with dBASE III.

dBASE II and III feature a universal translate function called CSV (Comma Separated Value) files, also known as DELImited files. These can be read and created by most programs. A CSV file is a file whose data is arranged a special way: the fields are listed across the line, with each field value

```
                Lotus Translate Utility   Version 2.00
       Copyright 1985 Lotus Development Corporation  All Rights Reserved


   What do you want to translate FROM?

           1-2-3, release 1A
           1-2-3, release 2
           dBase II
           dBase III
           DIF
           Jazz
           SYMPHONY, release 1.0
           SYMPHONY, release 1.1
           VISICALC



           Move the menu pointer to your selection and press [RETURN].
              Press [ESCAPE] to leave the Translate Utility.
                  Press [HELP] for more information.
```

Fig. 22-1. Lotus 1-2-3 Translate Utility screen 1.

```
                Lotus Translate Utility   Version 2.00
       Copyright 1985 Lotus Development Corporation  All Rights Reserved


   Translate FROM: 1-2-3, release 1A    What do you want to translate TO?

                                        1-2-3, release 2
                                        dBase II
                                        dBase III
                                        DIF
                                        SYMPHONY, release 1.0
                                        SYMPHONY, release 1.1







           Move the menu pointer to your selection and press [RETURN].
            Press [ESCAPE] to return to the source selection menu.
                  Press [HELP] for more information.
```

Fig. 22-2. Lotus 1-2-3 Translate Utility screen 2.

separated by a comma. Character fields are enclosed in quotation marks, while numeric values are not.

dBASE uses the command "COPY TO <filename> DELIMITED" to create a CSV file that other programs can use.

1-2-3 can read a CSV file, and has the capability of directly creating and reading dBASE files. Lotus 1-2-3 uses the following command to read CSV files:

/File Import

dBASE uses "APPEND FROM <filename> DELIMITED" to read a CSV file. dBASE can also read SDF files. SDF stands for System Data Format and means that the data file contains fields in exactly the same place on each line as they appear in the database. Each field in the dBASE database that will hold the data must contain the exact number of positions needed to read in the data. The format to read an SDF file is:

APPEND FROM <filename> SDF

FLASHCODE

The FlashCode screen editor was described in detail in Chapter 19. It is described once again in this section, because it does more than just display screens. FlashCode also allows you create and then display pop-up menus anywhere on the screen.

To create pop-up menus, you need Flashup, a program that is included with FlashCode. It is loaded before dBASE and sits in the background, accessible directly from your program without any intervention on your part.

FlashCode lets you generate text screens that can be used for on-line help. It also lets you generate menu screens that pop-up on command and allows the user to select from the choices that are given. Flashup passes a code to your dBASE program that indicates which menu items was selected. You can then take appropriate action in your program, based on the menu choice.

The pop-up screens can be as large as the whole screen or just take a tiny portion of it. You can create complete menu-based systems using the various size windows instead of the traditional dBASE code.

The Window Editor selection (on the Flash-Code main menu—see Fig. 19-8) lets you create a window. You are presented with a blank screen except for a box in the center. This box will contain your pop-up screen. Pressing function key F2 will cause the window shown in Fig. 22-3 to pop up. Before creating your window, you can move the window or resize it. The pop-up menu that allows you to do this is a good example of one of these windows in action. The bar moves between the lower three entries as you press the cursor keys. When you press the Enter key, FlashCode determines where the menu bar was when you pressed the Enter key and takes appropriate action.

Figure 22-4 shows a text screen after creation. The bar across the top of the window was created with the graphics editor of FlashCode as shown in Chapter 19. This might be a help screen for a menu-based general ledger system. The user, now knowing what the menu means, might request help. This screen would pop-up immediately.

The only difference between a text window and a menu window is the amount of definition. When you place text in a window, it is only text until you tell FlashCode to further redefine it. Figure 22-5 shows a window being defined as a menu. The cursor is placed on a line that contains text (not a blank line). Function key F4 is pressed to define a menu item. The line becomes a highlighted menu bar, where you can make selections. You then answer three questions: the first determines whether or not the line should be a menu item. When the dBASE code is generated, this will cause a menu bar listing the possible choices to be placed on that line in the window.

The Return Code is extremely important. FlashCode lets you set up a variable to hold the code. This code is a value that you set in your program. If you set three menu items, each with a code of A, B, and C respectively, you can pop-up the menu, let the user make the selection, and then test for A, B, or C. The dBASE code to do this is shown later in this section.

The final item to select is whether or not the

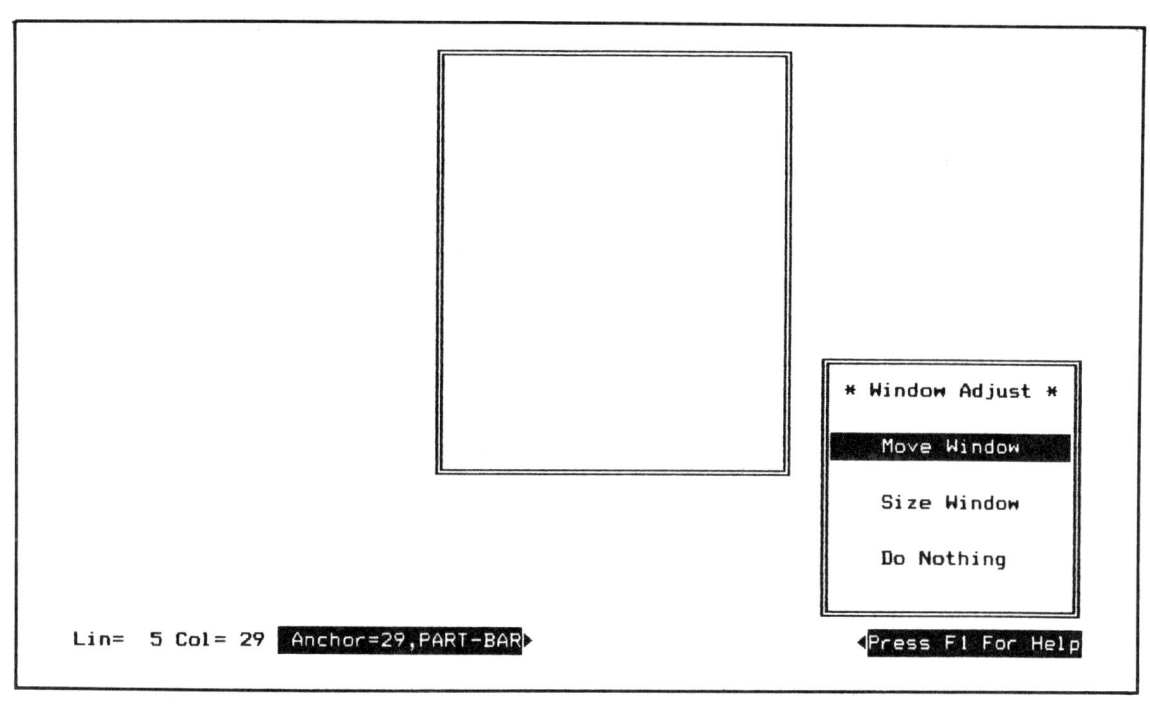

Fig. 22-3. FlashCode window screen.

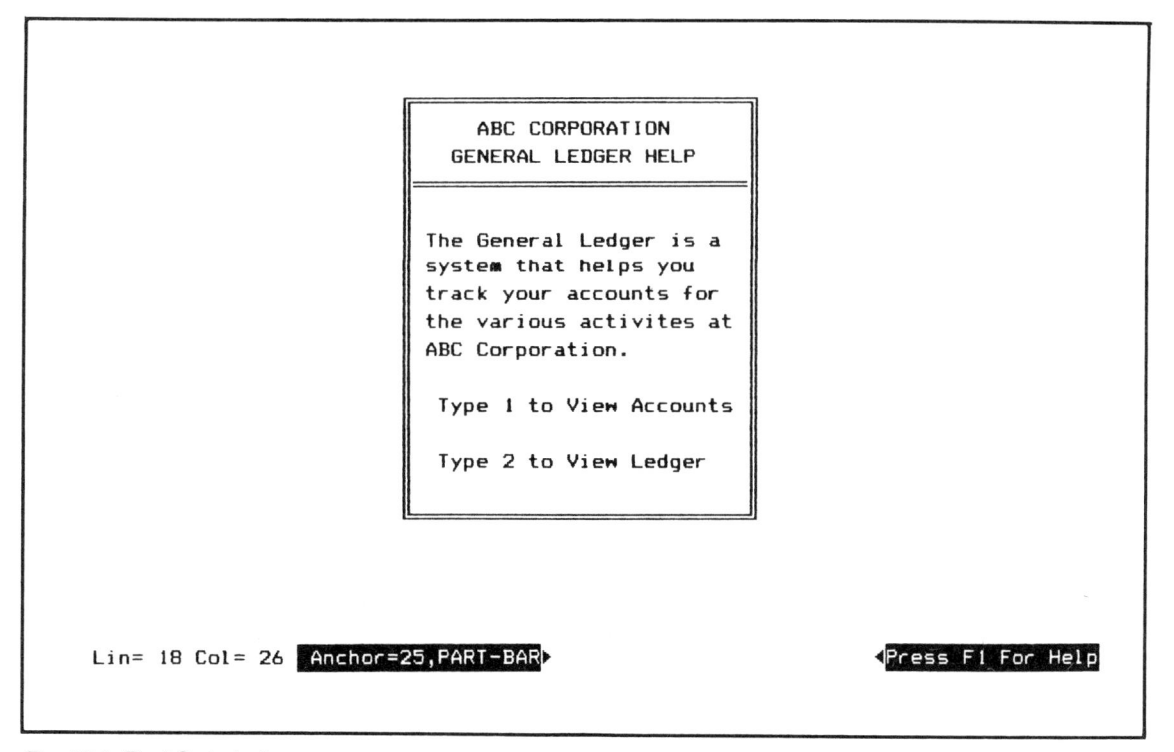

Fig. 22-4. FlashCode text screen.

185

menu bar will go to that item when the screen is first displayed. Once you have chosen these parameters, you are ready to code your program.

FlashCode windows can be positioned anywhere on the screen. You can also pop-up windows over screens that are currently being displayed. This is one of the nicest benefits of FlashCode. You cannot have multiple windows popped-up at the same time, however.

To use pop-up windows, you would write the same dBASE code you normally write, with a few exceptions. First, you must initially open the window library, which you only have to do once. Next, you must pop-up the window precisely when you want it to appear. After coding the pop-up command, you capture the menu selection (if it is a menu) and then usually take appropriate action with a CASE statement.

Here are some hints concerning the use of FlashCode windows.
- Normal dBASE Code goes anywhere.
- First load the window library.
- CHR(145) invokes Flashup.
- WINLIB is the name you create for the entire library.
- L. means "load the library."
- The double quotes and slash are mandatory.

$$??CHR(145) + ``L.WINLIB.WIN/''$$

- Next, display the window from the library.
- W. means "load a window" from an already loaded library.
- MINE is the name of the window that you create.

$$??CHR(145) + ``W.MINE/''$$

- Next capture the response.
- ANS can be named anything you desire.

SET CONSOLE OFF
WAIT TO ANS
SET CONSOLE ON

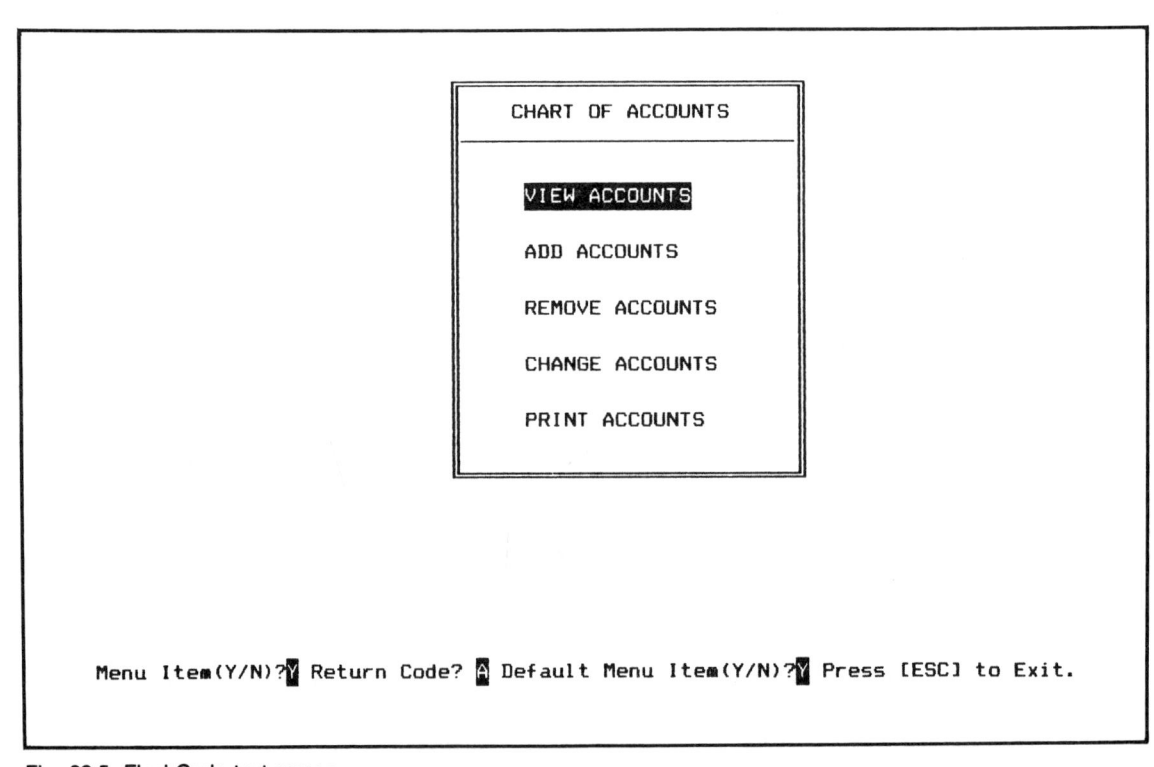

Fig. 22-5. FlashCode text screen.

- Finally, take appropriate action.

```
DO CASE
   CASE (ANS = 'A')
      take action # 1
   CASE (ANS = 'B')
      TAKE ACTION # 2
   CASE (ANS = 'C')
      TAKE ACTION # 2
ENDCASE
```

The above illustrates the dBASE code necessary for popping-up menu windows. When you pop-up text windows, there is no need to capture a response or take any action, as you are just displaying a message in a window.

FlashCode windows can add a lot of sophistication to any dBASE program. By mixing the type of menus you present to the user, you can create more flexible, easy to operate systems.

dWINDOW

There is another windowing product that, as of this writing, only works with dBASE II. dWindow is also an interesting package, and when translated for dBASE III should present another option for the user who desires flexible windowing in their programs.

Rather than allowing screen drawing and recall, dWindow features a set of windowing commands that let you accomplish the same tasks as FlashCode. The commands are "added" to dBASE by the dWindow software and become new statements that you can use in the program. This means that the code produced will be less portable, because the recipient must also have dWindow.

Figures 22-6 and 22-7 show some of the possibilities of dWindow, a package worth looking at.

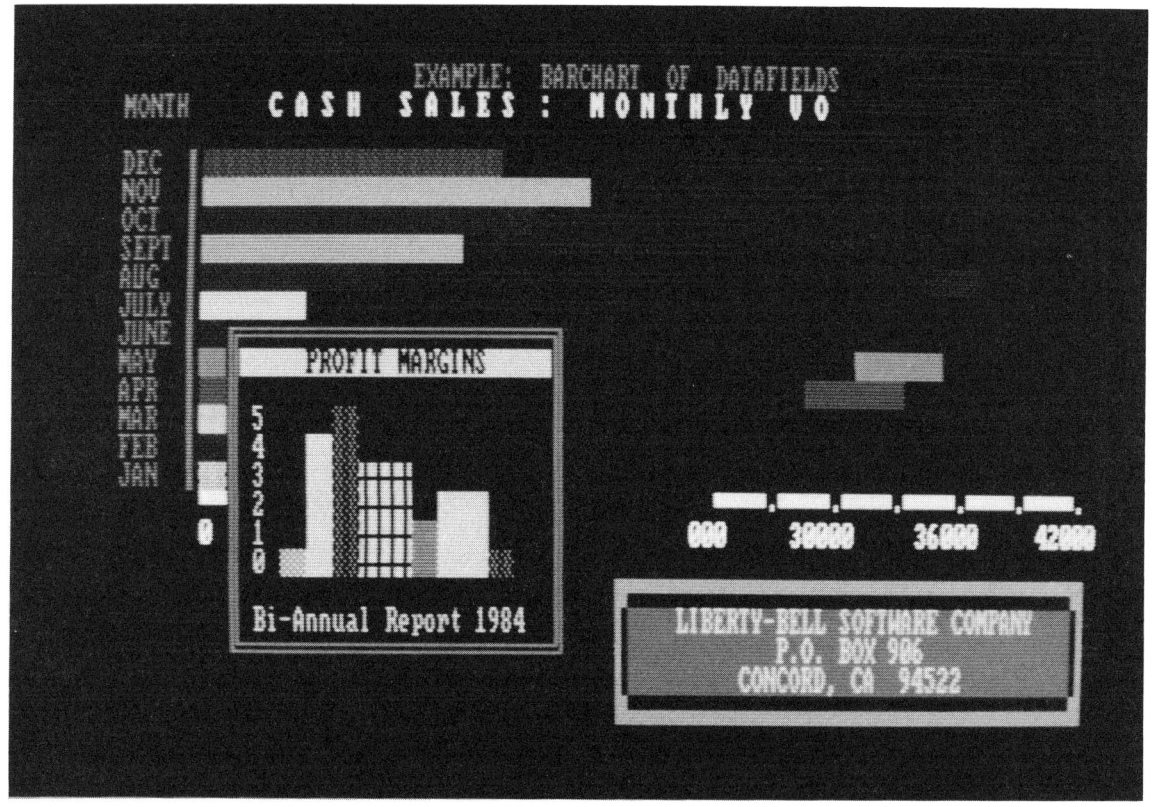

Fig. 22-6. dWindow example.

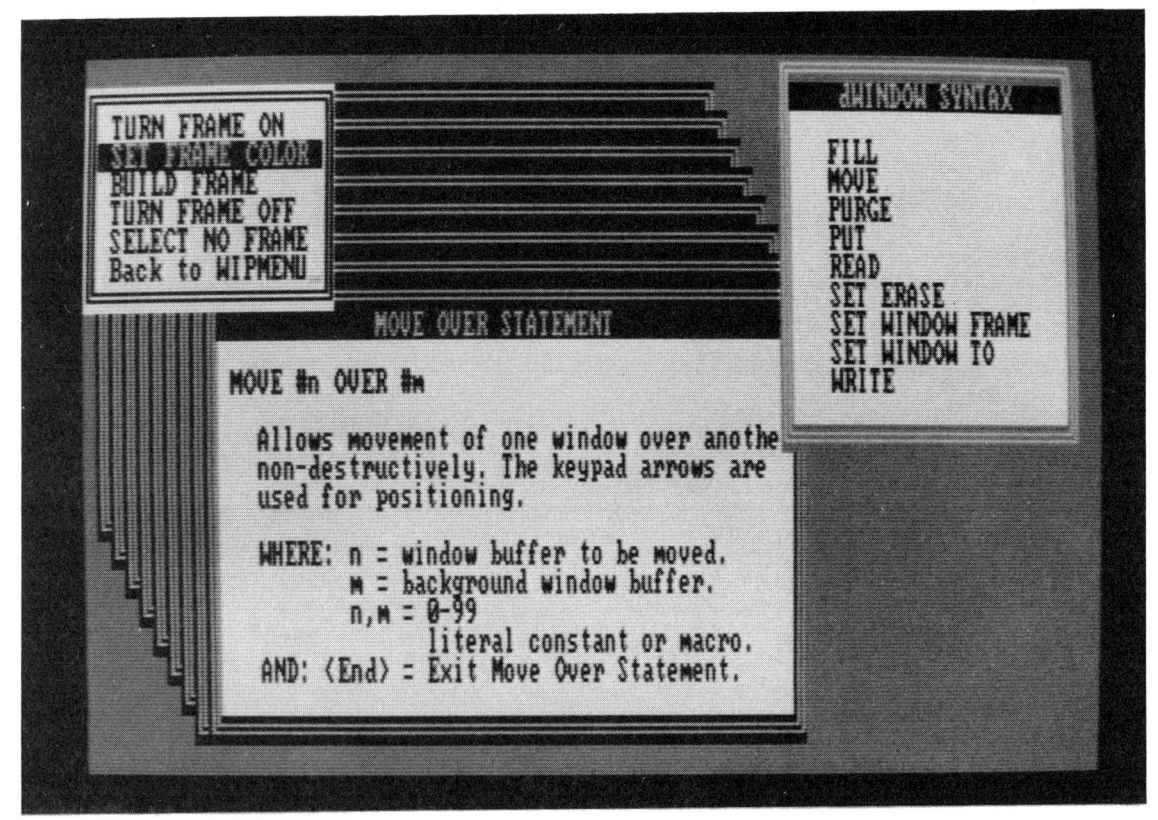

Fig. 22-7. dWindow example.

RUNNING dBASE CONCURRENTLY WITH OTHER SOFTWARE

dBASE can be run at the same time as other software by using several different methods. There are many reasons why you might want to run two or more programs simultaneously. You might want to use a text editor to view your dBASE code at the same time you are running the program. As you see errors occur in syntax or logic, you can switch to the editor to correct your dBASE code on the spot.

You might also want to work in dBASE and 1-2-3 at the same time. Suppose that during the day you use dBASE for your database tasks and 1-2-3 for spreadsheet tasks. Rather than having to switch from one to the other, you could just press a single key and change programs without loading and exiting either program.

You might want to create a document with a word processor and place some dBASE data in the middle of it or even attach a dBASE report. With concurrent processing, this is easily accomplished.

Concurrent processing means that the memory of the computer is split into two or more sections called *partitions*. Each partition can contain programs that are memory-resident. The programs can appear to be executing at the same time, although this is not really possible with a single computer CPU. The computer control is switched between concurrently executing programs while one or the other is waiting for response from the operator or waiting for some I/O operation.

Two products that allow this capability are Memory Shift by North American Business Systems, and Double DOS by SoftLogic Solutions.

Both products accomplish the same objective, which is letting you run two programs simultaneously. There are advantages to using both packages. Double DOS allows true concurrent processing; that is, each partition is active and two programs are executing apparently at the same time. You can be running a dBASE program in one partition while creating a Lotus 1-2-3 spreadsheet in the other. Memory Shift "freezes" a partition when you leave it; for example, if you were running a dBASE program and switched to the 1-2-3 partition, dBASE would "go to sleep." The dBASE partition would actually be suspended while you worked in other partitions. The moment you reenter the dBASE partition, it comes to life again exactly where it left off.

This switching capability is the major advantage of double DOS. Double DOS only lets you have two partitions and has no file transfer capability. Memory Shift features up to nine definable partitions. You can allocate precise amounts of memory for each partition. It also lets you capture any screen and "playback" the screen onto another program. Imagine capturing a screen of dBASE data and then dumping it into your word processor with no rekeying! Memory Shift can make this possible.

These are some of the advantages of concurrent processing. Double DOS or Memory Shift work with many of the finest programs, including dBASE II and III.

Chapter 23
dBASE Publications

There are a number of journals, books, and informative online services of interest to the dBASE III programmer available. This chapter describes some of the better known sources of information and ideas.

DATA BASED ADVISOR

Data Based Advisor is the best (and actually only) independent publication serving the world of microcomputer database products. Published by Data Based Solutions, a California-based consulting and software distribution company, it has earned the respect of most serious database enthusiasts.

It began serving the dBASE II community over two years ago and has maintained its quality over the years. They now feature all the major database packages, but still concentrate on dBASE.

A recent issue found articles on dBASE II, dBASE III, R:base 5000, Knowledgeman, Q-Pro 4, Revelation, FoxBase, ZIM, REFLEX, and ask SAM. Obviously, some of these packages are not yet enjoying the same status as dBASE and R:base, but all of the articles are well-written.

Data Based Advisor reviews almost all the new packages to keep the reader informed of any market changes. Peripheral packages that can save you time and money are also featured.

Data Based Advisor features a multitude of articles geared for all levels from novice to expert. There is something for both the casual user and the serious developer. Technical articles, tips, industry developments and even interviews make this monthly publication the most popular publication for the database user.

The magazine also contains a lot of advertising and can help you find the right package or utility at the right price. Comparisons of many packages are commonplace; the recent comparison between Nantucket's Clipper dBASE III compiler and WordTech's dBIII compiler attracted a great deal of attention.

If you need a monthly publication to keep on top of the latest developments in database, then *Data Based Advisor* is a necessity.

ASHTON-TATE QUARTERLY

The *Ashton-Tate Quarterly* is published (you guessed it) four times each year. It replaced the old *dNews* publication and contains articles on the Ashton-Tate product line, including dBASE and Framework.

Colorful and well written, it is aimed primarily at the novice. The *A-T Quarterly* features many technical tutorials that even the beginner can understand and put to good use.

Available at a nominal fee, it contains little advertising and presents many simple tricks that people have learned through the use of Ashton-Tate products.

One interesting set of recent articles feature an explanation of what a relational database is without even mentioning dBASE. Another article tells the latest trick for writing Fred programs in Framework.

New products are announced in the *Ashton-Tate Quarterly,* and news of Ashton-Tate in general is presented. It is a good publication for the Ashton-Tate user.

ASHTON-TATE TECH NOTES

Ashton-Tate Tech Notes is the undisputed guide for technical wizards. Written by the software support staff at Ashton-Tate, this is a monthly guide of tips, tricks, and traps. It is divided into several sections and categorized by products.

dBASE II, dBASE III, Friday!, and Framework are the product categories. The sections include the latest bugs (they call them anomalies) and bug fixes, technical tips, the latest versions of Ashton-Tate software and the methods you can use to update your copies, and more.

There are many tutorials that describe the programs in great depth for both the novice and the expert. *Tech Notes* is also an excellent tip guide. Because Ashton-Tate has a large support staff, they receive many calls from the user community. The best questions and suggestions usually make it into *Tech Notes*. Many tricks result in undocumented commands coming to light, and you may find ways to do things that the products cannot allegedly do.

Never tell a technical person that something cannot be done; they will find a way. The *Tech Notes* is the publication that reveals the most about using the products. It is aimed at the power-user, and it is well worth the yearly subscription charge.

APPLICATION JUNCTION

Application Junction is Ashton-Tate's list of software written in dBASE II or III by third-party developers. Covering vertical markets, industry specific programs, and other developed applications, this guide can be an excellent starting place when you want to purchase off-the-shelf applications.

In *Application Junction* you will find the applications listed by industry. They are described in a few paragraphs and list the dBASE environment (dBASE II, dBASE III, or Runtime). The price and the name and address of the developing companies are also listed.

COMPUSERVE—WORLD OF dBASE

CompuServe, the national on-line communications service maintains a dBASE user's group on the Programmer's Subscriber Interest Group (SIG). The CompuServe SIGs are bulletin boards where people from all over the United States and Canada meet and exchange ideas, programs, and tips. The Programmer's SIG (GO PCS-158 on C-serve) is the regular meeting place of a variety of dBASE users, from business people to the Ashton-Tate support staff themselves.

They have a weekly forum where they share ideas and get answers to problems. Also, a library of dBASE programs, Framework FRED routines, and add-on programs is maintained for the benefit of the SIG users, and the message board contains questions and answers from and to people in all walks of data processing life.

At the time of this writing, there is rumored to be an Ashton-Tate SIG that will soon be available on CompuServe. For a wide range of technical and nontechnical support, CompuServe is the meeting place of the 1980's.

THE BEST-SELLING dBASE BOOKS

The best-selling dBASE books are easy to

describe. The best books for learning dBASE are *Everyman's Database Primer for dBASE II* by Robert Byers and *Everyman's Database Primer for dBASE III* by Robert Byers published by Ashton-Tate.

The best books for learning programming with dBASE are *Programming with dBASE II* by Cary Prague and Jim Hammitt and *Programming with dBASE III* by Cary Prague and Jim Hammitt published by TAB BOOKS Inc.

The best book for advanced dBASE is *Advanced Programmers Guide featuring dBASE II and III* by Luis Castro, Jay Hanson, and Tom Rettig of the Ashton-Tate Support Center published by Ashton-Tate.

The best-selling dBASE books are *Using dBASE II* by Alan Simpson and *Using dBASE III* by Alan Simpson.

All of these books are essential to any serious dBASE library.

Chapter 24
dBASE User Groups

A new community has sprung up around the United States and even around the world: the community of dBASE programmers and business users. People in all walks of life who use dBASE II and/or dBASE III have gathered together to lend advice, programs, and techniques to others using the software.

This movement has been growing for several years, and is a constant source of information and mutual support. Members of such groups, like the Triangle dBASE User's Group (TDUG) in North Carolina, are providing programming services, libraries of dBASE programs, and advice on various add-on products to other members.

There are two major advantages to user's groups that make them well worth joining. The members can offer advice to people who are experiencing problems using software. This informal "problem desk" can help novice programmers and even experts.

The second advantage is that of bringing about change to the software itself. The user's groups post "wish lists" in their newsletters and other publications; Ashton-Tate and other large companies have found it extremely business-wise to listen to their complaints and suggestions.

In short, belonging to a user's group can enhance your knowledge and use of packages like dBASE III.

The following is a partial list of dBASE user's groups around the country:

Arizona

Phoenix Database User's Group
6803 S. Mitchell Dr.
Tempe, AZ 85283

California

dBASE II User's Group of Marin and North Bay
17 Angela Ave.
San Anselmo, CA 94960

dBUGS—dBASE II User's Group of Sacramento
(No address available)

dBASERS
5244 Edgepark Way
San Diego, CA 92124

Debasic Computer Groupies
c/o Applications Unlimited (Attn: Tom)
2153 Cooley Place
Pasadena, CA 91104

San Diego dBASERS Group
(No address available)

Colorado

Pike's Peak dBASE II User's Group
P.O. Box 4730
Woodland Park, CO 80866

Florida

dBASE II and III User's Group
119 Plantation Ct., Suite D.
Temple Terrace, FL 33617

Georgia

Atlanta Data Base User's Society
P.O. Box 19913
Atlanta, GA 30325

Hawaii

Oahu IBM PC User's Group
400 Hobron Lane
Honolulu, HI 96815

Maryland

dBASE User's Group
6200 Westchester Park Dr.
College Park, MD 20740

Missouri

dBASE II User's Club
8131 Indiana
Kansas City, MO 64132

New York

Rochester Area Data Base User Group
1459 Lake Rd.
Webster, NY 14580

North Carolina

Triangle dBASE User's Group
3304 Dell Drive
Raleigh, NC 27609

Ohio

dBASE II Society User's Club
210 Braunstein, ML #11
Cincinnati, OH 45221

South Dakota

Black Hills dBASE User's Group
1112 CrestRidge Ct.
Rapid City, SD 57701

Tennessee

Memphis dBASE User's Group
571 Buck St.
Memphis, TN 38111

Texas

Dallas-Ft Worth dBASE User's Group
1490 West Spring Valley Rd.
Richardson, TX 75080

Appendix A
Common dBASE III Error Messages

Alias name already in use. The ALIAS clause of the USE statement is referencing an alias name that is already in use. Use a different alias name.

Alias not found. A SELEct statement specified an alias that is not in use, or a letter value outside the range A to J.

Cannot erase open file. An ERASe command was issued for a database or other file that is currently in use.

Command file not found. A DO statement referenced a procedure name that is not in the current procedure file, and/or a .PRG file with the name specified could not be found.

Cyclic relation. The cyclic relation error occurs when one SELEcted area is related to another area via the SET RELAtion command, and the area that the relation is being set to already has a SET RELAtion pointing to the current file/area.

Data type mismatch. The operators in an expression are of different data types, and no conversion function was used.

Database is not indexed. A FIND or SEEK operation was attempted against a database that was opened by a USE statement with no INDEX clause specified, and no subsequent SET INDEX command was issued.

Directory is full. A file is being written to a disk or directory that already has the maximum number of files on it.

File already exists. A RENAme command was issued that specified a new filename that already exists on the current directory.

File does not exist. A filename was used in a file operation (APPEnd, DELEte, ERASe, RENAme, or USE) that does not exist on the current directory.

File is already open. This occurs when a USE statement specifies a file that was already USEd in a different SELEct area.

FOR and WHILE cannot both be specified. The FOR and WHILE clauses are mutually exclusive and cannot both be present in the same statement.

Insufficient memory. This is a kind of a catch-all error. It can occur when the RAM memory of the computer is not large enough to contain dBASE III, the program/procedure files, and the buffers for the databases and indexes. Be sure that you are using the recommended values for the BUFFERS and FILES parameters in CONFIG.-SYS.

Memo file cannot be opened. This error occurs when a memo field file was deleted or renamed, or does not exist on the current directory.

Memory variable file invalid. An attempt was made to RESTore FROM a file that is not a memory variable file. Valid files are only created by SAVE TO.

Out of memory variable memory. The combined sizes of the memory variables currently allocated exceeds the size of the memory variable area (default 6000 characters). This can be increased by adjusting the MVARSIZ parameter in CONFIG.DB.

SAY/GET position is off the screen. The row and column numbers specified in the @ . . . SAY . . . GET command were out of the screen area. Valid ranges (when device is set to SCREEN) are 0 to 24 for the row coordinate and 0 to 79 for the column coordinate.

Too many files are open. The total number of files that can be open at once in dBASE III is 15, but PC-DOS in conjunction with dBASE can use 20 only if that is specified in CONFIG.SYS. This effectively limits the number of open dBASE files to 13. This includes index files, database files, format files, memory variable files, and program files. PC-DOS issues a similar message when the number of open file handles exceeds the number specified in the FILES parameter of CONFIG.SYS (default 8).

Unrecognized command verb. The command was misspelled.

Unknown function. The first word on the command line was not a dBASE command keyword, or the statement was not a valid assignment statement in the alternate format (A = B).

Variable not found. A word was used on the command line that was neither a dBASE command nor an existing memory variable name.

Zero divide. Division by zero does not yield a real number as a result. The code should be written such that a divide operation is not tried if the divisor is zero.

Appendix B
A Sample Data Dictionary System

The following system is a sample for a data dictionary system. The database layouts, screen format, and a maintenance program are all included. Be sure to index the database as described in the program prior to running the program. You may, of course, modify this routine to your own individual needs and tastes.

DATABASE STRUCTURES

Structure for database   : B:ddict.dbf
Number of data records :   0
Date of last update   : 08/03/85

Field	Field name	Type	Width	Dec
1	FLDNAME	Character	11	
2	FLDTYPE	Character	1	
3	FLDLENGTH	Numeric	3	
4	FLDDECIML	Numeric	2	
5	FLDENTITY	Character	15	
6	FLDOWNER	Character	15	
7	FLDFILE	Character	12	
8	FLDPICT	Character	15	
9	FLDDESCR	Memo	10	

** Total **   85

```
********************************************************************************
Structure for database  : B:ddictsc.dbf
Number of data records :    0
Date of last update     : 08/03/85
    Field  Field name    Type              Width   Dec
      1    FLDNAME       Character           11
      2    SCREENID      Character            8

** Total **                                  20
********************************************************************************
Structure for database  : B:ddictp.dbf
Number of data records :    0
Date of last update     : 08/03/85
    Field  Field name    Type              Width   Dec
      1    FLDNAME       Character           11
      2    PROGNAME      Character            8

** Total **                                  20
********************************************************************************
```

SCREEN FORMAT FILE

```
*   B:DDICT1.PRG
*   ! '@!'
@   1,21 SAY "Data Dictionary Maintenance Screen"
@   2,2 SAY ;
    "= = = = = = = = = = = = = = = = = = = = = = = ="
@   2,57 SAY "= = = = = = = = = = = = = = = = = = ="
@   4,7 SAY "Field name:"
@   4,20 GET fldname PICTURE '@!'
@   4,46 SAY "Entity:"
@   4,55 GET fldentity PICTURE '@!'
@   6,7 SAY "Owner:"
@   6,15 GET fldowner PICTURE '@!'
@   6,46 SAY "File name:"
@   6,59 GET fldfile PICTURE '@!'
@   9,3 SAY "Field attributes:"
@   11,3 SAY "Data type (C,L,N,D,M):"
@   11,27 GET fldtype PICTURE '@!'
@   11,37 SAY "Length:"
@   11,46 GET fldlength
@   11,57 SAY "Decimals:"
@   11,68 GET flddeciml
@   14,24 SAY "Usual picture:"
@   14,40 GET fldpict PICTURE '@!'
@   16,23 SAY "Field description:"
@   16,43 GET flddescr
```

PROGRAM FILE
```
********************************************************************************
*   DATA DICTIONARY MAINTENANCE PROGRAM
********************************************************************************
*   Initialize memory variables
STORE .F. TO DDFINISH
STORE SPACE(11) TO SCROPT
STORE SPACE(1) TO ERRFLD1
STORE SPACE(1) TO ERRFLD2
STORE SPACE(78) TO ERRMSG1
STORE 'CLNDM' TO VALTYPE
*
*   Access database
SELECT A
USE DDICT INDEX FLDNAMEX
GO TOP
*
*   Processing loop
DO WHILE .NOT. DDFINISH
   CLEAR
   @ 5,5 SAY '—- Data Dictionary Maintenance —-'
   @ 7,5 SAY 'Enter field name or QUIT: ';
      GET SCROPT PICTURE '@!'
   READ
   IF SCROPT = 'QUIT       '
      STORE .T. TO DDFINISH
      LOOP
   ENDIF
   IF SCROPT = '           '
      LOOP
ENDIF
SEEK SCROPT
IF EOF( ) .OR. BOF( )
   APPEND BLANK
   REPLACE FLDNAME WITH SCROPT
ENDIF
STORE RECNO( ) TO HOLDREC
SET FORMAT TO DDICT2
STORE .F. TO DONE_RIGHT
DO WHILE .NOT. DONE_RIGHT
   CHANGE RECORD HOLDREC
   GO HOLDREC
   STORE SPACE(1) TO ERRFLD1
   STORE SPACE(1) TO ERRFLD2
   STORE SPACE(78) TO ERRMSG1
   DO CASE
```

```
      CASE FLDNAME = '     '
        STORE .F. TO DONE_RIGHT
        STORE '?' TO ERRFLD1
        STORE '*** FIELD NAME IS REQUIRED ***' TO ERRMSG1
      CASE AT (FLDTYPE, VALTYPE) = 0
        STORE .F. TO DONE_RIGHT
        STORE '?' TO ERRFLD2
        STORE '*** FLDTYPE MUST BE C,L,N,D,M ***' TO ERRMSG1
      OTHERWISE
        STORE .T. TO DONE_RIGHT
      ENDCASE
    ENDDO
    IF AT('/',FLDNAME) > 0
      DELETE
    ENDIF
    CLEAR GETS
    CLOSE FORMAT
  ENDDO
*
*  Clean up
  CLEAR GETS
  CLOSE FORMAT
  PACK
  CLOSE DATABASES
  RETURN
***************************************************************************
```

Appendix C

Some Development Tools

The programs included in this appendix are two useful development tools for use when writing and debugging dBASE III systems. They are not intended to be a replacement for any other software package on the market that performs these functions, but they are presented as an alternative to them.

The first program, written in Pascal, is CRUSHER, which will compress dBASE code into collapsed code that will be interpreted more quickly by dBASE. The collapsed procedure files are also up to 50 percent smaller than in their original source format.

```
PROGRAM Crusher;
{ }
{This program removes leading blanks and tabs, truncates}
{keywords joins continued lines, and removes comments from}
{a dBASE III prg file. The syntax is: }
{    CRUSHER <prg file name>   }
{Include drive identifier, but NOT file extension—}
{".PRG" assumed for input file, output file is ".CLN".}
{ }

TYPE
    InFileName          =   STRING[20];
    CommandString       =   STRING[127];
    KeyWordsArray       =   ARRAY[1 . . 64] OF STRING[10];
    Str80               =   STRING[80];
```

```
VAR
   InFile              : TEXT;
   OutFile             : TEXT;
   Search1             : INTEGER;
   Search2             : INTEGER;
   PrgFile             : InFileName;
   ClnFile             : InFileName;
   IOString            : STRING[255];
   OutLine             : STRING[255];
   CheckOut            : STRING[255];
   KeyWords            : KeyWordsArray;
   RingTheBell         : CHAR;
   SearchChar          : CHAR;
   SearchWord          : STRING[15];
   SearchSuccessful    : BOOLEAN;
   Buffer              : CommandString;
   CommLine            : CommandString ABSOLUTE CSEG:$80;

CONST
   Space       = ' ';
   Comma       = ',';
   Asterisk    = '*';
   SemiColon   = ';';
   DotPrg      = '.prg';
   DotCln      = '.cln';

FUNCTION UpcaseStr(S : Str80) : Str80;
{ }
{translate string to uppercase}
{ }
VAR
  P : INTEGER;
BEGIN
  FOR P := 1 to LENGTH(S) DO
    S[P] := UPCASE (S[P]);
  UpcaseStr := S;
END;

PROCEDURE DefineKeyWords;
{ }
{These are the keywords that are to be truncated to four}
{characters. If modification is required, be sure to change}
{the ARRAY[ ] definition and the FOR statement in the loop.}
{ }
BEGIN
  KeyWords[1]  := 'ACCEPT';
```

```
KeyWords[2]   := 'ALTERNATE';
KeyWords[3]   := 'APPEND';
KeyWords[4]   := 'AVERAGE';
KeyWords[5]   := 'BROWSE';
KeyWords[6]   := 'CANCEL';
KeyWords[7]   := 'CARRY';
KeyWords[8]   := 'CHANGE';
KeyWords[9]   := 'CLEAR';
KeyWords[10]  := 'CLOSE';
KeyWords[11]  := 'COLOR';
KeyWords[12]  := 'CONFIRM';
KeyWords[13]  := 'CONSOLE';
KeyWords[14]  := 'CONTINUE';
KeyWords[15]  := 'COUNT';
KeyWords[16]  := 'DEBUG';
KeyWords[17]  := 'DECIMALS';
KeyWords[18]  := 'DEFAULT';
KeyWords[19]  := 'DELETE';
KeyWords[20]  := 'DELETED';
KeyWords[21]  := 'DELIMITED';
KeyWords[22]  := 'DELIMITERS';
KeyWords[23]  := 'DEVICE';
KeyWords[24]  := 'DISPLAY';
KeyWords[25]  := 'ENDCASE';
KeyWords[26]  := 'ENDDO';
KeyWords[27]  := 'ENDIF';
KeyWords[28]  := 'ESCAPE';
KeyWords[29]  := 'EXACT';
KeyWords[30]  := 'FILTER';
KeyWords[31]  := 'FIXED';
KeyWords[32]  := 'FORMAT';
KeyWords[33]  := 'FUNCTION';
KeyWords[34]  := 'HEADING';
KeyWords[35]  := 'INDEX';
KeyWords[36]  := 'INSERT';
KeyWords[37]  := 'INTENSITY';
KeyWords[38]  := 'LOCATE';
KeyWords[39]  := 'MARGIN';
KeyWords[40]  := 'MEMORY';
KeyWords[41]  := 'MENUS';
KeyWords[42]  := 'MODIFY';
KeyWords[43]  := 'OTHERWISE';
KeyWords[44]  := 'PARAMETERS';
KeyWords[45]  := 'PRIVATE';
KeyWords[46]  := 'PROCEDURE';
KeyWords[47]  := 'PUBLIC';
```

```
KeyWords[48]   :=   'RECALL';
KeyWords[49]   :=   'REINDEX';
KeyWords[50]   :=   'RELATION';
KeyWords[51]   :=   'RELEASE';
KeyWords[52]   :=   'RENAME';
KeyWords[53]   :=   'REPLACE';
KeyWords[54]   :=   'REPORT';
KeyWords[55]   :=   'RESTORE';
KeyWords[56]   :=   'RETURN';
KeyWords[57]   :=   'SAFETY';
KeyWords[58]   :=   'SCOREBOARD';
KeyWords[59]   :=   'SELECT';
KeyWords[60]   :=   'STORE';
KeyWords[61]   :=   'STRUCTURE';
KeyWords[62]   :=   'TOTAL';
KeyWords[63]   :=   'UNIQUE';
KeyWords[64]   :=   'UPDATE';

END;


PROCEDURE CrunchKeyWords;
{ }
{This procedure searches for keywords to truncate}
{Lines beginning with "@" and "?" are passed unchanged}
{ }
VAR
  I      :   INTEGER;
  Fpos   :   INTEGER;
  Fchar  :   CHAR;
  Fstop  :   BOOLEAN;

BEGIN

  IF LENGTH (OutLine) > 0
  THEN
    Outline := OutLine + IOString
  ELSE
    Outline := IOString;
    SearchChar := COPY(OutLine,1,1);
  IF (SearchChar <> '@') AND (SearchChar <> '?')
  THEN FOR I := 1 TO 64 DO
  BEGIN

    Fpos := POS(KeyWords[I],OutLine);

    IF Fpos > 0
```

```
      THEN BEGIN

         Fpos := Fpos + 4;

         IF Fpos <= LENGTH(OutLine)
         THEN
           Fchar := COPY(OutLine,Fpos,1)
         ELSE
           Fchar := '!';

         IF Fchar IN ['A' .. 'Z']
         THEN BEGIN

            Fstop := FALSE;
            Fstop := (POS('SAY',OutLine) > 0);
            Fstop := Fstop OR (POS('WAIT',OutLine) > 0);
            Fstop := Fstop OR (POS('ACCEPT',OutLine) > 0);

            IF NOT Fstop
            THEN BEGIN
          REPEAT
            DELETE(OutLine,Fpos,1);

            IF Fpos <= LENGTH(OutLine)

            THEN
              Fchar := COPY(OutLine,Fpos,1)
            ELSE
              Fchar := '!';

            UNTIL NOT (Fchar IN ['A' .. 'Z']);

         END;
        END;
      END;
   END;
END;

***MAIN PROGRAM***}
{ }
{This is the main routine.}
{It performs the task of removing leading characters, and}
{handling the files.}
{ }
BEGIN

   Buffer := CommLine;
```

```
DELETE(Buffer,1,1);
PrgFile := COPY(Buffer,1,Length (Buffer)) + DotPrg;
ClnFile := COPY(Buffer,1,Length(Buffer)) + DotCln;
RingTheBell := CHR(7);
OutLine := '';
DefineKeyWords;

WRITELN(Space);
WRITELN('Crushing '+PrgFile+' to '+ClnFile+' . . . ');

ASSIGN(InFile,PrgFile);
RESET(InFile);

ASSIGN(OutFile,ClnFile);
REWRITE(OutFile);

READLN(InFile,IOString);

WHILE NOT Eof(InFile) DO BEGIN

   IF LENGTH(IOString) > 0
   THEN BEGIN

     IOString := UpcaseStr(IOString);
     SearchChar := COPY(IOString,1,1);
     SearchWord :=
       COPY(IOString,1,POS(Space,IOString));
  IF (SearchChar <> Asterisk)
  AND (SearchWord <> 'NOTE')
  AND (SearchWord <> '/*')
  THEN BEGIN

     IF NOT (SearchChar IN ['A' . . 'Z']+['@','?'])
     THEN BEGIN

       REPEAT
         DELETE(IOString,1,1);
         SearchChar := COPY(IOString,1,1);
         UNTIL SearchChar IN

         ['A' . . 'Z']+['@','?'];

     END;

     Search1 := POS(SemiColon,IOString);
     IF Search1 > 0
```

```
      THEN BEGIN

         CheckOut : =
         COPY(IOString,Search1,LENGTH(IOString));

         IF LENGTH(CheckOut) < = 2
         THEN BEGIN
   Search2 : = Search1 - 1;
   SearchChar : =
         COPY(IOString,Search2,1);

   IF SearchChar = Comma
   THEN
      OutLine : = OutLine +
         COPY(IOString,1,Search2)
   ELSE
      OutLine : = OutLine +
         COPY(IOString,1,Search2)
            + Space;

     END;
   END

ELSE BEGIN

   CrunchKeyWords;

   WRITELN(OutFile,OutLine);
   OutLine : = '';
   IOString : = '';

   END;

END;

      END;

   READLN(InFile,IOString);

   END;

WRITELN('Hey, I''m Done!!' + RingTheBell);

CLOSE(InFile);
CLOSE(OutFile);

END.
```

The following program, also written in Pascal, is a procedural cross reference for a dBASE .PRG program or procedure file. It will list all references of a dBASE subroutine and will show what parameters are passed and received.

```pascal
PROGRAM dXREF;
{ }
{This program produces a procedural cross-reference for a}
{dBASE III procedure file. The format of the command is}
{    DXREF <prg file name>   }
{Extension is included. The program assumes an output}
{file extension of ".XRF"}
{ }
TYPE
    InFileName          =       STRING[20];
    CommandString       =       STRING[127];
    Str80               =       STRING[80];

VAR
    InFile              :       TEXT;
    OutFile             :       TEXT;
    Search              :       ARRAY[1 . . 6] OF INTEGER
    LstFile             :       InFileName;
    PrgFile             :       InFileName;
    IOString            :       STRING[80];
    OutLine             :       STRING[80];
    TitleLine           :       STRING[80];
    FormFeed            :       CHAR;
    RingTheBell         :       CHAR;
    SearchChar          :       CHAR;
    LineCount           :       INTEGER;
    PageCount           :       INTEGER;
    PageNo              :       STRING[4];
    SplitPos            :       INTEGER;
    SearchSuccessful    :       BOOLEAN;
    Buffer              :       CommandString;
    CommLine            :       CommandString ABSOLUTE CSEG:$80;


CONST
    Period      =   '.';
    Space       =   ' ';
    Space6      =   '      ';
    Dash        =   '—';

FUNCTION UpcaseStr(S : Str80) : Str80;
{ }
```

```
{translate string to uppercase}
{ }
VAR
  P : INTEGER;
BEGIN
  FOR P := 1 to LENGTH(S) DO
    S[P] := UPCASE(S[P]);
  UpcaseStr := S;
END;

{***MAIN PROGRAM***}
{ }
{This is a one-routine Pascal program.}
{Each line of the procedure file is checked for the}
{commands that indicate that a subroutine is being called.}
{if so, an output report line is formatted to reflect the}
{information on the statement.}
{ }
BEGIN

Buffer := CommLine;
DELETE(Buffer,1,1);
SplitPos := POS(Space,Buffer);
PrgFile := COPY(Buffer,1,LENGTH(Buffer));
SplitPos := POS(Period,PrgFile);
LstFile := COPY(Buffer,1,(SplitPos - 1)) + '.xrf';

LineCount := 0;
PageCount := 1;
FormFeed := CHR (12);
RingTheBell := CHR(7);
OutLine := '';

WRITELN(Space);
WRITELN('Cross-referencing from'
     + PrgFile + 'to' + LstFile + ' . . . ');
TitleLine := 'dXREF of ' + PrgFile + ' . . . Page ';

ASSIGN(InFile,PrgFile);
RESET(InFile);

ASSIGN(OutFile,LstFile);
REWRITE(OutFile);

STR(PageCount,PageNo);
WRITELN(OutFile,TitleLine + PageNo);
```

```
READLN(InFile,IOString);
WHILE NOT Eof(InFile) DO BEGIN

IOString := UpcaseStr(IOString);
Search[1] := Pos('PROCEDURE',IOstring);
Search[2] := Pos('PARAMETERS',IOstring);
Search[3] := Pos('DO',IOstring);
Search[4] := Pos('WITH',IOstring);
Search[5] := Pos('WHILE',IOstring);
Search[6] := Pos('CASE',IOstring);
SearchSuccessful :=
     (Search[1] + Search[2] + Search[3] < > 0;

IF SearchSuccessful
THEN BEGIN

  SearchChar := Copy(IOString,1,1);

  IF NOT
    (SearchChar IN
       ['A' .. 'Z']+['0' .. '9']+['?','@','*'])
  THEN BEGIN

     REPEAT
       DELETE(IOString,1,1);
       SearchChar := COPY(IOString,1,1);
       UNTIL SearchChar IN
         ['A' .. 'Z']+['0' .. '9']+['?','@','*'];

     END;
  OutLine := '';

  IF   (Search[1] > 0)
  AND  (SearchChar = 'P')
  THEN BEGIN

     OutLine := Space+Space+IOString;
     WRITELN(OutFile,Space);
     LineCount := LineCount + 1;

     END;

  IF   (Search[2] > 0)
  AND  (SearchChar = 'P')
  THEN OutLine := Space+Space+Space+Space
       +'RECEIVED'+IOString;
```

```
        IF    (Search[3] > 0)
        AND   (Search[5] = 0)
        AND   (Search[6] = 0)
        AND   (SearchChar = 'D')
        THEN BEGIN
        DELETE(IOString,1,3);
        OutLine := Space6
                 + 'CALLED PROCEDURE' + IOString;

        END;

      IF LENGTH(OutLine) > 0
      THEN BEGIN

        WRITELN(OutFile,OutLine);
        LineCount := LineCount + 1;

        END;

      IF LineCount >= 50
      THEN BEGIN

        LineCount := 2;
        PageCount := PageCount + 1;
        WRITELN(OutFile,FormFeed);
        STR(PageCount,PageNo);
        WRITELN(OutFile,TitleLine + PageNo);
        WRITELN(OutFile,Space);

        END;

      END;

      ReadLn(InFile,IOString);

    END;

    WRITELN(OutFile,FormFeed);
    WRITELN('Hey, I''m Done!!' + RingTheBell);

    CLOSE(InFile);
    CLOSE(OutFile);

END.
```

The dXREF program listed above produces the following cross-reference listing:

dXREF of FRED20.prg . . . Page 1

PROCEDURE PAN2
    CALLED PROCEDURE PANHEAD

PROCEDURE CSMAINT
    CALLED PROCEDURE CDMAINT
    CALLED PROCEDURE PARMUPDT

PROCEDURE CONTACT
    CALLED PROCEDURE PAN22
    CALLED PROCEDURE CDMAINT
    CALLED PROCEDURE BADENTRY

PROCEDURE PAN22
    CALLED PROCEDURE PANHEAD

PROCEDURE CDMAINT
    CALLED PROCEDURE GETCUST
    CALLED PROCEDURE PARMUPDT
    CALLED PROCEDURE GETCUST

PROCEDURE GETCUST
    CALLED PROCEDURE PANHEAD

PROCEDURE PANHEAD

PROCEDURE BADENTRY

PROCEDURE PARMUPDT

    The following routine is a program that changes the file attribute byte on a PC-DOS directory file (PC-DOS 2.0 or later). The program may be entered using the DEBUG.COM program that is included with PC-DOS on the Supplemental Programs disk.
    The program thus created will "hide" a file from most directory listings. You may, however, still TYPE the file if you know the filename. The file will not be seen with the DIR command, so that the name must be discovered some other way.
    Hidden and protected files can be used to implement a level of physical security in a system by not allowing changes to the source code or by hiding databases that contain confidential information.

    This routine is entered by first placing DEBUG.COM on the logged disk drive, and typing the following:

```
a
xor bx,bx
mov bl,[80]
mov byte ptr [bx+81],0
mov ah,43
mov dx,82
mov cx,2
mov al,1
int 21
ret

r cx
117
n hide.com
w
q
```

    This is a quick way to enter a short assembler program. The w tells DEBUG to write the file to the disk with the name in the n command. When you have entered the sequence of commands, the file HIDE.COM will exist on the current disk drive. The syntax of the HIDE command is:

HIDE [drive:] [\path] [filename.ext]

    Please note that while this program will do the job, it is not the most sophisticated program of this type. There is no error checking done, so that if the file entered does not exist, nothing will happen. This is intentional; the program is meant to be short and easy to type in. Only one space should separate the HIDE command from the file name.
    The HIDE program may also be modified to change the file attribute to read-only. This is done by changing the statement "mov cx,2" to "mov cx,1" and changing the "n" statement to reflect the new name PROTECT.COM. Changing the statement to "mov cx,0" will undo all attributes, returning the file to a normal state. Call this program NORMAL.COM.

Appendix D

SOUNDEX Routines

The SOUNDEX algorithm was first described by W. L. Hewes and K. H. Stow in the article "Information Retrieval by Proper Name" in the June, 1965, issue of *Data Processing* magazine, page 18. It was further described by P. A. V. Hall and G. R. Dowling in "Approximate String Matching," *ACM Computing Surveys,* December, 1980, on page 388. Other descriptions include an article in the March, 1982, issue of *Byte* magazine titled "Finding Words That Sound Alike: the SOUNDEX Algorithm," by Jacob R. Jacobs. A letter by John Nesbit to the editor in the September, 1982 edition of that same magazine describes the enhancement of stripping duplicate codes before stripping the vowel codes (zeros). This is the version implemented in dBSOUND.PAS.

The following program code is written in Turbo Pascal by Borland International.

PROGRAM dBSOUND;

```
{ }
{This program reads a text input file, and writes a text}
{output file.}
{The syntax to call this program is: }
{    DBSOUND <infilename> <outfilename> }
{ }

TYPE
  SdxOut              =    STRING[4];
  Str30               =    STRING[30];
  FileName            =    STRING[20];
```

213

```
CommandString          =   STRING[127];

VARSdxLetters          :   STRING[18];
                           {array of letters with SOUNDEX values}

SdxNumbers             :   STRING[18];
                           {SOUNDEX values for letters}

SdxSet                 :   SET OF CHAR;
                           {set of letters with SOUNDEX values}

SdxOutput              :   SdxOut;
                           {final output field}

SplitPos               :   INTEGER;
                           {split between filenames on cmd line}

InString               :   STRING[30];
                           {input value to be SOUNDEXed}

InFile                 :   TEXT;              {input file declaration}

OutFile                :   TEXT;              {output file declaration}

InFileName             :   FileName;          {input file name}

OutFileName            :   FileName;          {output file name}

i,j                    :   INTEGER;           {counters}

LetterFound            :   BOOLEAN;
                           {true if letter is found in SdxLetters}

Buffer                 :   CommandString;     {command line work area}

CommLine               :   CommandString ABSOLUTE CSEG:$80;
                           {command line}

CONST
  Space = ' ';

FUNCTION UpcaseStr(s : Str30) : Str30;
{ }
```

{this function transforms the input string to all uppercase}
{letters}
{ }
VAR
  p : INTEGER;

BEGIN
  FOR p := 1 TO LENGTH(s) DO
    s[p] := UPCASE(s[p]);
  UpcaseStr := s;
END;

PROCEDURE InitVars;
{ }
{this procedure initializes the variables used in this}
{program}
{ }

BEGIN

```
    SdxLetters          := 'BPFVCGJKQSXZDTLMNR';
    SdxNumbers          := '111122222222334556';
    SdxSet              := ['B','P','F','V','C','G','J','K','Q',
                            'S','X','Z','D','T','L','M','N','R',];
    SplitPos            := 0;
    i                   := 0;
    j                   := 0;
    Letterfound         := FALSE;
    InString            := ' ';
    InFileName          := ' ';
    OutFileName         := ' ';
    SdxOutput           := ' ';
    Buffer              := ' ';
```

END;

PROCEDURE OpenFiles;
{ }
{open the files}
{NOTA BENE:}
{   no error checking is performed}
{   it is the responsibility of the user of this program}
{   to ensure that correct file names are passed to this}
{   routine.}
{END NOTE}
{ }

```
BEGIN
  ASSIGN(InFile,InFileName);
  RESET(InFile);
  ASSIGN(OutFile,OutFileName);
  REWRITE(OutFile);
END;

PROCEDURE CloseFiles:
{ }
{close the files}
{ }
BEGIN
  CLOSE(InFile);
  CLOSE(OutFile);
END;

PROCEDURE GetInput;
{ }
{read the input line}
{translate the input string to uppercase}
{ }
BEGIN
  READLN(InFile,InString);
  InString := UpcaseStr(InString);
END;

PROCEDURE TranslateStr;
{ }
{translate each character to its SOUNDEX value, starting}
{with the second}
{ }
BEGIN
  FOR i := 2 TO LENGTH(InString) DO
    BEGIN
      IF InString[i] IN SdxSet
      THEN BEGIN
          j := 1;
          LetterFound := FALSE;
          WHILE NOT LetterFound DO
            BEGIN
              IF InString[i] = SdxLetters[j]
              THEN BEGIN
                  InString[i] := SdxNumbers[j];
                  LetterFound: = TRUE;
                END;
              j := j + 1;
            END;
```

```
            END
        ELSE BEGIN
            InString[i] := '0';
          END;
    END;
END;

PROCEDURE StripDups;
{ }
{starting with the second character, strip consecutive}
{duplicate values}
{ }
BEGIN
  FOR i := 2 TO (LENGTH(InString) – 1) DO
    BEGIN
      IF InString[i] = Instring[i + 1]
      THEN BEGIN
          DELETE(InString,i,1);
          i := i – 1);
        END;
    END;
END;

PROCEDURE StripZeros;
{ }
{starting with the second character, delete zero values}
{from string}
{ }
BEGIN
  FOR i := 2 TO LENGTH(InString) DO
    BEGIN
      IF InString[i] = '0'
      THEN BEGIN
          DELETE(InString,i,1);
          i := i – 1;
        END;
    END;
END;

PROCEDURE DoSoundex;
{ }
{translate the characters into their SOUNDEX values}
{strip duplicate codes from the string}
{strip zeroes from the string}
{ }
BEGIN
  TranslateStr;
```

```
    StripDups;
    StripZeros;
  END;

  PROCEDURE PutOutput;
  { }
  {truncate the SOUNDEX code to four characters}
  {write the code to the output file}
  { }
  BEGIN
    SdxOutput := COPY(InString,1,4);
    WRITELN(OutFile,SdxOutput);
  END;

{***MAIN PROGRAM***}
{pseudocode **********************************************************************}
{initialize variables}
{get file names from command line}
{open the files}
{do while there are more input lines:}
{  get the input line}
{  SOUNDEX the line}
{  write the SOUNDEX code to the output file}
{endo}
{close files}
{end of program}
{ *********************************************************************************}
BEGIN
  InitVars;
  Buffer             := CommLine;
  DELETE(Buffer,1,1);
  SplitPos           := POS(Space,Buffer);
  InFileName         := COPY(Buffer,1,(SplitPos – 1));
  OutFileName        := COPY(Buffer,(SplitPos + 1),LENGTH(Buffer));
  OpenFiles;
  REPEAT
    GetInput;
    DoSoundex;
    PutOutput;
    UNTIL EOF(InFile);
  CloseFiles;
END.

{END OF PROGRAM}
```

The following routine is a dBASE III program to use the Turbo Pascal™ program above.

```
* test DBSOUND
* this routine creates a file of names which is passed to
* DBSOUND
* the output file is then appended to the original database
*


*
* this is the example of how to use the DBSOUND program
*

USE NAMEFILE

COPY TO SNDIN.TXT SDF

RUN B:DBSOUND B:SNDIN.TXT B:SNDOUT.TXT

APPEND FROM SNDOUT.TXT SDF

*
* end of example
*
USE
RETURN

* end of program
```

The following program is an implementation of SOUNDEX in dBASE III by James E. Hammitt.

```
PROCEDURE DBSOUND

PARAMETERS DBSNDIN,DBSNDOUT

* Initialize variables
STORE 'BPFVCGJKQSXZDTLMNRA' TO SNXLETS
STORE '11112222222223345560' TO SNXNUMS
STORE 0 TO SNDLOC
STORE SPACE(1) TO SNDTHIS, SNDNEXT

* Translate the string into SOUNDEX codes

STORE 2 TO I
STORE SUBSTR(DBSNDIN,1,1) TO DBSNDTMP, DBSNDTM2, DBSNDOUT

DO WHILE I < = LEN(DBSNDIN) .AND. SUBSTR(DBSNDIN,I,1 # ' '

   STORE AT (SUBSTR(DBSNDIN,I,1),SNXLETS) TO SNDLOC
```

```
   IF SNDLOC = 0
      STORE LEN(SNXLETS) TO SNDLOC
   ENDIF
   STORE DBSNDTMP + SUBSTR(SNXNUMS,SNDLOC,1) TO DBSNDTMP
   STORE (I + 1) TO I

ENDDO

* Remove consecutive duplicate codes
STORE 2 TO I

DO WHILE (I < = (LEN(DBSNDTMP) - 1))

   STORE SUBSTR(DBSNDTMP,I,1) TO SNDTHIS
   STORE SUBSTR(DBSNDTMP,(I+1),1) TO SNDNEXT

   IF SNDTHIS # SNDNEXT
      STORE DBSNDTM2 + SUBSTR(DBSNDTMP,I,1) TO DBSNDTM2
   ENDIF

   STORE (I + 1) TO I

ENDDO

* Remove the remaining zero (vowel) codes
STORE 2 TO I

DO WHILE (I < = LEN(DBSNDTM2))

   STORE SUBSTR(DBSNDTM2,I,1) TO SNDTHIS
   IF SNDTHIS # '0'
      STORE DBSNDOUT + SUBSTR(DBSNDTM2,I,1) TO DBSNDOUT
   ENDIF

   STORE (I + 1) TO I

ENDDO

* Truncate the SOUNDEX code to four positions

IF LEN(DBSNDOUT) > 4
   STORE SUBSTR(DBSNDOUT,1,4) TO DBSNDOUT
ENDIF

RETURN

* End of Program
```

Appendix E

A List of Peripheral Packages and Publications

The following is a list of dBASE utilities and add-ons that are available. This is in no way a complete list; new products are constantly being developed. Many software publishers that already manufacture a dBASE II package are rushing their dBASE III versions to the market at warp speed. For up-to-date information, keep an eye on the trade press, or call the company directly. Always be sure to ask 1) if it is right for your machine; 2) if it is being shipped at the present time; and 3) if you can get your money back if not satisfied. It is difficult to get assurances of number 3 because of copy-pirate paranoia.

Bailey and Associates
    dBMenu

Data Based Solutions, 1975 Fifth Ave., San Diego, CA 92101
    dNames, dBLink, dProgrammer, dCref, dQ, DValidate, dLineate, dEFlate, dNames Professional, Memory Shift, Memo Searcher, dBASE III dLetter Generator, dSolutions Pro-Pak

Fourcolor Data Systems, 7011 Malabar St., Dayton, OH 45459
    Fastbase

Fox & Geller, 604 Market St., Elmwood Park, NJ 07407
    Quickcode III, dGraph III, Quickreport III, dUtil III

General Corp.
    dBASE/Answer (micro-mainframe link software)

Global Technologies
    dBASE Professional Development System

Hilco Software
    Check, Art, Repair, Decode/Recode utilities

ITC, 9201 Penn Ave. S. Ste. 1, Bloomington, MN 55431

    dBXREF III

Liberty Bell Publishing, 4640 SW Macadam Ste. 150, Portland, OR 97201
    dWindow

Market Line International
    dNetwork, multi-user utility

Micro Software
    Autodate

Microclear
    dSecure

Monterey Computer Consulting
    dbRescue, Scrunch

Nantucket, 5995 S. Sepulveda Blvd., Culver City, CA 90230
    Clipper compiler for dBASE III

Nighhawk Computer Services
    dINLINE Calculator

O'Neill Software
    Electra-Find, file search utility

Pacer Business Automation
    dRecover, dShrink, dVerify

PostalSoft Inc.
    PostWare

Radix 2 Software
    dCross

Software Bottling Company of New York, The, 6600 LI Expressway, Maspeth, NY 11378
    FlashCode screen generator

Software Research Technology, 3757 Wilshire Blvd. 211, Los Angeles, CA 90010
    dFastest, utility package

Syscomp
    dBIII Translate (dB III to Symphony or 1-2-3)

Tylog Systems, 9805 SW 152 Terrace, Miami, FL 33157
    dB Window and dBDoor

WallSoft Systems, 233 Broadway, New York, NY 10279
    dFlow, debugging utility

WordTech Systems, P.O. Box 1747, Orinda, CA 94563
    dBIII Compiler

The following are selected dBASE II and III newsletters and publications around the country. They are a constant source of new techniques and support. Some, like dNOTICES, even list consultants who are available for questions and programming (at their usual rates, of course. Consultants are programming professionals and are paid for their services.) Consider subscribing to at least one of the following publications, or join your local user's group. Either way, it will be a big help to you.

Data Based Advisor
    1975 5th Ave., Suite 105
    San Diego, CA 92101

dNews
    10150 West Jefferson Blvd.
    Culver City, CA 90230

dNOTICES II
    Rich Slatta, Editor
    3304 Dell Drive
    Raleigh, NC 27609

Glossary

activity log—A sequential file detailing all actions made by an operator while using a system. The log can be used for security purposes or for the recreation of activity when you are recovering from a catastrophe using backup copies.

batch processing—The opposite of online processing. Batch processing was misnamed from the old practice of grouping cards for input to mainframe computers. Batch processing refers to any of noninteractive programming.

breakpoint—The point in time at which the computer's workload surpasses its ability to process the work in the required length of time. In other words, the breakpoint occurs when it takes the computer more than 24 hours to perform one day's worth of work. Usually this means that it's time to get a faster or bigger machine.

chaining—Relating databases in such a way that each relates to the next and so on.

change log—See Activity Log. This term is most often used to describe a file used for recovery.

checkpoint—A complete recording of the status, memory, and file positions of an executing program. A checkpoint is sometimes called a *snapshot*. See checkpoint-restart.

checkpoint-restart—The process of using a checkpoint to restart a program from the middle of its processing. This is possible because all values and file positions are stored on a file and used to reinstate the original environment as of the time of the checkpoint.

command shell—Another copy of PC-DOS started above an executing program like dBASE. This is the method used by dBASE to execute external commands with RUN/!.

concurrent processing—The ability to run two programs simultaneously on the same computer. This is made possible by dividing the computer's memory into discrete areas, called *partitions*, where the programs reside when running. Processing in one partition will not affect the others.

control break—A break in sequential processing to produce subtotals, eject to the next page, or perform some other function. A control break is caused by a field or fields changing value.

data dictionary—A document describing every field used in a database system. It is a central point of reference for developing new applications.

data entity—Something, real or abstract, about which data is to be stored. A data entity is the person, form, or item that exists in a one-for-one relationship with the records of the main data file of a system.

dependency—In normalization, a dependency describes relationships between data items on a record and the key of the record. If more than just the key of the record is needed to find the exact value of the data item, the item is said to be dependent on whatever other items are needed as well as the key.

disk cache—A buffer where large amounts of disk data are stored, so that when the data is required, there will not be a need to reaccess the disk. A disk cache is only useful for applications that are heavily bound by their disk I/O operations.

extract—The act of storing fields from several sources into one database that can more easily be processed or reported on.

freeing—The act of making more memory available by removing something from memory. The RELEase command frees the area used by memory variables.

generic—Something that is generic applies to all situations. A program or routine is generic if it can be used at several places in a system or even across different systems.

guidelines—A part of the computer plan of action. Guidelines are standards that can be broken for good reason. See Standards and Suggestions.

hackers—People who use a computer to the exclusion of almost everything else. Most hackers do not engage in criminal activity.

instance—One occurrence of an entity. For example, all database information that applies to the employee "Fred" make up one instance of the Employee entity.

macro—A dBASE variable preceded by an ampersand. The value of the macro may be larger than the string describing it. See Macro substitution.

macro substitution—Macros are replaced directly in the statement they appear in with their current value.

normalization—The process of reducing the interdependence of data items, thereby reducing redundancy. Unnormalized databases have a tendency to become out of synch with the real world, where normalized databases will never suffer redundancy problems.

partition—A segment of computer memory reserved for executing programs. This term is used to describe areas of memory used in concurrent processing.

pirates—People who don't pay for long distance calls (aka "phone phreakers"), and/or who steal software by copying and distributing this software without the approval of the copyright holder. Pirates also break into remote-access systems for illegal purposes.

pointer—An address of some routine or data in the memory of the computer, also called a vector.

positioning—Setting the current record number of the database, usually by using the GO command. FIND and SEEK also change this pointer.

print spool—A buffer that holds data going to the printer. The printer moves slowly, but a print spool exists in memory, so that transfers to that area are much faster than transfers directly to the printer would be.

prototype system—Refers to the practice of presenting a new application system to the users when only the screens and the necessary screen navigation have been programmed. This allows the users to examine the human interface in detail and offer suggestions for improvement.

run-time library—A file of routines used by a compiler or a compiled program. These routines are used in place of the dBASE statements that perform the function.

saving position—Refers to saving a record number in one database, closing it, moving to another database, and then reaccessing the first database at the record number stored.

scope—The programs and subroutines in which a variable exists. The general rule is that all variables are known in the routine where they are first used and in any routine lower in the hierarchy.

scratchpad—An area used by interactive programs to store information needed for communicating with the user. The use of a scratchpad is also referred to as conversational processing.

semaphore file—A file used to indicate records that are being updated in a multi-user system. The record is "flagged" by the program updating it, so that another user will not try to update the same record at the same time.

SOUNDEX—An algorithm for finding phonetically equivalent words.

SPOOL—Simultaneous Peripheral Operations On-Line. Spool refers to the process of saving output information in a memory or media area while a slower device is moving at its own pace.

standards—A set of rules that are specified in the computer plan of action. These are rules that are to be followed always. Only a radical situation should cause a system developer to violate a standard.

structured data design—The designing of the interface with the data separately from the rest of the system. This makes the program file-independent.

suggestions—In the computer plan of action, suggestions are just that: the system developer does not have to have a good reason to violate them.

transaction file—A file of activity records that are processed without operator interaction.

windowing—The process of overlaying a screen of information with another screen in such a way that the first screen can be returned to.

working storage—The area of memory where memory variables are stored.

Index

@ GET command, 12, 63
@ SAY command, 12, 63

A

active data dictionary, 5
activity log, 117
add-ons, 223
ADDItive option, 16, 52
algorithm, SOUNDEX, 92, 215
aliases, database, 6
alternate output file, 47
ampersand, 84
Application Junction, 191
archive backups, 23, 24
archive database, 34
arrays, 84
ASCII characters, 98
ASCII format, 14
Ashton-Tate Quarterly, 191
Ashton-Tate Tech Notes, 191
assignment statement, 56
ASSIST feature, 101
AT function, 11, 84, 93
attributes, file, 106, 126
audit trail, 104

B

B+ tree, 15, 123
backup files, 84
backups, archive, 23, 24

Baggage's disease, 30
batch processing, 83
binary switches, 11
bit switches, 11
books, dBASE, 191, 192
borders, graphic, 64
breakpoint, 87
breaks, control, 133
BUCKET, 17
buffer, 112
BUFFERS parameter, 44

C

cache, disk, 112
calculations, 87
call, subroutine, 54
canonical synthesis, 2
CDOW function, 22
chaining, 9
change log, 25, 117
character fields, 10
character-field data, 29
checkpoint-restart, 118
CHR function, 78
CLEAR GETS command, 67
CLEAR MEMOry command, 50
Clipper Compiler, 179, 180
computer plan of action, 127
computers, mainframe, 5
concurrent running of programs,

188, 189
CONFIG.DB file, 17, 54, 97
configuration database, 86
consonants, 92
control breaks, 133
control codes for printers, 77
control codes, file of, 80
control data, 104, 105
COPY TO command, 15
CREATE REPOrt command, 17, 72, 131
cross reference, 209
Crusher program, 201-209
CTOD function, 22

D

DASDS, 115
Data Based Advisor, 190
data dictionary, 31
data dictionary, sample, 197-200
data entity, 1
data entry, 60, 114
data item, 1
data protection, 103
data recovery, 116
data storage, 113
data transfer, 114
data type, field, 4
data, dictionary, 1, 4
data, extracting, 75, 87

data, importing, 99, 100
database aliases, 6
database fields, scope of 57
database file structure, 120
database files, 13, 14
database header, 14
database processing, random, 43
database schema, 5
database, archive, 34
database, configuration, 86
database, stack, 100
databases, 1, 5
databases, related, 6-9
date fields, 19
date, system, 85
DATE function, 21
dates used in variables, 23
dates, formats of, 20
dates, Julian, 20, 55
DAY function, 22
dBASE books, 191, 192
dBASE III SOUNDEX program, 221, 222
dBASE publications, 190
debugging tools, 170
debugging, 45
decimal places, 5, 11
declaration, 56
default values, 17
DELETE command, 12
DELETED function, 12
DELImited parameter, 98
dependencies, 31
dependency, functional, 2
design, screen, 59
design, structured data, 1
development tools, 53, 201
devices, future, 115
dFLOW, 170-178
dFORMAT, 69
dictionary, data, 1, 4, 197-200
direct-access storage device, 115
disasters, 116, 117
disk cache, 112
disk organization, 110
disk, floppy, 113
disk, hard, 111, 115
disk, laser video, 116
DISPlay command, 12
DISPlay MEMOry command, 45, 48
DISPlay RECOrd RECNO command, 45
DISPlay STATus command, 45
DISPLAY STRUCTURE report, 12
DO command, 16, 54
DO WHILE LOOP, 39
DO WITH command, 56
double striking, 78
documentation, system, 5
DOS, 97
DOW function, 22
drives, WORM, 116

drives, tape, 114
DTOC function, 22
duplicate files, 116
dWindow, 187
dXREF program, 209-214

E
editing, numeric, 68
editor, screen format, 69
editor, text, 53
editors, text, 17, 181, 182
edits, 66
efficiency of printing, 75
efficiency of systems, 107, 125
emphasizing, 78
end-of-the-day program, 82
ENDDO, 39
entity, data, 1, 5
entry, data, 60
environment, shifting, 90
Epson printer, 80
error messages, 44, 195, 196
errors, program, 170
escape character, 79
executing other programs, 97
EXIT command, 39
exporting data, 97, 98
external files, 27-29
extract program, 75
extracted files, 87
extracting data, 75, 87

F
Farley file, 35
field data type, 4
field name, 4
fields in reports, 136
field, 1
field, unseen, 12
fields, character, 10
fields, database, 121, 122
fields, date, 19
fields, logical, 11, 12
fields, numeric, 11
fields, standard, 86
fields, types of, 10, 13
filename, 5
file attributes, 106, 126
file Farley, 35
file maintenance, 81
file, CONFIG.DB
file, flat, 1
file, ISAM, 41
file, screen format, 59
file, semaphore, 81
file, transaction, 83
filenames, unique, 85
files, database, 13, 14
files, extracted, 87
files, index, 15, 16
files, memo field, 16
files, memory variable, 16

files, physical, 5
files, procedure, 16
files, program, 16
files, report format, 17
files, screen format, 16
FIND command, 7, 43
first normal form, 31
first-form normalized files, 2
fish market, 30
FlashCode, 146, 151-162, 184-187
flat file, 1
format file, screen, 59
format independence, 4
format of dates, 20
formatting, numeric, 68
Fox and Geller, 131
freeing variables, 50
fubar data, 45
function keys, 17
function, generic, 55
functional dependency, 2
functions, date, 21
future devices, 115

G
generator, report format, 72, 73
generators, screen and program, 146
GETS, 17
global memory variable, 86
GO command, 44
graphic borders, 64
graphics characters, 71
groups of data items, 2
groups, user, 193

H
hacker, 103
hard disk, 111
header, database, 14, 120
help function, 100-103, 125, 126
hidden attribute, 106
hybrid reports, 77

I
IBM PC/XT, 30
IBM printer, 80
importing data, 97-99
index files, 15, 16
INDEX ON . . . TO . . . command
index, structure of, 122, 123
Indexed Sequential Access Method file, 41
input, prompting for, 66
instances of entities, 2
interactive commands, 26
interface program, 6
interpreter, 108
ISAM file, 41
item, data, 1

J
Julian dates, 20, 55

227

justification of numbers, 11

K
key field, 2
keys, 34
keys, function, 17

L
laser video disk, 116
leaf node, 123
LEN function, 11
length, filed, 5
library, run-time, 108
LIST command, 12
LIST MEMOry command, 48
LOCATE statement, 7
log, activity, 117
logical fields, 11, 12
lookups, 42
LOOP command, 39
Lotus 1-2-3, 182
LOWER function, 67

M
machine language, 108
macro substitution, 84
mainframe computers, 5
maintenance, file, 81
manufacturers, 223
market, fish, 30
MAXMEM, 17, 97
memo field files, 16
memo field, 25, 29
memo fields, accessing, 26
memory variable files, 16
memory variables, 6, 48
menus, 54
messages, error, 44, 195, 196
modems, 104
MODIfy COMMand process, 54
MODIfy REPOrt command, 17, 73
module, 39
MONTH function, 22
multiple users, 81
MVARSIZ parameter, 17, 49

N
name, filed, 4
narrative description, 5
newsletters, 224
nodes, 123
NOEJECT option, 72
noninteractive processing, 83
nonreal-time processing, 82
numeric fields, 11

O
OCRs, 114
operator identification codes, 126
optical character readers, 114
organization, disk, 110
other programs, executing, 97

out of memory error, 44

P
page lengths, 77
PAGELEN, 77
PARAMETERS statement, 57
parent databases, databases, parent, 87
Pascal, 201
passive data dictionary, 5
passwords, 103, 104, 126
PATH searches, 109
payroll system, 31
peripheral packages, 223
phonetic spelling, 92
physical files, 5
PICTURE clauses, 10, 67
picture, template, 68
pirate, computer, 103
pitch, 78
PLAIN option, 72
plan of action, computer, 127
pointers, 25, 57
position, saving, 44
print spool, 112
printers, 79, 80
printers, control codes of, 78
printing reports, 75, 76
printing, efficiency of, 75
PRIVATE variable, 52, 56
prompt, 17
procedural cross-reference program, 209
procedure files, 16, 54
process, speeding up, 88
processing, batch, 83
processing, nonreal-time, 82
processing, real-time, 82
program files, 16, 53
program generators, 146
program, dBASE III SOUNDEX, 221, 222
program, dbSOUND, 215-220
program, end-of-the-day, 82
program, extract, 75
program, interface, 6
program, procedural cross-reference, 209
programming, 90
programs, development tool, 201
prompting for input, 66
protect attribute
protection of data, 103
prototype system, 61
pseudoconstants, 77
PUBLIC variable, 52
publications, dBASE, 190, 224

Q
QuickCode III, 146, 162-169
QuickCode, 146
QuickReport, 131, 137-145

R
random database processing, 43
range edits, 66
READ statement, 62
read-only attribute, 106
read-only files, 106
readers, optical character, 114
real time, 81
real-time processing, 82
reasonability edits, 66
RECALL command, 13
RECNO function, 15, 44
recovery, data, 116
reference lister, 209
related databases, 6-9
RELEase command, 49, 50
releases, new, 90
repeating groups of data items, 2
REPOrt FORM command, 17
report format files, 17
report format generator, 72
reports, 131-145
reports, printing, 76
report writers, 131
resources for programmers, 91
RESTore command, 16, 49
RETURN TO MASTER statement, 39
run-time library, 108
running of programs, concurrent, 188, 189

S
saboteur, 103
SAVE command, 16, 49
saving position, 44
schema, 5
scope of database fields, 57
scope of variables, 55
scratchpad, 48
screen design, 59
Screen Editor, 146-150
screen format editor, 69
screen format files, 16, 17, 59, 62
screen generators, 146
Screen Sculptor, 151
screen, programming, 59
SDF, 29, 98, 99
second-form normalization, 2
Second-System Syndrome, 30
security programs, 104
security, 103
SED, 69
SEEK statement, 7, 43
SELECT statement, 6
self-modifying programs, 84-86
semaphore file, 81
SET commands, 17
SET DELEted TO command, 12
SET ECHO ON command, 45
SET FORMAT command, 62
SET PATH command, 110

SET PROCedure to, 16
SET RELATION TO command, 7, 43
SET STEP ON command, 46
SET TALK ON command, 45
shell, command, 97
SORT command, 15
SOUNDEX algorithm, 92, 215
source code control system, 53
speed of execution, 41, 107
speeding up a process, 88
spelling, phonetic, 92
spool, print, 112
stack database, 100
Standard Data Format files, 29
standard data format, 98, 99
standard fields, 86
storage, physical, 117, 118
storage, working, 48
STORE command, 63
STR function, 23
structure, database file, 120
structured coding, 39
structured data design, 1
structure of an index, 122, 123
subdirectories, 109
subentities, 2
subroutine, 54
subroutine, generic, 55

subschema, 5
substitution, macro, 84
SUBSTR function, 11, 41, 84
switches, binary, 11
switches, bit, 11
system documentation, 5
system, prototype, 61
systems, efficiency of, 107

T

tape drives, 114
template, picture, 68
text editors, 53, 181, 182
text file, external, 29
third normal form, 33
TIME function, 22
tools, debugging, 170
tools, development, 53
transaction file, 83
transfer of data, 114
transitive dependency, 2, 33
tree, B+, 15, 123
TRIM function, 11
Turbo Pascal, 215, 151
types of files, 13

U

unseen field, 12
UPPER function, 67

USE command, 6, 8
user groups, 193
user-friendly, 103
users, multiple, 81
utilities, 223

V

VAL function, 84
validity edits, 66
variable, global memory, 86
variable, PRIVATE, 56
variables, dates used in, 23
variables, memory, 6
variables, scopes of, 55
vowels, 92

W

window, 5
windowing, 26
WITH clause, 16
word processor, 17
WordStar, 182
WordTech dBlll compiler, 180
working storage, 48
WORM drives, 116

Y

YEAR function, 19, 22

Other Bestsellers From TAB

☐ **ADVANCED dBASE III®
APPLICATIONS—Baker**

An invaluable collection of ready-to-use dBASE III applications for getting maximum productivity from Ashton Tate's state-of-the-art database management software! Includes how-to's for setting up and maintaining computerized files for managing employees, payroll, inventory, accounting applications, time management, tracking sales and performing marketing research, and more. 448 pp., 120 illus. 7" × 10".
Paper $21.95   **Hard $28.95**
Book No. 2618

☐ **JAZZ!™—Bolocan**

Let software expert David Bolocan guide your masterfully through all of Jazz's capabilities—word processing, spreadsheet analysis, database management, communications, and business graphics capabilities. Written in easy-to-understand, plain-English, this hands-on tutorial takes you from an introduction to using Jazz on the Macintosh and fundamental commands to exploring its tremendous applications and integrating them. 304 pp., 249 illus. 7" × 10".
Paper $17.95   **Hard $24.95**
Book No. 1978

☐ **MONEY MANAGEMENT WORKSHEETS
FOR 1-2-3™/SYMPHONY™—Maffei**

Turn your IBM PC® or PC-compatible into a full-time financial manager with the help of this huge collection of over 60 customized worksheets designed especially for the powerful 1-2-3/Symphony business software! Using these invaluable worksheets, you can do everything from balancing your checkbook and planning your budget to managing investments, even playing the stock market. 192 pp., 80 illus. 7" × 10".
Paper $14.95   **Hard $21.95**
Book No. 1968

☐ **MASTERING SYMPHONY™—Bolocan**

Anyone who's purchased the new Symphony package from Lotus . . . or who's thinking of trading up from Lotus 1-2-3™ . . . will find this an essential guide! Covering each of Symphony's functions separately and in depth, this unique guide clarifies and gives sample programs and diagrams to demonstrate the software's spreadsheet, word processing, data management, graphics, and communications features. 240 pp., 170 illus. 7" × 10".
Paper $16.95   **Hard $22.95**
Book No. 1948

☐ **ADVANCED APPLICATIONS FOR PFS®
AND THE IBM® ASSISTANT SERIES**

Capitalize on the power and flexibility of PFS® and IBM® Assistant Series software with this goldmine of ready-to-use applications! Each module is given extensive, indepth coverage, including predesigned applications organized around real-world applications and needs. It's an invaluable productivity tool for anyone using these bestselling software modules. 224 pp., 212 illus. 7" × 10".
Paper $16.95   **Hard $22.95**
Book No. 1989

☐ **PROGRAMMING WITH dBASE III™**

With this excellent sourcebook at your side, using dBASE III is a snap! You'll discover how to take advantage of all this fourth generation software's data handling capabilities *plus* learn how to unlock the power of dBASE III as a complete programming language! Also includes an appendix detailing the differences between dBASE II and dBASE III, with full instructions for using dConvert—the utility program used to convert dBASE II programs to dBASE III! 304 pp., 215 illus. 7" × 10".
Paper $17.95   **Book No. 1976**

☐ **USING FRAMEWORK™
—A PICTORIAL GUIDE**

Here's the hands-on, how-to explanations you need to take command of this all-new software package. From start-to-finish, this pictorial guide it packed with easy-to-follow, step-by-step explanations, examples, and programs for using all of Framework's functions: database management, spreadsheet, communications, word processing, and graphics. 320 pp., 300 illus. 7" × 10". Printed in 2-Colors.
Paper $18.95   **Hard $26.95**
Book No. 1966

☐ **NETWORKING WITH THE IBM®
NETWORK™ AND CLUSTER™**

A complete guide to installing, using, and programming IBM's new state-of-the-art Network™ and Cluster™! Written in easy-to-understand terminology and packed with plenty of examples and illustrations, it provides easy entry into LAN's for anyone who is just getting started—and in particular for those who have or are considering the purchase of IBM's Network or Cluster. 480 pp., 225 illus. 7" × 10".
Paper $19.95   **Hard $29.95**
Book No. 1929

Other Bestsellers From TAB

☐ **SERIOUS PROGRAMMING FOR THE IBM® PC™/XT™/AT®**

Here's your key to learning how programs can be developed and designed for your own specific purposes to really do the job you need accomplished. You'll cover different aspects of program design, including using subroutines to build an effective subroutine library of your own, get special tips on learning to write a user's guide and creating help screens. 208 pp., 113 illus. 7" × 10".
Paper $14.95   Hard $21.95
Book No. 1921

☐ **dBASE II® —A COMPREHENSIVE USER'S MANUAL—Bharucha**

A logical, easy-to-follow guide that takes you from computer novice to expert programmer in dBASE II! Just some of the unique features that set this guide apart from ordinary user manuals include: How to create and maintain a database; Explanations of dBASE functions; Details on how to use COPY to create standard text files from dBASE files . . . a requirement of communicating with other software; and much more. 320 pp., 7" × 10".
Paper $18.95   Hard $24.95
Book No. 1884

☐ **INCREASING PRODUCTIVITY WITH PFS® —Burton**

Here's an important money-saving guide that provides expert guidance on the most effective ways to use all six PFS modules to increase efficiency and productivity in your business, nonprofit agency, or service organization! Plus there are 10 time- and money-saving templates or applications models that make it possible for you to prepare more than 20 specific forms and reports! 192 pp., 92 illus. 7" × 10".
Paper $14.95   Hard $21.95
Book No. 1789

☐ **LOTUS 1-2-3™ SIMPLIFIED—Bolocan**

Lotus 1-2-3 is the dynamic new business software that offers an incredible range of data-handling capabilities. Now, here's an outstanding guide that can make it really as simple as 1, 2, 3. From the very first steps of installing and using Lotus 1-2-3 to the procedures for designing and using your own spreadsheets, this user-friendly manual gives you the understanding necessary to utilize the capabilities of Lotus 1-2-3. 192 pp., 195 illus. 7" × 10".
Paper $10.95   Book No. 1748

☐ **HOW TO RUN YOUR BUSINESS WITH dBASE II® —Baker**

With this book at your side, you can set up personnel records, perform payroll duties, keep inventory, pay bills, and more. You can actually incorporate big business management techniques into your small business, easily and profitably. Everything you need to run your business with dBASE is included . . . what dBASE II can do and how you can get professional results. 320 pp., 144 illus. 7" × 10".
Paper $16.95   Hard $26.95
Book No. 1918

☐ **MAKING MS-DOS AND PC-DOS WORK FOR YOU—The Human Connection**

Here's a clear, plain English description of MS-DOS (Microsoft Disk Operating System) and PC-DOS (the IBM PC disk operating system). This outstanding guide also includes a special programmers section listing commands needed to create, run, and "debug" programs, and a handy "commands at a glance" that gives you fast reference to all MC/PC-DOS commands! 224 pp., 93 illus. 7" × 10".
Papor $14.95   Hard $19.95
Book No. 1848

☐ **PROGRAMMING WITH dBASE II®**

If you've invested in dBASE II—or are thinking of doing so—here's an invaluable sourcebook that can show you how to get the most from its powerful, fourth generation data handling capabilities! Here's where you'll discover how to use dBASE II as a full programming language . . . one that's far easier to use than traditional languages (like BASIC, Pascal, even COBOL or FORTRAN). 228 pp., 292 illus. 7" × 10".
Paper $16.95   Hard $26.95
Book No. 1776

☐ **MASTERING MULTIPLAN™**

If you want practical, expert advice on how to get the most performance from your software . . . this book is an essential programming tool. Guiding you from the very first step to advanced commands designed to give your spreadsheet maximum versatility, you'll get the hands-on guidance on how to use Multiplan's extraordinary data-handling capabilities to arrange your own sophisticated spreadsheets. 128 pp., 60 illus. 7" × 10".
Paper $11.50   Hard $16.95
Book No. 1743

*Prices subject to change without notice.

Look for these and other TAB BOOKS at your local bookstore.

TAB BOOKS Inc.
P.O. Box 40
Blue Ridge Summit, PA 17214

Send for FREE TAB Catalog describing over 900 current titles in print.